Forest and Forest Villagers

Forest and Forest Villagers

Tarun Das

RAJESH PUBLICATIONS
NEW DELHI - 110 002

Forest and Forest Villagers

Published by :
Sanjay Gupta
RAJESH PUBLICATIONS
1, Ansari Road, Darya Ganj, New Delhi - 110002
Ph.: 011-23274550, 43084725
Website : www.rajeshpublications.com
Email : rajeshpublications@gmail.com,
rajeshpubdelhi@gmail.com

First Published in India : 2022

ISBN : 978-93-91139-16-2

Printed in India by :
Aryan Digital Press
Delhi - 110002

Book is dedicated to

My parents, wife (Alpana Roy), and my dear son (Ankit Das), who gave their uncounted support and also all my respected teachers, friends, colleagues and students who encouraged and supported me.

Preface

The UN Forum on forests has always recognized the strong role of Indigenous Peoples in achieving sustainable forest management. In 2007, the Forum adopted the Non-Legally Binding Instrument (NLBI) on all types of forests, the first ever inter-governmental instrument on sustainable forest management for enhanced access to forest resources and relevant support to the livelihoods of forests dependent local and indigenous communities, living in and outside forest areas. The IUFRO (The International Union of Forest Research Organizations, French) promotes global cooperation in forest-related research and enhances the understanding of the ecological, economic and social aspects of forests and trees. It disseminates scientific knowledge to stakeholders and decision-makers and contributes to forest policy and on the ground forest management. IUFRO's vision is of science-based sustainable management of the world's forest resources for economic, environmental and social benefits.

Here the District Alipurduar, situated in the northern eastern part of West Bengal has international borders with Bhutan and Bangladesh in the north and south respectively. The forest of Alipurduar, assign its significance roll in the international context for providing shelter and protection to various species of wildlife along with forest villagers as it has huge forests cover in respect of the West Bengal and India. This research work can be compared the socio-economic and livelihood status of forest villagers as well as activities of JFM prevailing in Alipurduar, with the other countries of the world. The position of socio-economy of forest villagers as well as activities of JFM can be marked out in respect of international context. Therefore, this research work has international importance and may be assists worldwide interaction with poly makers, administrators, and others forest participatory activity concerned. So this research work has international values and will help in proper documentation of management level of forest for sustainable livelihood of society. Nationally the Alipurduar District has got a great credence being one of the important forest cover district in India where National protected areas include the Buxa National Park (which includes the Buxa Tiger Reserve), the Gorumara National park and part of the Jaldapara National Park and unclassed forests are located.

There are numerous forest villages around these forests and these settlements are growing continuously by extracting forest resource in the uncontrolled and unsustainable way which is considerable matter for national level environmentalists. Therefore forest covered area of Alipurduar District which constitute near about 9.86 % of West Bengal's forest cover land is an important subject matter of considerations in environmental issues along with sustainable livelihood of forest inhabitants. Sustainable management through JFM action directly or indirectly reflects the overall environmental quality of West Bengal and in India. Further the study about the sustainable livelihood of forest villagers through JFM prevailing in the this district can be compared with the JFM as well as forest participatory management prevailing in other states of India like in Assam, Madhya Pradesh, Jharkhand, Chhattisgarh, and Kerala. Therefore, this research work has national importance in broad perspective and more specifically to direct the forest rural area development programme within the country. In this research, various assessments will be reviewed that are conducting in Alipurduar District at national, state and forest division level. This study could generate information to assess the impact of JFM policies, issues that need to be addressed and new challenges. An attempt will be made here to review Monitoring and Evaluation (M & E) studies conducted in the district. The major goal is to understand the life style and adaptation of villagers in forest ecosystem, functioning of JFM institutions, and regeneration of vegetation and non-timber forest product (NTFP), issues involved in implementing and sustaining the programme. Also the study will highlight few important points, which would enhance forest villagers' socio-economic conditions and improve active participation in the JFMC meetings through sustainable management. Further proper planning by the Government and the non-governmental organization would be possible through this study.

My efforts will be worthwhile if the students, researchers, academicians and policy makers find this volume useful.

July, 2022
Siliguri

Dr. Tarun Das
Siliguri, Balai Das Chatterjee Road
Hakim Para, Paul Para (Ward No. 16)
Darjeeling, West Bengal

Acknowledgement

I thank to the Divisional Forest Officer, Jalpaiguri Forest Division; Ranger, Dalgaon Range Office; Ranger, Hamiltongaunge Range Office, Buxa Tiger Reserve for their valuable support for this work. In spite of busy schedule their valuable suggestions have really been an inspiration and driving force for me. They have constantly provided valuable inputs for carrying out this research thesis successfully.

I would like to thank all the DFOs, SDOs, Range, Beat Officers and other officials of the forest department of district of Jalpaiguri and Alipurduar who helped and rendered their valuable time, knowledge and information during the field trips. I take this opportunity to thank all the forest villagers for patiently co-operating me and helping me to fulfil the research objective.

I would like to thank my guide Dr. Deepak Kumar Mandal, Professor for the proper presentation of this long pursuit and for the real autonomy, he has given to me, so that I could explore the topic and enrich my own views. I express my sincere thanks to my parents, my wife, son and all the family members for all their sacrifices they have made in supporting and motivating me through all difficult moments.

I would like to thank University of North Bengal for support and also providing the institutional facilities whenever needed. I am thankful to all the faculty members especially professor Dr. Subir Sarkar for their valuable suggestions and also other staff members of the Department of Geography & Applied Geography, University of North Bengal for their kind cooperation.

Lastly, I am grateful to my family members, well wishers and followers for their co-operation and encouragement.

July, 2022
Siliguri

Dr. Tarun Das

Abstract

Forest and Forest Villagers

There is no doubt that management of forest resources is extremely important in developing and underdeveloped countries for providing sustainable management of livelihood to forest villagers as well as fringe people. In countries like Bangladesh, Sri Lanka and India, improper property right, economic insecurity, regulation violence and failure, poverty and heterogeneity in socio-economic characteristics of households had often led to unsustainable management of forest resource and deforestation. So protection of forest resources is one of the precaution and preconditions of taking sustainable benefit from forest resources, particularly in countries where forests fulfilled livelihood needs of million forests villagers.

This writtings tried to generate the information of impact of forest on forest villagers' socio-economy, and other forest related issue that need to be addressed. Here the study of forest villages and dependency of villagers on to forest has been summarized on the basis of data and information collected from the field survey of sample households. For this study, face-to-face survey was conducted amongst 878 head of forest village households of the 39 forest villages in the Alipurduar District of West Bengal. It is noticed that forest plays an important role to get shape of villagers separate socio-economic as well as cultural life. The site and location of forest villagers' has a profound impact on livelihood which they have been adapted according to their capacity and needs. So the manner, customs and behaviour related to forest environment as well as forest based economy have been studied to observe livelihood adaptation power and economy of forest villagers in locality of the study area. It is also investigated that villagers are primarily depend on forests for number of forest resources and needs like fodder, fuel, fruit, timber, flower, tubers, roots, leaves, medicines, firewood and minor forest products etc. The effort has been made to show the details of collection of forest resources such consumption of Non-Timber Forest Product (NTFPs), fodder, timber, fuel wood as well as time spent and distanced covered for collection of these resources and it is notice that there is a negative relation between consumption of fuel-wood and distance.

For the purpose of assuring a healthy forest resources management, there must be contribution of idea of local inhabitants mainly forest villagers who have close interaction with forests along with their attitudes, perspectives, suggestions and ideas concerning sustainable forests protection on their locality. Based on a participatory approach, the prime aim of this study was to identify villagers' perception about change in forest cover in the years, period of tree felled, perception about present and future forest stock, about forest values as well as environment related views such as perception about the effect of forests on ecological changes, reasons for shrinkage of forest area, destruction, its responsibilities and solutions. It is noticed that villagers were consented about the influence of forest on the environmental vulnerability such as increasing normal temperature and decreasing amount of normal rainfall over last few years, the river bank erosion and landslides in the high altitude area, and large scale tree felling as the single reason for forest destruction and shrinkage. Villagers also opined that more and more afforestation is one and only good way of solution of environmental and other forests related problems in the area. The study indicated that forest villagers preferred more economic value as well as ecological values of forests than social values. Respondents believed that the ecological values of the forests is being very relevant in present days due to phenomenal change of local environment, and predicted that the forests cover will have increased for their livelihoods, health and future generation.

It is also identified that different anthropogenic activities such as changes in land use pattern, jhum cultivation, tea garden extension, conversion of forest cover area into agricultural and habitat lands etc. has become a primary issue for loss natural corridors of animals and are the main causes for man-animal conflict in this area. Man-animal conflict has over the few years become a major concern for wildlife management in North Bengal-Duars region. The conflicts of villagers with elephant, tiger, leopard, monkeys, gaur, wild boar, and rhino have become a regular feature. So immediately Government should ensure proper amount of compensation for victims and take up effective preventive measure against conflicts. Besides, forest authority must take steps to enrich trees of animal food as well as corridors to reduce crop raid and animals attack.

The study also highlighted the coherent relation between socio-economic conditions of forest villagers and their participation in different programmes of the Joint Forest Management (JFM) as well as different important activities of JFMC programs such as horticulture, NTFPs processing, nursery of small plants and medical plants, cleaning of forest, sal and teak plantation of felling area, seed handling which are related with forest villagers' socio-economic condition and participation through sustainable management. But it is noticed that JFMC members are not properly appointed to work in these working circles and less number of members sometimes had been engaged in these schemes. The EDCs, FPCs and other communities' leadership is not observed more in number. It is also observed that only 13.48% women were engaged as JFM member where JFM aims is to involve 50% women as major actors in forest management participatory programme, so there is a clear gender disparity occurred which should be eradicate to success the aims of the JFM project. Besides the JFM members are getting less interest as there is no regular source of income and employment opportunity in this programme. Although JFM project opened up many avenues for forests as well villagers development but a number of difficulties and issues have been identified that is need to be addressed by the Government and the non-governmental organization to overcome the problems. Lastly they are convinced that only central and state forests organizations are not successful enough in terms of forest protection and sustainable development. So in terms of managing and protecting local forests, it has been understood that forest villagers are more willing to protect forest resources through participatory and cooperative approach with central and state forests organization.

Contents

List of Abbreviations

BTR	Buxa Tiger Reserve
CCF	Chief Conservator of Forest
DFD	Deputy Field Director
DFO	Divisional Forest Officer
EDC	Eco-Development Committee
FV	Forest Village
FD	Forest Department
FPC	Forest Protection Committee
JFM	Joint Forest Management
JFMC	Joint Forest Management Committee
LUP	Land Use Planning
MOEF	Ministry of Environment and Forests
NABARD	National Bank for Agriculture and Rural Development
NBSS	National Bureau of Soil Survey
NGO	Non-Governmental Organisation
NREGA	National Rural Employment Guarantee Act
NTFP	Non-Timber Forest Product
PA	Protected Area
PCCF	Principal Chief Conservator of Forest
PMRY	Pradhaan Mantri Rozgaar Yojna
PRA	Participatory Rural Appraisal
RO	Range Officer
SHG	Self Help Group
SME	Small and Medium Enterprises
TE	Tea Estate
VFC	Village Forest Committees

List of Appendices

1 Chapter Introduction

1.1 Problem and Issues

The socio-economic life of the forest villagers is nearly intermixed and interrelated with the forests that by now forests and villagers have become unseparated word. The forest being a permanent home for the villagers, they think it as their ancestral home and in that way there is an emotional attachment of forest villagers with forests. The forests form an integral part of the physical, economic, social and spiritual lives of forest villagers. The forest resources add to villagers' livelihood security, especially for forest villagers and those living people on the fringe area. The forest constitutes a natural asset of immense value which contributing directly and indirectly to the well-being of forest villagers as well as for inhabitants of surrounding area. Directly the forest, as a renewable productive resource, provides fuel wood and woods for house construction, a variety of minor forest product such as dry branches, bamboo, cane, katha, khair-gilta, resin, grasses, gums, wax, leaves and medicinal herbs. Indirectly, the forest performs protective functions and accounts for a large number of environmental and ecological advantages like preserving the air quality clean, moderating climates, checking soil erosion and landslides, mitigating floods, working as reserves for wildlife etc. Like millions of people in the world living in forest environment for livelihood, India, too, has a huge population living near to the forest with their livelihood linked to the forests. There are around 1.73 lakh villages residing in and around forests (Ministry of Environment and Forests, 2006). Although there is no official census figures for the forest dependent population in the country, different estimates put the figures from 275 million

(Bhattacharya, et al., 2008) to 350-400 million population (Ministry of Environment and Forests, 2009) live in forests. Moreover, a significant percentage of the country's underprivileged villagers happen to be living in its forested area (Mahapatra, 1992). It has been estimated that more than 40 % among the poor of the country are living in forest (Ministry of Environment and Forests, 2006). The forest villagers do not only collect forest resources (minor forest product) for their own consumption but also for commercial purpose, which bring them some income opportunity (Kolay, 2000). The income from sale of the forest resources for households living in and around forest constitutes 40 to 60 % of their total income (Malhotra, et al., 1991). About 80 % of their food comes either directly from the forest or through shifting cultivation (Philip, et al., 1985). A variety of mushroom, tubers, tender bamboo shoots and green leafy vegetables are collected and eaten or stored for future use. The study of Niyamatullah (1984) identified 83 edible items that are available in the forest of Madhya Pradesh alone. Studies in Orissa, Madhya Pradesh, Himachal Pradesh and Bihar indicate that over 80 % of the forest villagers depend on the forest for 25% to 50 % of their food. Besides these, forest also supplies to the villagers with their requirements for building material, fuel and fodder. In addition, villagers also collect minor forest produce like leaves honey, gum, flowers and sell these to earn an income. Villagers also derive their medicines from the herbs, trees, animals and birds. The study on forest tribal medicine in Kerala identified at least 30 varieties of leaves, 39 species of roots, 12 species of barks, 15 types of fruits, and many kinds of flowers and latex and nine entire plants that are consumed by the forest villagers (Gadgil et al., 1982). The same is noticed in other parts of the country. For instance, more than 900 plants and herbs are used for medical purposes by the forest villagers in West Bengal (Fernandes, et al, 1988). A study on the extent of use of Non-Timber Forest Products (NTFPs) in north east India suggests that the tribal villagers use 343 NTFPs for diverse purposes like edible fruits (75 species), medicinal (163 species) and vegetables (65 species) and others. Besides, the dependency for house construction, firewood and other materials is hundred and more in number; and NTFPs contribute 19% - 32 % of total household income for the forest villagers under study in the Buxa Tiger Reserve (Das, 2005). Considering the socio-cultural importance of NTFPs in forest livelihoods, Wickens (1991) believes that NTFPs are:

> All the biological components that may be collected from forest ecosystems, managed plantations etc. and be utilized within the household have social, cultural or religious significance, be marketed. Thus, non-timber forest products include plants used for fodder, medicine, food, fibres, fuel, bio-chemical, etc.

So it is clear that forest have been strongly linked with the development of man and his society. From the emergence of the primitive man on this earth in the Eolithic age (a million years ago) to the modern times, man has been heavily dependent on forest.

In Alipurduar district, the study area of the present work, forests are not only a source of income for more than twenty thousand households but it also provides employment opportunities for the forest villagers. This makes forest an important contributor to the forest villagers' economy. The villagers living in forest of this district depend upon forests for variety of goods and services. These includes collection of edible fruits, flowers, tubers, roots and leaves for food and medicines; firewood for both cooking and selling in the market; wood materials for agricultural implements, house construction and fencing; fodder i.e. grass and leaves for livestock and grazing of livestock in forest; and collection of a large amount of marketable non-timber forest products. These activities of villagers are continuous from their ancestral period till now. But their extensive dependence pattern of villagers on forests, over exploitation of forest resources and unsustainable harvest practice, increasing population and changing standards of living have brought increasing pressure on forests. Therefore whatever resources were considered free gift of nature of unlimited quantity is now presently considered shrinkage and limited resources because of excessive exploitation that is greater than regeneration and growth, a trend which potentially degrades the forests of the district and due to which forest villagers face a serious shortage of livelihood needs or resources such as fruits, flowers, tubers, roots and leaves for food and medicines; fuel wood for both cooking, wood materials for agricultural, house construction and fencing; grass, leaves for livestock and grazing of livestock field; and non-timber forest products. The increasing awareness about the limited supply of forest raw-material, their renewable nature resources being constrained because of more exploitation than regeneration, has brought into focus the need for forest development strategies with reference to environmental degradation.

Earlier, the forest village economy was self-supporting subsistence economy and villagers could satisfy their meagre wants by hunting, food-gathering, minor forest produce and primitive cultivation. But now, due to laws enforced by the Forest Department, the rights of villagers on forests and forest resource are reduced day by day along with their chances of making a livelihood from their natural habitat. Now forest villagers in the plains and low altitude areas depend only on traditional agriculture, mainly food crops with livestock grazing which found in Gadadhar, Garobasti, Balapara, Suni and other villages. But in high altitude areas, villagers practised horticulture farming throughout the year. It has to be mentioned that the Forest Department gave each family 2 to 3 acre of land as agreement holder for cultivation in 1998 but now due to extension and separation of family members less quantity of land comes to them without any agreement. Moreover, forest villagers have little opportunity to work in the tea gardens that are close to the tea gardens. Therefore the villagers are forced to work as wage earners outside the forest to earn their livelihood needs. As a result, few of them have reverted to shifting cultivation while some have left the forest habitat and have shifted to urban areas for searching of jobs and became slum-inhabitants facing all the miseries and trouble of the urban poor. However most of the landless and jobless young generation are going to nearby states and countries for employment and better opportunities resulting in inter-state and international migration among the villagers. Such inhabitants are from Pana, Bhutri, Gangutia, Garopara, Poro basti (North), Bhutiabasti, Adma, Chunabati, Lepchakhawa and Tashi, where villagers are going to Bhutan, Assam and other states for employment (Das, 2000). The agriculture is the primary source of livelihood for most of the forest villagers in this District. But villagers still practised primitive agriculture using traditional modes of cultivation. Lacking knowledge of modern agricultural practices and the money to buy the necessary equipment, the villagers rarely use modern techniques of cultivation and therefore their agricultural outputs are not at the satisfactory level. On the other hand, they do not get agriculture loan from the government or other non-government organisations as they do not have proper documents of land-ownership and other properties. Lack of irrigation is another common problem and it is severe in high altitude horticulture practice areas that are apparent in Adma, Gangutia, Chunabati, Raimatang and other such villages. Apart from this a vast acreage of land is infertile and waste, rocky, barren and unirrigated and therefore the forest villagers are not interested to cultivate their land attentively.

The average cultivable land-holdings among the forest villagers have decreased because forest villages occupied vested land without any proper document or patta. Most of the inhabitants do not enjoy tenancy or legal rights on the residential land or on the agricultural land, which they or their ancestors cleared once. As a result, they always live with the fear of eradication by the Forest Department. In some cases the Forest Department possessed some of their land for departmental purpose and made them landless or labourers on their own lands. Although the State Government provided a few of them with 'patta' of land in Gudamdabri and Poro (North) forest villages in 2015 but still most of the villagers have not been provided with 'land patta' or other related papers for further benefit. Therefore they are unable to get financial assistance from Government schemes, NGOs or institutional sources as they have no recognized right or proper documents on land and other properties. Being the inhabitants of remote forests area untouched by revenue department, they hardly come under the purview of the development administration of the Block and whatever development schemes have been implemented; the benefits either do not reach the forest villages in remote areas or do not reach in time. For that reason, despite development schemes launched by the state or central governments, the forest villagers face a large number of socio-economic problems such as economic exploitation, social and cultural exploitation, unemployment, land alienation and lack of education. Since most of the villages are located in the interior of forests, on hilly areas or at high altitudes-e.g. Jayanti (inside the forest), Bhutri forest basti and Raimatang basti (inside the forest and in hilly area), Adma and Chunabati (forest and at high altitude) villagers are exploited by outsiders, money-lenders and vendors who buy at cheap prices of agricultural and other commodities that they produce from the land or collect from the forests. Due to undulating land, dense forest cover, huge number of small and big rivers and springs across un-metalled road, the transport network is poor in situation. Only one or two mini buses/ jeep/ auto ply between nearby markets and the forest villages; in some cases there is no bus, auto or jeep plying directly from market to village, that is noticed in Jayanti, Bhutri forest basti, Raimatangbasti, Adma, Chunabati. As a result villagers are isolated from the mainstream of life; therefore brokers, vendors from Kalchini, Hamitlonganj, Alipurduar and other parts travelling to the forest villages to sell daily products at highest prices and purchase at cheaper rates whatever the villagers produce. These include food grains e.g. corn, spices e.g. ginger, pepper, chilly, and vegetables such as brinjal, squash, cucumber, kochu (an esculent edible root), beans and non-timber forest product such as fuel wood, grass, bamboo, wax, gums, tree leaves, medicinal plants, etc. The only other alternative for the forest villagers is the weekly market. In some places there is no local market. In that way day by day the villagers are economically exploited by outsiders. Besides due to lack of money in their hand, most of the villagers borrow from private money-lenders for cultivation and livestock rearing. The money-lenders charge high rates of interest by which they are indebted. If they cannot repay their debt, they are forced to repay with their cultivable products or forest collections, and as a result they are pulled further below the poverty line. Even in some cases they have to work as bonded labourers outside the village. Tribal women/girls of forest villages are victims of social and cultural exploitation and gender harassments. Tribal culture is misconceived. Their traditional dress and free behaviour are wrongly understood. Outsiders such as contractors, truck drivers, tourists, social workers, etc. belittle their culture and consider it cheap and vulnerable. Girls are lured or enticed and fall victim to allurements.

Conflict of villagers over forest rights, forest products (timber and non-timber forest products) and with animals (man-elephant conflict, man-leopard conflict, and man-bison conflict) are common and it occurs at regular intervals. As a result villagers often lose their cultivated food crops and vegetables and in some cases elephants and bison damage their standing crops. Moreover, elephants have been known to injure or even kill villagers as well as damaging their houses. Besides cattle-predation by leopards is also happens frequently. On the other hand, forest villagers' accelerate increasing demands of land and forests resources has affected this ecosystem to a great extent and made overall environment vulnerable as well as unsustainable. High rate of illiteracy among both male and female inhabitants is a prominent picture among the villagers. Hence illiteracy and ignorance are the main hurdles for village development. The illiterate villagers often look at their children as assets to their family and they are made to support their parents' income by working as labourers collecting forest resources or working in the agriculture sector as labour. Therefore, traditionally they are not being educated or their education is confined to the primary level; even the children themselves are not interested to go to school. More or less each forest village has a free primary school but there is no secondary or higher secondary school for upper primary and high school education in the surrounding areas. Flash floods occur during every monsoon period due to sudden excess rainfall in the Bhutan hills, damaging the forest villagers' houses and properties which are located near river banks. In that period some villages are totally isolated and disconnected due to sudden overflowing of the rivers as there are no bridges across the rivers. For example, Gangutia forest village is disconnecting by Raimatang non-perennial river and Bhutri forest basti by Panna Non-perennial River. Villagers do not get medical facilities because there are no sub-centers or primary health centres within village territory. As a result, the villagers have moved towards Alipurduar, Kochbehar, or even Siliguri for treatment. Mal nutrition among the villagers presents a severe problem and in some places villagers have died due to lack of sufficient food which is an unfortunate incident to modern society. Moreover lack of proper drinking water, only one source of fuel wood (non-timber forest wood), inappropriate livestock grazing and shortage of livestock grazing fields are also prominent challenges among the villagers. All the above problems are simultaneously pulling the forest villagers in this district back and their daily lives are directly and indirectly affected by these social and economic problems. As a result, the forest villagers are still remaining backward in all sense.

1.2 Study Area

Alipurduar District is the new district of North Bengal, covering an area of 2526.30 sq. km. (Statistical Hand Book of Jalpaiguri District, 2011). It is situated between 26°23'11" and 26°52'30" north latitudes and 89°02'30" and 89°53'07" east longitudes. The District was established in 25th June of 2014. The headquarter of the District is at Alipurduar town, and has its special importance in respect of tourism, forests, hill, tea gardens, scenic beauty and a wide variety of tribes like the Totos, Dukpa, Mech, Rava, Santal etc. (Grunning, 1911).

The area is bounded by Assam in the east and Jalpaiguri district in the west and the Bhutan in the north, Kochbehar district in the south. Topographically, the whole area is crisscrossed with springs, rivers and hills; northern part of

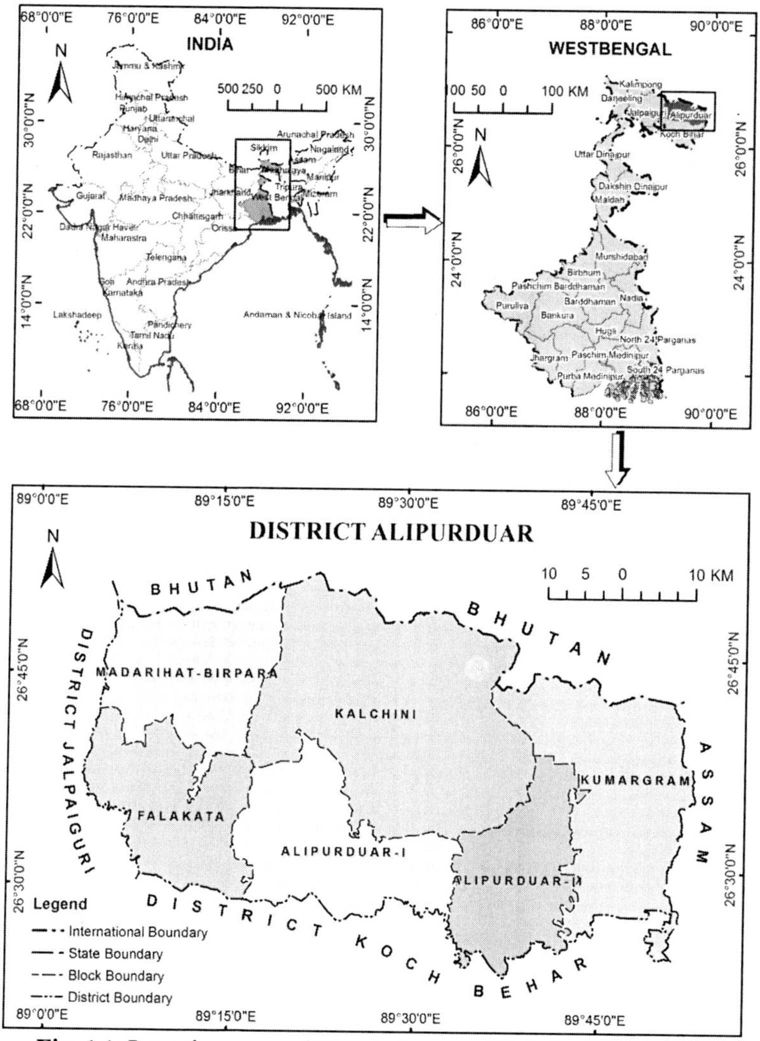

Fig. 1.1: Location map of the study area, District Alipurduar

the district is adjacent to the Bhutan hill relatively with high altitude. Comparatively low lying plain cultivated lands are extended in the southern part of the district. The area is drained by number of rivers; important are being the Torsa, Kaljani, Raidak, Sonkosh, Mujnai, Gaburbasra, Dima, Pana, Bala and Jainti which are also subjected to occasional flooding (Grunning, 1911). This piece of land has been properly named as the land of 'Tea, Timber and Tourism'. A major extension of area is bordered in the north by the Bhutan country and hence the name 'Duars' which mean 'Door of Bhutan'. Climatically, the area experiences the south-west monsoon and south-east monsoon. So heavy rainfall comes in between June to September and average rainfall varies from 2800 to 3300 mm and the average temperature ranges from 31.9°C to 11.8°C throughout the year (Statistical Hand book of Jalpaiguri District, 2018). The soil status of the district is sandy to sandy loam having low water holding capacity. The main kharif crops are Aus and Amon. Besides, some vegetables, namely brinjal tomato, cauliflower, cabbage, beans, cucumber, pumpkin, chilli etc. have gained as exporting quality. The only important tree of this area is sal. Other valuable trees which are fairly numerous are teak, sissoo, chair, kamjal and simul (Grunning, 1911). The forest may be divided into different types; these are (i) Deciduous forests (sal, sissoo, schimawallichii), (ii) Mixed forests of which sal is found scattered here and there, (iii) Evergreen forests species are numerous including Luqinia, Glaeocarpus, Echinocarpus, Michelia and canes, (iv) Savannah forests (Saccharum, Erianthus, Imperata cylindrical). This forests average height is in between 25 m to 45 m. In fact it is a store house of bio-diversity for which tourists very often visit North Bengal. There are two important pockets of wilderness which have been reserved carefully in Alipurduar District where wild animals can wander without disturbance. These are i) Buxa wildlife sanctuary & tiger reserve: 761.09 sq. km ii) Jaldapara wildlife sanctuary: 216.51 sq. km, (State Forest Report, 2013). Most of the area is connected by roads and are found as metalled and non-metalled, also there are railways of broad gauge, but many areas of this district are still suffering from inadequate transport and communication which influences the marketing system. The region was inhabited by 1337575 persons (Census, 2001) and it is 1491250 persons (Census, 2011). The density of population was 471 persons/sq. km (Census, 2001) and now it is 525 persons/sq. km (Census, 2011). Major ethnic groups are Ravas, Mechs, Rajbanshi, Santals, Totos, Garos, Oraons, Nepalees, etc. (Kar, 2003). There are 39 forest villages of 2948 households with the population of more than twenty thousand in Alipurduar District (Das, 2000) and more than 90% of the forest villages belongs to ST community who are economically, culturally and socially backward (9th working plan of Jalpaiguri Forest Division, vol. I, 2008-09). The Alipurduar District consists of Alipurduar Municipality and six Community Development (CD) blocks: Alipurduar-I, Kalchini, Alipurduar-II, Madarihat-Birpara, Falakata and Kumargram. Alipurduar Sadar (town) is the districts headquarter along with Alipurduar municipality and other office. At present there is no subdivision formed in the district. But according to the forest administration area, there are three administrative divisions fall in this district and these are Jalpaiguri forest division, Alipurduar forest division and Kochbehar forest division.

1.3 Objectives

In proposed work the following objectives are considered:

a. To examine socio-economic condition of forest villagers in relation to the forest ecology.
b. To analyze how the forest villagers depend on forest as well as for Non-Timber Forest Product (NTFPs) and other resources for livelihood.
c. To highlight the role of JFM on the protection of forests and villagers development.
d. To consider relevant suggestions and recommendations for further development.

1.4 Research Methods and Tools of Data Collection

To fulfil the above objectives, the methodologies used in the research have been discussed below. Qualitative as well as quantitative methodologies are applied not only to collect data but also for the synthesis of those data. The techniques for the analysis of data, issues and problems faced during fieldwork are also examined here. For this research finding, the collection of qualitative and quantitative data and information, both primary and secondary sources received equal priority. To discuss primary and secondary data, qualitative as well as quantitative methodologies have been used concurrently.

1.4.1 Data and Information Source

1.4.1.1 Secondary Sources

This study started with detailed work at the North Bengal University, Birpara College and Siliguri College Library. This research work provided data and information on socio-economic characteristics of forest village and other related details of forest livelihoods of Alipurduar District. Although, there is not sufficient official record or document of forest villages and their livelihoods in colonial period of Bengal and Alipurduar District, the books, articles and correspondence of different forest officers of the West Bengal and new formed Alipurduar District were consulted for information. To synthesis the socio-economic characteristics such as ethnic composition, economy, anthropogenic activities, and other details of forest village of the study area, the state Government's annual forest reports such as '*Ninth Working plan of Jalpaiguri Forest Division*, Directorate of Forests, Volume-I (2008-09)'; '*State Forest Report, 2005 to 2013*', Directorate of Forests; '*Management-cum-working plan of Buxa Tiger Reserve*', Forest Department, Govt. of West Bengal, Vol. 1(2000); 'Tiger Conservation Plan', BTR, 2016-17 to 2026-27; '*Statistical Handbook of Jalpaiguri District*', 2011 to 2018; *Eastern Bengal and Assam District Gazetteers, Jalpaiguri*, 2008, and the West Bengal Tribal Development Cooperative Corporation Ltd. (WBTDCC) annual reports (1990-2005) have been examined.

Although, a limited amount of topic related relevant

previous research work has been done on forest livelihoods and NTFPs in East Indian states, therefore, during the analysis of livelihood need of forest village, NTFPs, Joint Forest Management (JFM) and other related details of the research area, in addition to the annual reports of different government organizations, previous project reports by organizations such as '*Annual Report of Ministry of Environment and Forest' (2005 to 09)*, '*Kirat Bhumi, Jalpaiguri Zila Sankalan*' (2003) and National Afforestation and Eco-Development Board (NAEB) have been consulted. Books and articles on forest villagers' demography, activities of JFM, NTFPs and forest livelihoods in West Bengal and other state of the country such as '*Joint Forest Management in India*' (2008), '*Role of NTFPs among forest villagers in a protected area of West Bengal*' (2005) were followed. Besides online information such as web maps, web journals, web books and newspaper articles have been referred as the source of secondary data and information. For the identification of villages and households targeted for semi-structured interviews, forest village map and other thematic maps were used. To get a clear view of the socio-physical features of the sampled villages, site map of forest village, land-use and land-cover maps (including forest cover), soil map, drainage and water-body maps were also referred. For this purpose, the State Forest Offices such as Beat and Range (Department of Forest, Government of West Bengal), the Chief Conservator of Forests, North Bengal, Forest Survey of India (FSI), Kolkata, and Divisional Forest Office (Alipurduar, Jalpaiguri, Kochbehar) were contacted. Google image maps, topographical maps and cadastral map of the Survey of India at the scale of 1:50,000 and 1: 3960 were used during fieldwork. The National Atlas and Thematic Mapping Organization (NATMO) published the 'District Planning Map' of Jalpaiguri and Kochbehar District using remote sensing technologies. All these maps were used during fieldwork. Jalpaiguri District was divided into two separate Districts (Jalpaiguri and Alipurduar) on 25th June 2014. As most of the reserved, protected forest areas and forest villages are in the District of Alipurduar, the fieldwork was arranged in Alipurduar District for research purpose. However, in the 'Annual Forest Report' from 2005 to 2013 of West Bengal both Districts have been considered as one District that is Jalpaiguri and all data and information related to forest have been considered as of Jalpaiguri District only, so for this research, data and information on Alipurduar District as a single was used after sorting carefully (as research work considered after 25th June 2015). Census data (which includes socio-economic information on households) and the voter lists were also useful sources for the selection of interviewee/participants to be interviewed. Census data also provided information about demography, literacy, landholding and occupation and other socio-economic information of the interviewees and villages.

1.4.1.2 Primary Sources

For the collection of primary data and information, predominantly qualitative methods were used. These included interviews such as semi-structured interviews, group discussions and elite interviews. The semi-structured interviews were organised with forest villagers, Ranger Officers, Forest guards, Beat Officers. To get data and information from forest officers, elite interviews were arranged. Questionnaires were used for the household survey among sampled forest villagers to obtain qualitative as well as quantitative data such as demography, economy, adaptation habits, dependency and perception on forests. In addition to these methodologies, discussion with local villagers and direct observation as well as participatory appraisal were undertaken to get information on the collection, storage, marketing and impacts of NTFPs on forest livelihoods.

1.4.2 Methodologies for Primary Data Collection

The semi-structured interviews, elite interviews and group discussions were used in this research for generating more qualitative information whereas questionnaires were used to collect both qualitative as well as quantitative data from forest villagers (Appendix B, C). Finally, both qualitative and quantitative data were compared to obtain accurate picture of the contemporary situation regarding socio-economic, ecological adaptation, dependency on NTFPs, perception and participation in the Joint Forest Management. Using these methodologies, a huge amount of data and information were generated which cover many subjects of forest villagers' livelihoods and their dependence on forest. The survey was designed to explore data or information regarding the demography, social status, economy, dependency on forest. Also it was try to discuss villagers' feelings, their understandings of the surrounding environments and their perception using related questions in the questionnaire.

Table–1.1
Methodologies used for empirical data collection

Methodologies used for empirical data collection		
Interviews	Interviewees and places visited for empirical data collection with date	
	Elite interviews	Chief Conservator of Forest (CCF), Wildlife (North Bengal), Government of West Bengal (02-03-2015); Chief Conservator of Forest (CCF), North Bengal, Government of West Bengal (05-03-2015); Divisional Forest Officer, Jalpaiguri Forest Division, Jalpaiguri (08-03-2015); Field Director (FD), Buxa Tiger Reserve (12-03-2015); Deputy Field Director (DFD), Buxa Tiger Reserve, East (17-03-2015); Deputy Field Director (DFD), Buxa Tiger Reserve, West (22-03-2015).
	Semi-structured interviews	Ranger, Dalgaon range, Jalpaiguri Forest Division (29-03-2015); Members of JFM, Lehra village, Dalgaon range, Jalpaiguri Forest Division (02-04-2015); Forest guard, Bandapani beat, Jalpaiguri Forest Division (5-04-2015); Ranger, West

	Raja Bhatkhawa range, Buxa Tiger Reserve, West (9-04-2015); Ranger, Nimati range, Buxa Tiger Reserve, West (13-04-2015); Ranger, Hamiltonganj range, Buxa Tiger Reserve, West (17-04-2015); Ranger, Buxaduar range, Buxa Tiger Reserve, East (21-04-2015); Ranger, Jainty range, Buxa Tiger Reserve, East (25-04-2015); Ranger, Kumargram range, Buxa Tiger Reserve, East (29-04-2015).
Group discussions	Ranger and forest staffs of Dalgaon range, Jalpaiguri Forest Division (04-05-2015); Ranger and Forest staffs, Hamiltonganj range office (06-05-2015); Lehra villagers, Dalgaon range, Jalpaiguri Forest Division (08-05-2015) ; Sankosh villagers, Kumargram range, Buxa Tiger Reserve, East (10-05-2015); Lapraguri villagers, Barobhisa beat, Buxa Tiger Reserve, East (11-05-2015); Bhutri forest basti, Hamiltonganj range, Buxa Tiger Reserve, West (13-05-2015); Poro villagers, West Damanpur range, Buxa Tiger Reserve, West (14-05-2015); JFM groups of Dalgaon range, Jalpaiguri Forest Division (17-05-2015); JFM groups of Hamiltonganj range, Buxa Tiger Reserve, West (21-05-2015); JFM groups of Nimati range (24-05-2015), Buxa Tiger Reserve, West; JFM groups of Pana range (26-05-2015), Buxa Tiger Reserve, West; JFM groups of Bholka range, Buxa Tiger Reserve, East (30-05-2015).

Questionnaires survey of sample household with date			
Forest Division	**Range office**	**Beat office**	**Forest village**
Jalpaiguri Forest Division	Dalgaon range	Bandapani	Lehra village (No. of Household-22), 17-06-2015 to 19-06-2015.
			Suni village (No. of Household-28), 09-06-2015 to 16-06-2015.
Buxa Tiger Reserve, West Division	West Raja-bhatkhowa	West Raja-bhatkhowa	Garo Basti (No. of Household -72), 18-08-2015 to 24-08-2015
	East Damanpur	Gadhadhar	Gadhadhar (No. of Household-63), 01-10-2015 to 06-10-2015.
	West Damanpur	East Poro	Poro (N) (No. of Household-61), 09-10-2015 to 15-10-2015.
	Nimati	West Poro	Nimati and Dabri (No. of Household - 68), 25-12-2015 to 31-12- 2015.
	Pana	Gangutia	Gangutia (No. of Household -55), 01-01-2016 to 05-01-2016.
		Adma	Adma (No. of Household -55), 31-03-2016 to 04-03-2016.
		Raimatang	Raimatang (No. of

			Household -55), 07-05-2016 to 12-05-2016.
	Hamiltonganj	Bhutri	Bhutri forest basti (No. of Household - 45), 15-08-2016 to 20-08- 2016.
		Hamiltonganj	Gudamdabri (No. of Household -63), 18-10-2016 to 23-10-2016.
Buxa Tiger Reserve, East Division	Buxaduar	Chunabati	Chunabati (No. of Household -54), 25-12-2016 to 31-12-2016.
	Jainty (south)	Bhutiabasti	Bhutiabasti (No. of Household -30), 01-01-2017 to 04-01-2017.
	Kumargram	Sankosh	Sankosh (No. of Household -60), 17-04-2017 to 22-04-2017.
	Bholka	Barobhisa	Lapraguri (No. of Household -47), 25-08-2017 to 29-08-2017.
	Buxaduar	Santrabari	Santrabari (No. of Household - 65), 01-10-2017 to 06-10-2017.
	Bholka	Balapara	Balapara (No. of Household -35), 25-12-2017 to 31-12-2017.

Source: Prepared based on field survey, 2017

1.4.2.1 Elite Interviews

This type of interview is connected with an 'elite person' in their respective field, who has a good knowledge of the research topic. The elite interviewee (persons of officer rank) is in a position to provide a maximum amount of data and information to the researcher in a very short period of time. For this research elite interviews were organized with the Chief Conservator of Forest (CCF), Wildlife (North Bengal), Government of West Bengal (02-03-2015); Chief Conservator of Forest (CCF), North Bengal, Government of West Bengal (05-03-2015); Divisional Forest Officer, Jalpaiguri Forest Division, Jalpaiguri (08-03-2015); Field Director (FD), Buxa Tiger Reserve (12-03-2015); Deputy Field Director (DFD), Buxa Tiger Reserve, East (17-03-2015); Deputy Field Director (DFD), Buxa Tiger Reserve, West (22-03-2015); A total of six (6) elite interviews were conducted during fieldwork.

1.4.2.2 Semi-Structured Interviews

Semi-structured interviews were chosen because it does not follows any inflexible or specific order and at the same time, new questions as well as topics related to the research area, could also be added and discussed. For this study, semi-structured interviews were held with forest villagers, Ranger Officers, Forest guards, Beat Officers, other Forest Department staff, villagers/members of Joint Forest Management Committee who have knowledge about villagers' background, need, activities, cultures, social and economic condition, and involvement in plantation, NTFPs business at the ground level. Nine (9) semi-structured interviews were arranged. In this case, interviewees were able to share own views and knowledge in a flexible and informal environment. All answers were written at the time and simultaneously recoded by mobile recorder.

During field survey, to overcome the language problem between researcher and interviewees (villagers), an interpreter was used at the time of interview from villagers' community who had good knowledge of their native language that is

Nepali and Adivasi as well as Bengali, thus the comments from local people were translated to English language at the time of interviews. Interpreters, however, also helped the researcher to be friendly between the researcher and forest villagers as interpreters were mostly selected from the sampled villages and mostly young people from forest communities, who were college students and had very good relationships with other forest villagers and knowledge about the forest community, were selected as interpreters.

1.4.2.3 Group Discussion

Group discussions were applied in this research for several causes such as group discussions were normally organised in a relaxed environment for participant compared to semi-structured or elite interviews; and participants felt and acted more naturally in this case. Through such discussion, several common views and opinions have been exposed on complex questions and subjects. Besides as most of the participants in a group were from the same background, they were free from hesitation and happy to consult the same topic from different points of view. This provided some extra information for the research topic. Finally, for 'group discussions' the group worked as a very popular methodology as it generates new and unexpected information on topic. For this research, 12 (twelve) group discussions were arranged. These were two with the Ranger and forest staffs of Dalgaon (Jalpaiguri Forest Division) and Hamiltonganj range office (Buxa Tiger Reserve, West Division). Five group discussions were organized with forest villagers, two in both from Buxa Tiger Reserve, West and East Division and another one taken from Jalpaiguri Forest Division. Another five group discussions were organized with members of Joint Forest Management Committee (JFMC) of which three were taken from Buxa Tiger Reserve, West Division, one from each of Buxa Tiger Reserve, East Division and Jalpaiguri Forest Division respectively. There were six to ten participants in each group.

Each group discussion ran from an hour to two hours. Open questions were discussed during this time. The topics of discussion were revealed to all the group members at the time of discussion. All information of group discussions were noted down and recorded by mobile recorder. Important points had also been taken as special notes during discussions session. The researcher tried to shorten the problems associated with group discussions. Sensitive issues (such as collection of forest product legally or illegally, conflict between foresters and villagers) were normally avoid in discussion. It was very common that some of the participants took a more active role and gave more ideas than others. Therefore, the researcher targeted to give all the participants an equal opportunity to express own ideas by supplied each of all the group participants with a pre-formatted sample of questions; which were consulted during group discussions. This helped participants to take fast preparations and their decisions. However, not all the participants viewed the group discussions with equal importance. To solve this problem, the researcher tried to make all participants understand the importance of this research from the perspective of forest preservation and forest livelihoods. To discuss all the research related subjects and to arrange local environment, an assistant was also taken from the same community who had good ideas about other language to run the discussion.

1.4.2.4 Questionnaires

Questionnaire (Appendix B) surveys were conducted among forest villagers mainly for the generation of quantitative data. Through such surveys, large amounts of data were generated in a short period of time for chapter 4, 5, 6, 7 and chapter 8. Some open questions, which generated qualitative data, were included in the questionnaire to share forest villagers' opinions on the research related subject. Questionnaires were used in 17 sample forest villages (44% of total number, i.e. 39) of three forest divisions. The questionnaire was divided into two parts. The first part deals with the demographic features of sampled forest village (Appendix B). Whereas the second part associates with the household schedule (Appendix C) or socio-economic part including resources for livestock feeding, kind of forest resources uses, house building materials, consumption pattern and dependence on NTFPs, kind of fuel and its use, reasons for forest destruction from villagers point of view, perception on forest, wood collection and consumption by villagers, participation to activities of Joint Forest Management and various other problems of agriculture and stock breeding, suggestions for further improvement forest etc.

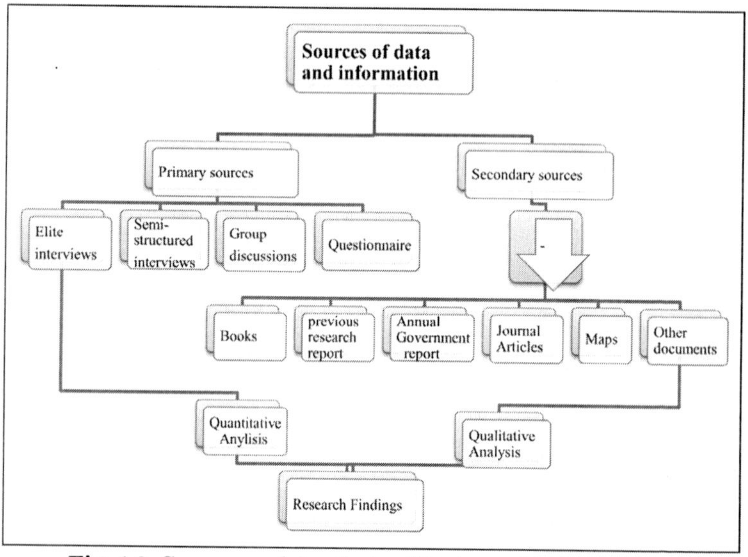

Fig. 1.2: Source and Analysis of Data and Information.

Questionnaire surveys were arranged throughout the whole day but preferred given to the morning and afternoon, so that all types of household members could take part. During field study on consumption of fodder, timber collection, tree felling and storage related questions were asked to the respondents at the time of survey through questionnaire. The questionnaire survey was started from 17th June, 2015 and continued until 31st December, 2017. This long fieldwork period was also useful in providing information on the different aspects of villages and villagers socio-economic characteristics. There are some limitations in using this technique. For example, respondents may not give their opinions or thoughts in a flexible way if most of the answers are of the 'yes' or 'no' type. To avoid this error researcher organized semi-structured interviews and group discussions where villagers were able to share their ideas giving own words.

1.4.2.5 Criterion for Selection of the Sample Villages

The Alipurduar District of West Bengal form the study area which covers 2526.30 sq.km and accommodate a population of 14 lac 91 thousand (Census, 2011), spread over more than 15,000 villages and one municipal town. The majority of the forest villages are small with a population size of less than 300 persons. As the study area has large geographical extent, it is necessary to have representative samples of villages in order to provide wider representation to area as well as villagers. The region has large variations in its altitudinal setting. The villages of Dalgaon forests differ from Buxa and valley slope differs from the other with the corresponding changes in altitude. The changing altitude has influence on vegetation, climate and human settlements. The nature of village eco-system mainly depends upon the altitude on which they are situated. The altitudinal gradient, in fact, is the base on which numerous other environmental gradients are established. Therefore, the most important criterion for selection of sampled villages adopted in the present study is the altitude. The population size of the settlements is another basis of village selection. The altitude helped in the selection of the villages as the villages in their physical setting are located indifferent altitudinal zones. The location aspects like distance of the village from transport lines and the village site such as valley, hill-slope and hill-top, inside of forest is presumed to be taken care of by the random selection of sample villages. It was initially decided to select 17 villages to represent 39 villages, thus, taking one village as representative of more than two villages. However, the 17 villages selected to cover the whole region in a representative manner; hence villages were considered to cover different altitudinal and location sites. The sample villages were selected on the basis of random sampling method where the villages were classified into 3 categories according to population size and the villages with less than 350 populations, the village population between 350-650, and the villages with more than 650 populations. And for such observation random sampling survey were been adopted through questionnaire of 878 household (30% of total household, i.e. 2948) of forest villagers.

1.4.2.6 Analysis of Data

For this research finding, to analyse primary data as well as secondary data and information, qualitative and quantitative methodologies were used simultaneously. For the quantitative analysis of the data on rainfall, temperature were been analyzed by adopting different cartographic techniques to determine climatic condition of the study area. Besides different statistical methods such as central tendency, measures of dispersions, correlation were employed for comparative analysis of the socio-economic conditions of the forest villagers along with different parameters and for calculation and computation of data, MS word and EXCEL software packages were used. For qualitative data analysis, interpretation and table coding were applied. The interpretation includes the copying of interviews, which were arranged through semi-structured interviews, group discussions and elite interviews. Important comments of interviewee, other researchers have been taken during the time of data analysis. Different opinions of forest villagers were collected in the native languages (mainly Nepali, Hindi, and Bengali) and afterwards their comments and views of mother languages were translated into English. Software such as M.S word, MapInfo and Arc GIS were used during the time of qualitative analysis of data. Preparation of maps were been done with the help of MapInfo, Arc GIS software and GPS tool to show the location of study area and other details of forest villages as well as to show the relationship between different components of physical and cultural aspects. Illustrative photographs, videos as well as field-notes were taken during the time of interview and field survey. All of these visual documents, as well as field-notes, were considered during data analysis to find out the differences between the actual situations and the participants' given information.

During this research work following limitations were identified such as secondary data of all kinds were not available in the respective Government office. Some secondary data were not always reliable as it was irrelevant, outdated and partially manipulated. At the time of primary data collection, problems were faced during the period of field survey for this research area. The problems of sampling villages or households were very common in respect of location, language, economy and politics. Therefore, before starting field survey, the researcher considered some issues carefully such as, the socio-economic status, culture, language and ethnicity. Sampling survey was prepared after visiting the research area i.e. location; however, after starting fieldwork, particularly in dense remote villages, several issues such as poor transportation, sudden attack of wild animals (elephants, leopard, bison) in some areas, floods and flash floods in springs and rivers, political disturbances were emerged which the researcher did not expect earlier.

1.5 Meaning and Definition of Forest Village

The genesis of forest villages was a part of forest management in the early part of the last century. The British Government had to fulfil the supply of raw material for wideness of railway lines and collection of revenue to support the British Imperial Government. The need for extraction of forest resources required keeping a regular supply of human labour. In the early time of forest resource occlusion and demand was met through the introduction of 'taungya' system as was earlier practiced in Malaysia and Burma. This process consists of the cutting down and the forest growth, firing it when dry and sowing the areas thus arranged with field crops. When crops have been harvested and, as the case may be, after two or three year's use, the open area is deserted, and a new piece of forest cover is clear felled. This goes on till a forest growth adequate to offer a good flame and enough of ashes have grown upon the place first attacked and felled. The rotational system continued from ten to thirty years. In Burma these clearings are called taungya. The inclusion of local tribal people into the scheme of taungya was very effective for Forest Department. The villagers had become habituated to the employment thus offered, which provide a regular earnings, in addition to the crops which they were able to cultivate just as in former times; and it became possible to pracctice over massive areas, and at the same time to declare better average results. In India, the practice of taungya system was followed mainly in the areas where the local villagers denied sharing labour for Government silvicultural programmes. Primarily, the forest labours were considered as bondsman by the government as they were bound to give free service for forests work for a number of days in a year as specified. Afterwards, the circumstances changed slightly as the migrant labours were offered homesteads and one hector of land in place of services rendered by them to the Forest Department. These hamlets or settlements came to be known as forest villages (Sonowal, 2007). Either existing habitations in the forest were declared as forest villages or people were brought from outside to set up forest villages. The report of the committee on Forestry Programmes for Alleviation of Poverty, GOI (1984), shows that there are five thousand forest villages where two lakhs scheduled tribe (ST) family resideing who are still in the category of inaccessible from the planning process. Individuals in forest villages were allowed to construct small temporary huts and also cultivate some food crops to supplement their earnings. The land thus utilized legally continues to remain 'reserved' forests and the villages were expected to be replaced when there was no forest work. There are also evidences especially from Madhya Pradesh and Gujarat (Prasad and Jahagirdar, 1993) that some revenue villages were transferred to Forest Department to form forest villages. These types of forest villages are technically or administratively known as 'Revenue Forest Village'. The typical forest villages are on the other hand the ones where the labour camps have been replaced into semi-permanent or permanent settlements.

1.6 Forest Policy of India

1.6.1 The First Forest Act of 1865

This act was the first attempts in the direction of regulation of collection of forest produces by the forest villagers. The act empowered the states to declare any land covered with brush or trees cover as state forest and to make rules regarding the management of the same by notification, provided that such notification should not affect or summarize any existing rights of villagers or communities. The government was empowered to prescribe penalty for the violation of provisions or for infringing rules and for the arrest of offenders. In the process, the socially regulated practices of the local people were restrained by law.

1.6.2 The Forest Act of 1878

This Act was more comprehensive than earlier one and divided forest into reserved forests, protected forests and village forests. Villagers or dwellers were to be notified to record their claims over land and forest produce in the proposed reserved and protected forest. Certain activities like trespassing or pasturing of cattle were prohibited and declared certain activities as forest offences and imprisonment and fines were also prescribed. Provisions were made to impose a duty on timber. Some provisions were also made to control private forest. Thus, the 1878 Act continued and extended the Government policy of establishing control over forests.

1.6.3 The First Forest Policy 1894

The Indian Government brought out a wide forest policy in 1894 that clearly spelt out the supremacy of the State's interest over that of villager's interest. By the resolution, forest were divided into 4 divisions: (i) forests, the preservation of which was essential on physical or climatic grounds; (ii) forests, which give a supply of expensive timbers for business purposes; (iii) minor and non-forests and (iv) pasture or feeding land. The above mentioned classification was applicable only to forest under the management of the State. This policy considered the release of forest land for cultivation, subjected to certain safe guards. Also the policy had left a margin of outlying areas of reserved forest for the supply of the villager's needs.

1.6.4 The Indian Forest Act 1927

This was an attempt to formalize all the practices of the forest officials and to regulate further villagers rights over forest lands and produce. The forests were divided into protected, reserved and village forest and elaborate provisions were made to extend State control over forest. The Act removes the reference to communities' rights over forest, which was made in the 1878 Act. This Act has put some control on the shifting or Jhum cultivation with certain special provisions. The State Government was finally to fix on the issue of permission or prohibition. If the state government sanctioned the practice wholly or in part, the Forest Settlement Officer (F.S.O) was to arrange for the dividing of land for such practice. This act created a powerful and adequately protected executive consisting of forest officers of Indian Forest Service (IFS), State Forest Service, Rangers, Beat Officers and Forest Guards. These officers enjoyed legal powers. The provisions prepared in respect of the protected forest and the power of arrest any persons without warrant to certain offences or reasonable doubt of movement.

1.6.5 The National Forest Policy 1952

The relevance of forest to meet the needs of defence, reconstruction schemes such as river valley projects, development of industries and communications was asserted by the first national forest policy of Independent India in 1952 based on national interest. The act followed, by and large, the limes of the British administration where the tribals had virtually no right but enjoyed only certain concessions such as right to take water for agriculture purposes, digging of wells and canals for agricultureal purpose, free grazing in open forests, removal of timber, bamboo, canes for construction of houses and agricultural impliments, collection of grass, dry and dead branch for domestic uses as fuel. The president of India under the article 339 of the constitution of India appointed the Scheduled Area and Scheduled Tribes Commission in 1960 under the chairmanship of U.N. Dhebar. The report of the commission analysis forest policy and vis- a-vis tribals. The commission under scored the importance of forest in the life of the tribals in providing them with all kinds of food, fodder, tubers and fish, timber, fuel, wood for construction of houses and other needs even income from the sale of forest produce (minor forest) besides fuel. The commission recommended that the policy of 1952 should be reconsidered and that, subject to safeguards, tribals should be permitted to cultivate forest lands and that their needs should be met from outlying areas in the reserve forest and that their requirements for shifting cultivation and livestock rearing should be accepted.

1.6.6 NCA Report on Forests 1976

The commission recommended a drastic reduction in the forest villager's rights over forests and forest produce. The commission recommended the strengthening of forestry legislation for effective implementation of forest policy and law for the revision of all Indian forest acts and drastic reduction in people's rights over forests. It was stated, free supply of forest produce to the inhabitants and their rights and advantages have brought destruction to the forests and so it is necessary to severe the process. The local people have not contributed much towards the maintenance or regeneration of the forests. The commission recommended strengthening of the forest legislation by the enactment of a revised all India Forest Act. In 1976 itself a major change taken in that the subject of forest was transferred from the State list to the concurrent list through the 42nd amendment of the constitution. This resulted in the decrese of the state's powers and the inerese of the centre's power over forest.

1.6.7 The Forest Draft Bill 1980

Based on the recommendations of the NCA a draft forests bill was circulated in 1980. Provisions were prepared in the bill to reduce villagers' rights over forest lands and produce. In states that the principal aim of the forest policy must be ensure environmental stability and the maintenance of ecological balance including atmospheric equilibrium, which are vital to the sustenance of all life forms such as human, animal and plant. Besides safe guarding the customary rights and interests of such people the forestry programmes should pay special attention to the following– To reduce the illegal cutting, contractors should be replaced by the forest as well as tribal cooperative basis, attention should be paid to the protection, regeneration and optimum collection of NTFPs, family oriented schemes for improving the status of tribals, integrated area development programmes to meet the needs of the tribals economy.

1.6.8 The National Forest Policy 1988

The resolution stated the primary objectives of forest policy as follows: the principal aim of forest policy must be to ensure environmental stability and maintenance of ecological balance including atmospheric balance and whatever possible, degraded lands should be made available for tree farming on either lease or the basis of a tree patta scheme. The policy statement asserts that existing forest and forest lands should be fully protected and their productivity should be improved normally. Minor forest produce should be developed and protected, so as to continue to provide sustenance to the tribal population livelihood needs. The national good should be to have a minimum of 1/3rd of the total area in the country under forest or tree cover. A large need-based and time-bound programme of afforestation and tree planting should be undertaken. The important provision taken in this act is the inclusion of farm forestry on private lands of mostly absentee landlords as well as degraded forest land as part of 'Social Forestry' programme. The species most developed in this scheme was eucalyptus and the Forest

Department supplied seedlings, technical help and soft loom, all under the so called 'social forestry' which was anything but social as well as environmental purpose. In the last import and captive exotic plantation under joint sector was promoted by this act.

1.6.9 Scheduled Tribes and Others Traditional Forest Dwellers (Recognition of Forest Rights) Act, 2006

This Act of 2006 was included in the gazette of Government of India on 31st December, 2007. It is also known as Tribal Rights Act, 'Forests Rights Act', Tribal Land Act and Tribal Bill. The act was passed 18th December, 2006 by the parliament of India and Government of India has notified the Forests Dweller Rules, 2007 on 1st January, 2008. The act aims to recognize and protect forest rights and other related subjects to scheduled tribes and other forest villagers residing in forest for long generations. This act provides that no member of forest villagers of ST or other traditional forest villagers shall be evicted or removed from the land under his occupation till the recognition and verification is complete. In doing so, the act also makes the responsibility to protect, conserve and regenerate of wildlife, forests, biodiversity on people who get this right. The act also seeks to endow title on holders of leases and pattas on forest land and endowing title to land and homesteads to residents of forest village and other old habitations on forest land. In addition to this the right to access and collect NTFPs also provides the forest villagers to develop income generating activities such as dry branches, honey collection, tassar cultivation, tendu leaves collection. Such activities could be developed as common occupation for these people based on the model of cooperatives or JFMC members could be engaged in such operations to aid to build such enterprises.

Chapter 2 Geographical Aspects

2.1 Administrative Set-up

The administrative set up of Alipurduar District consists of one sub-division i.e. Alipurduar with District headquarter at Alipurduar municipal town which has 7 police stations under this jurisdiction. There are 6 CD blocks (Birpara-Madarihat, Falakata, Kalchini, Kumargram, Alipurduar-I and Alipurduar-II) or panchayat samities and 2 municipalities (Alipurduar and Falakata) in the District where 3 blocks and 1 municipality belongs to Alipurduar sub-division, other 3 blocks and 1 municipality in proposed Falakata sub-division. But according to the forest administration there are three forest divisions fallen in this District and these are Alipurduar forest division, Jalpaiguri forest division and Koch Behar forest division.

Table–2.1
The Administrative Particulars of Alipurduar District

Geographical area (sq. km)	**2526.30 sq. km**
Geographical location	Between 26°23'11" and 26°52'30" North latitudes and 89°02'30" and 89°53'07" East longitudes
District headquarter	Alipurduar
Parliamentary constituency	1
Assembly area	1
Sub-Division	1
Blocks	6
Panchayat samities	6
Gram panchayat	66
Gram samsad	902

Municipality	2
Mouza's	340
Police Station	7
Police outpost	3
Inhabited villages	338
Forest villages	39

Source: District Planning & Development Office, DM, Alipurduar, 2018

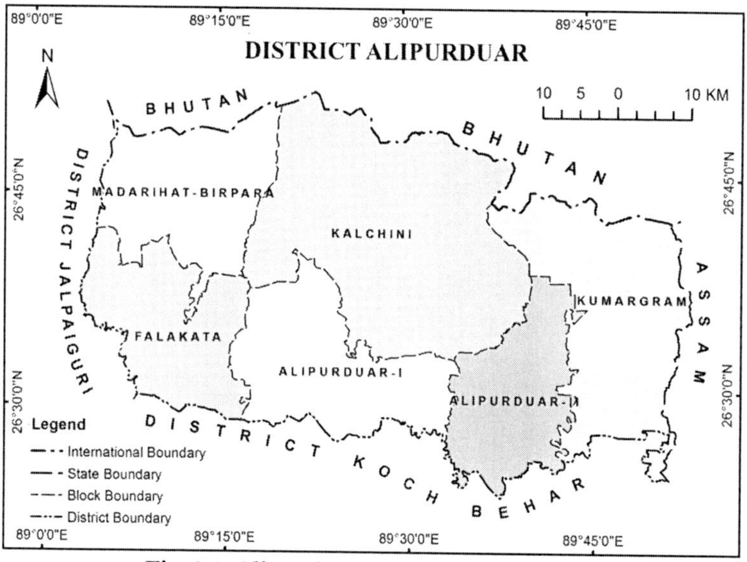

Fig. 2.1: Alipurduar District (Block-wise)

2.2 Relief

The surface of the District is wavy plain at the foot of the Eastern Himalayas where slope gradually declines from north to south. The District covers entire 'duars' which means doors to the Bhutan/or mountain (Grunning, 1911). It refers to the area at the immediate foot of the Bhutan hills and the tract forms a very irregular belt, scantily clothed and intersected by innumerable rivulets from the Bhutan hills. A rough plain part from north to south resembles it as a gigantic staircase running step by step down from the lofty Eastern Himalayas to the south of the District. The formation and geological development of 'Duars' have been summarized by Dr. B. Banerjee in 'Morphological Regions of West Bengal,' in

Geographical Review of India, vol. 26, as follows– 'There is another type of plain lying at the foot hill of the Himalayas. This is the typical piedmont plain or the alluvial fan surface of the Himalayan foot hills. This tract is known as the Duars, the general elevation of which is over 250 feet'. A major parts of this plain is built up of debris washed down from the Himalayan slopes. The immense loads of materials carried down by the rivers are gathered as soon as the streams get down to the plain region. The erosion and deposition is occurred repeatedly every year. A general southerly slope of 2 to 3 feet per mile is characteristics feature of the landscape where the rivers came down from the hill; huge number of semi-circular fans also formed by the deposition of boulders and coarse sandy soil particles.

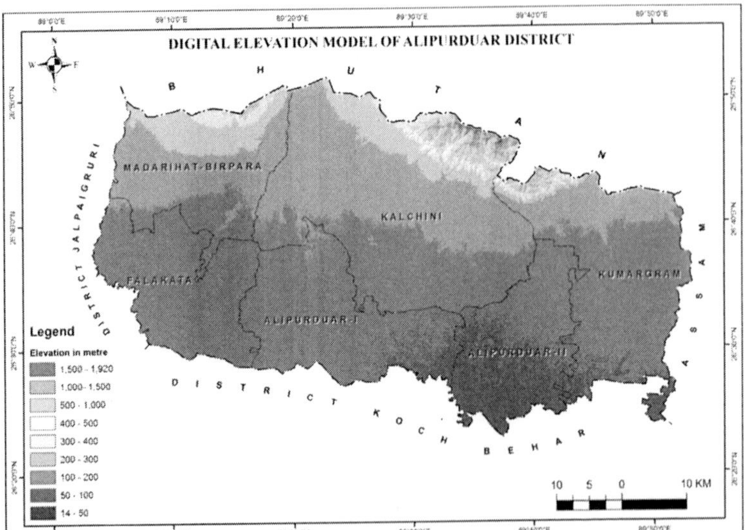

Fig. 2.2: Digital Elevation Model (DEM) of Alipurduar District

2.3 Drainage

The forest area is intercepted by many rivers, streams and jhoras of varying sizes which normally originate in the hills of the Bhutan and flow southwards. They rise and fall with great rapidity and frequently change their course which causing damage of forest. Drainage system is one of the important components of the physical environment which affects the agriculture directly and indirectly (Chauhan, 1987). The principal rivers that flow through this District are Sankosh, Rydak, Phaskhawa, Jayanti, Bala, Dima, Mujnai, Pana and Gaburbasra. The rivers become full and fierce with torrents in the rainy season (July to September) but are shallow and tame in the dry season (December to April).

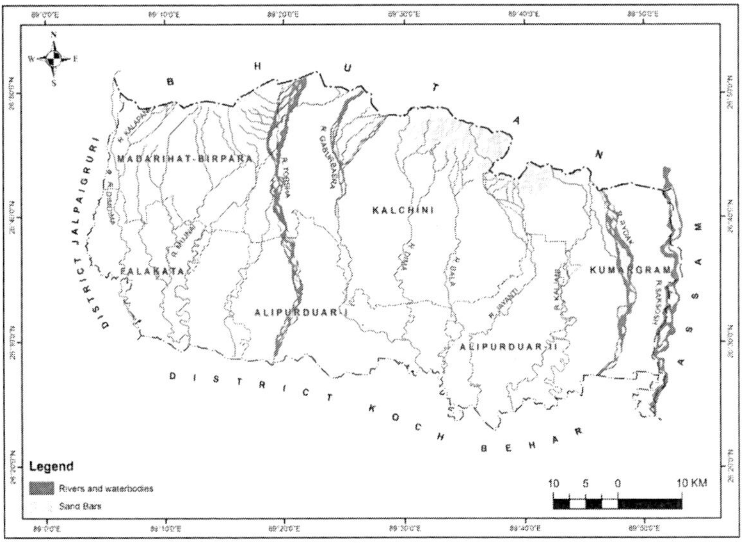

Fig. 2.3: Rivers in Alipurduar District

2.4 Climatic Characteristics

The seasons in Alipurduar District follow the course of those of other Districts in the plains but, owing to its proximity to the Bhutan hills, the rainfall is much heavier and the temperature is rarely excessive. Oppressive heat, high humidity and heavy precipitation are the principal characteristics of the climate of this District.

2.4.1 Seasons

The Alipurduar District experiences five dominant seasons with altitudinal variations both in duration and extent. The important seasons are as follows:

i. Summer season (May to June)
ii. Rainy season (July to September)
iii. Autumn season (October to November)
iv. Winter season (December to February)
v. Spring season (March to April)

The summer is tropical and hot, rainy season is severe with high amount of rainfall and sometimes flood occurs due to sudden heavy rain in the Bhutan hill. The autumn is experienced for a very short period. The sky remains clear in this season and temperature is mild and gradually decreases. This is a favorite season for inhabitants and within this period several festivals are celebrated them. The winter season is again severe and coldly. A short period of spring season also developed after ending of winter where temperature again gradually increases.

2.4.2 Temperature

Temperature is lowest in January; by April the temperature rises and it gradually increases till it reaches its highest point in July and August in 2018 (Table–2.2). The mean minimum temperature is lowest in January which is recorded 12°C in 2018 and the mean maximum temperature is highest in May which is recorded 33°C in 2018 (Table–2.3). At Buxa-Jainty hill forests and other forests of the District the climate is somewhat exceptional; the rainfall is heavier and even in the hottest weather fans are not used and blankets are necessary at midnight. The north of the region is generally cooler than southern plains area.

Table–2.2
Maximum and Minimum Temperature (°C) by month in the District of Alipurduar

Month	2014		2015		2016		2017		2018	
	Max.	Min.	Max.	Min.	Max.	Min.	Max.	Min.	Max.	Min.
January	27	9	27	11	28	9	28	8	27	9
February	31	9	32	12	30	12	28	10	28	9
March	37	16	34	16	35	15	35	13	33	15
April	35	19	34	17	37	17	36	18	35	17

May	37	20	35	20	37	20	37	20	36	20
June	37	23	37	21	36	23	28	22	36	23
July	35	23	37	23	36	23	36	23	36	23
August	37	24	36	23	37	23	38	23	37	23
September	35	23	37	23	36	21	36	23	36	22
October	35	18	34	17	35	17	35	20	35	18
November	33	14	33	14	33	13	32	14	33	13
December	31	8	29	10	29	11	29	10	31	12
Average	**34.17**	**17.17**	**33.75**	**17.25**	**34.08**	**17**	**33.17**	**17**	**33.58**	**17**

Source: India Meteorological Department, Govt. of India (2018) & District Statistical, Handbook, Jalpaiguri District.

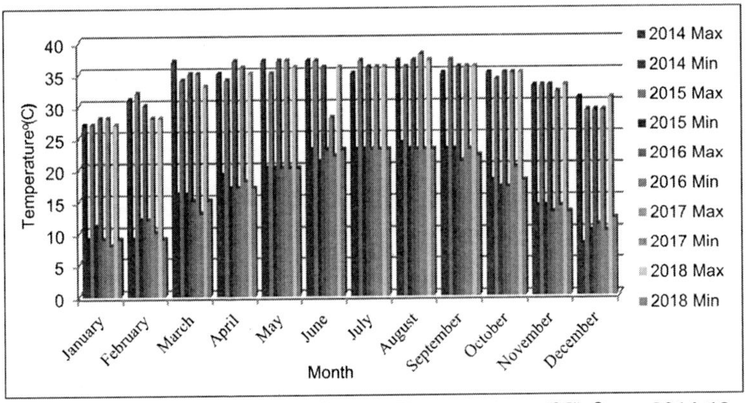

Fig. 2.4: Maximum and Minimum Temperature (°C) from 2014-18 (Ref. Table 2.2)

Table–2.3
Mean Maximum and Mean Minimum Temperature (°C) by Month in the District of Alipurduar

Month	2014		2015		2016		2017		2018	
	Max.	Min.	Max.	Min.	Max.	Min.	Max.	Min.	Max.	Min.
January	23	12	24	12	24	12	23	11	23	12
February	27	14	27	15	29	16	24	14	24	12
March	31	20	30	18	31	17	30	17	29	19
April	30	21	32	21	32	21	31	21	32	21
May	32	23	31	23	33	23	34	24	33	23
June	32	25	33	24	32	25	32	25	32	25
July	31	25	32	25	33	25	32	25	32	25
August	34	26	32	25	34	25	33	25	32	25
September	32	25	34	25	32	24	32	25	33	25
October	31	22	30	21	32	21	32	23	32	22

November	30	16	30	16	28	17	31	18	30	16
December	27	14	28	13	26	13	26	13	26	15
Average	**30**	**20.25**	**30.25**	**19.83**	**30.50**	**19.92**	**30**	**20.08**	**29.83**	**20**

Source: India Meteorological Department, Govt. of India (2018) & District Statistical Handbook, Jalpaiguri District.

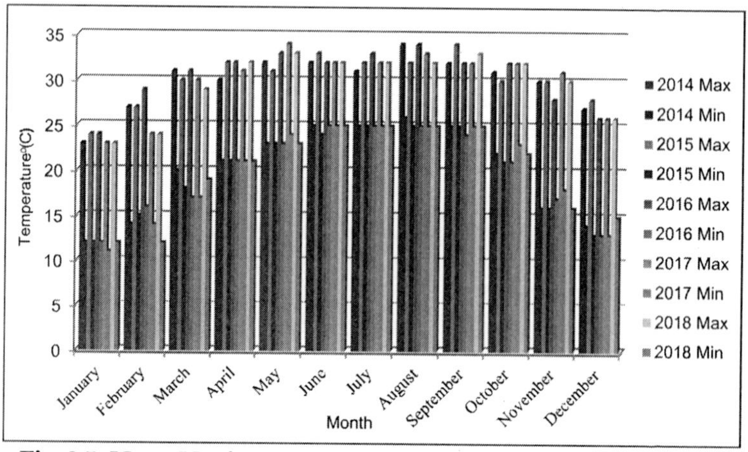

Fig. 2.5: Mean Maximum and Mean Minimum Temperature (°C) by Month from 2014-18 (Ref. table 2.3).

2.4.3 Rainfall

The rainfall is the single dominant weather parameter that affects plant growth, plant production, location of farming system and farmers selection of crops. Failures of rains or excessive of rainfall in a short period have brought repeated crop failures (Vyas, 1994). The heaviest rainfall in this District is at the foot of the Bhutan hills, and the lowest in the south on the plain of Falakata, Alipurduar. November, December, and January are the driest month although in these months rainfall sometimes occurred due to western disturbance. In consequence of this heavy rain and widespread rainfall the area never dried up and is always green and the growth of vegetation is most luxuriant.

The rainfall is lightest in the cold weather months, but more in April and increases considerably in between May to October in every year. From June to September the monsoon wind flow north-east wards and is deflected towards in North

Bengal which is responsible for heavy rain. During this period the rainfall at this area is 1195 mm in July which was highest recorded in 2018, 1109 mm in August, 597 mm in June, 273 mm in September, 167 mm in May (table 2.4). The lowest recorded rainfall was 9 mm in February of 2018.

Table–2.4
Monthly Rainfalls (mm) of the District Alipurduar

Months	Actual					Normal
	2014	2015	2016	2017	2018	
January	15	17	0	0	12	9
February	8	5	7	63	9	17
March	35	132	17	45	49	54
April	208	207	98	201	132	172
May	416	230	404	222	167	305
June	647	438	625	511	597	606
July	1307	782	760	946	1195	989
August	436	648	242	717	1109	600
September	668	254	637	701	273	461
October	171	353	201	82	72	224
November	9	7	15	0	73	23
December	4	0	11	0	0	5
Total	**3924**	**3073**	**3017**	**3488**	**3688**	**3465**

Source: India Meteorological Department, Govt. of India (2018) & District Statistical, Handbook, Jalpaiguri District.

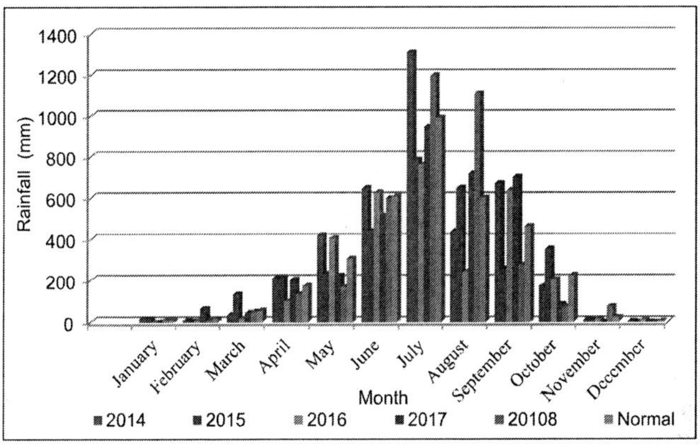

Fig. 2.6: Monthly Rainfall (mm) from 2015-18. (Ref. table 2.4)

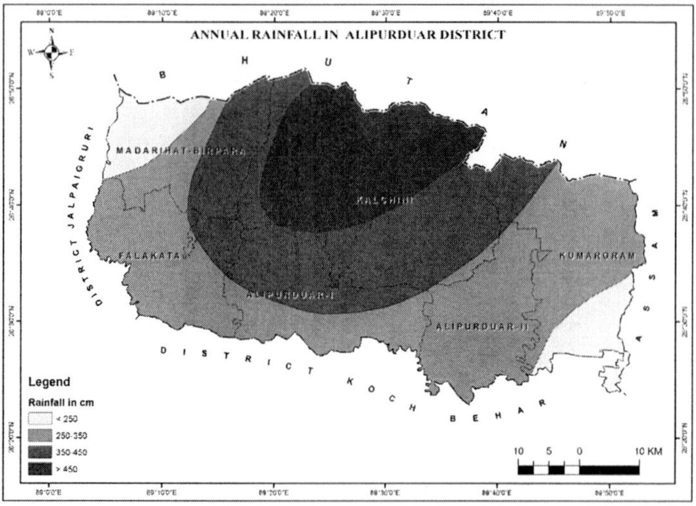

Fig. 2.7: Annual Rainfall Zones, 2018

2.5 Soil and Rock

The greater part of the District is covered with alluvium ranging from pure sandy to clay. Over most of the area the soil is sandy loam but in the river basin areas such as the Torsa, Raydak, Kaljani, Dima, Pana and Sankosh it is bard, black, and clay (Das, 2000); excellent bricks and earthenware can be made in this part of the soil and the land furnishes good pasture and fine crops of paddy, wheat, and tobacco. In the north of the District the soil is ferruginous clay and is particularly well suited to the growth of the tea plants. The District contains numerous old river beds which have been deserted by the streams which used to flow along them; near the hills they are strewn with stone and boulders, lower down they contain gravel, and in the pains sand. These deserted river-beds are unprofitable wastes, of little use to anyone. The north of the hill portion are composed of a series of beds, which consists of variegated slates, quartzite and dolomites, and are fringed on the south by low hills of upper tertiary strata. Limestone occurs in considerable amount in the Buxa hills and masses of calcareous tufa are found along their base (Grunning, 1911). Copper are occurs in greenish slate with quartzite layers to the west of Buxa.

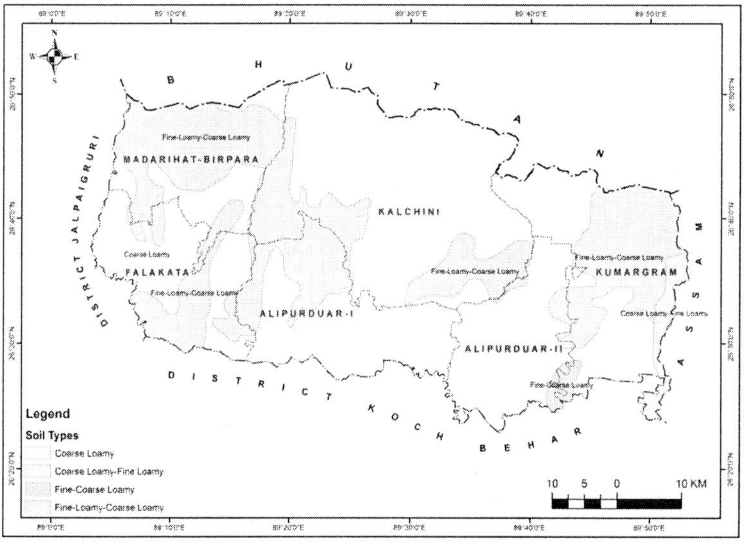

Fig. 2.8: Soil Map of Alipurduar District

Source: NBSS & LUP, Regional Centre, Kolkata

2.6 Vegetation

A major part of Alipurduar District is covered by forests. Even today this area remains one of the most prominent wildlife areas of the country and bears the best sal, teak and other forest in India. The main forest cover comprises of semi-moist-deciduous vegetation. Apart from this high rise forest, there are floodplains of rivers like Kaljani, Pana, Torsa etc. covered with grasslands which nourish a wide spectrum of wildlife. The forests of this region are home to many rare and endangered species of mammals and birds. The Indian one horned rhinoceros is found in Jaldapara National Park. Near extinct species like the hispid hare, pygmy hog, floricanan endangered bird have been reported from the Jaldapara National Park and Buxa Jayanti Forest. Apart from this species like tiger, leopard, Asian elephant, gaur, wild boar, sambar, cheetah, hog deer, barking deer are also found in the various forest tracts of Alipurduar. A number of divisions of Forest Department of Govt. of West Bengal are working over this area. Forests like Jaldapara, Buxa Jayanti are declared as sanctuaries and national park to protect wildlife.

The forests of this area extend from south of the plains to north of the Duars regions of the Bhutan hills and is located in the flood plains of different main hill rivers and other medium and small rivers and rivulets which have created a pocket of grass land. Apart from national parks and sanctuaries a significant small forests area of this District is covered by forest such as Dalgaon, Titi-Rehti, Dhumpara, Bhakla, Raidak, Sankosh forest etc. Some where it has such a luxurious growth that even the sun light finds it difficult to reach the surface of land. The forest of this District are predominately sal (Shorea robusta) with associates viz., schima wallichii, michelia champaca and chukrasia tabularis (State Forest Report, 2012-2013).

The forest of the district may be classified into the following main types:

i. Riverine forests
ii. Plains forests
iii. Hill forests
iv. Savannah forests

The riverine forests are of mixed type, main trees are khair (acacia catechu), sissoo (dalbergia sissoo), premna

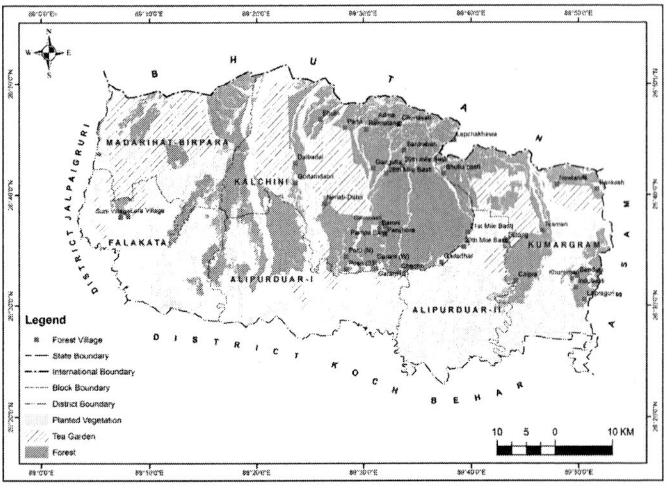

Fig. 2.9: Vegetation cover and tea gardens of Alipurduar District

species, salmalia malabarica, albizzzia species, and gmelina arborea etc. Besides bauhinia, wrightia tomentosa, toona ciliate and grewia species are found in the riverine forests areas (Roy, 1961). At some places odal and sidha are found in good proportion.

The plains forests are semal, khair, asathwa (ficus religios), neem (melia azadirachta), amlaki (phyllanthus emblica), radha chura (poinciana regia), debdaru (polyalthia longifolia), guava (psideim guyava), Arjuna (terminalia Arjuna), hartaki (terminalia Arjuna) etc.

Close to the streams and moist pockets occurs a type of evergreen forests known as tropical evergreen forests, typical trees of which are aesculus assamica, Eugenia Formosa, dillenia indica, castanopsis species, talauma hodgsoni, pinanga gracilis, and myristica species (Forest survey of India, Eastern Zone, Calcutta, 1999).

The hill forests of this District include some important species of toona ciliate, castanopsis specia, acrocarpus fraxinifolius, durabanga sonneratioides, and ailanthus grandis and mours laevigata. These are sporadic in nature.

Savannah forests are covered small area in the District. Common savannah forests species of grasses that are found include the saccharum species, erianthus species, imperata cylindrical, phragmites karka, and arundo donax and neyraudia reynaudiana. Apart from these, numerous other species are surrounded by thickets of trees and shrubs, partly planted and partly of spontaneous growth, in which mango, jack, papal and tamarind trees frequently occur; bamboos thrive luxuriantly and the numerous clumps of these form a conspicuous feature in the landscape and add greatly to its beauty (Grunning, 1911).

2.7 Population

In 2011 the District have population of about 14, 91,250 people, among them about 7, 976212 (53.49%) are male and about 6, 93,629 (46.51%) are female. But in 2001 census, it was about 1337575 of which males were 686490 (51.32%) and remaining 651085 (48.68%) were females. The decadal growth rate is 11.49% which is compared increased to population census of 1991 to 2001 that was 10.45%. According to 2011 census about 44.57% of the total populations are from general caste, 29.84% are from schedule caste and 25.59% are schedule tribes. The Child (aged under 6 years) population of Alipurduar District is 13.34%, among them 52.12% are boys and 47.88% are girls. The majority of the population, nearly 79.38% (about 11.83 lakh) lives in rural area and 20.62% (about 3.07 lakh) population live in the urban area in Alipurduar District. There are about 3.19 lac households in the District and an average 4 persons live in every family.

Table–2.5
Demography of Alipurduar District

Description	2011	2001
Actual Population	1491250	1337575
Male	732395	686490
Female	693629	651085
Decadal population growth	11.49 %	-
Area (sq. km)	2526.30 sq. km	-
Density/sq. km	590 persons/sq.km	-
Sex ratio (per 1000)	949	-
Child sex ratio (0-6 age)	953	-
Average literacy	72.29 %	-
Male literacy	56.27	-
Female literacy	43.73	-
Total child population (0-6 Age)	167071	-
Male population (0-6 Age)	85541	-
Female population (0-6 Age)	81530	-
Literates	908622 person	-
Male literates	511206 person	-
Female literates	397416 person	-

Source: District Census Handbook, Jalpaiguri District, Directorate of Census Operations, West Bengal and Statistical Handbook of Jalpaiguri District, 2011

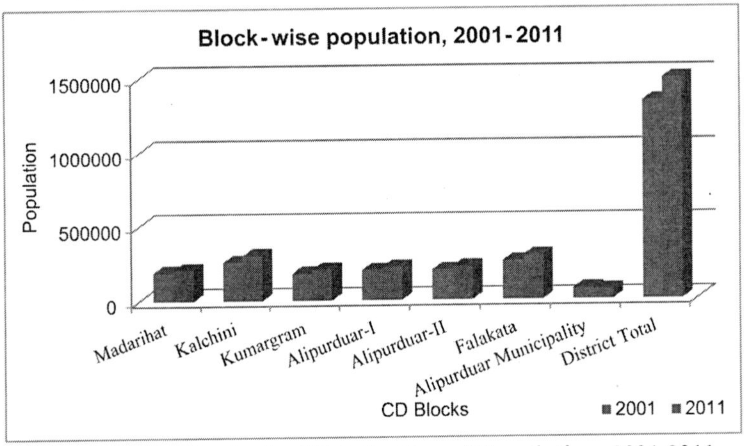

Fig. 2.10: CD Block-wise Distribution of Population, 2001-2011

Table–2.6

Block-wise Distribution of Population, 2001 and 2011

S.No.	CD Block	Population	
		2001	2011
1	Madarihat	185470	202026
2	Kalchini	252571	298458
3	Kumargram	178047	199609
4	Alipurduar-I	197231	216931
5	Alipurduar-II	196984	218272
6	Falakata	254273	290722
7	Alipurduar Municipality	72999	65232
	District Total	**1337575**	**1491250**

Source: District Census Handbook, Jalpaiguri District, Directorate of Census Operations, West Bengal, 2011

Table–2.7

Category-wise male and female population, 2011

Category	General	SC	ST	Total
Male	376815	229153	191653	797621
Female	287881	215785	189963	693629
Total	664696	444938	381616	1491250

Source: District Census Handbook, Jalpaiguri District, Directorate of Census Operations, West Bengal, 2011

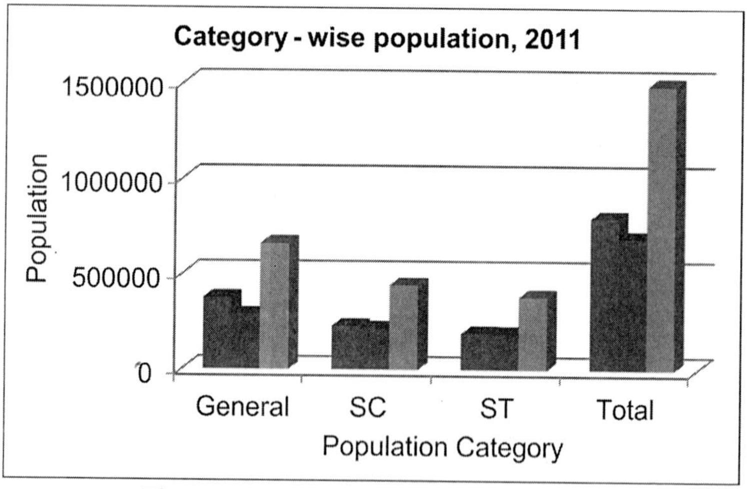

Fig. 2.11: Category-wise Populations, 2011

2.7.1 Religion wise Distribution of Population

It is observed from the table below (table 2.8) that as per 2011 census, the Hindu religion contribute 1201315 population (80%) of the total population and are the highest religious community in the District followed by the Muslims which contribute 130144 population (9%) of the total population and Christians is the third largest religious community with 117128 (8%) population all other religious communities contribute 3% of the total population.

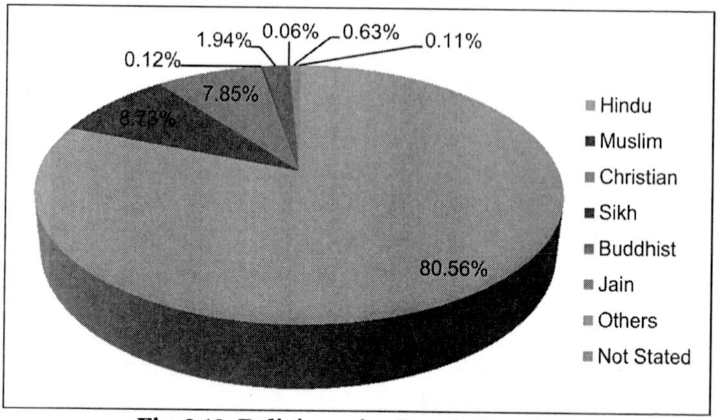

Fig. 2.12: Religion-wise Population, 2011

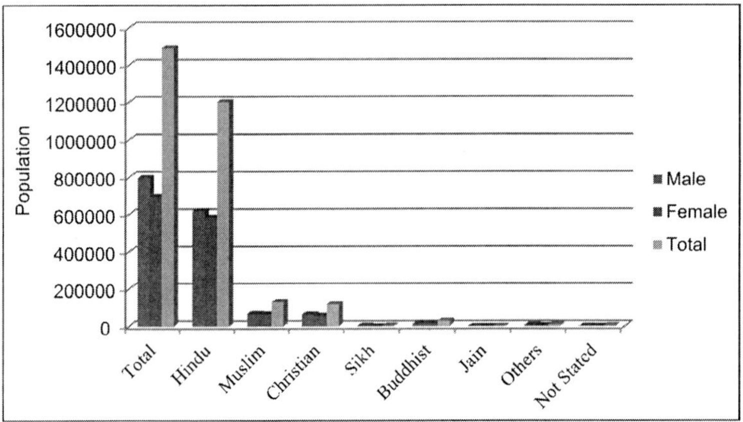

Fig. 2.13: Sex-wise Religious Population, 2011

Table–2.8
Religion-wise Population, 2011

	Total	Hindu	Muslim	Christian	Sikh	Buddhist	Jain	Others	Not Stated
Male	797621	618958	66320	61903	1330	14926	571	5437	889
Female	693629	582357	63824	55225	471	14055	308	3947	729
Total	**1491250**	**1201315**	**130144**	**117128**	**1801**	**28981**	**879**	**9384**	**1618**
%	**100**	**80.56**	**8.73**	**7.85**	**0.12**	**1.94**	**0.06**	**0.63**	**0.11**

Source: District Census Handbook, Jalpaiguri District, Directorate of Census Operations, West Bengal, 2011

2.7.2 Growth of Population

The population of the District has increased by 11.49% in last 10 years. The yearly growth rate of the District is 0.96%. In 2001 census total population were about 1337575 lakh. The decadal growth rate has increased from 8.93 to 18.67% among the six C.D Blocks. The maximum rate has increased in Kalchini block by 18.67% and minimum in Madarihat block by 8.93%. Except Alipurduar municipality where negative growth rate has been developed and which has decreased by '-10.64%' in last ten years.

Table–2.9
Growth of Population, 2001-2011

S. No.	CD Block	Population		Growth of Population	Decadal Growth Rate	Yearly Growth Rate
		2001	2011			
1	Madarihat	185470	202026	16556	8.93	0.89
2	Kalchini	252571	298458	45887	18.67	1.87
3	Kumargram	178047	199609	21562	12.11	1.21
4	Alipurduar-I	197231	216931	19700	9.99	0.99
5	Alipurduar-II	196984	218272	21288	10.81	1.08
6	Falakata	254273	290722	36449	14.33	1.43
7	Alipurduar Municipality	72999	65232	-7767	-10.64	-1.06
	District Total	**1337575**	**1491250**	**153675**	**64.2**	**6.41**

Source: District Census Handbook, Jalpaiguri District, Directorate of Census Operations, West Bengal, 2011

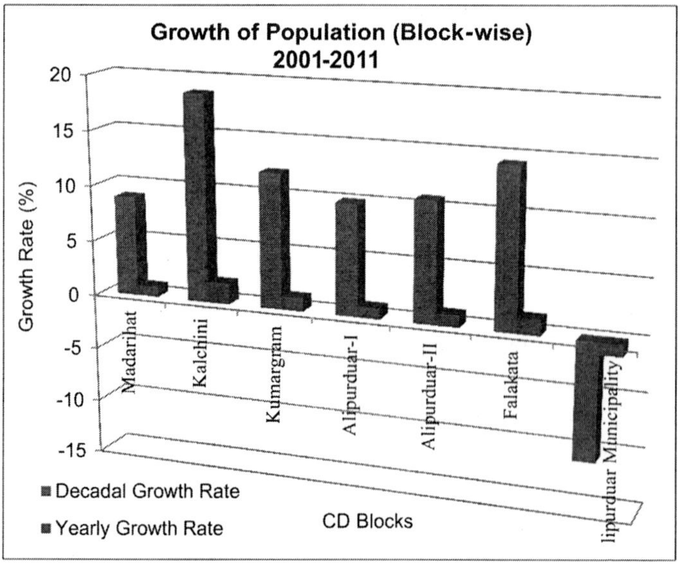

Fig. 2.14: Growth of population, Block-wise, 2011

2.7.3 Sex Ratio

The sex ratio is an important demographic indicator for ascertaining the gender balance of the population. The following table shows the sex ratio of Alipurduar District.

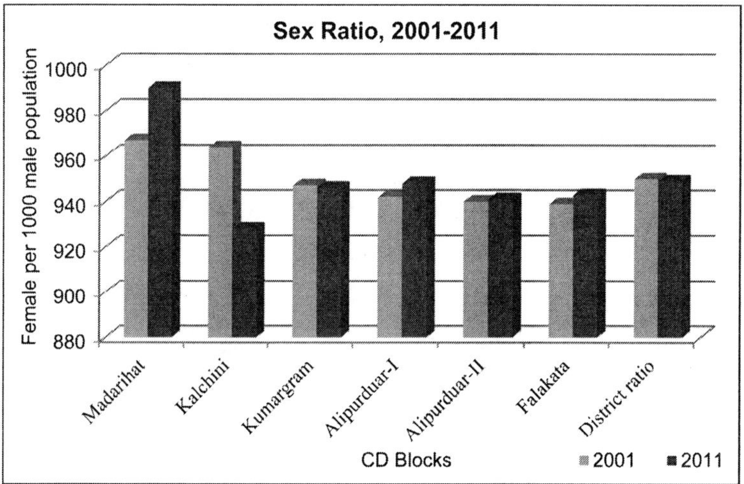

Fig. 2.15: Block-wise sex ratio, 2001-2011

Table–2.10

Change in Sex Ratio from 2001 to 2011

S. No.	Name of the Block	Sex Ratio					
		Total		Rural		Urban	
		2001	2011	2001	2011	2001	2011
1	Madarihat	967	990	967	992	-	964
2	Kalchini	964	928	973	1005	928	761
3	Kumargram	947	946	946	946	953	945
4	Alipurduar-I	942	948	944	940	936	971
5	Alipurduar-II	940	941	940	942	937	937
6	Falakata	939	943	941	943	920	945
	District ratio	**950**	**949**	**952**	**961**	**935**	**921**

Note: Sex ratio has been defined here as the number of female per 1000 male.

Source: District Census Handbook, Jalpaiguri District, Directorate of Census Operations, West Bengal, 2011

It is observed from the above table no. 2.10, that the sex ratio of this District in 2011 census is 949 and for urban it is 921. But it is observed that the sex ratio of rural area is higher (961) than the sex ratio of total and urban. The total sex ratio in the District has decreased by 1 female per 1000 male during the years from 2001 to 2011. The urban sex ratio of the District reveals a decreasing trend from 935 in 2001 to 921 in 2011census thinkable situation.

2.7.4 Literacy

Total about 72.29% people in the District are literate, among them about 70.01% are belonged to the rural area, and about 83.41% are from urban area.

Table–2.11
Percentage of Literacy, 2011

S.No.	Name of the Block	Literacy Rate (%)		
		Total	Rural	Urban
1	Madarihat	67.77	66.89	79.76
2	Kalchini	68.96	65.32	77.87
3	Kumargram	72.42	69.79	89.71
4	Alipurduar-I	76.19	72.26	87.02
5	Alipurduar-II	75.76	75.29	82.79
6	Falakata	72.64	70.56	83.30
	District	**72.29**	**70.01**	**83.41**

Source: District Census Handbook, Jalpaiguri District, Directorate of Census Operations, West Bengal, 2011

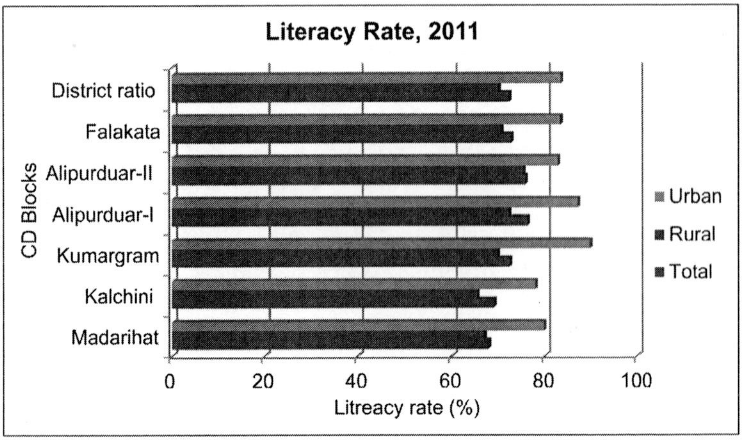

Fig. 2.16: Block-wise Literacy Rate, 2011

2.7.5 Workers Profile

The Alipurduar District has 39.96 % (about 5.9 lac)

population engaged in either main or marginal works. Among them 67.75% (about 4.04 lac) are male and 24.41% (1.45 lac) are female working population. Besides from total main worker about 82.06% (3.31 lac) are male workers (full time) and 21.95% (88.6 thousand) are female workers as well as about 49.76% are male and 52.84% are female among total marginal workers. All details are given below in the table 2.12.

Table–2.12
Percentage of Workers and Non-Workers (Block-wise), 2011

S. No.	Name of the Block	Total Workers (Main & Marginal Workers)	Non-Workers	Main Workers	Marginal Workers
1	Madarihat	40.42	59.58	28.38	12.04
2	Kalchini	40.29	59.71	30.04	10.25
3	Kumargram	39.63	60.37	27.09	12.53
4	Alipurduar-I	41.13	58.87	31.12	10.01
5	Alipurduar-II	39.53	60.47	28.42	11.10
6	Falakata	38.76	61.24	30.71	8.05
	District	**39.96**	**60.04**	**29.29**	**10.66**

Source: District Census Handbook, Jalpaiguri District, Directorate of Census Operations, West Bengal, 2011.

2.8 Economy

The economy of the study area is based on three 'T's-that is Tea, Tourism and Timber (Debnath, 2010). Besides agriculture and businesses are other livelihood activities of peoples. The main industry of the region is the tea industry. Based on the tea gardens and tea making factories thousands of people are engaged in the tea estates and factories as permanent or temporary labour. Several people are also engaged in the cultivation of betel nuts which also contributes to their economy. Cultivation of other crops has been practicing mainly for local people consumption. The timber industry flourishes and enhance economic in this region. A number of saw mills, plywood industries, tourism activities as well as other allied business also act as an important factor to the economy of this District.

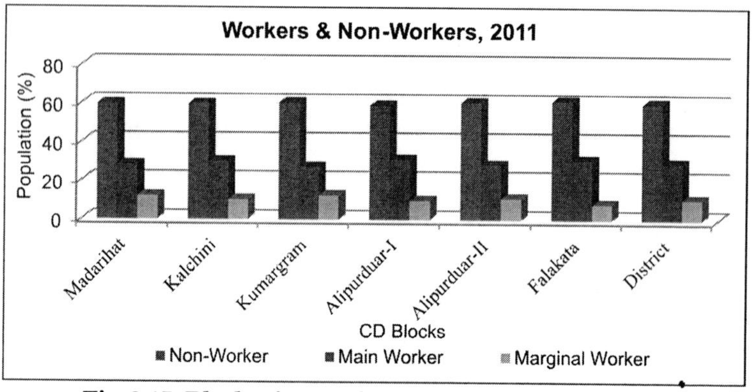

Fig. 2.17: Block-wise Workers and Non-Workers, 2011

Table–2.13
Percentage of male and female workers and non-workers (Block-wise), 2011

S. No.	Name of the Block	Total Workers (%)				Non-Worker (%)	
		Main Worker		Marginal Worker			
		Male	Female	Male	Female	Male	Female
1	Madarihat	39.02	17.63	12.75	11.33	48.23	71.03
2	Kalchini	42.52	16.59	11.30	9.11	46.18	74.03
3	Kumargram	41.58	11.78	12.57	12.50	45.86	75.72
4	Alipurduar-I	49.44	11.79	7.40	12.77	43.16	75.45
5	Alipurduar-II	47.13	8.55	9.60	12.71	43.27	78.74
6	Falakata	50.23	10.02	6.71	9.47	43.06	80.51
	District	**44.99**	**12.73**	**10.05**	**11.32**	**44.96**	**75.91**

Source: District Census Handbook, Jalpaiguri District, Directorate of Census Operations, West Bengal, 2011

2.8.1 Agriculture

The majority of the people are engaged in agricultural activities. Therefore the economy of the area is mainly dependent on agriculture as well as plantation farming. The rice is the principal food crop and tea is one and only most valuable economic plantation farming of the District. Lots of people are employed as tea garden labour, tea factory labour. Three types of rice i.e. aush, aman and boro are practicing in a year. Other important crops are tobacco, jute, mustard seeds, corn and wheat. Now it is noticed that gradually more and more areas are covering under corn and wheat production in the plain area of the District. Pulses like musur, mug, gram, maskalai, khesari and arhar are also grown. The largest cultivated area in this region is the tract between Madarihat-Birpara and Falakata where fields of rice and mustard can be found lying here and there. The tea plantation practicing as well as pump nut cultivation covered total northern foot hill zone of the District. The horticulture practice such as cauliflower, cabbage, tomato, and potato are also cultivated in the high altitude though the year.

2.8.2 Minerals & Mining

There is no mine in the District. The northern part of the hill consists of variegated slates, quartzite and dolomites. The minerals include limestone, tufa, graphite; lignite, iron ore copper etc. are quarried along the base of the Bhutan hill. Among them the limestone occurs in considerable amount in the Buxa hills and masses of calcareous tufa are found along their base (Grunning, 1911). Copper are occurs in greenish slate with quartzite layers to the west of Buxa. A small copper mine a 'chunabati' two miles from Buxa was formerly worked by Nepalis.

2.8.3 Industry

The most important manufacturing industry in the District is the manufacture of tea. The tea is grown and manufactured within the District area. Presently the tea planters have learnt how to improve the quality of tea as well as its production compared to the other countries. Organic fertilizer uses, thoughtful and scientific uses of fewer fertilizers have also helped improvement in the field of tea cultivation. Apart from tea, the District is well known for its handicraft products. Manufacturing of cane and bamboo products, cotton weaving, mat weaving, silver and gold ornaments, clay toys etc. are worth mentioning. The District cannot be proud of being in a very favorable position as far as the industrial factors are concerned. Although it's significant deposits of dolomite and other minerals like limestone, coal, stone makes the District prospective for industrial development. The District is rich in agricultural and forest resources, so there is a chance for setting up agrarian and forest based industries for further industrial development.

2.8.4 Trade and Commerce

As there are no major industries in the District, it has direct effect in the field of trade and commerce and indirect effect on economy of the District. In spite of that, the trade is connected with an international trading point at Jaigaon town of Bhutan border under Kalchini Block. The towns of Jaigaon of Indian border side and Phuentsholing of Bhutan border side are important hubs of the export-import industry of this area. The principal exports goods are tea, sal timber, wooden furniture, and many food crops and imports goods are ply wood, cloths, beverages, open mining minerals such as dolomites etc. which are exported and imported through this point.

2.8.5 Forestry

The District is fortunately blessed with rich reserves of forest resources due to its relief and natural climate. The presence of vast hill and foothill tracts covered with dense mixed forest with sparkling springs and streams flowing through them attract tourists from different location of state as well as outside of country. The forest, covering about 1171.6622 sq. km of land which is 46.38% of the total geographical areas of the District, is home to an attracting variety of fauna and flora. The vegetation is mostly deciduous semi-ever green with teak, sisoo, sal as the dominant species. The timber produced in these forests is valuable and is used for home furniture, doors, windows and other wooden equipment. Once timbers used for sleeper of train line and for wooden bridge. Social forestry is also becoming popular now-a-days with trees like eucalyptus, simul, krishnachura etc. being widely planted or cultivated through local people personally or by the Government. The forested hilly ranges have also augmented growth of several major Wildlife Reserves. These are Jaldapara Wildlife Sanctuary: 216.51 sq. km, Bauxa W.L.S & tiger reserve: 761.09 sq. km, (Karmakar, 2011). Minor forest produces like bamboo, cane, honey, fodder, firewood; flower, seeds, roots, wax etc. are also found in the forest areas. Bamboo and cane furniture is manufactured both in the rural and urban areas. The timber and fuel wood are the major forest produce.

2.8.6 Tourism

Economic transformation through tourism has now been accepted by all countries and thus tourism has been recognized as an industry. It invites foreign exchange for earnings; enhance income and employment opportunity at local, regional and national level. Karmakar (2011) pointed out that in India, tourism provides direct employment to 9 million people and indirect employment to another 13 million persons, thus provide a livelihood to 22 million persons. It contributes an estimated 2.4% of the gross national product. The tourism plays an important role in the economy of North Bengal after tea industry. The northern hill and foothill panoramic views, rolling topography, fascinate streams and springs, foaming torrents, lakes, river valleys, ethnic diversity, undulating attractive tea gardens, rich natural forest and comfortable climate etc. all these natural and cultural component have built the framework of tourism in Alipurduar District. Besides some rich tourism spots such as Jaldapara W.L.S, Buxa Tiger Reserve and W.L.S, Kunganagar, South Khairbari are the forest based tourist spot that have been developed in this area which attracted lots of tourists from all over India and abroad, making it an important contributor to the economy as well as created employment opportunity of local people.

The study of the physical and cultural aspects of the region reveals that, the surface of the area is undulating where slope gradually declines from north to south. Major parts of the area built up of debris washed down from the Bhutan hill slopes. The immense loads of materials carried down by the streams and jhoras are gathered as soon as the streams get down towards southern plain. The hill portion are composed of a series of beds, which consists of variegated slates, quartzite's and dolomites, and are fringed on the south by low hills of upper tertiary strata. Limestone occurs in considerable amount in the Buxa hills. The major part of the District is covered with alluvium soil ranging from pure sandy to clay although some place the soil is sandy loam but in the river basin areas it is bard, black, and clay. The climatic characteristics have wide variation which is depend on altitude and presence of forest although four seasons are very prominent here and the summer is tropical and hot, rainy season is severe with high amount of rainfall. The autumn is experienced for a very short period. The winter season is again severe and coldly. A short period of spring season also developed after ending of winter. Temperature is lowest in January; by April the temperature rises and it gradually increases till it reaches its highest point in July and August. A major part of the District is covered by forest. The forests area is intercepted by many rivers, streams and jhoras of varying sizes which normally originate in the hills of the Bhutan and flow southwards. The main forest cover comprises of semi-moist-deciduous and mixed vegetation. Apart from these high rise forests, there are floodplains of rivers covered with grasslands which nourish a wide spectrum of wildlife. Even today this area remains one of the most prominent wildlife areas of the country. This wild life sanctuaries, beautiful scenario of tea gardens, natural beauty of foothill landscape are the main tourist spot which are attracted lots of tourists from all over India and abroad. The majority of the population lives in rural area in this District among them most of the inhabitants are scheduled caste and scheduled tribe and they belongs to Hindu and Christian community. The inhabitants primarily engaged in agriculture, agriculture labour as well as tea plantation labour activity. The economy of the area depends on natural resources as well as on tea, tourism and timber. But there are many environmental challenges and issues which are arisen due to the large scale human induced activities on those natural agents. Its consequential hazards are deforestation, flooding though frequently river shifting, soil erosion and degrade of water resource system due to intensive used of chemical fertilizers and pesticides of tea garden belts for increasing production. Thus it can be concluded that, different physical elements are being vulnerable due to bulk pressure of inhabitants' livelihood and unsustainable way of consumption of natural resources.

Chapter 3 Forest and Forest Villages

3.1 Administrative Set-up of Forests

The administrative set up of forests of Alipurduar District consists of three division viz. Buxa Tiger Reserve (under Field Director), Jalpaiguri Forest Division (under Divisional Forest Officer) and Koch Behar Forest Division (under Divisional Forest Officer). The Districts' maximum part of forest area under the Buxa Tiger Reserve (BTR), and it is controlled by Field Director, BTR. Only Dalgaon range and Madarihat range belongs to the Jalpaiguri and Koch Behar Forest Division respectively. Other details of administrative setup are given in the Fig. 3.1 and table 3.1 below.

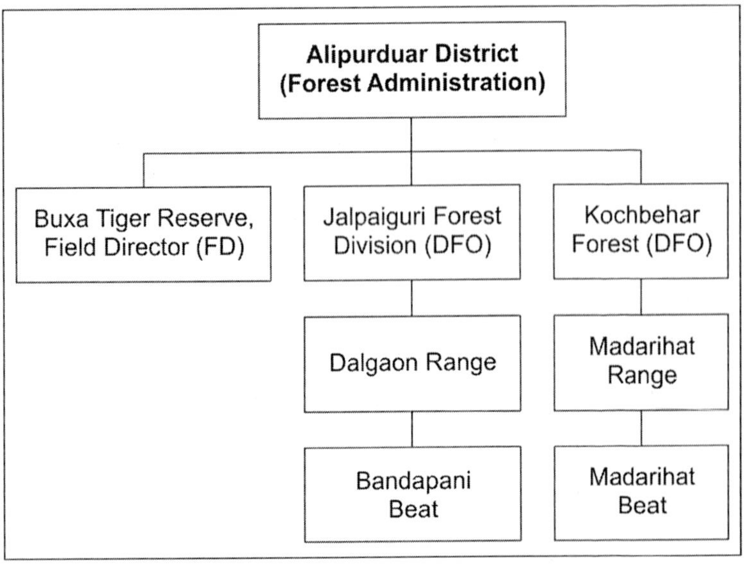

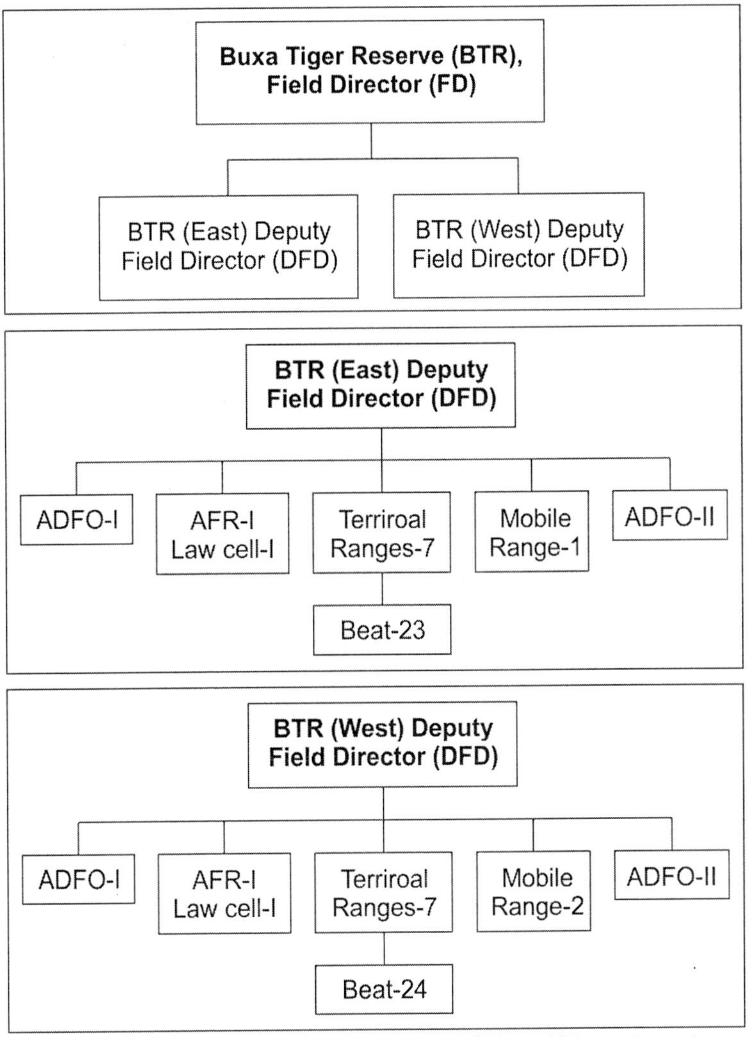

Chart 3.1: Administrative Structure of Forest Department, Alipurduar District

Source: State Forest Report, 2012-2013 & Tiger conservation plan, 2016-17 to 2026-2027.

The administrative setup of the Buxa Tiger Reserve (BTR) is based on the erstwhile Buxa Division. This came under the control of Field Director, BTR on 27-04-1992. As per reorganization vide Govt. Order No. 4983-for dated

Calcutta, 25th September 1995 (Das, 2000), the entire area of BTR has come under the control of BTR (East) and BTR (West) division headed by two Field Director (FD) with separate jurisdiction. The overall control of the entire project lies under the Field Director and Conservator of Forests BTR (Fig. 3.1). The Headquarter of the two Field Directors is at Alipurduar town. The Field Director of the forest is assisted by two Deputy Field Director (DFD). The following is the present administrative set up in field level. The details of forests divisions, ranges, beats, components with area of beats are given below in the table 3.1.

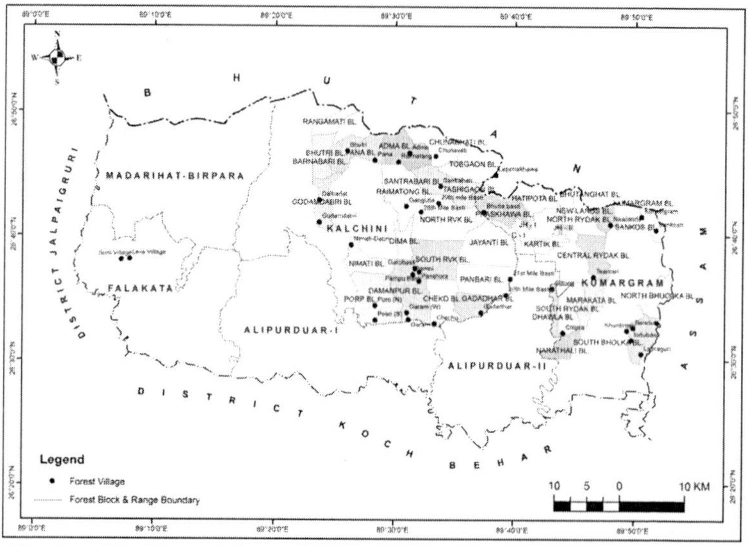

Fig. 3.1: Division of forest blocks and ranges, Alipurduar District

3.2 Forest Coverage

The forests of the Alipurduar District belongs to four forest divisions which are Buxa Tiger Reserve (East), Buxa Tiger Reserve (West), Jalpaiguri Forest Division and Kochbehar Forest Division. It cover an area of 1162.76 sq. km and are situated entirely in the Duars between west of Madarihat block to Sankosh river in the east of Kumargram block (State Forest Report, 2012-2013). All the forests are plain forest, exception Buxa forests which occupies foot hilly

Table–3.1
Forest Division, Range, Beat and Components of Beats with Area

Division	Range	Beats	Components (Division)	Area (Ha)
Jalpaiguri Forest Division (DFO)	Dalgaon	1. Dalgaon 2. Bandapani 3. Dalmore	-	2069.87
Kochbehar Forest Division (DFO)	Madarihat	1. Madarihat	-	
Buxa Tiger Reserve (BTR), East	Kumargram	1. Sankosh	SNK-1, 2, 3	1105.17
		2. Kumargram	KGM-1, 2	1051.37
		3. Newlands	NLS-1, 2; NLS - USF	942.42
	Bholka	1. Barobisha	SBH-5, 6; D. Rampur-PF	688.47
		2. Ghoramara	SBH-1, 2b, 3a, 4	1201.94
		3. Balapara	SBH- 2a, 3b, NBH-5	805.62
		4. Chengmari	NBH- 1, 2, 3, 4; M- Haldibari- PF	1133.2
	South Rydak	1. Narathali	NTR-1, 2	1288.12
		2. Marakata	MKT-1, 2, 3, 4	1352.04
		3. S. Rydak	SRD -1, 2, 3, 4; DH-1, 2	1858.38
		4. Chipra	SRD -5, 6, 7; DH- 3	1146.92

Division	Range	Beats	Components (Division)	Area (Ha)
	North Rydak	1. Karthika	KRT- P.F, KRT- USF, Rahimabad- PF, Rydak- USF, Loknathpur- PF; C-J-II	815.37
		2. Mainabari	BGT-1, 2; NRD -1,2,3; CRD-1, 2; Turturi-PF; J.H-II; T-Khanda	3511.95
		3.Tiamari	CRD -3, 4, 5, 6; U. Rampur - PF	1297.26
		4. Hatipota	HP-1, 2; J-H-1	1745.67
	Jainti	1. S. Jainti	JNT-3, 4, 5, 6, 7, 8, 9; C- Jhora- I	3393.02
		2. N. Jainti	NRVK- 6, 7, 12, 13, 14; JNT-1, 2	2397.58
		3. Phashkwa	Tashigaon-1, 2; NRVK-5	1717.99
		4. Bhutia Basti	PHK-1, 2, 3; PHK- RF	2735.80
	Buxaduar	1. Santalabari	STB -1, 2, 3, 4	2299.85
		2. Buxa Road	NRVK -1, 2, 3, 4	1219.33
		3. Chunabhati	CNBT-1, 2, 3	2001.58
		4. Buxaduar	Tobgaon -1, 2, 3, 4	3135.95
Buxa Tiger Reserve (BTR), West	Damanpur East	1. Damanpur	DPO - 3, 4, 7, 8	1233.48
		2. Checko	Checko -3, 4, 5, 6, 7, 8, 9	1751.12
		3. Gadadhar	Gada -1, 2, 3, 4, 5, 6	1433.86

Division	Range	Beats	Components (Division)	Area (Ha)
	Damanpur West	1. Garam (East)	DPO -1, 2, 5, 6, 9	2419.17
		2. Garam (West)	Poro - 3, 8, 9	1077.67
		3. Poro (East)	Poro -2, 7, 10; Phoskadanga - PF	920.27
	Rajabhatkawa East	1. Panabari (South)	Pan - 6, 7, 8, 9, 10	1573.10
		2. Panbari (North)	Pan -1, 2, 3, 4, 5	1599.28
		3. SRVK	SRVK - 11, 12, 13, 14	984.38
	Rajabhatkawa West	1. WRVK	SRVK -7, 8, 9, 10, 15, 16	2470.70
		2. NRVK	SRVK-1, 2; NRVK- 10, 11, 15, 16	1986.68
		3. CRVK	SRVK- 3, 4, 5, 6	1252.27
		4. Dima	Dima -1, 2, 3, 4; Dima - RF	1081.25
	Nimati	1. Nimati (East)	Nimati -3,4,5,6	1170.78
		2. Nimati (West)	Nimati -1,2,7	1189.01

Division	Range	Beats	Components (Division)	Area (Ha)
		3. Poro (West)	Poro -1, 5, 6, 11; Nimti- Domohani- PF	1366.90
	Hamiltongunj	1. Gudamdabri	GDB -1, 2, 3, 4	1613.42
		2. Bharnabari	BNB -1, 2, 3, 4	1685.44
		3. Rangamati	RMT-1, 2, 3; RMT-Extn.	1017.49
		4. Bhutri	Bhutri -1, 2, 3, 4, 5	1526.62
	Pana	1. Pana	Pana -1, 2, 3, 4	1336.66
		2. Gangutia	RTG -6, 7, 8, 9, 10	1542.26
		3. Raimatang	RTG -1, 2, 3, 4, 5	1962.00
		4. Adma	Adma -1, 2, 3, 4, 5	2507.44

Source: 9th Working plan of Jalpaiguri Forest Division, vol. 1, 2008-09 & Tiger conservation plan, 2016-17 to 2026-2027

ground rising rapidly from 150 meter to 1000 meter. The table–3.2 showed the area of Alinagar forests which is covered 6.4146 sq. km, Jaldapara wild life sanctuary 220.249 sq. km, Buxa 721.659 sq. km, Rydak 35.5018 sq. km, Dalgaon 78.1529 sq. km, Titi 63.1041 sq.km, Dalmore 17.2549 sq.km, and Dhumpara-Bhalka 29.3241 sq.km. In percentage (Table–3.2) highest forests cover is found in the Buxa wild life sanctuary (61.59 %), other followers are Jaldapara WLS (18.79 %), Dalgaon (6.68 %), and Titi forest (5.39 %), Rydak (3.03 %) and so on. To take necessary administrative works of forest in the District, all together there are sixteen (16) forest range office within that District, these are Buxaduar, Hatipota, Jainti, North Rydak, South Rydak, Bhokla, Kumargram, Hamiltonganj, Pana, Nimti, West Dananpur, East Damanpur, East Rajabhatkhawa, West Rajabhatkhawa, Madarihat and Dalgaon.

Table–3.2
Forest Area of Alipurduar District

S.No.	Name of the forest	Area (sq.km)	Percentage
1	Alinagar	6.4146	0.55
2	Jaldapara WLS	220.249	18.79
3	Buxa Tiger Reserve	721.659	61.59
4	Rydak	35.5018	3.03
5	Dalgaon	78.1529	6.68
6	Titi	63.1041	5.39
7	Dalmore	17.2549	1.47
8	Dhumpara & Bhalka	29.3241	2.50
	Total	**1171.66**	**100**

Source: Google Earth Image, 2017, area calculated by using Arc GIS

3.3 Forest Villages

By definition, forest villages does not mean the villages situated in the forest, but means such colony of collies or villages or labours settled by the Forest Department for maintenance of assured supply of labour required in forest works done departmentally (Sinha, 1987). In 1894 cultivators were first allowed to settle in the forest in connection with the scheme of taungya sowings. About 1904 establishment of forest villages became a regular policy and very large numbers of forest villagers were allowed to settle in the forest. Forest villagers were found very useful for undertaking cultural operations in the forest and also for fire protection purpose. Initially there was no sufficient control over the amount of land, a villager might cultivate and number of cattle they might keep (Ninth working plan of Jalpaiguri Forest Division, vol. I, 2009). In 1912 rules were made to limiting the cultivation and homestead land to 2.5 acres in plains, and 1.5 acres in hills per family. Each household was allowed to keep not more than two (2) plough cattle, two (2) milk cow and four (4) calves; two (2) got/sheep may be allowed provided that they are always stall feed (Das, 2000). As a result of this restriction all the undesirable villagers left but the useful villagers in nearly all cases returned shortly agreeing to abide by the rules. This has to be read with the definition of 'forest village' given in section 2(f): According to the Forests Rights Act 2006 (FRA), 2(f) forest villages means the settlements which have been settled inside the forest by the Forest Department of any State Government for forestry

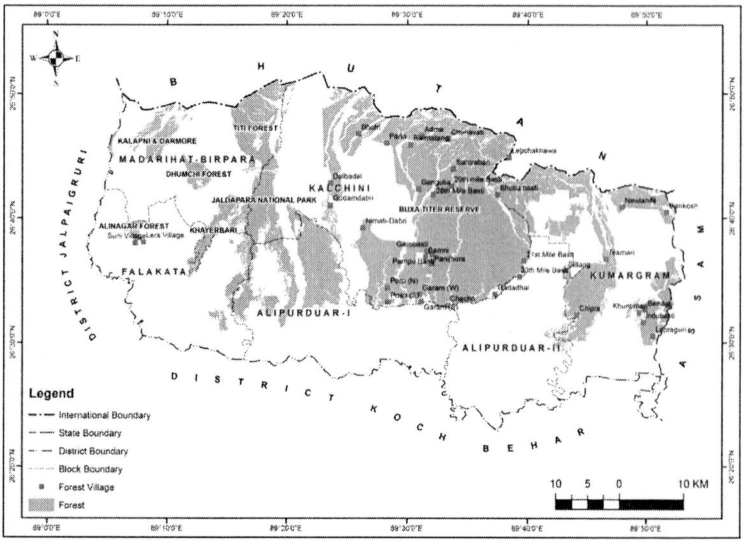

Fig. 3.2: Location of Forest Villages of Alipurduar District

activities or which were shifted into forest villages through the forest reservation process and includes fixed demand holdings, forest settlement villages, all types of taungya settlements, by whatever name called, for such villages and includes lands for cultivation and other uses, allowed by the Government (Sarin and Springate, 2010).

At present there are 39 forest villages existing in this District with a total strength of 2948 families of which 1011 are agreement holder. These forest villagers are looked after by the forest village development division created in 1988 with HQ at Jalpaiguri (Das, 2000). The forest villagers have been provided with wooden departmental quarters in most cases. Constructions of wooden huts have been started from the year 1947-48 and have continued till 1960-61. Further welfare measures have been undertaken in the forest villages by providing ring wells, construction of pipelines for supply of water and also by providing primary schools and teachers' quarters to cater to the requirement of forests villagers. Forest villages come under the panchayet system from 1998 through tiger reserve provides villagers with amenities through Joint Forest Management system. Forest villagers cultivate their land and rare large number of cattle. Reduction in forest harvesting, extent of creation and maintenance of plantations meant substantial reduction in employment of both forest villagers and fringe villagers.

3.3.1 Ethnic Identities of Forest Villagers

A substantial proportion of the population comprises of scheduled tribes (ST) such as Rava, Mechia, Garo, Santal, Nepali, Bhutia, Oraon etc. are the prime community. Nepali and Santhal community is proportionally higher among all forest villagers. Villagers live in complete communal harmony. Relationship of villagers within their own community and with other community is good. They marry socially although love marriage is also allowed within the society. They generally arrange their marriage within the same community. Durga puja, Shyama puja, Saraswati puja etc. are the festival of villagers who are Hindu; and Christmas is

Table–3.3
Name and location of forest villages within Alipurduar District

Name of Forest Division	Range office	Beat office	Forest village	Population 1991	Population 2001	Population 2011
Jalpaiguri Forest Division	Dalgaon range	Bandapani	Lehra village	104	122	145
			Suni village	154	182	207
Buxa Tiger Reserve, West Division	West	West	Garo Basti	752	911	1129
	Rajabhatkhowa	Rajabhatkhowa	Pumpu Basti	190	215	243
			Bamni Bsati	84	102	122
	East Damanpur	Gadhadhar	Gadhadhar	1125	1279	1436
		Damanpur	Panijhora	210	247	276
		Checko	Kalkut	702	842	997
	West Damanpur	East Poro	Poro (N)	643	776	934
			Poro (S)	428	513	627
		Garam (West)	Garam (West)	375	483	591
		Garam (East)	Garam (East)	605	722	876
	Nimati	West Poro	Nimati &Dabri	590	696	798
	Pana	Gangutia	Gangutia	383	443	523
		Adma	Adma	298	349	413

Name of Forest Division	Range office	Beat office	Forest village	Population 1991	Population 2001	Population 2011
		Raimatang	Raimatang	409	489	578
		Pana	Pana	446	548	671
	Hamiltonganj	Bhutri	Bhutri basti	251	223	258
		Gudamdabri	Gudamdabri	867	971	1102
			Dalbada	152	174	202
	East	Panabari (S)	20th Mile	200	226	261
	Rajabhatkhowa	Panabari (N)	21st Mile	133	163	203
Buxa Tiger Reserve, East Division	Jainty (south)	Bhutiabasti	Bhutiabasti	415	389	279
	Kumargram	Sankosh	Sankosh	602	697	792
			Newlands	165	198	246
		Kumargram	Kumargram	401	479	594
	Bholka	Balapara	Balapara	216	261	317
		Ghoramara	Khutimari	251	307	364
			Bengdoba	201	274	354
			Indu basti	177	219	267
		Barobhisa	Lapraguri	276	342	397
	North Rydak	Teamari	Teamari	182	213	265

Name of Forest Division	Range office	Beat office	Forest village	Population		
				1991	2001	2011
	South Rydak	South Rydak	Shiltong	383	445	509
		Chipra	Chipra	225	297	387
	Buxaduar	BDR road	28th Mile	300	377	472
			29th Mile	126	173	238
			Lepchakhawa	300	349	401
		Chunabati	Chunabati	274	316	359
		Santrabari	Santrabari	339	403	497

Source: Census of India, 2001, 2011

the main festival among Christians. All communities are living peacefully and help one another; and gathered to help for social activities such as marriage and other social ceremony each other. The tribal population includes mainly Rava, Mechia, Oraon, and Madeshia on southern and comparatively low height area, Dukpas/Bhutia tribes are lived on extreme north hill of Buxa and Nepalese are scattered all around. There are good numbers of Bangali too live in the proximity of the forest villages (table–3.4).

3.3.1.1 Rava

The Ravas are believed to enter into the Alipurduar District of West Bengal from china through Tibet and Burma. Their language is Bhot-Burmese. They also belong to mongoloid. The Ravas are divided into different clans, such as Koch, Bongdania, Mytori, Dhahuripati, Bitliya, Hema, Sanga, Totla and Madahi. 'The Ravas living in Jalpaiguri are mostly Koches' (Roy, 2010). The mother has the highest respect in the society. The Ravas of this District are economically very poor and lived inside or fringe area of forest. They have very small quantity of land who is agreement holder with Forest Department and others are landless. The Rava women are good weavers of handloom. Their taste of colour combination is praiseworthy. Their bamboo made handloom instruments are attractive. These instruments are traditional and with the help of these they weave lufun, kambang, faakcheck, soloylone, kalai etc. (Kar, 2003). They are making traditional cloths for their own use. The culture of the Ravas is full of variety. They like to sing and dance together and especially women take part in dancing with the traditional musical instruments. The Ravas worship Kamakhsha Devi during Ambubachi. They sacrifice bamboo to goddess Kamaksha.

3.3.1.2 Garo

The Garos of the North Bengal are chiefly concentrated in Kochbihar, Alipurduar and Jalpaiguri District. Linguistically the Garos belong to the Bodo group, and there seem good grounds for supporting that their members of the great Tibeto-Burman race (Allen, Gait, Allen & Howard, 2001). They belongs to Mongoloid group and are divided into different sub castes such as; Dedoi, Champek, Maji, Uni, Lokbok, Banda, Kama etc. A man and woman of the same caste cannot marry and for that one caste must marry into another caste. Relationship is traced in the female line. The main food of the Garos is rice. Fish of every kind is eaten; also flesh of pig, deer, goat, ducks, fowls, and pigeons. Large grasshoppers and locusts are also their food. Vegetables of all kinds are eaten. Men wear a cotton dhoti called gumcha and a coat to cover their bodies called bukhchili; others are pagga, kalai, lofoon, kambang etc. which are used to cover different parts of the body both of male and female.

The chief deity of the Garos is Rishi. Juggo is said to be the husband of Rishi, and is also worshiped. In the month of March and April a new bamboo is cut and planted in the courtyard to represent Rishi, in order that the house or village may be safe from enemies, fire, sickness and other troubles. The bamboo is called Sirfak. Rishi is said to eat flesh of pig and fowls. She also drinks liquor called chokot. Juggo eats no flesh; but drinks liquor (Kar, 2003). They are cultivating cotton, bhadoi paddy, mustard seed, a little tobacco of inferior quality, brinjals, chillies, cucumbers, and melons called bangi. Fish are caught in small streams which are blocked up and the water is poisoned with various articles. To capture fish in streams they used bamboo traps called Dingir, Dhoska, Darika and Burung also used long fishing net called kheolic-hek and bamboo trap called pallao.

3.3.1.3 Santal

The santals are an important tribe in forest and tea belt area of the Alipurduar District. They descend from the pre-Dravidian who migrated to the regions of Jharkhand, Chhattisgarh, and Orissa. The Santals were made their way into the North Bengal as tea garden coolies and in 1901 they numbered 10,857 (Grunning, 1911). They were used for the purpose of opening out land in the terai for tea (Dash, 1947). They have some clans among which Hansdak, Murmu,

Hembrom, Soren, Kisku, Tudu, Besra, Bedea etc. are found. The Santal culture has attracted many scholars and anthropologists for decades. This culture is depicted in the paintings and art works in the walls of their houses. They love traditional music and dance. Like other Indian ethnic groups, their culture has been influenced by mainstream Indian and Western culture. In spite of that their traditional music and dance still remain in the society. Santhals believe in supernatural beings and ancestral spirits. The society is devoid of caste hierarchy and therefore, the Santal's is casteless society. In their language marriage is called Bapla. There are different forms of marriage among the couples, such as Raibar Bapla, Sanga Bapla, Kudam Bapla, Tunki Dipil Bapla etc. They have separate religion and it is called 'Sarna'. Image or idol worship is absent and there is no as such traditional temple that exists in Santal society.

3.3.1.4 Mechia

The Meches of the Alipurduar District is close to the Bodos and the Kacharies of Assam. They are probably the original inhabitants of the Darjeeling Terai, and are a distinctly Mongolian race, with fair skins and large bones and limbs' (Grunning, 1911). The river Mechi in the India and Nepal border area is named after the Meches as per the opinions of some scholars. The Meches are known as good hunter and cultivator also love to live in forest and fringe areas. Among Mechia, Batho Puja is famous and it is celebrated during the month of Baisakh. Batho is a male God and his wife Mainas is a goddess of wealth of them. This puja is done whole of the month of Baisakh to please God. Bihu– mainly Baisakhi bihu is celebrated on 1st day of Baisakh. Drinking of local made liquor is common which they called 'Bokha-Jao' and it is winter drink (Kar, 2003). They have liquor called 'Hasa-Jao' which is drunk only during the summer. Some other community who lived among them also suffers from this practice.

3.3.1.5 Nepali

Nepalese are the dominant ethnic group in the hilly tracts

of Duars. They hail from different castes and dialect groups like the Gurungs, the Mangars, the Limbus, the Tamangs, the Khas or Chettri, the Newars, the Subbas, the Muramis, the Sherpa, the Kamis, the Damai etc. Various castes and tribes that immigrated to the area during the 18th and 19th century from Nepal are submerged under this group. Today they are permanent settlers inside the forest or tea garden areas. Gurungs are innocence, simple mindedness. The khas are the Nepali Brahmins who have a large admixture of Aryan blood. Muramis are a Mongolian or semi Mongolian caste who has been modified by intermixture with Nepalese races (Malley, 1907). Sherpa, Tamang came from Tibet and followed Tibetan language and Buddhism religion. Limbus, Gurungs, Gorkhas, Mangers are lower caste among Nepalese. Most of them follow Buddhism as their major religion, but Christian and Hinduism also found among them. At present they engage in agriculture, trade, labour and other activities. They love music, specially drink of liquor in any kind of festivals.

3.3.1.6 Bhutia

Bhutias live in Chunabati and Buxa areas of Alipurduar District. The word Bhutia signifies an inhabitants of Bhot or Tibet; Bhot is the Sanskrit form of Bod, which is the native name of Tibet, and Bhutia means the end of Bhot. The Sanskritic speaking peoples of India consequently call the inhabitants of Tibet and Bhutan, 'Bhutias' (Grunning, 1911). The Bhutias or Dukpas, as they are called, belonged to the country known as Bhutan. The number of tall men among them is very few; but all are very robust as compared with the people of the plains. The main foods are rice, pork, beef, fowls, deer, marua, fish, both dried and fresh and vegetables of all sorts. Tea is a favourite drink of this society and taken it frequently during whole of the day. But it is never drunk or served without some eatable food. Rice-beer, called arra or biachang, is prepared by the Bhutias for feasts and religious ceremonies. The old and young, men and women drink liquor. The women wear a long cloak with loose sleeves called kira or moki and men wear a loose woolen, or cotton, or endi silk coat called KO. The Bhutia people are Buddhist, and generally confine themselves to repeating the words Om-Mani-Padine-Hom (Kar, 2003). There is no marriage ceremony among the Bhutias. The houses of are built on stone walls, wooden, as also on posts and are from 8 to 10 feet off the ground. The domestic animals found in the houses are pig, they called phup; fowls, dogs, cows, ponies and cats.

3.3.1.7 Oraon

The Oraons are spread over the tea belt and forest belt of this study area. According to the historical report they have been transmigrated from middle India as well as from Bihar and Orissa towards the middle of 19th century, with the establishment of tea gardens in Duars (Kar, 2003). The history of the Oraons belongs to properly to the Ranchi District, from which most of them came up to the tea gardens. They converse with each other in kurukh, a popular language. It belongs to the Dravidian family group and has got a close relation with other languages including Brahui and Paharia (Ghosh, 2003). Oraon tribes are religious minded mostly following the customs of Hinduism, but many Oraons are today Christians. They have a rich and vast range of folk songs, dances and tales, as well as traditional musical instruments. Mandar, Nagara and kartal are the main musical instruments. Their songs and music are changed according to seasons and festivals. Majority of Oraon who have converted to christianism write their title Kerkatta, Xalxo, Xaxa, Xesss, Tirkey, Kujur, Minz, Indwar, Kindo, Kistoper, Lakra etc.

3.3.2 Relationship with Forest

Forests provide significant social and economic benefits at all levels, especially in developing countries. Economics of people living in forest and fringe area have traditionally been dominated by subsistence agriculture. Forest villagers are totally depends on the forests for firewood, small timber, grazing and Non-Wood Forest Products (NWFP). Now villagers used to be employed in timber harvesting and

Table–3.4
List of Forest Villages with Their Composition

S.No.	Name of Forest village	Total No. of Family	No. of Agreement holders Family	No. of Family belongs to							
				R	O	S	M	G	N	B	OT
1	Lehra village	31	13	-	-	31	-	-	-	-	-
2	Suni village	27	7	27	-	-	-	-	-	-	-
3	Garo Basti	216	71	87	93	-	-	5	31	-	-
4	Pumpu Basti	41	14	-	7	-	2	-	32	-	-
5	Bamni Bsati	15	6	-	1	5	-	-	7	-	2
6	Gadhadhar	257	71	187	27	33	-	-	-	-	10
7	Panijhora	41	21	13	2	2	13		5	-	6
8	Kalkut	98	42	-	-	-	30	-	-	-	58
9	Poro (N)	135	54	135	-	-	-	-	-	-	-
10	Poro (S)	78	27	78	-	-	-	-	-	-	-
11	Garam (West)	34	17	-	18	5	-	-	-	-	11
12	Garam (East)	110	33	-	-	10	61	-	-	-	39
13	Nimati & Dabri	115+15	30+5	85	-	-	-	-	-	-	45
14	Gangutia	68	23	-	-	-	-	-	68	-	-
15	Adma	64	13	-	-	-	-	-	-	64	
16	Raimatang	81	22	-	-	-	-	-	80		1

S.No.	Name of Forest village	Total No. of Family	No. of Agreement holders Family	No. of Family belongs to							
				R	O	S	M	G	N	B	OT
17	Pana	86	41	-	-	-	-	-	86	-	-
18	Bhutri basti	50	23	-	-	-	-	-	68	-	-
19	Gudamdabri	142	71	-	-	-	40	-	12	-	90
20	Dalbada	45	19	-	-	-	-	-	33	-	12
21	20th Mile	58	11	54	-	3	-	-	1	-	-
22	21st Mile	23	9	-	-	20	-	-	-	-	3
23	Bhutiabasti	72	31	-	-	-	-	-	40	-	32
24	Sankosh	98	44	-	-	-	-	-	30	68	-
25	Newlands	40	12	-	12	-	-	-	17	11	-
26	Kumargram	56	28	-	-	-	-	-	13	43	-
27	Balapara	40	17	-	-	3	32	-	5	-	-
28	Khutimari	99	22	35	-	-	-	-	54	10	-
29	Bengdoba	56	25	12	-	17	-	-	27	-	-
30	Indu basti	37	10	-	-	-	37	-	-	-	-
31	Lapraguri	52	11	45	7	-	-	-	-	-	-
32	Tiamari	34	10	-	2	3	-	-	8	-	21
33	Shiltong	144	27	120	11	-	-	-	13	-	-
34	Chipra	44	14	44	-	-	-	-	-	-	-

S.No.	Name of Forest village	Total No. of Family	No. of Agreement holders Family	No. of Family belongs to							
				R	O	S	M	G	N	B	OT
35	28th Mile	51	27	-	-	-	-	-	46	5	-
36	29th Mile	25	10	-	-	-	-	-	17	8	-
37	Lepchakhawa	86	40	-	-	-	-	-	15	71	-
38	Chunabati	70	18	-	-	-	-	-	6	64	-
39	Santrabari	96	20	-	2	-	-	-	84	10	-

Note: R=Rava, O=Oraon, S=Santal, M=Mech, G=Garo, N=Nepali, B=Bhutia/Dukpa, OT= Others,
Source: 9th working plan, 2008-09 & Tiger conservation plan, 2016-17 to 2026-2027

plantation work for more than 100 days in a year through Joint Forest Management (JFM) scheme. Fringe villagers and tea garden labourers are also dependent on forests for wood, small timbers, thatch grass, cattle grazing and collection of NWFPs to a considerable extent. Villagers also depend on some rivers and streams such as Rydak, Sankosh, Gadhadhar, Pana for irrigation and for fishing. Landless and marginal farmers get employment as a daily labour in different forestry and panchayet development works. Some persons among tea garden and fringe villagers are involved in illegal felling of timber and poaching. This leads to occasional conflicts with forest officials.

3.3.3 Villagers Economy and Occupation

Villagers residing in and around the forests are very poor in all sense. There is no industry except tea. Subsistence agriculture, horticulture is the main occupation and majority of the families is small and marginal farmers. Most of the families have less than 3 acre land where they gave huge labour force for livelihood. Villagers follow the traditional agricultural practices. Irrigation facilities are totally absent, few of them arrange own self and majority of the agriculture lands are mono-cropped. The existing source of employment that shown in the area is forest plantation works, annual felling and thinning coupes, cane products, soil conservation and river bank dam construction, fishing in rivers, honey and other NWFP collection, labour works in tea gardens, boulder collection, livestock rearing etc. The main seasons of considered as unemployment are winter and rainy. Villagers maintain large number of cattle and most of them are scrub cattle. Cow dung is used mainly for manure in agriculture field. For fuel wood villagers depends on forest besides some fuel also comes from agricultural wastes. Vocations of villagers living and around the forest are agriculture, animal husbandry and agro-based, forestry-based cottage industries. Number of regularly employed is very little, except school teaching, there is little scope of getting job. Few are engaged in banking, cottage industries and some are in private and business. Tea gardens labour gets job from April to November and other December to March is lean period where few are engaged. During this lean period tea garden and fringe people also depends on cutting firewood from forest. There are 37 saw mills including 5 veneer mills in the vicinity. There are 279 recognised firewood dealers and 85 furniture shops operating around this District forest (Das, 2000). Moreover villagers migrated to the Bhutan, Meghalaya, Arunachal Pradesh and Assam in search of work.

3.4 Anthropogenic Intervention in Forest

In the present study attempt has been made to collect the information on anthropogenic intervention on forests. For that purpose the researcher looks on the subject of collection of NTFPs, illegal activities on forests, livestock grazing, forest fire, wildlife health attack etc.

3.4.1 Illegal Activities

Illegal cutting of trees, illegal removal of firewood & NWFP, poaching of wild animals, boulder collection, illegal grazing and encroachment are the main illegal activities in Buxa Tiger Reserve and surrounding forests area of the District.

3.4.1.1 Poaching

Poaching is one of the illegal activities in BTR due to its peculiar location. Its northern boundary runs along Bhutan and eastern boundary with Assam, international boundary with Bangladesh is 20 km away from its southern boundary wild animals in BTR are vulnerable to poaching. Currently, elephants are most susceptible to poaching. From 1991 to 2013, total 23 animals were poached in Alipurduar District (table–3.5). Labourers mainly from nearly tea estates are reported to indulge in poaching for deer, wild boar, jungle fowl, etc. It is suspected that poaching of bears for their bile & gallstones takes place in Jaigaon. Fishing also takes place in Rydak, Gholani, Dhawla, Poro & other rivers. It is also suspected that poachers enter BTR through Indo-Bhutan boundary (65 km, open boundary). As the Indo-Bhutan boundary is inaccessible due to hilly terrain (outer Himalayas), effective patrolling lacks. During 1994, three elephants were poached by Arunachal tribes in S. Rydak Range. They poached by arrow poisoning (vegetative poison). One male elephant calf was poached in 1997 at Tashigaon for supplying "two small tusks with jaw" by specific order from Bhutan.

Table–3.5
Year-wise Poaching of Wildlife in BTR, Alipurduar District

S.No.	Year	Species	No. of Animals
1	1991	Elephant	-
2	1992	Elephant	1
3	1993	Elephant	1
4	1994	Elephant, Pangolin	3
5	1995	Elephant	1
6	1996	Elephant, Chital Bison, Leopard	3
7	1997	Elephant	1
8	1998	Samber	1
9	2005	Leopard	1
10	2006	Elephant, Barking deer	1
11	2007	Sambar	1
12	2008	Spotted deer	1
13	2009	Wild boar, Hill myna	4
14	2010	Tortoise	1
15	2011	-	-
16	2012	Baison, Spotted deer, Wildboar	1
17	2013	Elephant	2
	Total		**23**

Source: Tiger Conservation plan, 2016-17 to 2026-2027.

In the Figure 3.4, the location of tea gardens as well as forest covers shown clearly where it is noticed that most of the tea gardens boundary are attached with forest which means tea gardens labours have an intervention to the forests for livelihood needs.

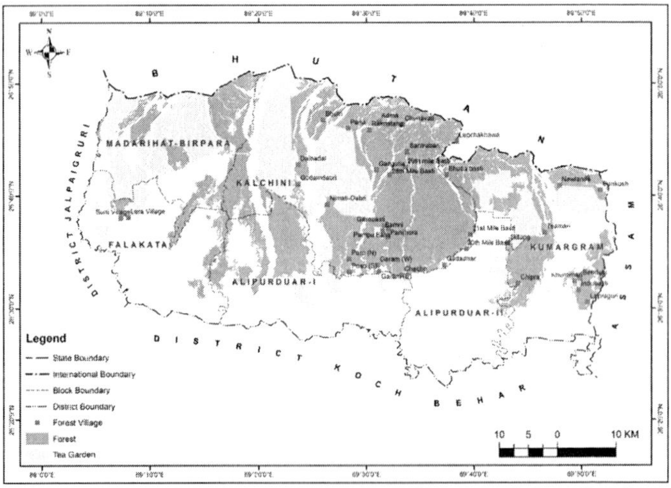

Fig. 3.3 : Location of Forest, Forest Village and Tea Gardens

The table–3.6 shows the details of tea gardens as well as their inhabitants and cattle population. There are huge number of human and cattle population. This population directly and indirectly involved in forest resource extraction, besides for livestock rearing tea estate villagers totally depend on nearby forests.

3.4.1.2 Illegal Cutting of Trees

It's a common illegal activities and a serious problem in forest area of Alipurduar District. The forest offences recorded during the period of 1993-1994 to 2012-2013 and quantity of timber seized in both the divisions of BTR is given in table–3.7. The most valuable areas are Bhutri, Bharnabari, Rangamati, parts of Raimatang along T.E., Dima, Poro, Nimati, Gadadhar, parts of Panbari, parts of SRVK, Chuniajhora, Raydak & Newlands. There are many saw mills, veneer mills and furniture shops present in Alipurduar, Kalchini (Jaigaon) & Kumargram P.S. and adjoining areas. A part of illicit timber is sold to these mills. A part of these, illicit timbers goes to Coach Behar, Dinhata & Baxirhat and even to Bangladesh. A part is going to Bhutan through Jaigaon. Timber mafias are very active in this region. They

Table–3.6

Name and Location of Tea Estate Situated near BTR

S.No.	Name of Tea Estate	J.L No.	Population Human (1991)	Population Cattle (1991)	S.No.	Name of Tea Estate	J.L No.	Population Human (1991)	Population Cattle (1991)
				BTR, East Division					
Kumargram ps					**Kalchini p.s**				
1	Phaskhawa T.E	2	1096	600	17	Nimtijhora T.E	11	4014	1234
2	Chuia Jhora T.E	3	2237	865	18	Atiabari T.E	41	5538	1858
3	Kartick T.E	4	4140	1073	19	Bhatkhawa T.E	40	5927	1431
4	Rahimabad T.E	5	3061	1166	20	Rajabhat T.E	42	3696	826
5	Jainti-I T.E	6	4601	1545	21	Dima T.E	39	4906	1012
6	Jainti-II T.E	8	937	450	22	Gangutia	38	4500	972
7	Turturi T.E	9	2163	2200	23	Kalchini T.E	37	11998	2959
8	Rydak T.E	10	6492	1766	24	Bhatpara T.E	36	8037	1466
9	Newlands New T.E	31	5581	2580	25	Chupara T.E	33	6337	1681
10	Kumargram T.E	33	5291	1225	26	Radharani T.E	32	1203	431
11	Sankosh T.E	34	5709	1920	27	Madhu T.E	18	4573	790
	Alipurduar ps				28	Dalsinghpara T.E	23	12226	2514
12	Kohinoor T.E	120	2070	994	29	Bharnabari T.E	22	5682	1621
13	Dhawla Jhora T.E	118	2907	1152	30	Torsa T.E	24	4354	811

S.No.	Name of Tea Estate	J.L No.	Population Human (1991)	Population Cattle (1991)	S.No.	Name of Tea Estate	J.L No.	Population Human (1991)	Population Cattle (1991)
BTR, West Division									
14	Patkapara T.E	39	3914	1900	31	Satali T.E	19	4906	1012
15	Majherdabri (E) T.E	58	2272	891	32	Rangamati T.E	30	7604	2578
16	Srinathpur T.E	81	1232	485	33	Raimatang T.E		3673	1001
					34	Mechpara T.E	35	5742	1359

Source: Management-cum-working plan of BTR, 2000

Table–3.7

Offence Cases & Illegal Timber Seized in BTR

Year	BTR, West Division				BTR, East Division				Total no. of offences in BTR	Total quantity of timber
	No. of offence seized (m^3)			Quantity of timber seized (m^3)	No. of offences		UDOR	Quantity of timber seized (m^3)		
	COR	POR	UDOR		COR	POR				
1993-94	218	21	512	760.913	---	---	---	---	751	760.913
1994-95	261	19	538	647.112	---	---	---	---	818	647.112
1995-96	169	26	625	670.153	---	---	---	---	820	670.153
1996-97	73	3	364	523.12	281	27	648	696.742	1396	1219.862
1997-98	56	30	1188	1175.8	459	16	653	797.437	2402	1973.237
1998-99	90	108	1476	1173.767	318	11	815	1190.565	2818	2364.332
2005-06	70	44	1003	1182.03	329	116	964	1431.97	2526	2613.98
2006-07	76	29	1046	1572.89	311	21	745	1119.69	2228	2692.58
2007-08	87	43	1182	1426.23	287	13	777	942.07	2389	2368.30
2008-09	98	37	1058	1050.43	218	17	731	1006.52	2159	2056.95
2009-10	86	25	1322	1381.77	181	19	887	1264.13	2520	2645.9
2010-11	65	39	1440	1219.6	230	15	1004	1618.26	2793	2837.86
2011-12	147	34	2099	2841.0	188	23	983	1455.75	3474	4296.7
2012-13	78	21	1584	1736.2	235	14	984	1534.70	2916	3270.9
Total	**1574**	**479**	**15437**	**17361.02**	**3037**	**292**	**9191**	**13057.83**	**30010**	**30418.78**

Source: Tiger conservation plan, 2016-17 to 2026-2027.

mislead poor villagers into the act.

Firewood is collected by people not only for their own use but also for sale in local markets. For this purpose they even fill green trees. Removal of timber from forest by wood poachers is done by 'Thela' & river rafting. Truck is rarely used. Firewood is removed by head load, cycle & thela. During rainy season most of the areas of BTR become inaccessible due to the presence of water current flow of numerous rivers & streams. River rafting of illegal timbers is a common feature in BTR. Although later two permanent river camp of Sankosh & Rydak and 4 temporary river camps on Poro, Dima and Gholani rivers operate to check river rafting during rainy season.

3.4.1.3 Illegal Removal of NTFPs

The NTFPs collection by FPCs/EDCs members is legally permissible as per Govt. order. But there is no definite harvesting procedure for it. The FPCs/EDCs members, many tea garden labourers are also involved in its collection. Lot of thatch is collected from grasslands for thatching roofs. Due to cutting of thatch unscientifically, grassland habitat is destroyed. Many birds including Bengal florican lay eggs and rear chicks in these grasslands. Illegally many people enter into the forest for collection of simul floss and decorative fungi (cheu) and thereby create a lot of disturbance to wild animals including birds in their natural habitat.

3.4.1.4 Illegal Boulder Collection inside of Forest

Alipurduar sub-division is situated in the flood plain of many rivers & streams. Lot of boulder & bed materials are required annually by the irrigation department, P.W.D., railways & panchayets for soil conservation, bed protection, road side protection etc. works. Boulder is also available in rivers flowing through Buxa Tiger Reserve, Titi forest and other forests. Legally boulder collection permission is not given to anybody from 1996-97 to protect natural flows of rivers, to control of river bank erosion of forest. There is some illicit collection of surface boulder and bed material. Smuggling of

BTR boulders to these parts is also in evidence which enhanced soil erosion and flash flood surrounding of forest.

3.4.2 Domestic Livestock Grazing

As per rules no grazing allowed inside the forests. Nevertheless the reserve forest suffers from illicit grazing. It is most severe in Rangamati, Bharnbari, Bhutri, Raimatang, Nimati, Poro, Damanpur, Checko, Gadadhar, Rydak, Newlands, Sankosh & Bholka block. The reserve forest has 46 fringe villages, 34 tea gardens, 37 forest villages and 4 F.D holding hamlets in and around it. These villages and tea gardens have approximate 1.5 lakh domestic livestock (table–3.7 and 3.9). Fair percentage of these graze illegally inside the forest grazing during dry season (March-April) affects habitat quality severely. The domestic cattle compete directly with the wild herbivores for fodder. They share the common water holes with the wild animals. So, there is a fair chance of dissemination of cattle borne diseases (Anthrax, FMD, HSBQ, etc.) to the wild animal.

3.4.3 Forest Fire

Fire is not uncommon in BTR. The occurrence of the fire particularly in the month of January to April is common in foothill areas above 23rd mile towards North and in areas occupied by pure teak plantations. The vulnerable areas are Bhutanghat, Phaskhawa, Santrabari, NRVK, Raimatang blocks also the riverine tract of Rydak blocks and grasslands of Narathali, Marakata & Bholka blocks. Illicit fellers, grazier, thatch collectors & other NWFP collectors knowingly/ unknowingly lit the fire. Sometimes poachers lit fire to expose the wild animals.

3.4.3.1 Type of Fire

Crown fire is not reported from BTR except in few patches in hilly tract of Tashigaon lock. Ground fire is common in BTR from January to April every year.

3.4.3.2 Causes of Fire

In Buxa Tiger Reserve the reason for forest fire is purely men-made either deliberately or accidentally. Following are the main reasons of forest fires in this District.

3.4.3.2.1 Fire due to Grazers

The cowboys or cattle grazers lit fire in forest. Sometimes these grazers deliberately fire the areas to get new flush of grasses. It is estimated that near about one lakh cattle graze in BTR every day. Lot of cowboys enters into the forest with those cattle. They are serious source of fire hazards.

3.4.3.2.2 Fire due to Pedestrians

Large number of forest paths is used by local people for their day to day activities. While passing through the forest, knowingly/unknowingly they throw the burning butts of cigarette/bidis, causing fire to forest.

3.4.3.2.3 Fire due to Poachers

Poachers who set fire in the forest areas have two aims in their minds:

i. To deviate attention of forest department staff from targeted timber felling areas to other areas, so that staff gets involved in fire fighting giving them access to targeted areas.
ii. To flush out wild animals from forest, for easy hunting.

3.4.3.2.4 Fire due to NWFP Collectors

Fire is also being caused by forest produce collectors especially by people who collect "Phooljharu", as by fire clearing the area; they get, fresh/flush of Phooljharu and also an increased growth of the same for their business.

3.4.3.3 Fire Affected Areas

Most fires affected areas in BTR are the north of 23rd mile, mainly Bhabar & hilly tracts. The survey conducted by

Table–3.8

Burnt Category-wise Affected Ranges in BTR Showing Devastation Percentage

Range	Affected area (Ha)	Affected compartments	Total % burnt	Burnt percentage in affected class				
				0 -20 %	21-40 %	41-60 %	61-80 %	81-100 %
BTR, West division								
Pana	378	AD-1,4;Pana-1,4; RTG-2,3,9	1.85	1.09	0.75	0	0	0
Hamiltonganj	1005	GDB-1,3; BNB-1,2,3,4; BH-1,2,3,4,5	4.92	1.66	1.56	1.69	0	0
East Damanpur	1346	CH-5,6,7,8,9; GD-1,2,3,4,5,6; DPO-3,4,7,8	6.59	0.77	3.39	0	0	2.41
West Damanpur	1081	PORO-5,7,10; DPO-1,2,5,6,9	5.29	1.04	2.39	1.85	0	0
East Rajabhatkhawa	478	PANA-4,5; PAN-6,10; SRVK-11,14	2.34	0.86	0.66	0.80	0	0
West Rajabhatkhawa	1215	SRVK-1,2,7,8,10, 15; DIMA-1,2,3,4	5.95	0.26	3.35	0	0	2.33

Range	Affected area (Ha)	Affected compartments	Total % burnt	Burnt percentage in affected class				
				0 -20 %	21-40 %	41-60 %	61-80 %	81-100 %
Nimati	2218	NMT-1,2,3,4,5,6,7; SRVK-9,16; PORO-1,5,6,7,11	10.86	0	2.36	3.34	1.24	3.91
BTR, East division Jainty	4562	NRVK-5,6,7,12, 13,14;TGN-1,2; JNT-1,2,3,4,8,9; PH-2,3;CHU-RF	22.34	0	0.58	7.50	4.62	9.63
Buxaduar	3288	TG-1,2,3; NRVK-1,2,3,4,8,9; STB-1,2,3,4; CHU-2,3	16.1	1.54	2.57	3.09	4.64	4.24
Bholka	1449	SB-1,2a,2b,3a,3b, 4,5,6;NB-1,2,3,4,5	7.09	0.08	5.41	0	0	1.60
South Rydak	1102	NRT-1,2;MKT-,2, 3,4;SR-1,2,3,6,7; DH-1,2	5.39	0.84	1.60	2.94	0	0

Range	Affected area (Ha)	Affected compartments	Total % burnt	Burnt percentage in affected class				
				0 -20 %	21-40 %	41-60 %	61-80 %	81-100 %
North Rydak	1772	HP-1,2;JH-1; BHT-1,2; NRD-1,2,3; CR-1,2,3,4,5,6,7	8.67	3.61	2.35	0	2.71	0
Kumargram	521	NR-3;KGM-1,2; SNK-1,2,3	2.55	1.57	0.97	0	0	0
Total				**13.36**	**28**	**21.24**	**13.23**	**24.14**
Ranking				**IV**	**I**	**III**	**V**	**II**

Source: Tiger conservation plan, 2016-17 to 2026-2027.

M.P.O. & Ecology of BTR in 2016 reveals the following facts as stated in Table–3.8. Total fire affected areas in BTR is 2045 (27% of total BTR). Most affected ranges are Jainty, Rjabhatkhawa (West), Santrabari and North Rydak.

3.4.4 Wildlife Health Attack

Foot & Mouth Disease (FMD) & Anthrax are pathological diseases. No case has been recorded for FMD. During 1994 one (1) bison & four (4) elephants died due to anthrax in BTR. This was the first incidence of anthrax outbreak. Entire North Bengal is affected. These diseases are transmitted through domestic cattle. Cattle in fringes are regularly immunized against these.

3.4.4.1 Illegal Trade in Wildlife and Wildlife Products

This study was conducted under the West Bengal forestry project by Wildlife Protection Society of India (W.P.S.I.), New Delhi during 1996-97. This study covered BTR study aimed at compiling wildlife offences in the past, identifying extent and routes of illicit wildlife trade etc. in North Bengal. Findings of study relevant to BTR are emergence of North Bengal as a crucial trade route in wildlife articles. Wildlife articles from Assam too pass through North Bengal. Proximity of such trade routes to BTR exposes it to great danger of poaching. The study identifies tiger skins & bones, leopard skins & bones, ivory, rhino horn, bear bile, reptile skins, clouded & snow leopards, lesser cat skins, deer skins, turtle & tortoise, orchids & medicinal plants as the major wildlife products that are traded. A total of 27 elephants have been poached during 1979-1997, where 15 were poached in BTR. Substantial seizures have also been done in BTR (Table–3.9).

Table–3.9
Seizures of elephant products in West Bengal during 1979-1997

Species	Location	District	Item seized	Quantity seized
Elephant	Calcutta	Calcutta	Ivory articles	243 pcs. + 2.28 kg

		Ivory carving Raw Ivory	6 pcs. + 0.15 kg 40.4 kg
Cooch Behar	Cooch Behar	Raw Ivory	9.45 kg
Baikunthapur	Jalpaiguri	Raw Ivory	6.1 kg
Buxa Tiger Reserve		Raw Ivory Bones (carved as tusk) Tusks Raw Ivory	24.295 kg 6 pcs 2 pcs 15 pcs
Other divisions	Murshidabad	Raw Ivory	6.5 pcs

Source: Tiger conservation plan, 2016-17 to 2026-2027.

3.4.4.2 Threatened on Monitor Lizards

Shri Brij Bhushan Sharma-a scientist of Jiwaji University, Gwalior (M.P.), carried out a survey of monitor lizards in Buxa Tiger Reserve (BTR) during August 1994 under MOEF project "Conservation status survey of monitor lizards in India" (Das, 2000). He has reported the presence of three species of monitor lizards in BTR viz.-Bengal Monitor Lizard (Veranus Bengalensis), Yellow Monitor Lizard (Veranus Flavescens) and Water Monitor Lizard (Veranus Salvator). The forests areas near rivers and wet lands in east Rajabhatkhawa, S. Rydak, Kumargram and Nimati Range have been indicated as potential areas for monitor lizard. Now monitor lizards are threatened. They are killed for skin. Yellow Monitor Lizard is included in Schedule I, while Bengal Monitor and Water Monitor Lizard are included in Part-II of Schedule II of the Wildlife (Protection) Act, 1972.

3.4.4.3 Men-animal Conflict

Human-wildlife conflict can be defined as any interaction between humans and wildlife that results in negative impacts on human social, economic or cultural life, on the conservation of wildlife populations, or on the environment (Manoj, K., et al., 2013). 'During 2011-12, in West Bengal, a compensation of Rs 3.20 crs. had to be paid against 71 human casualties, 317 injuries, 311 death of cattle or cattle lifting, damage of 4283 huts & crop damage over 5285 hectare' (Das, 2013). Forest habitat loss largely taken place due to human interferes and changes in land use pattern in the present study area. Fragmentation and loss of natural corridors of animals are main cause for man-animal conflict regularly. Bio-diversity is continuously threatened due to loss of forest habitats. Habitat loss has led to decline in several species, like otter, Bengal jackal, pangolin, mongoose, porcupine which are not frequently sighted today here and there. The forest of Duars was an extremely rich bio-diversity zone but today facing challenging moment due to man-animal conflict. Declining one-horn rhino population, political violence in the entire Duars, Jhum-cultivation, tea garden extension etc. are responsible for disturbance of its bio-diversity. Besides incidences of elephants being hit by speeding trains in their migratory corridors are some of the very burning issues and challenges. Conversion of forests cover area into agricultural and habitat land, land acquisition has become a serious issue. The fringe area villagers are least concerned about preserving the forest ecosystem as they are mostly tribal communities and less educated. The conflicts among human and wild animals such as elephant, tiger, leopard, monkeys, gaur, wild boar, crocodile, rhino etc. have become a regular scenario in this place. In table–3.10 details of elephant death by speeding trains is given below.

Table–3.10

No. of Elephant death by broad gauge speeding trains in BTR

S. No.	Date	Time of incident	Division	Location	Sex of animal	No. of animal killed
1	04.06.96	23.00 PM	BTR, West	Adjacent forest	Adult female	1
2	09.06.01	00.45 AM	BTR, West	T.E	Adult female	1
3	28.05.06	19.30 PM	BTR, West	T.E	Adult makna	1
4	11.04.07	4.40 AM	BTR, West	Forest	Adult	1

					makna	
5	09.11.07	1.20 PM	BTR, West	Forest	Male calf	1
6	15.01.08	4.30 AM	BTR, West	Forest	Male calf	1
7	03.06.10	2.08 AM	Garo para, BTR	Corridor	Sub-adult male	1
8	03.06.10	5.00 AM	BTR, West	Forest	Female	1
9	05.01.13	18.14 PM	BTR, West	Forest Three	adult male, one female	4
10	05.03.13	6.40 AM	BTR, West	Forest	Tusker	1
	Total					**13**

Source: Tiger conservation plan, 2016-17 to 2026-2027.

3.5 Forest Products and their Utilization

There are 39 forest villages within or nearby forests and the forest area bordering by either agricultural land or tea estates. As a result huge number of population consists of hunting, rearing, cultivator or tea estate labours that have different kinds of demands from the forests. Besides a sophisticated section of the nearby urban and semi-urban population also require some quantities of timber for construction of house and for furniture. The Jalpaiguri, Alipurduar, Kochbehar and Siliguri are the main markets for major forest product. The produce of this forest has a very ready and established market particularly for sal and teak. The major marketable products are structural wood, plywood, box wood, fuel wood, benches and minor produces. There are innumerable saw mills in the periphery of the forest and these mills have a good demand of timbers.

Besides 34 tea gardens are situated in the vicinity of the forest area and they have well demand of firewood, house construction and house post, agricultural equipment, thatch etc. The produce of the forest mainly timber is exported not only to Calcutta and Bihar but also sent to the Bhutan, Bangladesh and to the some areas in the Northern India. In the 19th century the Indian Railway bought large number of timber for sleepers of railway lines. The entire production of the plywood timber is also very saleable and a few factories situated in the Duars and Siliguri consume the plywood. Presently plywood is allotted to West Bengal plywood and Allied Products Ltd (WBPAPL). The match wood timber is purchased by the Western India Match Co. (WIMCO) of Calcutta. There is also a very keen demand for Khair trees for manufacture of Katha. The entire produce of fire wood is readily taken by the neighboring tea estates and yet their demands are not completely fulfilled. At present the demand for each and every produce, both major and minor, is more than the supply, and as a result there is no problem for the disposal of the produce and the other hand accelerate deforestation, lacking of density of trees increasing.

3.5.1 Structural Wood

The sal timber has been recognized as the best structural wood since long time past for purposes where strength and durability are the prime considerations. Sal timber is the most important and maximum revenue earning produce of the forest. The list of timber of depots and their location is given in the table–3.11. Through this depot all kind of out turn of timber are arranged. Before 2000, railways sleepers of various sizes were sawn by the purchasers and largely by the Government saw mill, Siliguri, for supply to the Indian Railways.

Table–3.11
List of Timber Depots with Location

S.No.	Name of Depot	Location
1	Godamdabri	Godamdabri Office campus
2	Hamilton	Pana Range Office campus
3	Nimati	Nimati Range Office campus
4	Rajabhatkhawa	West Rajabhatkhawa Range Office campus
5	Damanpur	Damanpur Range Office campus
6	Poro	East Poro Beat Office campus
7	Gadadhar	Gadadhar Beat Office campus
8	Jainty	Jainty Range Office campus
9	Buxa Road	Buxa Road Beat Office campus

10	Karticka	North Rydak Range Office campus
11	Samuktala	South Rydak Range Office campus
12	Marakata	Marakata Office campus
13	Kamashyaguri	Kamakshyaguri Mobile Range Office campus
14	Barobisha	Bholka Range Office campus
15	Shil Bunglow	Barobisha Beat Office campus
16	Chengmari	Chengmari Beat Office campus
17	Kumargram	Kumargram Range Office campus

Source: Management-cum-working plan of BTR, 2000

3.5.2 Plywood

In recent years the plywood and veneer industry has come to limelight amongst the wood-based industries. The present trend of demand in the market is for strong, durable and light timber. As a result the veneer industry has earned immense popularity in the market so far the furniture; decorative paneling and flush doors etc are concerned.

3.5.3 Bamboo and Cane

The bamboo is called 'poor man's timber' due to its less price and versatile utility and distribution of bamboo is mainly restricted to Santrabari, Tashigaon, Adma, Lera and Suni block of the forests. There are other areas where bamboo is available, such as Chunabati block, Dandapani block, Topgaon block and Bhutanghat etc. To regulate cutting and to afford rest for further growth, a cutting cycle of 5 years had been adopted and the programme of bamboo cutting in the entire District had been drawn up on that basis. Presently no bamboo extraction is done. Cane holds an important place in the tea industries as it is used for basket making. Some quantities of cane are being exposed for making furniture and other home and kitchen articles. Canes are available mainly in Nimti, Poro, Damanpur, Checko, Panabari, SRVK, S. Rydak and Dalgaon block. To regulate cutting and afford rest for further growth a cutting of cycle have been adopted and like bamboo the programme of cane cutting in the entire District have been restricted on that basis.

3.5.4 Firewood Collection

Large quantity of firewood is required annually the forest villagers, neighbouring tea estates and fringe population for industrial and domestic use. This demand was earlier met from the clear felling coupes by allotting areas to each tea estate. Normally the entire area ear-marked for a particular tea estates are not allotted all at a time. Only a portion of the area is allotted at first. Further area would allot only when the already allotted area is completely workout. The following table–3.12 will give an idea about the firewood demand of tea gardens situated in the fringe of the forest area. Besides table–3.13 (Appendix D) will depict details of out turn of timber and firewood in different forest blocks.

Forest villagers for their daily firewood need, go inside the forest and collected it according to their needs. Mainly they used the dead trees, dry branches, wind fallen produces etc. Sometimes they illegally cut small trees/branches and collect it after drying. Mainly women folk and children do this work. Illegal collection of firewood sometimes reaches to the extent that younger plantation are being damaged.

3.5.5 Non-Timber Forest Produces (NTFPs)

As per the forest working plan prescription, collection of Minor Forest Produce (MFP) or Non-Timber Forest Produce (NTFP) of any kind was allowed from any part of the forests but no quarry for sand, gravel and stone should be made without previous approval of the Divisional Forest Officer or local range or beat officer. There are many NTFPs available in the forests of this study area but no systematic study was conducted regarding the quantity of NTFPs available and its regeneration status. There is no definite extraction procedure adopted for its collection. Forest villagers go inside the forest and collect NTFPs according to their demand. The chief NTFP items which are collected by villagers are Cane fruits, Purundi fruits, Pan leaves, Naglata, Lycopodium stick, Totola pods and Seeds, Golden and Sponge mushrooms, Odal fruit, Fern bud, Mahogony floral axis, Lali fruit, Simul floss and

Table–3.12
Requirement of firewood of 15 tea gardens (out of 34) during 2009-2010 located in the fringes of BTR

Name of Gardens	Daily rated workers @2.5 stacks per worker/ annum	Monthly rated workers @3 stacks per worker/ annum	Monthly rated workers & Tech. C @4 stacks per worker/ annum	Clerical & medical staff & Tech. A & B @12 stacks per worker/ annum	Managerial, hospital & other stacks	Total domestic use stacks	Factory use stacks	Total requirement stacks
BTR, West Division								
Atiabari	2790	150	552	0	560	4020	500	4520
Bhatpara	2787	537	292	336	12	3964	0	4146
Bhatkhawa	2750	0	680	360	463	4253	200	4265
Chuapara	2042	273	312	84	484	2737	12	3137
Nimtijhora	1847	48	440	276	176	3096	400	3176
Dima	3155	189	60	0	124	3580	80	3680
Kalchini	3744	63	664	312	12	4907	100	4907
Paktapara	1450	276	36	156	304	1930	0	1935
Rajabhat	1452	240	40	280		2316	5	2316
TOTAL BTR(W)						**30803**	**1297**	**32100**

Name of Gardens	Daily rated workers @2.5 stacks per worker/ annum	Monthly rated workers @3 stacks per worker/ annum	Monthly rated workers & Tech. C @4 stacks per worker/ annum	Clerical & medical staff & Tech. A & B @12 stacks per worker/ annum	Managerial, hospital & other stacks	Total domestic use stacks	Factory use stacks	Total requirement stacks
BTR, East Division								
Jainti	1370	448	56	36	46	1956	0	4838
Kartick	1210	180	52	228	2900	4570	2882	5020
Phaskhawa	452	93	24	96	450	1115	450	3176
Sankosh	2367	0	552	248	2226	5393	2061	5591
New Lands	2040	312	52	0	246	2650	198	2848
Rydak						3333	2061	5394
Total BTR(E)						**19017**	**7652**	**26867**
Grand Total						**49820**	**8049**	**58967**

Source: Tiger conservation plan, 2016-17 to 2026-2027.

Floral axis, Broom stick, Thatch etc. There are many medical herbs in this forest region. Some are collected by the villagers who are used to remove fever, bone fracture join etc. A large number of forest villagers were interviewed by foresters (Sri Tapan Katham) to assess the items of NTFPs and other details. As seen in the forest report of the project plan of 2000, 43 species have been used for collection. Almost 50% are the tree species. The second most important category is climbers. A total of 624.05 metric tons of NTFP has been collected. The market price in the primary market is over Rs. 26.00 lakes. But foresters/exporter sell at more than four times of that price of villagers.

Inflorescence is collected from 7 species. The account for 28 % of the total value and collection of other plant parts are quite small. Almost 3/ 4th collection of NTFP from 20 different species is for decorative purpose. Dyes, Resins, Detergents along with species are also collected from 8 species. Medicinal NTFP is collected from 6 species and it constitutes 6 % of the total value at exporter's level. In this connection it can be said that 'NTFPs, especially medicinal plants, rattans and bamboos are the alternative sources of income for these people' (Sarmah, 2010).

In this study it is clear that it is a mini store house of bio-diversity for which tourists very often visit Duars. Some pockets of wilderness have been reserved carefully where wild animals can wander without disturbance. These are Jaldapara wild life sanctuary, Buxa wild life sanctuary & tiger reserve, Titi forest, Rhiti forests, Dalgaon forests, Dhumpara & Bhalka forests. Within these forest environments, forest villagers are resided since their ancestors' period where a major proportion of the villagers comprises of scheduled tribes (ST) among them Nepali Rava and Santhal community is proportionally higher than others. The villagers residing in and around the forests are economically poor. They practicing subsistence agriculture, horticulture and others are engaged as agriculture labour, marginal worker, and tea garden labour. Although agriculture is the main livelihood support, but

Table–3.14

Collection of NTFPs from Forest during 1999-2000

Nature of plants	No. of species used	Quantity Collected (Metric ton)	Value of collection at primary collector's level (Rs. Lakh)	Value of exporters level (Rs. Lakh)	%	Remarks (Species)
Climber	9	30.60	4.90	11.87	11	Satmula, Manjito, Bantarul, Gila, Sikakai, Dhundhal, Jangli San, Bet.
Shrub	5	25.25	2.33	15.33	15	Jangli sojna, Ulta, Kamal, Hartaki, Hydrocial etc.
Tree	20	231.20	11.36	51.19	48	Jarul, Lotka, Pata, Chilauni, Chikrasi, Narkeli, Sal, Tinfali, Ritha, Simul, Bohera, Odal, Phata lali, Gota lali, Dalchini, Kowla, Lampata, Amloki Etc.
Grass	3	310.00	2.40	3. 70	4	Kucho, Kans, Thatch etc.
Others	6	27.00	5.10	23.90	22	Includes Orchards, bamboo, mushrooms, and edible herbs.
Total	**43**	**624.05**	**26.09**	**105.99**	**100**	

Source: Tiger conservation plan, 2016-17 to 2026-2027.

Table–3.15

Collection of NTFPs from Forest during 1999-2000

Utility class of NWFP collected	No. of species used	Quantity Collected (Metric ton)	Value at primary collection level (Rs. in Lakh)	Value at exporters level (Rs. in Lakh)	%	Remarks
Decorative purpose	20	204.00	10.88	77.19	73	For selling
Edible products	4	36.00	3.30	5.35	5	Local use
Commercial products (Dyes, Resins, Detergents)	6	53.00	4.45	9.25	9	For selling
Household utility products (Grass, thatch, Bamboo)	5	310.00	4.00	6.95	7	Local use
Medicinal products	6	20.85	3.45	6.85	6	Mostly selling
Species	2	0.20	0.01	0.40	-	selling
Total	**43**	**624.05**	**26.09**	**105.99**	**100**	

Source: Tiger conservation plan, 2016-17 to 2026-2027.

inhabitants are finally depends on the forests since it provides significant economic benefits for forest villagers, especially for tribal communities. However, non-timber forest products (NTFPs) is playing vital role to provide income and subsistence living. Such Non-Timber Forest Products are fuel wood, timber, medicinal plants, tree leaves, wild edible routes, fruits, vegetables; house building materials etc which are integral part of day-to-day livelihood activities for forest villagers. But due to some large scale anthropogenic legal and illegal pressure such as collection of NTFPs, forest cutting, grazing, forest fire, wildlife health attack etc. are giving a question on imbalance of bio-diversity. Therefore there are men-animal conflicts especially men with leopards and elephants conflicts occurred frequently. Due to this reason many villagers afraid to go inside the forest for NTFP collection. Besides the wild animals attack their fields and damage their crops. Villagers admitted that they lived in a constant fear of encountering wild animals and very agitated in letting their family members outside alone. In the end, it can be said that presently NTFPs are more and more importance as it is creating more employment and income generating opportunities to the economically downtrodden forest villagers. So with the increasing of scientific and sustainable way of harvesting of NTFPs, the financial bad condition can be increased to some extent. At the same time, it will also reduce their over dependency on wood and timber collection which might be efficient to resolve the problem of forest degradation of this area.

4 Chapter — Demography and Social Status: Sample Analysis

4.1 Demography

Presently, analysis of demographic parameters becomes important in a dynamic sense in order to understand the qualitative and quantitative aspects of the population that interacts with the environment for all-round development. Therefore population characteristics affect the rate of development both in the economic and social sphere on the one side and at the same time it also influenced of overall development of any area or country. The population characteristics always influenced the nature and natural resources, and level of resource use although it depends on knowledge of technology and perception level. Thus analysis of demographic parameters have crucial significance, and refers mainly to the study of size, territorial distribution and composition of population, changes therein and the components of such changes (Hauser, 1959) most important in Population Geography. The demographic analysis deals with the numbers population, spatial distribution and other characteristics of the human population and these phenomena continuously changing which are concerned with the relationship between demographic processes on one side and economic, social, political, biological and ecological sphere on the other side. Therefore, in this chapter an attempt has been taken to analyse the qualitative and quantitative aspects of the population in Alipurduar District, such as the size of family and growth of population in the villages, through which natural increases of population can be explain. The population structure in terms of age sex composition and sex ratio, which disclose important aptitude in fertility, migration, labour availability and other socio-economic conditions, and literacy rates that pointed clearly the level of social awareness, thus, some of the qualitative aspects of the population discussed carefully.

4.1.1 Demographic Profile of Forest Villages

There were total of 878 households in the 17 sampled study villages. The total population size was 4071 of which 2102 (51.63%) were male and 1969 (48.37%) were female during the survey in 2017 (table–4.1). Among the total households, 776 (88.38%) households were of cultivators; where about 668 (76.08%) cultivators were their own land for cultivation. From the observation the researcher has noticed that the villagers have agricultural as well as labour power potentiality.

Table–4.1

Demographic Characteristics of Sampled Forest Villages

S.No.	Forest village	Total house-hold	Total popu-lation	Male	Female	Cultiva-tors	Cultiva-ted land owner
1	Lehra	22	93	49	44	21	21
2	Suni	28	127	69	58	28	25
3	Garo Basti	72	329	170	159	70	63
4	Balapara	35	152	78	74	32	29
5	Poro (N)	61	301	155	146	61	57
6	Gadhadhar	63	348	179	169	63	60
7	Gudamdabri	63	251	129	122	63	61
8	Nimati & Dabri	68	368	191	177	68	63
9	Gangutia H.A	55	210	112	98	32	24
10	Adma H.A	55	184	95	89	31	20
11	Raimatang H.A	55	271	139	132	43	32
12	Bhutri F. basti H.A	45	221	113	108	40	36
13	Chunabati H.A	54	211	109	102	34	24
14	Santrabari H.A	65	310	159	151	53	37
15	Bhutiabasti	30	133	68	65	30	21
16	Sankosh	60	331	169	162	60	54
17	Lapraguri	47	231	118	113	47	41
	Total	**878**	**4071**	**2102** (51.63 %)	**1969** (48.37 %)	**776** (88.38 %)	**668** (76.08 %)

H.A=High Altitude, (Prepared based on field survey, 2017)

Among the sampled forest villages only one village have below 200 inhabitants according to the census of India namely it is Lehra village, and other 8 village have population between 200 - 500 persons as well as population more than 500 hundred persons also belongs to other 8 villages (table–4.2).

Table–4.2
Number of sampled villages in different population size

Number of sampled villages in different population size, according to 2011			
Forest village	**Population less than 200 persons**	**Population between 200-500 persons**	**Population more than 500 hundred persons**
Lehra village	✓		
Suni village		✓	
Garo Basti			✓
Gadhadhar			✓
Poro (N)			✓
Nimati and Dabri			✓
Gangutia H.A			✓
Adma H.A		✓	
Raimatang H.A			✓
Bhutri forest basti H.A		✓	
Gudamdabri			✓
Chunabati H.A		✓	
Bhutiabasti		✓	
Sankosh			✓
Lapraguri		✓	
Santrabari H.A		✓	
Balapara		✓	
Total	**01**	**08**	**08**

H.A=High Altitude, (Prepared based on field survey, 2017)

The other detailed profile of the forest villagers in the area understudy consisting of the age, caste, ethnic composition, dominant tribal group, literacy status, and working condition are given below.

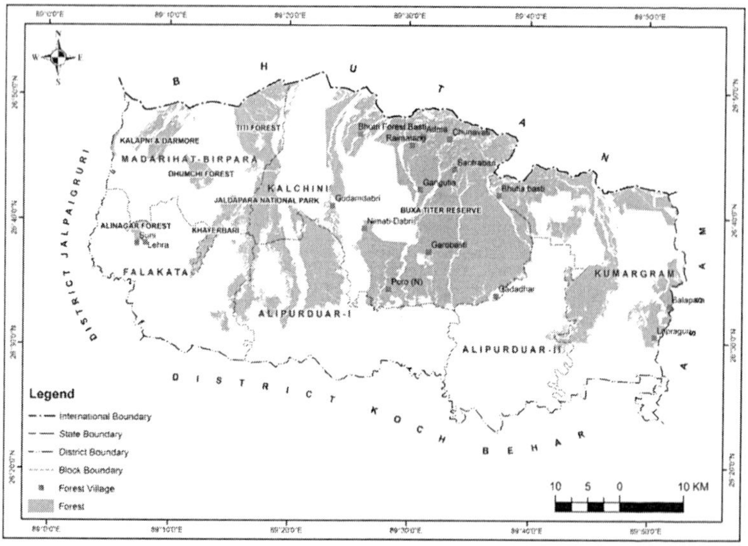

Fig. 4.1: Alipurduar District map with site of sampled forest villages

4.1.1.1 Age Group

The table–4.3 reveals the age group of forest villagers where the highest percentage is 24.83% which is observed in the age group of 0 to 14 years and lowest is belongs to the group of above 60 years age which is only 11.38%. Besides about 24.71% of them are in the age group of 15 to 29 years, 22.16% of them are in the age group of 30 to 44 years, 16.92% of them are in the age group of 45 to 59 years. From the above observation it has been noticed that due to less education among head of households as well as villagers economy totally depends on primary activities such as agriculture, livestock and NTFPs collection etc. so more infant growth is a result of illiteracy and poor economic society where excess children would be later converted future labour power potentiality in their society.

Table–4.3
Age Group of Sampled Forest Villages

S.No.	Forest village	Age Group					
		Up to 14 years	15 to 29 years	30 to 44 years	45 to 59 years	Above 60 years	Total popu-lation
1	Lehra	20	30	24	11	08	93
2	Suni	29	34	25	25	14	127
3	Garo Basti	73	88	79	49	40	329
4	Gadhadhar	84	98	71	54	41	348
5	Poro (N)	61	70	84	48	38	301
6	Nimati and Dabri	86	90	81	71	40	368
7	Gangutia H.A	66	56	42	28	18	210
8	Adma H.A	51	45	43	31	14	184
9	Raimatang H.A	69	67	65	47	23	271
10	Bhutri forest basti H.A	59	52	50	36	24	221
11	Gudamdabri	69	53	55	40	34	251
12	Chunabati H.A	49	55	40	38	29	211
13	Bhutiabasti	33	32	27	24	17	133
14	Sankosh	84	76	75	65	31	331
15	Lapraguri	57	53	46	42	33	231
16	Santrabari H.A	76	72	63	54	45	310
17	Balapara	45	35	32	26	14	152
	Total	**1011 (24.83%)**	**1006 (24.71%)**	**902 (22.16%)**	**689 (16.92%)**	**463 (11.38 %)**	**4071 (100 %)**

H.A=High Altitude, (Prepared based on field survey, 2017)

4.1.1.2 Age-Sex Composition

The total population of the Lehra village sample household is 93 persons of which males account for 49 (52.69%) and females for 44 (47.1%). The age and sex composition pattern of the village population reveals that 9.68% males and 11.83 females are in the age group of 0-14 years, 17.20% males and 15.05% of females are in the age group of 15-29 years. In 30-44 years age group, 15.05% and 10.75% males and females population respectively and 7.53% and 4.30% males and females population are in the 45-59 years age group. Only 3.23% of male and 5.38% of female population fall in the age group of 60 and above. The sex ratio of this village has 897.96 (table–4.4 from Appendix D).

From total 127 population of the Suni households, males account for 69 (54.33%) and females for 58 (45.67%). The age and sex composition pattern of this village population reveals that 12.60% of the male and 10.23% of female in the age group of 0-14 years, 14.17% males and 12.60% females are in the age group of 15-29 years, 11.02% and 8.66% are in the group of 30-44 years and 9.45% and 10.24% are in the group of 45-59 years. In the age group of 60 and above there are only 7.09% males and 11.81% females in this village. The sex ratio of this village has 840.57.

The total population of the Garo Basti village households is 329 persons of which males belongs to 170 (51.67%) and females for 159 (48.33%). About 11.55% male and 10.64% female of the village population are in the age group of 0-14 years and; 13.68% male and 13.07% female are in the age groups 15-29 years respectively. About 12.46%, 7.59%, and 6.38 % of this village population are in the age group of 30-44, 45-59, and 60 and above years for male population, on the other side 11.55%, 7.29% and 5.78% population are belongs to the female population. The sex ration of this village population is 935.29.

The total population of the Gadhadhar village households is 348 persons of which males account for 179 (51.44%) and females for 169 (48.56%). The age and sex composition pattern of the village population reveals that 12.93% males and 11. 20% females are in the age group of 0-14 years, 14.66% males and 13.51% of females are in the age group of 15-29 years. About 9.77% and 10.63% males and females populations are belong to the 30-44 years age group and 8.05% and 7.47% males and females population are in the 45-59 years age group. Only 6.03% of male and 5.75% female population fall in the age group of 60 and above. The sex ratio of this village has 944.13.

There are 301 total population in the Poro (N) village of which males account for 155 (51.49%) and females for 146 (48.50%). The age and sex composition pattern of this village population reveals that 10.63% of the male and 9.63% of female are in the age group of 0-14 years, 11.96% males and 11.29% females are in the age group of 15-29 years, 14. 29% and 13.62% are in the group of 30-44 years and 8.64% and 7.31% are in the group of 45-59 years. In the age group of 60 and above there are only 5.98% males and 6.64% females in this village. The sex ratio of this village has 941.94. In the same way a total population of the Nimati and Dabri sample household is 368 persons, of which males account for 191 (51.90%) and females for 177 (48.09%). The age and sex composition pattern of this village population reveals that 12.22% of the male and 11.14% of female in the age group of 0-14 years, 12.77% males and 11.68% females are in the age group of 15-29 years, 11.41% and 10.59% are in the group of 30-44 years and 9.78% and 9.51% are in the group of 45-59 years. In the age group of 60 and above there are only 5.70% males and 5.16% females belongs to this village. The sex ratio of this village has 926.70.

The total population of the Gangutia village households is 210 persons of which males account for 112 (53.33%) and females for 98 (46.67%). The age and sex composition pattern of the village population reveals that 12.86% males and 13.81% females are in the age group of 0-14 years, 15.23% males and 12.38% of females are in the age group of 15-29 years. About 10.95% and 9.99% males and females population are in the 30-44 years age group and; 8.57% and 6.67% males and females population belongs to the 45-59 years age group. Only 5.71% of male and 3.81% female population fall in the age group of 60 and above. The sex ratio of this village has 875.

The total population of the Adma hill forest village households is 184 persons of which males account for 95 (51.63%) and females for 89 (48.37%). The age and sex composition pattern of this village population reveals that 12.50% of the male and 13.04% of female in the age group of 0-14 years, 14.13% males and 12.50% females are in the age group of 15-29 years, 11. 41% and 11.96% are in the group of 30-44 years and 9.24% and 7.61% are in the group of 45-59 years. In the age group of 60 and above there are only 4.35%

males and 3.26% females in this village. The sex ratio of this village has 936.84.

The total population of the Raimatang village households is 271 persons, of which males account for 139 (51.29%) and females for 132 (48.71%). The age and sex composition pattern of this village population reveals that 12.55% of the male and 11.44% of female in the age group of 0-14 years, 13.65% males and 11.81% females are in the age group of 15-29 years, 12.18% and 12.55% are in the group of 30-44 years and 8.49% and 8.86% are in the group of 45-59 years. In the age group of 60 and above there are only 4.43% males and 4.06% females in this village. The sex ratio of this village has 949.64.

The total population of the Bhutri forest basti village households is 221 persons of which males belongs to 113 (51.13%) and females for 108 (48.87%). About 13.57% male and 13.12% female of the village population are in the age group of 0-14 years and; 11.31% male and 12.22% female are in the age groups 15-29 years respectively. About 11.76%, 8.59%, and 5.88% of this village population are in the age group of 30-44, 45-59, and 60 and above years for male population, on the other side 10.86%, 7.69% and 4.98% population are belongs to the female population. The sex ration of this village population is 955.75.

The total population of the Gudamdabri village households is 251 persons of which males account for 129 (51.39%) and females for 122 (48.61%). The age and sex composition pattern of this village population reveals that 13.55% of the male and 13.94% of female in the age group of 0-14 years, 11.16% males and 9.96% females are in the age group of 15-29 years, 11.16% and 10.76% are in the group of 30-44 years and 8.37% and 7.57% are in the group of 45-59 years. In the age group of 60 and above there are only 7.17% males and 6.37% females in this village. The sex ratio of this village has 945.74.

The total population of the Chunabati hill forest village households is 211 persons of which males belongs to 109

(51.66%) and females for 102 (48.34%). About 12.32% male and 9.16% female of the village population are in the age group of 0-14 years and; 13.74% male and 10.36% female are in the age groups 15-29 years respectively, 9.00%, 9.95%, and 6.64% of this village population are in the age group of 30-44, 45-59, and 60 and above years for male population, on the other side 8.37%, 6.77% and 5.98% population are belongs to the female population. The sex ration of this village population is 935.78.

The total population of the Bhutiabasti village households is 133 persons of which males account for 68 (51.13%) and females for 65 (48.87%). The age and sex composition pattern of this village population reveals that 12.03% of the male and 12.78% of female in the age group of 0-14 years, 12.78% males and 11.28% females are in the age group of 15-29 years, 11.28% and 9.02% are in the group of 30-44 years and 9.77% and 8.27% are in the group of 45-59 years. In the age group of 60 and above there are only 5.26% males and 7.52% females in this village. The sex ratio of this village has 955.89.

The total population of the Sankosh village households is 331 persons of which males belongs to 169 (51.06%) and females for 162 (48.94%). About 13.29% male and 12.08% female of the village population are in the age group of 0-14 years and; 11.78% male and 11.18% female are in the age groups 15-29 years respectively. About 11.18%, 10.27%, and 4.53% of this village population are in the age group of 30-44, 45-59, and 60 and above years for male population, on the other side 11.48%, 9.37% and 4.83% population are belongs to the female population. The sex ration of this village population is 958.58.

The total population of the Lapraguri village households is 231 persons of which males account for 118 (51.08%) and females for 113 (48.92%). The age and sex composition pattern of this village population reveals that 12.99% of the male and 11.69% of female in the age group of 0-14 years, 11.26% males and 11.69% females are in the age group of 15-29 years, 10.39% and 9.53% are in the group of 30-44 years and 9.52% and

8.66% are in the group of 45-59 years. In the age group of 60 and above there are only 6.93% males and 7.26% females belongs to this village. The sex ratio of this village has 957.63.

The total population of the Santrabari hill village households is 310 persons of which males belongs to 159 (51.67%) and females for 151 (48.33%). About 11.94% male and 12.58% female of the village population are in the age group of 0-14 years and; 12.26% male and 10.97% female are in the age groups 15-29 years respectively. About 10.32%, 9.03%, and 7.74% of this village population are in the age group of 30-44, 45-59, and 60 and above years for male population, and about 9.99%, 8.39% and 6.77% population are belongs to the female population. The sex ration of this village population is 949.68.

The total population of the Balapara village households is 152 persons of which males account for 78 (51.63%) and females for 74 (48.37%). The age and sex composition pattern of this village population reveals that 14.47% of the male and 15.13% of female in the age group of 0-14 years, 11.84% males and 11.18% females are in the age group of 15-29 years, 11.18% and 9.87% are in the group of 30-44 years and 9.21% and 7.89% are in the group of 45-59 years. In the age group of 60 and above there are only 4.61% males and 4.61% females in this village. The sex ratio of this village has 948.73.

A total population of the households are 4071 persons of which males account for 2102 (51.63%) and females for 1969 (48.37%). The age and sex composition of sampled villages population indicates that 24.83% villagers associates with the age group of up to14 years where 12.36% is female and 12.48% is male, about 24.71% population are belongs to the age group of 15-29 years of which 11.74% is females and 12.97% is males, 22.16% are pertains in the age group of 30 to 44 years of which 10.78% females and 11.37% is males, as well as 16.93% are associates in the group of 45 to 59 years where 7.98% is females and 8.94% is males. There are only 11.38% population is in the age group of 60 and above, of which 5.50% is females 5.87% is males of sampled villages. Besides, the sex ratio of population is normally expressed as the number of females' population per 1000 males' population. The overall sex ratio between male and female is 936.73 (Table–4.5).

Table 4.5
Overall Age-Sex Composition

Overall age-sex composition							
Age Group	**Male**		**Female**		**Both**		**Sex Ratio**
	No. of persons	**%**	**No. of persons**	**%**	**No. of persons**	**%**	
0-14	508	12.48	503	12.37	1011	24.83	990.16
15-29	528	12.97	478	11.74	1006	24.71	905.30
30-44	463	11.37	439	10.78	902	22.16	948.16
45-59	364	8.94	325	7.98	689	16.93	892.86
60+	239	5.87	224	5.50	463	11.37	937.24
Total	**2102**	**51.63**	**1969**	**48.37**	**4071**	**100.00**	**936.73**

(Prepared based on field survey, 2017)

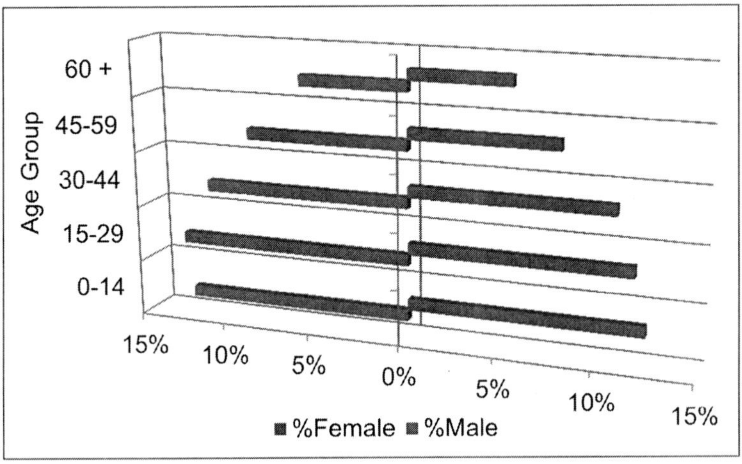

Fig. 4.2: Age-wise Male & Female Population

4.1.1.3 Ethnic Composition

The table–4.6 shows that about 3009 (73.91%) of forest-villagers area belonging to the ST community which is found as a dominant community of forest villagers. It is followed by General 667 (16.38%), and OBC 346 (8.51%) of forest villagers respectively. However it is also noticed that only 49

(1.20%) villagers are associates to SC community. So from the above observation, it is identified that majority of villagers are belongs to ST, which indicates that the area is resided by socially, economically and educationally belongs to backward class population.

Table–4.6
Ethnic Composition of Sampled Forest Villages

S.No.	Forest village	Ethnic composition				
		SC	ST	OBC	GEN	Total
1	Lehra	-	93	-	-	93
2	Suni	-	127	-	-	127
3	Garo Basti	05	304	12	08	329
4	Gadhadhar	-	331	06	11	348
5	Poro (N)	-	301	-	-	301
6	Nimati and Dabri	21	306	24	17	368
7	Gangutia H.A	-	13	48	149	210
8	Adma H.A	-	184	-	-	184
9	Raimatang H.A	05	176	24	66	271
10	Bhutri forest basti H.A	-	09	63	149	221
11	Gudamdabri	18	116	69	48	251
12	Chunabati H.A	-	211	-	-	211
13	Bhutiabasti	-	84	17	32	133
14	Sankosh	-	195	49	87	331
15	Lapraguri	-	231	-	-	231
16	Santrabari H.A	-	184	34	92	310
17	Balapara	-	144	-	08	152
	Total	**49 (1.20%)**	**3009 (73.91%)**	**346 (8.51%)**	**667 (16.38%)**	**4071 (100%)**

H.A=High Altitude, (Prepared based on field survey, 2017)

4.1.1.4 The Dominant Communities in the Study Villages

There were a total of 6 prime communities among the 17 study villages. The dominant communities such as the Nepali, Rava and Dukpa/ Bhutia were the landowning agreement holder predominantly native communities and were the commonest in the area. The Nepalis are first major community and dominant in 5 villages i.e. in Garo basti, Adma, Raimatang, Bhutri and Santrabari village, Ravas in 5 villages i.e. in Suni, Gadhadhar, Poro, Nimati and Dabri, and Lapraguri, Dukpa/ Bhutias in 3 villages i.e. in Adma, Chunabati and Sankosh; others were dominated in few villages. All communities are considered as backward castes and poor in the sense of education, living standard and income level.

4.1.1.5 Dominant Tribal Groups

A substantial proportion of the villagers are comprises of scheduled tribes (ST) which is found as a dominant community of forest villagers and it is about 3009 persons (73.91%). Among them the prime communities are Santal, Rava, Mechia, Nepali, Bhutia, and Oraon. The Rava about 1290 (42.87%), Tamang (Nepali) about 560 (18.62%), Dukpa/ Bhutia about 541 (17.98%) and Mech about 233 persons (7.74%) community are proportionally higher among forest villagers (Table–4.7 & 4.8). Villagers living altogether in complete communal harmony. Relationship of villagers within their own community and with other community is good. They marry socially although love marriage is also allowed within the society. They generally arrange their

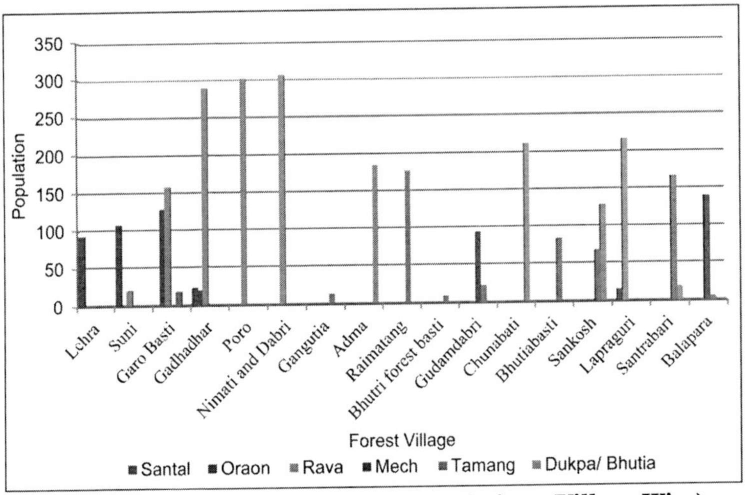

Fig. 4.3: Dominant Tribal Group Populations (Village-Wise)

marriage within the same community. Durga puja, Shyama puja, Saraswati puja etc. are the festival of villagers who are Hindu and Christmas is the main festival among Christians. All communities are living peacefully and help one another; and gathered to help for social activities each other. The tribal population mainly Rava, Mechia, Oraon, and Madeshia are concentrated in southern and comparatively low lying and plain area, while Dukpas/ Bhutia tribes are lived on extreme North Buxa Hill and Nepalese are scattered all around (Das, 2000). There are good numbers of Bangali too live in the proximity of the forest villages.

Table–4.7

Dominant Communities in the Study Villages

S.No.	Forest village	Major communities			
		First major commu-nity	Second major commu-nity	Third major commu-nity	Forth major commu nity
1	Lehra	Santal	Rava	Oraon	-
2	Suni	Rava	Oraon	-	-
3	Garo Basti	Oraon	Rava	Nepali	-
4	Gadhadhar	Rava	Santal	Oraon	
5	Poro (N)	Rava	-	-	-
6	Nimati and Dabri	Rava	Bihari	Bengali	
7	Gangutia H.A	Nepali	-	-	-
8	Adma H.A	Dukpa/ Bhutia	Nepali	-	-
9	Raimatang H.A	Nepali	-	-	-
10	Bhutri forest basti H.A	Nepali	-	-	-
11	Gudamdabri	Mech	Bengali	Nepali	-
12	Chunabati H.A	Dukpa/ Bhutia	Nepali	-	-
13	Bhutiabasti	Nepali	Bihari	-	-
14	Sankosh	Dukpa/ Bhutia	Nepali	Santal	-
15	Lapraguri	Rava	Oraon	-	-
16	Santrabari H.A	Nepali	Dukpa/ Bhutia	Oraon	
17	Balapara	Mech	Nepali	Santal	-

H.A=High Altitude, Source: Source: Tiger conservation plan, 2016-17 to 2026-2027.

Table–4.8

Dominant tribal group population of sampled forest villages

S.No.	Forest Village	Dominant tribal group						
		Santal	Oraon	Rava	Mech	Tamang	Dukpa/Bhutia	Total
1	Lehra	93		-	-	-	-	93
2	Suni	107		20	-	-	-	127
3	Garo Basti	-	128	158	-	18	-	304
4	Gadhadhar	23	19	289	-	-	-	331
5	Poro (N)	-	-	301	-	-	-	301
6	Nimati and Dabri	-	-	306	-	-	-	306
7	Gangutia H.A	-	-	-	-	13	-	13
8	Adma H.A	-	-		-	-	184	184
9	Raimatang H.A	-	-	-	-	176	-	176
10	Bhutri forest basti H.A	-	-	-	-	09	-	09
11	Gudamdabri	-	-	-	94	22	-	116
12	Chunabati H.A	-	-	-	-	-	211	211
13	Bhutiabasti	-	-	-	-	84	-	84
14	Sankosh	-	-	-	-	67	128	195
15	Lapraguri	-	15	216	-	-	-	231
16	Santrabari H.A	-	-	-	-	166	18	184
17	Balapara	-	-	-	139	05	-	144
	Total	**223 (7.41%)**	**162 (5.38%)**	**1290 (42.87%)**	**233 (7.74%)**	**560 (18.62%)**	**541 (17.98%)**	**3009 (100%)**

H.A=High Altitude, (Prepared based on field survey, 2017)

4.1.1.6 Occupation

In the table–4.9, it is noticed that about 1443 (35.45%) of forest villagers engaged in agriculture & livestock as their primary occupation. It is the highest percentages among villagers engaged in agriculture and livestock. The forest villagers are lowest in number of 19 (0.46%) who are working in service as Govt. or private sector. It has also been observed that 1198 (29.43%) are employed in agriculture labour and livestock, 424 (10.42%) is in horticulture, agriculture and livestock, 424 (10.42%) is in daily labour, forest product collection and livestock; and remaining 549 (13.48 %) belongs as students and other job. So, it is considered that for livelihood needs villagers are mainly depend on different kinds of primary activities due to lack of opportunities of manufacturing and service jobs which have less importance for them.

4.1.2 Migration

The tribal migration may be understood from two angles. The first is through pushed out factors and the second is pulled out factors that force the tribals to leave their lands (Hasnain, 2005). Generally migration among the forest villagers is uncommon since they are meant own self as son of soil. They love to stay within the silence forest environment and doing their daily day works for livelihood peacefully. However, the temporary migration has observed as common matter for rehabilitation, employment and education. The details are presented in table–4.10. The highest number of temporary migration has been experienced in case of employment purpose where members of 352 household (40.09%) are connected with temporary migration and it is shown almost in all village.

For education purpose, particularly in the level of higher secondary, and college education, only 40 families (4.46%) of the sampled households attached with temporary migration and it is noticed mainly in case of hill top villages such as Adma, Chunabati, Raimatang, Gangutia who are located far

Table–4.9

Occupational Structure of Sampled Forest Villagers

S.No.	Forest village	Occupation						
		Agriculture & Livestock	Agricultural Labour & Livestock	Daily Labour, Forest Product collection & Livestock	Agriculture, Horticulture & Livestock	Service	Student & Other	Total
1	Lehra	47	31	-	-	01	14	93
2	Suni	52	36	11	15	01	12	127
3	Garo Basti	101	87	39	48	03	51	329
4	Gadhadhar	137	98	31	27	-	55	348
5	Poro (N)	89	78	37	56	-	41	301
6	Nimati and Dabri	146	85	41	48	02	46	368
7	Gangutia H.A	83	44	28	21	01	33	210
8	Adma H.A	55	53	31	24	-	21	184
9	Raimatang H.A	81	93	34	23	04	36	271
10	Bhutri F. basti H.A	84	71	24	16	01	25	221
11	Gudamdabri	104	83	21	11	01	31	251
12	Chunabati H.A	62	79	23	24	01	22	211
13	Bhutiabasti	41	46	14	11	-	21	133
14	Sankosh	129	98	24	31	02	47	331
15	Lapraguri	81	75	26	22	-	27	231
16	Santrabari H.A	93	89	28	50	02	48	310
17	Balapara	58	52	12	11	-	19	152
	Total	**1443**	**1198**	**424**	**438**	**19**	**549**	**4071**
	%	**35.45**	**29.43**	**10.42**	**10.76**	**0.46**	**13.48**	**100**

H.A=High Altitude, (Prepared based on field survey, 2017)

Table–4.10
Migration of the Sample Households

S.No.	Forest village	Number of households connected with migration					
		Cause of migration					
		Rehabilitation		Education		Employment	
		Temporary migration	Permanent migration	Permanent migration	Temporary migration	Permanent migration	Temporary migration
1	Lehra	0	0	0	0	0	7
2	Suni	0	0	0	0	0	9
3	Garo Basti	0	0	0	0	0	23
4	Gadhadhar	0	0	0	0	0	29
5	Poro (N)	0	0	0	0	0	25
6	Nimati and Dabri	0	0	0	0	0	29
7	Gangutia H.A	0	0	0	3	0	12
8	Adma H.A	0	0	0	6	0	23
9	Raimatang H.A	0	0	0	4	0	26
10	Bhutri F. basti H.A	0	0	0	6	0	18
11	Gudamdabri	0	0	0	0	0	28
12	Chunabati H.A	0	0	0	9	0	21
13	Bhutiabasti	0	23	0	3	0	11
14	Sankosh	0	0	0	5	0	36
15	Lapraguri	0	0	0	0	0	17
16	Santrabari H.A	0	0	0	4	0	24
17	Balapara	0	0	0	0	0	14
	Total	**0**	**23 (2.62%)**	**0**	**40 (4.46%)**	**0**	**352 (40.09%)**

H.A=High Altitude, (Prepared based on field survey, 2017)

from transport line. It is only 2.62 % household (23 household) where villagers were moved and rehabilitated permanently outside from village as well as forest. The permanent migration also occurred towards village area but in little number due to marriage of females who are from outside of forest and fringe area. So it is noticed that the households practiced temporary migration mainly for employment, education and health related problems.

4.1.3 Family Size

The table–4.11 shows the type of family size of the sample households of the forest villages. Out of the total 878 sample households, 432 households (49.20%) are of 4 to 6 family, followed by 7 to 9 members, 3 members and 10 and above members which constitute 25.75%, 24.49% and 0.57% respectively. So it is clear that above 70% of the households are belongs to the family of 4 to 9 members which is the result of economically and socially backwardness of the area where there is no idea regarding family planning among villagers hence they are less education and other social welfare related government project are not focused properly among this villages.

Table–4.11
Family Size of the Sample Households

S.No.	Forest village	Family Size (members)				
		Up to 3 family member	4 to 6 family member	7 to 9 family member	10 and above family member	Total house-holds
1	Lehra	07	12	03	-	22
2	Suni	09	13	06	-	28
3	Garo Basti	20	30	22	-	72
4	Gadhadhar	09	29	25	-	63
5	Poro (N)	13	28	20	-	61
6	Nimati and Dabri	08	33	27		68
7	Gangutia H.A	26	24	05	-	55
8	Adma H.A	21	32	02	-	55
9	Raimatang H.A	08	29	18	-	55
10	Bhutri F. basti H.A	07	23	14	01	45

11	Gudamdabri	21	34	08	-	63
12	Chunabati H.A	21	30	03	-	54
13	Bhutiabasti	09	15	06	-	30
14	Sankosh	06	29	23	02	60
15	Lapraguri	07	23	15	02	47
16	Santrabari H.A	14	29	22	-	65
17	Balapara	09	19	07	-	35
	Total	**215 (24.49%)**	**432 (49.20%)**	**226 (25.74%)**	**05 (0.57%)**	**878 (100%)**

H.A=High Altitude, (Prepared based on field survey, 2017)

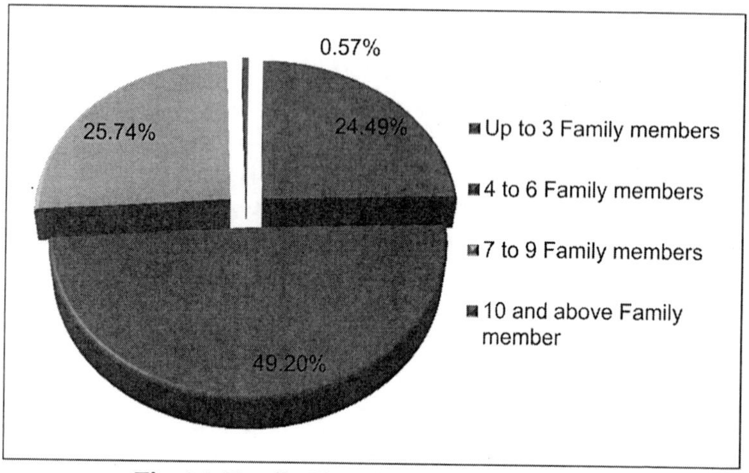

Fig. 4.4: Family Size of Sample Households

4.1.4 Type of Family

The table 4.12 shows the type of family type of the sample households. Out of the total 878 sample households, 462 families (52.62 %) are joint families, followed by 403 nuclear families (45.90 %), and 13 extended families (1.48 %). It is noticed that above fifty percent of the total family belongs to joint family which convey that the villagers still believes traditional way of livelihood. On the other hand nearly fifty percent of the family comes to the touch of modern culture and chosen nuclear family system for the betterment of family.

Table–4.12
Family Type of the Sample Households

S.No.	Forest village	Family type			
		Joint Family	Nuclear Family	Extended Family	Total house-holds
1	Lehra	17	05	-	22
2	Suni	24	04	-	28
3	Garo Basti	35	34	3	72
4	Gadhadhar	37	26	-	63
5	Poro (N)	30	31		61
6	Nimati and Dabri	31	34	03	68
7	Gangutia H.A	29	26	-	55
8	Adma H.A	21	32	02	55
9	Raimatang H.A	24	28	03	55
10	Bhutri forest basti H.A	27	18	-	45
11	Gudamdabri	30	33	-	63
12	Chunabati H.A	25	27	02	54
13	Bhutiabasti	17	13	-	30
14	Sankosh	33	27	-	60
15	Lapraguri	34	13	-	47
16	Santrabari H.A	29	36	-	65
17	Balapara	19	16	-	35
	Total	**462 (52.62%)**	**403 (45.90%)**	**13 (1.48%)**	**878 (100%)**

H.A=High Altitude, (Prepared based on field survey, 2017)

4.2 Social Status

4.2.1 Language

The dialect which the Lehra and Gadhadhar villagers are speaking is Santali language among them since almost all are belongs to the santal community. The Santali language is part of the Austro-Asiatic language family (Grunning, 1911). Most of the villagers communicating through Santali but they used other regional languages to interact with outsiders nearby such as Bengali, Hindi and Rajbanshi. The Rava tribes of Suni, Garo Basti, Gadhadhar, Poro, Nimti-Dabri and Lapraguri villagers' speaking Rava language among them which is their mother language. The Rava language belongs to Maituri, Rongdani category of Sino-Tibetan language family (Jose, 2000). They also speak in Bengali language in markets, schools and office but for neighbours they follow local language such as Rajbanshi, Nepali and Sadri.

The villagers' of Garo Basti, Gadhadhar and Lapraguri who are Oraon, converse with each other in Kurukh, a popular language. This language belongs to the Dravidian family group and has got a relation with other language including Brahui and Paharia (Karmakar, 2011). They also speak in Bengali and other local language such as Rajbanshi, Nepali and Sadri. The villagers' of Gangutia, Raimatang, Bhutri forest basti, Bhutiabasti, Sankosh and Santrabari are speaking Nepali as prime conversation language. This language belongs to the Indo-Aryan, Indo European and Sino-Tibetan language family group formally it is called as Khaskura and Gorkhali and has got a relation with other language including Paharia (Karmakar, 2011). They also speak in Bengali and other local language such as Rajbanshi and Sadri. The villagers' of Gudamdabri, Balapara who are Mech, converse with each other in Bodo language, which is Tibeto-Burman dialect, and this language belongs to the Indo European family group and has got a relation with Assamese language (Debnath, 2010). They also speak in Bengali and other local language such as Rajbanshi and Nepali.

The villagers' of Adma, Chunabati, and few of Sankosh and Santrabari, who are Dukpa/Bhutia, are speaking Dzongkha as prime conversation language. Besides this they are speaking various language of the Tibeto-Burman branch of Sino-Tibetan language family group and have got a relation with other language including Khowa, Hruso (Karmakar, 2011). They also speak in Nepali and Hindi, some of them able to speak in Bengali and Sadri.

4.2.2 Educational Status

Educational qualification is one prime indicator of the levels of living standard and development. A minimum level of education is necessary to acquire knowledge, to perceive and to solve daily day social problems. It is admitted that education and occupations are always interrelated with poverty, and it also proved that the jobs requiring the most education have high income opportunity and low poverty incidence. So richness/poverty concentrated among employment with high/low educational requirements. It can be said that education and literacy have a real bonding to change socio-economic status and also to increase the level of participation in developmental activities in the society. Since the state and central governments have been initiated numerous education related project for the development of backward class peoples such as Govt. running tribal residential schools exclusively meant for the Scheduled Tribes. The students are also provided with boarding and lodging facilities. The schools are established within respective backward class habitat area.

Hence, analyzing the education level of the forest villagers is one of the important variables to know the socio-economic conditions. The education scenario of the sample households were given in table–4.13 (Appendix D). Out of 4071 total inhabitants, 25.59% are illiterates of which males constitute 13.31% and female constitutes 12.28%. About 48.87% are primary school educations of which 25.79% of the male and 23.07% of the female, it is also mentioned that each every forest village have a primary education institution or school but for secondary, higher secondary and higher education there is not a single educational institute is noticed nearby any villages. Therefore in secondary, higher secondary and graduate level it is only 16.80% (8.35% male and 8.45% female), 7.61% (3.59% male and 4.03% female) and 1.13% (0.59% male and 0.54% female) respectively which is too poor. It is also noticed that not a single villager has occupied P.G or other technical diploma.

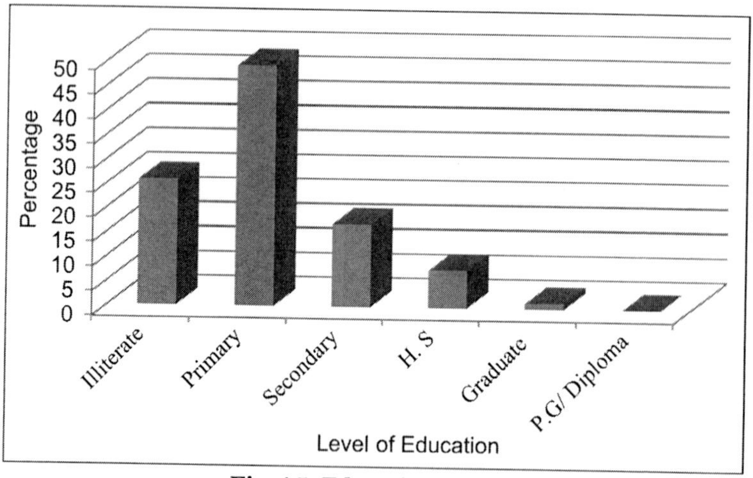

Fig. 4.5: Educational level

4.2.3 Educational Level of the Head of the Households

Among the total 878 households, 70.73% of the household's heads are illiterate and only 29.27% are literate in which about 22.89% of the total literate household head have studied to the primary school education, 5.24% have touched their education up to secondary level and only 1.14% household's head educated up to higher secondary and graduate (table–4.14). From the observation it is also noticed that among literate household's head, about 78.21% of the head household have only primary education which had direct effect in their family and surrounding socio-economic activities.

4.2.4 Education with Reference to Occupation

In this study, an attempt has been made to know how far the occupational structure helped for education and other development. From the table–4.15 (Appendix D) it is clear that out of 4071 inhabitants, 25.59% are illiterates of which males constitute 13.31% and female constitutes 12.28%. Among both of them 10.71% are employed as labour of agriculture and MFP (Minor forest product collection), 5.94% in labour and MFP collection, 4.54% in labour, livestock and MFP collection and 4.39% are engaged in own agricultural

Table–4.14

Educational Level of the Head of the Sampled Households

S.No.	Forest village	Illiterate	Literate	Literate			Total
		Households	Households	Primary (I-V)	Secondary (VI-X)	H.S. (XI--XII) & Graduate	Households
1	Lehra	15	7	5	2	-	22
2	Suni	17	11	7	2	2	28
3	Garo Basti	51	21	16	4	1	72
4	Gadhadhar	45	18	14	3	1	63
5	Poro (N)	45	16	13	3	-	61
6	Nimati & Dabri	49	19	15	4	-	68
7	Gangutia H.A	39	16	14	2	-	55
8	Adma H.A	41	14	14	-	-	55
9	Raimatang H.A	34	21	15	4	2	55
10	Bhutri F. basti H.A	30	15	13	2	-	45
11	Gudamdabri	46	17	15	2	-	63
12	Chunabati H.A	41	13	10	3	-	54
13	Bhutiabasti	21	9	6	3	-	30
14	Sankosh	41	19	15	2	2	60
15	Lapraguri	35	12	9	3	-	47
16	Santrabari H.A	45	20	14	5	1	65
17	Balapara	26	9	6	2	1	35
	Total	**621** (70.73%)	**257** (29.27%)	**201** (22.89%)	**46** (5.24%)	**10** (1.14%)	**878** (100%)

H.A=High Altitude, (Prepared based on field survey, 2017)

field for cultivation. About 48.87% are primary school educations of which 25.79% of the male and 23.07% of the female. Among them 15.82% are engaged as labour of agriculture and MFP, 10.02% in Labour and MFP collection, 8.72% are students, 7.79% are of in labour, livestock and MFP collection and 6.51% are engaged in own agricultural field for cultivation. In secondary education it is only about 16.80% (8.35% male and 8.45% female) of which 5.31% belongs to labour of agriculture and MFP, 4.10% in labour and MFP collection, 3.49% in students, 2.46% labour, livestock and MFP collection and 1.45% are engaged for cultivation of own land. In case of higher secondary it is about 7.61% (3.59% male and 4.03% female) of which 2.58% employed to labour of agriculture and MFP, 1.57% in labour and MFP Collection, 1.30% labour, livestock and MFP collection, 1.20% in students and 0.71% are engaged for cultivation of own land. Besides only 0.25% are employed as service job in different government sectors. About 1.13% (0.59% male and 0.54% female) are graduate which is too poor. Among them 0.42% are engaged as labour of agriculture and MFP, 0.19% in labour and MFP collection, 0.17% in service, 0.15% are of in labour, livestock and MFP collection, 0.122% in agriculture respectively. It is noticed that not a single villager belongs post graduate or other technical diploma.

4.2.5 Religious and Beliefs

From the table–4.8, it is observed that about 162 (5.38 %) Oraon tribe of this study area followed the 'Sarna Dharma (Sarna religion) but due to influence of Hinduism and Christianity some of them started following Sarna in Hindu style. The Oraon believe in nature and its power. The Dharti (the earth), Chando (the moon) and Biri (the Sun) are its representative divine powers, which are the prime sources of supernatural powers. Most of inhabitants are Sarna Dharma, in which Dharmesh is the supreme almighty (Ghosh, 2003). They called the earth Dharti Aayo (Earth as mother), worship nature and believe that the consciousness or the God is nature itself. The Rava community occupies

1290 (42.87%) inhabitants of total household of which all of them worship Kamakhsha Devi during Ambubachi. They sacrifice bamboo to Goddess Kamaksha. Besides, they worship an evil God for the good health and prosperity of the children and for having the grace of bearing child. The name of evil God is Tukini. The Nepalese are dominant ethnic group in Tarai and Duars region. They have different caste and dialect among them Tamang are dominant in this study area. Their social practices and customs are based on Buddhism and they have own language, tamang and 560 (18.62%) villagers of the study household belief Buddhism principle. The Santals are an important inhabitant tribal who belongs to 7.41% (223 villagers) of total sampled household. They believe in supernatural beings and ancestral spirits and rituals consist mainly of sacrificial offerings and invocations to the spirits, or bongas. It is believed by some scholars that bongas means the same as Bhaga (or Bhagavan). About 233 (7.74%) Meches of this study area worship the following deities: Mohes tacur-This is the God who watches the moral character of people and villagers believe that he punishes man who commits a fault. The Bato-according to the villagers, this God lives in the Siju tree. This tree is planted in the courtyard of every Mach homestead and is regularly worshiped. Mahakal-It is the God of good spirit and is believed to be ever watching the action of the people. Biso-Hari- she lives in a small house of owner of east. Minao-this God remains in the north hut, and Grajjo- this God is known as Kali. The Bhutias live in only Chunabati village of Buxa in North Bengal. The Bhutias or Dukpa as they called belongs to the country of the Bhutan. In the sampled study they have 541(17.98%) inhabitants who are Buddhist, and generally confine themselves to repeating the words Om-Mani-Padine-Horn. In their village, have a small temple at which Lama offers prayers daily for the people.

4.2.6 Marital Status

To know the demographic status of any community, it is very important to examine the marital situation of population

Table–4.16
Marital status of villagers (household-wise)

S.No.	Marital Status	Unmarried			Married			Widow			Divorce			Total		
	Village	M	F	T	M	F	T	M	F	T	M	F	T	M	F	T
1	Lehra	14	12	26	31	28	59	3	4	7	1	-	1	49	44	93
2	Suni	21	17	38	45	38	83	2	3	5	1	-	1	69	58	127
3	Garo Basti	54	47	101	113	110	223	-	2	2	3	-	3	170	159	329
4	Gadhadhar	55	50	105	121	114	235	3	2	5	-	3	3	179	169	348
5	Poro (N)	48	43	91	104	96	200	1	4	5	2	3	5	155	146	301
6	Nimati and Dabri	50	47	97	136	124	260	-	6	6	5	-	5	191	177	368
7	Gangutia H.A	36	34	70	76	63	139	-	1	1	-	-	-	112	98	210
8	Adma H.A	22	19	41	71	66	137	2	-	2	-	4	4	95	89	184
9	Raimatang H.A	26	24	50	106	97	203	4	6	10	3	5	8	139	132	271
10	Bhutri forest basti H.A	19	23	42	94	82	176	-	2	2	-	1	1	113	108	221
11	Gudamdabri	27	22	49	99	95	194	3	-	3	-	5	5	129	122	251
12	Chunabati H.A	21	17	38	86	84	170	1	1	2	1	-	1	109	102	211
13	Bhutiabasti	20	17	37	48	48	96	-	-	-	-	-	-	68	65	133
14	Sankosh	40	38	78	127	121	248	2	3	5	-	-	-	169	162	331
15	Lapraguri	24	22	46	94	89	183	-	1	1	-	1	1	118	113	231
16	Santrabari H.A	44	31	75	112	114	226	3	2	5	-	4	4	159	151	310
17	Balapara	20	18	38	56	54	110	-	-	-	2	2	4	78	74	152
	Total	**541**	**481**	**1022**	**1519**	**1423**	**2942**	**24**	**37**	**61**	**18**	**28**	**46**	**2102**	**1969**	**4071**
	%	**13.29**	**11.82**	**25.11**	**37.31**	**34.95**	**72.27**	**0.59**	**0.91**	**1.49**	**0.44**	**0.69**	**1.13**	**51.63**	**48.37**	**100**

H.A=High Altitude, (Prepared based on field survey, 2017)

of the study area. Because the percentage of married, widow, divorce helps to study the reproductive population as well as important to examine how far this status is related with varied ecology and environment. From the table–4.16, it has been observed that the number of married person is more than unmarried person and number of widowed, divorce or separated persons are significantly low. Numerically the married persons account for 2942 (72.27%) while 1022 (25.11%) are unmarried of the total 4071 population. There are 1519 married persons, 541unmarried person, 24 widowers and 18 divorces among the males constituting 37.31%, 13.29%, 0.59% and 0.44% of the total male population respectively. On the side there are 1423 married persons, 481 unmarried persons 37 widows and 28 divorces among the females constituting 34.95%, 11.82%, 0.91% and 0.69% of the total female population respectively.

Here important aspects of the forest villagers' demography, social and culture life have been depicted. The various tables have been documented to have a very clear idea about demographic characteristics of forest villagers such as their age group, age-sex composition, ethnic variation, family size and family type; and social customs i.e. education, migration, occupation, language, marital status, religious festivals associated with agriculture and traits related with the forest environment have been describe carefully. The changes of family types have been noticed among villagers and it is trends into joint to single/nuclear family type. The situation of marital status is not indicates the good social condition of villagers and it is observed that early marriage is a common matter both for girls and boys in every community. In respect of occupation of the villagers it has been identified that only primary occupation is the main source of income which has been in a pinpointed situation. It has also been observed that occupation pattern of the villagers are not uniform. There is a variation of agricultural practices in respect of geographical settings which is clearly depicted between high altitude and plain area villages. The economy is still based on primitive agriculture to a great extent in the high altitude villages. The higher education is not having a good position and it is happened only for remote location as well as far distance of main transport line of villages. So residential/ashram type high and higher secondary school are needed by which new generation will be in a position to complete all sorts of situations through education.

5 Chapter — Adaptation to Environment and Economy

5.1 Adaptation to Environment

In this chapter effort has been drawn up to show the impact of nature (physiography) on the socio-economic as well as cultural environment of forest villagers of the study area. The relief and geomorphology are responsible factor for the development of settlement pattern, population distribution, road and communication, land use, agriculture and other socio-economic activities. In fact, life in this hilly, rugged and dense forests area is tough and quite expensive. To a great extent, these natural parameters/factors determine the level of economic development as it is clear that, due to ruggedness terrain conditions; there is no scope for better livelihood such as development of large-scale marketing, agricultural farming, communication network system etc. In this connection it can be mentioned that as different physical factors or parameters have its own effective role, which directly and indirectly determines the form, type, location and shape of settlements as well as cultural landscape. Here it has been tried to deals how villagers adapted in different physical situations and obstacles; and physiographic-economic relation in different activities along with separate altitude location of villages.

5.1.1 The Physical Characteristics of Sample Villages

There are some parameters which are used to describe the physical character of the sample villages. Since the purpose of the study is to show relation among forest and villagers, so only those physical parameters have been considered into account which has direct relation of the forest related activities. The type of forests, relief and slope, settlement type and site, type of soil around the village, altitude of village, climate etc. are the prime characteristics which have been taken into consideration during the time of field observation.

5.1.2 The Site Characteristics

The table–5.1 shows the different nature of physical characteristics of sample villages. Locationally, villages are situated in valley slope, inside the forest, beside river bank, on hill slopes and flat hill-tops. Out of 17 villages, 2 have valley sites, 2 are located on hill-slopes, 8 are located inside the forests (core area), and 5 villages are beside the forests and 2 on the hill-tops. Out of the 17 sample villages, 9 villages have scattered type of settlement 2 are linear and rest 6 have compact and semi compact type. The site of the settlement has been the main factor responsible for this type of settlement. The dispersed settlements are sited beside the forest area; besides two settlements is located Buxa hill top such as Adma and Chunabati village. Due to lack of land, settlements inside the forest area are compact and two linear settlements also formed along unmetalled road inside the forest.

5.1.3 The Characteristics of Natural Vegetation

The natural vegetation cover acts as rain banker and rain holder of the earth. It is mentioned that the trees also act like millions of tiny damps and check the flow of water like a barrage (Khullar, 2002). The study area covered by huge dense forest of evergreen, deciduous, coniferous, savannah and other forest. The sample villages are located in the areas covered by four types of vegetation regimes, namely, the sub-tropical moist deciduous, savannah forests, plains forests, riverine forests. There are 10 villages in the zone of sub-tropical deciduous type, 5 villages are in the zone of plain forests, and 3 are in the zone of riverine forests and left are in the zone of savanna moist type and mix type.

The pattern of altitude-vegetation is coincidence according to relief height (table-5.1) as the sub-tropical forests

Table–5.1
Physical Characteristics of the Sample Villages

S.No.	Forest village	Site of the Settlement	Type of settlement	Type of natural vegetation	Valley type	Soil type	Relief	Altitude
1	Lehra	B.F	SCA	P.F	-	Sandy clay	EV	156 m
2	Suni	B.F	SCA	P.F	FLA	Sandy clay	EV	156 m
3	Garo Basti	W.F	COM	STD	-	Sandy clay	EV	202 m
4	Gadhadhar	B.F	SCA	PF	WID	Silt clay	EV	212 m
5	Poro	W.F	COM	STD	-	Sandy clay	UND	235 m
6	Nimati and Dabri	W.F	SCA	STD	-	Silt clay	UEV	235 m
7	Gangutia H.A	W.F & V.S	COM	STD	NAR	Sandy rocky	UND	306 m
8	Adma H.A	H.T	SCA	STD	-	Sandy rocky	HRUG	846 m
9	Raimatang H.A	H.S	SCA	STD		Sandy rocky	RUG	487 m
10	Bhutri forest basti H.A	H.S	LIN	STD	NAR	Sandy clay	UND	367 m
11	Gudamdabri	B.F	LIN	RF	-	Sandy clay	EV	179 m
12	Chunabati H.A	H.T	SCA	STD	-	Sandy rocky	HRUG	887 m
13	Bhutiabasti	W. F and R.B.A	COM	RF	FLA	Sandy Rocky	UEV	256 m
14	Sankosh	W.F and V.S	SCA	STD and RF	WID	Sandy loam	UND	312 m
15	Lapraguri	W.F	COM	PF	-	Sandy clay	EV	257 m
16	Santrabari H.A	W.F	SCA	STD	-	Sandy rocky	UND	467 m
17	Balapara	B.F	COM	PF	-	Sandy clay	EV	233 m

H.A=High Altitude, (Prepared based on field survey, 2017)

Note: Settlement site: B.F=Beside forests, W.F=Within forests, H.T=Hill fop, H.S=Hill slope, R.B.A=River bank area, V.S=Valley slope; Type of settlement: LIN=Linear settlement, COM=Compact settlement, SCA=Scattered settlement; Type of natural vegetation: STD=Sub-tropical moist deciduous, S.F=Savannah forests, P.F = Plain forests, R.F=Riverine forests; Valley type: WID=Wide valley, NAR=Narrow valley, FLA: Flat valley; Relief: EV=Even relief, UEV=Uneven relief, UND=Undulating plain relief, RUG= Rugged relief, HRUG= Highly rugged relief.

such as sal, teak, sisoo, khair etc. are found to occur at a height of above 500 m and the villages around this are Adma, Chunabati, Bhutri, Gangutia of Buxa hill forests. In the middle and lower altitude (below 500 m), there are villages having plain forest and riverine forests vegetation and it is found within 8 villages that belong to the trees such as semal, khair, asathwa, neem, amlaki, radha chura, debdaru and villages namely Sankosh, Lapraguri, Balapara. Besides mixed and savanna forests are covered around the villages that located in the lower flat surface namely Gudamdabri, Lerha, Suni, Garo Basti etc.

5.1.4 The Soil Characteristics

The other physical aspect which influences the forest and forest village is the soil. The soil is the primary factor of land use is any region. The formation of soil is influenced by the local climate and topography. The agriculture and agricultural pattern is also depended on the physical and chemical characteristics of soil as well as altitude, thick and distribution of soil. In order to know the relationship between the characteristics of soil and land use pattern, soils have been studied on the basis of types and composition status. The locations of villages, altitude, nearby flat surface and valley areas of villages' have been selected randomly to observe these characteristics. While the type of soil in the valley and nearby area of the villages' remains almost the same, there are obvious differences in their depth and erosional status at different locations. The soils are generally sandy dominated with mixtures of boulder, rock, clay and silt in varying degree. The sandy clay soil is found in 8 village locations, whereas, sandy rocky is available in 6 villages. There are 2 villages with silt clay and sandy loam soils in one village (table–5.1). Most of the valley soils are found steep hard sandy rocks soil. The high altitude soil in these villages' is sandy rocky and loam. The average depth of the soils is between 10 and 25 cm. but it varies from less than 10 cm. in high altitude soil to more than 40 cm. in the flat plain surface and river valley soil. The erosional status also shows the marked difference between valley and high locations. In valleys, moderate to high erosion is noticed. There are only 5 villages having no erosion of soil in their valley portion while all other villages' located in valley suffers from severe erosion. In case of highland locations, however, 4 villages (Chunabati, Adma, Raimatang, Bhutri village) have severe erosion while 2 (Ganguitia, Santrabari) villages have moderate erosion.

5.1.5 Pattern of Land Use

Man is a bio-geographical factor and has greatly modified the natural landscape. Therefore, it is essential to deal with both, the physical as well as cultural landscape before any enquiry is made regarding the use of the land (Giri, 1976). Land use pattern directly or indirectly controlled by relief. In this context it can be said that the relief indirectly influences farming by modifying the climate and by affecting the degree of accessibility, the case of cultivation and the consequential changes in soil, erosion and patterns (Singh, 1974). Also the type of soil and thickness, size and distribution of arable land, selection of crops ultimately depended on the relief. The land use pattern of the villages is important in order to know their adaptation with relief, dense forests environment and other works such as cultivation as well as the land lying unused and other practice etc. The type of land use pattern presented in table–5.2. There are large areas under the categories of cultivable waste and area not capable for cultivation and it is apparent among highland village area.

From the table 5.2 it is noticed that the majority of lands uses were recorded under food crop and it accounted for about 69.68% of the total owned land of sample household. The higher proportion of land under agriculture means it shows better scope for livestock rearing. In case of horticulture field, the land holding size has been recorded 134.20 acre (16%), for cultivable waste land, it is 72.66 acre (8.67%); for uncultivated land and barren land it is observed 19.54 acre (2.33%) and 27.81 acre (3.32%) respectively.

Table–5.2
Land use Pattern of Sample Villages

S.No.	Forest village	Area under different land use categories (Village-wise in acre), 2015								
		Food crop		Horti-culture		Cultivable waste land		Unculti-vated land	Barren land	Total land (acre) IR/UIR
		IR	UIR	IR	UIR	IR	UIR			
1	Lehra	-	14.42	-	2.57	-	3.21	-	-	20.20
2	Suni	-	19.27	-	2.21	-	4.50	2.1	-	28.08
3	Garo Basti	-	57.78	-	4.51		8.23	-	1.3	71.82
4	Gadhadhar	-	68.19	-	2.12	-	3.34	2.45	-	76.10
5	Poro	-	51.29	-	3.45	-	2.57	1.09	-	58.40
6	Nimati and Dabri	-	70.91	-	4.13	-	4.98	-	2.10	82.12
7	Gangutia H.A	-	23.47	-	17.02	-	3.61	3.95	2.80	50.85
8	Adma H.A	-	17.89	-	14.62	-	3.92	2.87	1.79	41.09
9	Raimatang H.A	-	19.16	-	9.59	-	4.67	3.23	1.99	38.64
10	Bhutri forest	-	12.04	-	11.31	-	3.93	2.59	2.17	32.04
11	Gudamdabri	-	53.75	-	2.23	-	5.12	-	3.27	64.37
12	Chunabati H.A	-	15.71	-	10.45	-	4.34	-	2.98	33.48
13	Bhutiabasti	-	11.39	-	8.94	-	3.07	-	4.31	27.71
14	Sankosh	-	65.85	-	8.67	-	4.32	-	-	78.84
15	Lapraguri	-	27.42	-	5.88	-	6.96	-	2.21	42.47
16	Santrabari H.A	-	36.73	-	23.67	-	2.78	1.26	2.89	67.33
17	Balapara	-	19.02	-	2.83	-	3.11	-	-	24.96
	Total	**-**	**584.29**		**134.2**		**72.66**	**19.54**	**27.81**	**838.50**
	%		**69.68**		**16.00**		**8.67**	**2.33**	**3.32**	**100.00**

H.A=High Altitude, (Prepared based on field survey, 2017)

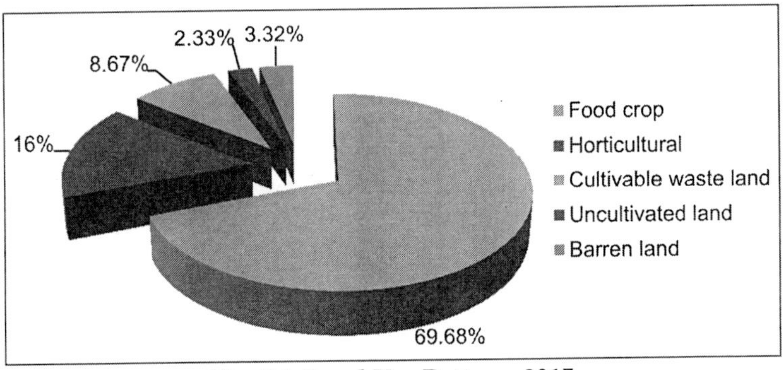

Fig. 5.1: Land Use Pattern, 2017

The uncultivated land mainly observed in surrounding of the high altitude forest villages as well as barren land noticed in low land or plain area villages and villagers referred that along rivers side sandy land and stony waste land as barren land. The horticulture practice is found more in number among high altitude villagers such as Amda, Bhutri, Chunabati, Santrabari etc. and comparatively less practice noticed in plain area villagers. It is totally opposite in case of food crop practice.

5.1.6 Food Habit

The main food of the Meches of Gudamdabri and Balapara villagers, are rice, fish, goat's meat, duck, fowl, pigeon, buffalo meat, pig and a variety of vegetables. They also drink milk and used mustard oil for cooking food. The blood of pig is cooked with vegetable curry. 'Marrow' is obtained from bones of pig, deer and goats. 'Kharodoi-bodai' is used for flavouring curries. It is made from the twigs of one kinds of pulse called 'kalai' and mustard plant, the roots of the cotton plant and root of plantain trees. These are well dried and burnt; the ashes (Kharodoi) are put in to a bamboo basket called 'Khardoi-Kholong' and water is poured over the ashes. This water drips through into a vessel and is called Khardoi-bedai. Roselle is eaten and is cooked with khardoi-bedai, with diminishes the acid taste. Along with the rice, they eat various types of wild edible, tubers, green leaves, fruits, especially Jackfruit.

Bhutias live in Chunabati, Adma and Buxa areas of this study area. The staple food of the Bhutias are rice, pork, beef, ducks, fowls, deer, barley, marua, fish, both dried and fresh, butter, cheese, Indian corn, and vegetables of all sorts. Oranges, pineapples, jack, plantains and other fruits are eaten. Milk is seldom drunk even by the sick. There is a marked preference for dried fish, pork and beef; the latter is often cut into strips and dried, and is used from day to day. Marrow, whenever obtainable, is used. In this case bones are broken and marrow is taken from them and is cooked eaten with vegetables. Blood is also used as an item of food, especially the blood of pig. It is mixed with meat finely minced which is made into 'sausages'. Along with these they consume different types of fruits, roots, leaves from the nearby forest.

The main food of the Ravas of Suni, Ghadhar, Poro (N), Garo Bsati villagers' is rice. Fish of every kind is eaten; also flesh of pig, deer, goat, ducks, fowls and pigeons. Large grasshoppers and locusts are also their food. Vegetables of all kinds are eaten. Indian corn is grown by the Ravas and is eaten raw, when tender or is boiled, roosted or parched when too ripe. Milk is drunk by few Ravas. They enjoy curd and eat it with beaten rice. The blood of pig is cooked up with vegetable curry and is much relished. Mustard oil is used for making curries. Vegetable curries are cooked with 'hari and cheka'.

The main staple food of Nepalese's of Gangutia, Raimatang, Sankosh, Santrabari, Bhutia basti, Bhutri forest basti villagers' is rice and wheat; besides they consume different vegetables, roots and tubers, tender stem of bamboos and mushrooms that are collected from the forest. They also eat meat, generally goat, cow, pig, poultry and fish of all kinds. Women eat the same food as men and there are no restrictions on the widows of any kind. Oranges, mangos, bananas, apples, and other fruits are eaten. All Nepalese community people use mustard oil food, sometimes cooked in butter or lard. The men use tobacco to smoke differently. Both men and women were addicted to alcohol consumption.

Santals of Lehra and Gadhadhar villagers' are animal eaters for a long time. Their usual food includes rice, frogs, snakes, rats, earthworms, shells and snails. Now rice and wheat is their main food. They also eat meat, generally goat, pig, poultry and fish of all kinds. Santals prefer having 'Tari and Haria' wine (one kinds of country wine made of decaying rice) on the various occasions. They also consume wine, brandy, arrack and toddy, which are available from the nearby towns. They consume pulses, roots and tubers which are available in the forest, and the vegetables that are available in the local markets and which are grown by them, same times they purchase the vegetables that are all available in the local market. They also consume non-alcoholic drinks such as coffee, tea and milk. Men smoke cigarettes and beedies.

The Oraons of Garo basti and Gadhadhar are non-vegetarians; they are animal eaters for a long time. Their usual food includes rice, wheat, frogs, snakes, earthworms, shells and snails. Besides they consume pulses, roots and tubers which are available in the forest, and the vegetables that are common in the local area and produce by locals. Oraons consumes local drinks such as 'Tari' and 'Haria' wine (one kind of local wine made of decaying rice) on the occasions. Men and women both smoke tobacco, cigarettes and beedies.

5.1.7 Fuel Used

It is observed from the table (table–5.3) that villagers are using forests wood, dry benches, leaves as fuel for cooking. About 99.20% of the households are using wood for cooking which collected from the forests. And almost all of household of Lehra, Suni, Poro, Nimti & debri, Adma, Raimatang, Butri forest basti, Gudamdabri, Chunabati, Lapraguri and Balapara villagers are using wood as fuel for cooking and other purpose. Only six of the all sampled household (0.80%) are using gas as fuel for cooking and for other purpose they are also using forest wood as fuel. In this context it is reported that 61.60% of the total village energy requirement was met by wood fuel of forests, during 1992-93 and 30.35% met by other commercial fuel and bio-fuel contributed only 8.05% (Natarajan, 1996). The table–5.3, below shows that in the study area majority of the villagers' are depending on the nearby forests for cooking and other purpose.

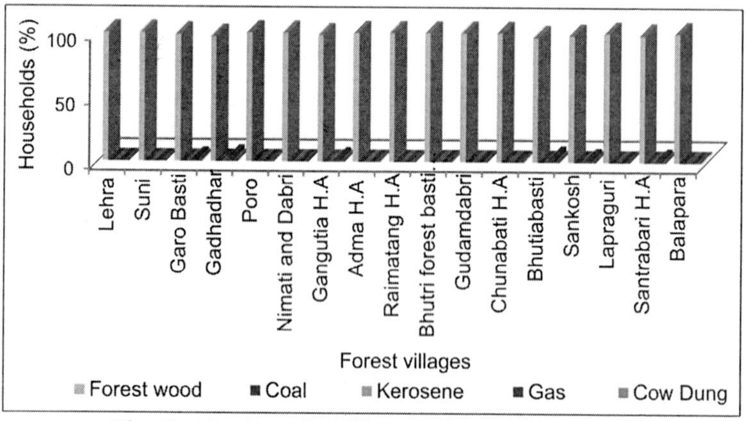

Fig. 5.2: Fuel used of Households (Village-wise)

Table–5.4
Fuel wood used for cooking (kg)

S. No.	Forest village	Fuel wood for domestic use (kg)			
		Total surveyed house-holds	Total fuel demand in a month	Fuel wood from forest	Fuel wood from other sources
1	Lehra	22	3300	3300	-
2	Suni	28	4620	4620	-
3	Garo Basti	72	12960	12780	180
4	Gadhadhar	63	10395	10065	330
5	Poro (N)	61	10065	10065	-
6	Nimati and Dabri	68	11220	11220	-
7	Gangutia H.A	55	11550	11340	210
8	Adma H.A	55	8250	8250	-
9	Raimatang H.A	55	9075	9075	-
10	Bhutri forest basti H.A	45	8100	8100	-
11	Gudamdabri	63	9450	9450	-
12	Chunabati H.A	54	8910	8910	-
13	Bhutiabasti	30	4500	4350	150
14	Sankosh	60	11700	11505	195
15	Lapraguri	47	7050	7050	-

Table–5.3
Fuel Used for Cooking (Households-wise)

S. No.	Forest village	Fuel used for cooking (Sampled households)					
		Forest wood	Coal	Kerosene	Gas	Cow Dung	Total sampled households
1	Lehra	22 (100)	-	-	-	-	22 (100%)
2	Suni	28 (100)	-	-	-	-	28 (100%)
3	Garo Basti	71 (98.61)	-	-	1 (1.39)		72 (100%)
4	Gadhadhar	61 (96.83)	-	-	2(3.17)	-	63 (100%)
5	Poro	61 (100)	-	-	-	-	61(100%)
6	Nimati and Dabri	68(100)	-	-	-	-	68 (100%)
7	Gangutia H.A	54 (98.18)	-	-	1 (1.82)	-	55 (100%)
8	Adma H.A	55 (100)	-	-	-	-	55 (100%)
9	Raimatang H.A	55 (100)	-	-	-	-	55 (100%)
10	Bhutri F. basti H.A	45 (100)	-	-	-	-	45 (100%)
11	Gudamdabri	63 (100)	-	-	-	-	63 (100%)
12	Chunabati H.A	54 (100)	-	-	-	-	54 (100%)
13	Bhutiabasti	29 (96.67)	-	-	1(3.33)	-	30 (100%)
14	Sankosh	59 (98.33)	-	-	1 (1.67)	-	60 (100%)
15	Lapraguri	47 (100)	-	-	-	-	47 (100%)
16	Santrabari H.A	64 (98.46)	-	-	1 (1.54	-	65 (100%)
17	Balapara	35 (100)	-	-	-	-	35 (100%)
	Total	**871 (99.20)**			**7 (0.80)**		**878 (100%)**

H.A=High Altitude, (Prepared based on field survey, 2017)

16	Santrabari H.A	65	8775	8640	135
17	Balapara	35	5775	5775	
	Total	**878 (100 %)**	**145695**	**144495 (99.18 %)**	**1200 (0.82 %)**

H.A=High Altitude, (Prepared based on field survey, 2017)

A total of 145.695 ton of fuel wood (table–5.4) was used by the study villagers in a month and of this 144.495 ton of wood originated from the contagious forest and rest from non-forest sources. Beside fodder, green manure, dry branches etc. were extracted from forests source in a daily or weekly basis throughout the year. All the villagers used fuel wood extracted from the forest where 99.18% fuel used from forest wood in a month by the villagers and only 0.82% of fuel is used from different sources such as gas, cow dung and others. This suggests that the most important forest product used by the villagers is forests' wood, whereas the other products were not regularly used throughout the year except rainy season.

5.1.8 Water Facilities

Primarily the villagers depend on their traditional water resource such as river, natural reservoir and spring. During winter and summer season they face difficulty to get water, since many of the springs, rivers and reservoirs are dried up. The table below explains the source of available water facilities based on village wise.

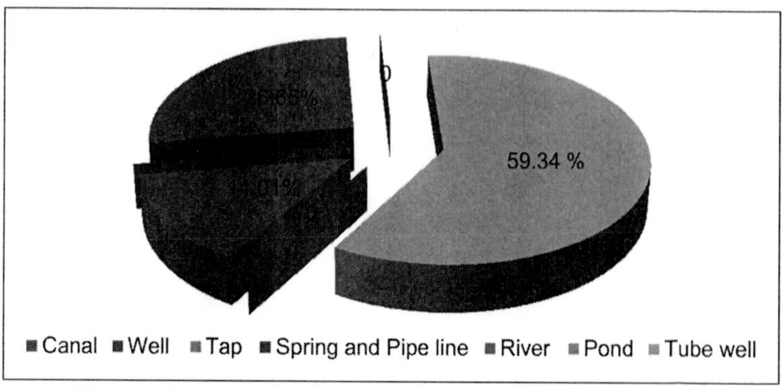

Fig. 5.3: Source of Water Facilities used by Households

Table–5.5
Availability of Water Facilities (village-wise)

S.No.	Forest village	Source of water facilities (Sampled house hold)							
		Canal	Well	Tap	Spring and Pipe line	River	Pond	Tube well	Total sampled households
1	Lehra	-	5 (22.73)	-	-	-	-	17 (77.27)	22 (100%)
2	Suni	-	4 (14.29)	-	-	-	-	24 (85.71)	28 (100%)
3	Garo Basti	-	8 (11.11)	-	-	-	-	64 (88.99)	72 (100%)
4	Gadhadhar	-	6 (9.52)	-	-	-	-	57 (90.48)	63 (100%)
5	Poro	-	14 (22.95)	-	-	-	-	47 (77.05)	61 (100%)
6	Nimati and Dabri	-	11 (16.18)	-	-	-	-	57 (83.82)	68 (100%)
7	Gangutia H.A	-	9 (16.36)	-	40 (72.72)	-		6 (10.91)	55 (100%)
8	Adma H.A	-	-	-	55 (100)	-	-	-	55 (100%)
9	Raimatang H.A	-	-	-	55 (100)	-	-	-	55 (100%)

S.No.	Forest village	Source of water facilities (Sampled house hold)							
		Canal	Well	Tap	Spring and Pipe line	River	Pond	Tube well	Total sampled households
10	Bhutri forest basti H.A	-	45 (100)	-	-	-	-	-	45 (100%)
11	Gudamdabri	-	7 (11.11)	-	-	-	-	56 (88.88)	63 (100%)
12	Chunabati H.A	-	-	-	54 (100)	-	-	-	54 (100%)
13	Bhutiabasti	-	-	-	30 (100)	-	-	-	30 (100%)
14	Sankosh	-	6 (10)	-	-	-	-	54 (90)	60 (100%)
15	Lapraguri	-	-	-	-	-	-	47 (100)	47 (100%)
16	Santrabari H.A	-	8 (12.31)	-	-	-	-	57 (87.69)	65 (100%)
17	Balapara	-	-	-	-	-	-	35 (100)	35 (100%)
	Total	**-**	**123 (14.01)**		**234 (26.65)**	**-**	**-**	**521 (59.34)**	**878 (100%)**

H.A=High Altitude, (Prepared based on field survey, 2017)

The table–5.5 shows that all villages are using tube well water, spring and pine line water and well water by 59.34%, 26.42% and 14.24% respectively. In high altitude and hill villages all households are depending on spring and pipe line for water facilities, such as Adma, Chunabati, Raimatang, Santrabari and Bhutia basti. Above 80% households of nine villages are having water facilities by tube well and such villages are Balapara, Santarabari, Sankosh, Gudamdabri etc. So above table shows that very remote villages, high altitude and hilly area villages are not getting protected water for drinking and other domestic purpose. Even there is no water tank or canal facility.

5.1.8.1 Proximity of Water Sources

The table–5.6 shows that contiguity of source water based on the sampled household of villagers. Out of the 878 households, about 822 (93.62%) households (taking both of street pipe and street tube well or well) are having proximity of source of water from outside. Only 56 households (6.38%) having water provision within the house premise and surrounding.

The villagers' of Gangutia, Adma, Raimatang, Chunabati, Bhutia basti, Suni, and Bhutri forest Basti having water provision from outside. Only 15 households (32.06 %) of Nimti and Dabri have the proximity of water source inside the house which is more among all the villages.

5.1.8.2 Water Storage Facilities

Polluted water storage and consume is the prime causes of unhealthy and water related disease of the villagers. The households in the study area store the water in cistern, drum, utensil, bucket and pitchers. The table–5.7 shows village wise water storage facilities of the households.

Out of the 878 households, about 398 households (45.33%) and 365 households (41.57%) are used buckets and drums as water storage facilities respectively. Only about 6.95%, 4.78%, and 1.37% households are using pitcher, utensil and cistern

Table–5.6
Proximity of source of water facilities
(Sampled households)

S.No.	Forest village	Premises of House	Out side		Total sampled households
			Street pipe	Street Tube well or well	
1	Lehra	3 (13.64)	-	19 (86.36)	22 (100%)
2	Suni	-	-	28 (100)	28 (100%)
3	Garo Basti	13 (18.06)	-	59 (81.94)	72 (100%)
4	Gadhadhar	7 (11.11)	-	56 (88.89)	63 (100%)
5	Poro (N)	2 (3.28)	-	59 (96.72)	61(100%)
6	Nimati and Dabri	15 (32.06)	-	53 (77.94)	68 (100%)
7	Gangutia H.A	-	55(100)		55 (100%)
8	Adma H.A		55(100)		55 (100%)
9	Raimatang H.A		55(100)		55 (100%)
10	Bhutri F. basti H.A		-	45 (100)	45 (100%)
11	Gudamdabri	2 (3.17)	-	61 (96.83)	63 (100%)
12	Chunabati H.A		54 (100)		54 (100%)
13	Bhutiabasti		30 (100)		30 (100%)
14	Sankosh	3 (5)	-	57 (95)	60 (100%)
15	Lapraguri	2 (4.26)	-	45 (95.74)	47 (100%)
16	Santrabari H.A	5 (7.69)	-	60 (92.31)	65 (100%)
17	Balapara	4 (11.43)	-	31 (88.57)	35 (100%)
	Total	**56 (6.38%)**	**249 (28.36%)**	**573 (65.26%)**	**878 (100%)**

H.A=High Altitude, (Prepared based on field survey, 2017)

Table–5.7
Water Storage Facilities (village-wise)

S.No.	Forest village	Cistern	Drum	Utensil	Bucket	Pitcher	Total sampled households
1	Lehra	-	-	7 (31.82)	11 (50)	4 (18.18)	22 (100 %)
2	Suni	-	-	11 (39.29)	15 (53.57)	2 (7.14)	28 (100 %)
3	Garo Basti	-	15(20.83)	7 (9.73)	50 (69.44)	-	72 (100 %)
4	Gadhadhar	-	-	10 (15.87)	47 (74.60)	6 (9.52)	63 (100 %)
5	Poro (N)	-	11 (18.03)	4 (6.56)	37 (60.66)	9 (14.75)	61(100 %)
6	Nimati and Dabri	-	16 (23.53)	-	44 (64.71)	8 (11.76)	68 (100 %)
7	Gangutia H.A	-	51 (92.73)	-	4 (7.27)	-	55 (100 %)
8	Adma H.A	-	55 (100)		-	-	55 (100 %)
9	Raimatang H.A	-	55 (100)	-	-	-	55 (100 %)
10	Bhutri forest basti H.A	-	35 (77.78)	-	10 (22.22)	-	45 (100 %)
11	Gudamdabri	-	-	3(4.76)	46 (73.02)	14 (2.19)	63 (100 %)
12	Chunabati H.A	-	54 (100)	-	-	-	54 (100 %)
13	Bhutiabasti	8 (26.67)	22 (73.33)	-	-	-	30 (100 %)
14	Sankosh	-	-	-	55 (91.67)	5 (8.33)	60 (100 %)
15	Lapraguri	-	-	-	39 (82.98)	8 (17.02)	47 (100 %)
16	Santrabari H.A	4 (6.15)	51(78.46)	-	8 (12.31)	2 (3.07)	65 (100 %)
17	Balapara	-	-	-	32 (91.43)	3 (8.57)	35 (100 %)
	Total	**12 (1.37%)**	**365 (41.57%)**	**42 (4.78%)**	**398 (45.33%)**	**61 (6.95%)**	**878 (100%)**

H.A=High Altitude, (Prepared based on field survey, 2017)

to store collected water. In village wise figure, it has been mentioned that in high altitude hill villages' 90 to 100% villagers followed drums to store water since they have lot of scarcity of water and only within a particular time water has been supplied through pipe line. Such villagers are of Gangutia (92.73%), Adma (100%), Raimatang (100%), and Chunabati (100%). For Chunabati and Adma villages', water has been taken through water pipe line from the Bhutan hill water reservoir.

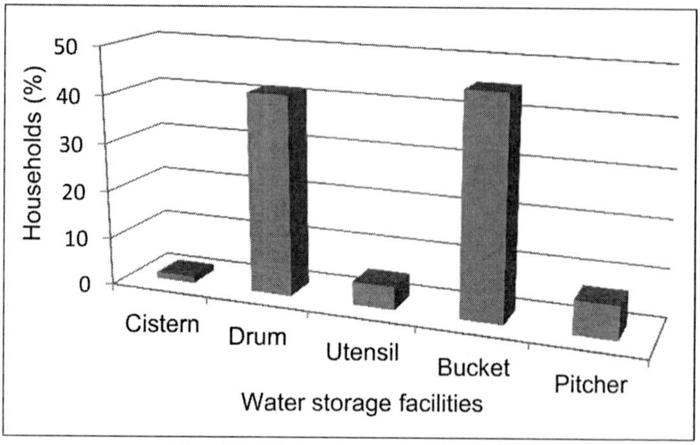

Fig. 5.4: Water Storage Facilities

5.1.9 House Type

The table–5.8 shows the type of houses of 878 households in the study area. It is observed from the table that majority of the households that is about 770 household (87.70 %) are living in the wood and tin house. Only about 58 (6.61 %) and 50 (5.69 %) households are living in the thatched and pacca house. Due to easy and good availability of wood, most of the house used wood to make walls, windows, door even stage like floor or platform for environmental adaptation. For roof, villagers used tin which has long serviceable than wood. The number of pacca house are seen more than others in the Lera (68.18 %) and Suni (82.14 %) village, because only this two forest village has taken under 'Gitanjali Project' through which beneficiaries got pacca house. There is no stone and tiled house observed in the study village.

Table–5.8
Types of House (village-wise)

S.No.	Forest village	Stone & Tin	Wood and Tin	Pucca (concrete with tin)	Thatched and wood	Tiled	Total sampled households
1	Lehra	-	7 (31.82)	15 (68.18)	-	-	22 (100 %)
2	Suni	-	5 (17.86)	23 (82.14)	-	-	28 (100 %)
3	Garo Basti	-	65 (90.28)	-	7 (9.72)	-	72 (100 %)
4	Gadhadhar	-	45 (71.43)	-	18 (28.57)	-	63 (100 %)
5	Poro (N)	-	57 (93.44)	4 (6.56)	-	-	61(100 %)
6	Nimati and Dabri	-	61(89.71)	-	7 (10.29)		68 (100 %)
7	Gangutia H.A	-	55 (100)	-	-	-	55 (100 %)
8	Adma H.A	-	51 (92.73)	-	4 (7.27)	-	55 (100 %)
9	Raimatang H.A	-	47 (85.45)	-	8 (14.55)	-	55 (100 %)
10	Bhutri forest basti H.A	-	45 (100)	-	-	-	45 (100 %)
11	Gudamdabri	-	58 (92.06)	-	5 (7.94)		63 (100 %)
12	Chunabati H.A	-	52 (96.30)	-	2 (3.70)	-	54 (100 %)
13	Bhutiabasti		30 (100)	-	-	-	30 (100 %)
14	Sankosh	-	53 (88.33)	4 (6.67)	3 (5)	-	60 (100 %)
15	Lapraguri	-	47 (100)	-	-	-	47 (100 %)
16	Santrabari H.A		61 (93.85)	4 (6.15)	-	-	65 (100 %)
17	Balapara	-	31 (88.57)	-	4 (11.42)	-	35 (100 %)
	Total		**770 (87.70%)**	**50 (5.69%)**	**58 (6.61%)**		**878 (100%)**

H.A=High Altitude, (Prepared based on field survey, 2017)

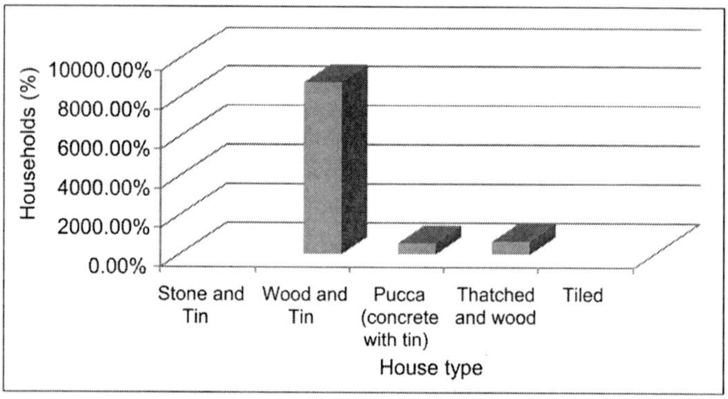

Fig. 5.5: House Types of Villagers

5.1.10 Dependency on Forest Produces

Generally forest villagers are found in interior and fringe forest areas with dense and fair forest. Hence villagers' economy is closely connected with the forest. The forests not only provide them food, materials to build houses, fuel for cooking and lightening but also satisfy deep rooted sentiments with forest environment. It is stated that in Gujarat, forest possessed a central position in the village economy through a provision of a variety of minor forest products (NTFPs) and other goods and services for local use like fuel fodder, wood, materials for agricultural implements and bulbs and wild tubers as vegetables, etc. (Kant et al., 1993). The forests products are numerous and available seasonally, their pattern and collection of the use differs with economic and socio-cultural condition of each household (Malhotra et al., 1991). Here villagers are isolated with their own economy and culture as well as small forest society due to their remote location and untouched with others world. Ravi et al., (2006) reported that NTFPs acts a key role in the economy and life of the tribal community residing in and around the protected areas of Kote region. The income derived from NTFPs was the single largest source but it was not sufficient to meet even their subsistence requirement of food. So different kinds of forest products are prime lifeline and collection of forest products is one of the ways of life. Regularly villagers go inside the forest and collect forest product according to their demand and local sell. The chief collected items are cane, cane fruits, dry branches and leaves, purundi fruits, pan leaves, naglata, lycopodium stick, totola pods and seeds, golden and sponge mushrooms, odal fruit, fern bud, mahogony floral axis, lali fruit, simul floss and floral axis, broom stick, thatch etc. There are many medical herbs in this region which are also used by inhabitants to remove fever, stomach problem, jadish, asthma, skin disease, bone fracture join etc.

The table–5.9 shows the villagers dependency on forest produce where out of 878 household, 818 (93.17%) depends on forest produce for livelihood needs and only 60 household (6.83%) depends on other sources. The dependency on forest produce is more among villagers of interior area and such villagers are Gangutia, Adma, Raimatang, Bhutri Forest basti, Chunabati and Bhutia basti, Santrabari where 100% dependency were observed during field survey.

Table–5.9
Dependency on Forest Produce (village-wise)

S.No.	Forest village	Yes	No	Total sampled households
1	Lehra	18 (81.82)	4 (18.18)	22 (100%)
2	Suni	25 (89.29)	3 (10.71)	28 (100%)
3	Garo Basti	66 (91.67)	6 (8.33)	72 (100%)
4	Gadhadhar	53 (84.13)	10 (15.87)	63 (100%)
5	Poro (N)	61 (100)	-	61(100%)
6	Nimati and Dabri	56 (82.35)	12 (17.65)	68 (100%)
7	Gangutia H.A	55 (100)	-	55 (100%)
8	Adma H.A	55 (100)	-	55 (100%)
9	Raimatang H.A	55 (100)	-	55 (100%)
10	Bhutri forest basti H.A	45 (100)	-	45 (100%)
11	Gudamdabri	54 (85.71)	9 (14.29)	63 (100%)
12	Chunabati H.A	54 (100)	-	54 (100%)
13	Bhutiabasti	30 (100)	-	30 (100%)
14	Sankosh	58 (96.67)	2 (3.33)	60 (100%)
15	Lapraguri	43 (91.49)	4 (8.51)	47 (100%)
16	Santrabari H.A	61 (93.85)	4 (6.15)	65 (100%)
17	Balapara	29 (82.86)	6 (17.14)	35 (100%)
	Total	**818 (93.17%)**	**60 (6.83%)**	**878 (100%)**

H.A=High Altitude, (Prepared based on field survey, 2017)

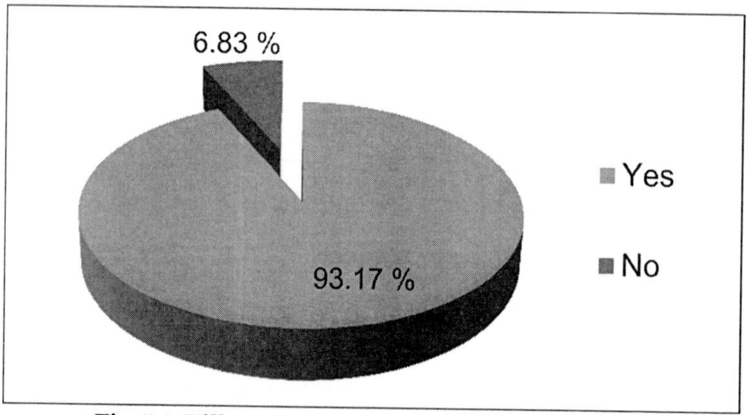

Fig. 5.6: Villagers Dependency on Forest Produces

5.1.11 Conflict with Wildlife

The forests of Alipurduar District are an extremely rich bio-diversity zone but today facing challenging moment due to regular man-animal conflict. Human interferes such as changes in land use pattern, Jhum cultivation, tea garden extension, conversion of forest cover area into agricultural and habitat lands etc. has become a primary issue for loss natural corridors of animals and are the main causes for man-animal conflict in this study area. Besides tea gardens serves as ideal dens for breeding leopard; illicit liquor, brewing attracts wild animals mainly elephants in nearby tea gardens, forest villages as well as revenue villages and caused conflicts. The conflicts of humans with tiger, elephant, leopard, wild boar, monkeys, gaur, and rhino have become a regular feature (Das, 2013). In this respect the table–5.10 shows the conflict of men and wildlife based on the sampled household of villagers. Out of the 878 households 759 (86.45%) households gave positive option and 119 (13.55%) household gave negative approach regarding of wild animal conflict. Except hill top villagers such as Adma, Chunabati, Raimatang other villagers gave their 100% positive option on men animal conflict.

Table–5.10
Villagers' Response on Man-Wildlife Conflict (village-wise)

S.No.	Forest village	Yes	No	Total sampled households
1	Lehra	22 (100)	-	22 (100%)
2	Suni	28 (100)	-	28 (100%)
3	Garo Basti	72 (100)	-	72 (100%)
4	Gadhadhar	63 (100)	-	63 (100%)
5	Poro (N)	61 (100)	-	61(100%)
6	Nimati and Dabri	68 (100)	-	68 (100%)
7	Gangutia H.A	55 (100)	-	55 (100%)
8	Adma H.A	12 (21.82)	43 (78.18)	55 (100%)
9	Raimatang H.A	23 (41.82)	32 (58.18)	55 (100%)
10	Bhutri forest basti H.A	45 (100)	-	45 (100%)
11	Gudamdabri	63 (100)	-	63 (100%)
12	Chunabati H.A	10 (18.52)	44 (81.48)	54 (100%)
13	Bhutiabasti	30 (100)	-	30 (100%)
14	Sankosh	60 (100)	-	60 (100%)
15	Lapraguri	47 (100)	-	47 (100%)
16	Santrabari H.A	65 (100)	-	65 (100%)
17	Balapara	35 (100)	-	35 (100%)
	Total	**759 (86.45%)**	**119 (13.55%)**	**878 (100%)**

H.A=High Altitude, (Prepared based on field survey, 2017)

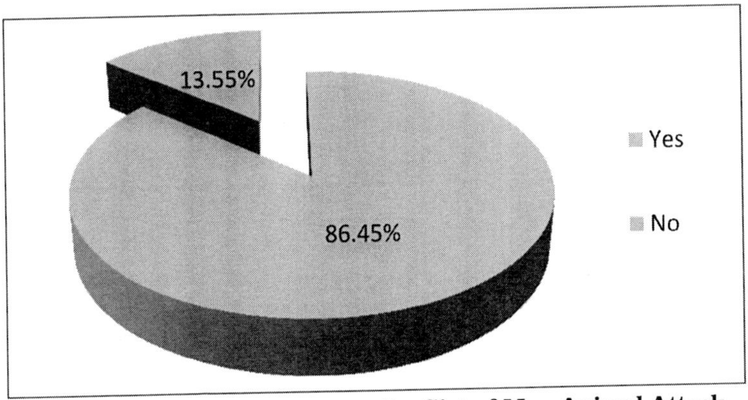

Fig. 5.7: Villagers' Response on Conflict of Men-Animal Attack

The table–5.11 shows the cattle lifting figure of different ranges in BTR of this District. It is mentioned that most affected area of ranges are N. Rydak, Jainti, Buxaduar, Kumargram, S. Raidak, Hailtongaunj, Hatipota and Pana where maximum number of cattle lifted by wildlife.

Human death and injuries are reported in BTR mainly from tea gardens and fringe villages. Forest villages were also affected. Human death and injuries are caused due to elephants and leopards attack. The following table 5.12 shows the range wise human death and injuries figures in BTR of this area by elephants and leopards.

Table–5.12
Human death and Injury by elephant and leopard/tiger in BTR (2005-13)

Year	BTR, West Division		BTR, East Division		Total	
	Person killed	Person injured	Person killed	Person injured	Person killed	Person injured
2005-06	4	10	13	8	17	18
2006-07	4	6	5	4	9	10
2007-08	2	7	5	9	7	16
2008-09	4	15	8	10	12	25
2009-10	6	0	4	8	10	8
2010-11	3	8	2	5	5	13
2011-12	4	16	3	17	7	23
2012-13	6	23	10	11	16	34
Total	**33**	**85**	**50**	**72**	**83**	**157**

Source: Tiger conservation plan, 2016-17 to 2026-27, DFD, East & West BTR Forest Office, Alipurduar

Elephant, wild boar, bison and monkey damages agricultural crops in peripheral and forest villages. Maximum damage to the crop takes place from August-September to December-January. They damage mainly paddy, maize, wheat, mallets etc. The table–5.13 will give an idea about the magnitude of crop and hut damage in Buxa Tiger Reserve of this District. Elephants are involved in house/hut damage in forests villages, peripheral villages and tea garden labour lines.

Table–5.11
Cattle Lifting in Buxa Tiger Reserve by Tiger and Leopard

Year	BTR (West) Division							BTR (East) Division							Total
	PANA	HMTG	NMT	EDPO	WDPO	ERVK	WRVK	JNT	BDR	NRD	SRD	BH	KGM	HPA	
2004	-	-	-	-	-	-	-	8	11	23	-		5	-	47
2005	3	-	1	-	-	1	-	24	9	26	6		11	-	81
2006	6	-	3	1	-	1	-	8	12	24	5		8	-	68
2007	10	-	1	-	-	1	4	7	10	27	2	2	13	-	77
2008	4	-	-	1	-	1	-	10	8	26	2	-	8	-	60
2009	2	1	2	-	-	1	4	-	-	-	-	1	1	2	14
2010	3	2	3	-	-	1	1	-	-	2	-		2	5	19
2011	-	2	-	2	2	1	-	-	-	4	-		1	-	12
2012	-	3	-	-	5	-	-	27	-	-	4		3	-	42
2013	1	2	-	-	-	1	1	-	2	-	1	1	1	1	11
Total	**29**	**10**	**10**	**4**	**7**	**8**	**10**	**84**	**52**	**132**	**20**	**4**	**53**	**8**	**431**

Source: Tiger conservation plan, 2016-17 to 2026-27, DFD, East & West BTR Forest Office, Alipurduar

Table–5.13
Crop and Hut Damages by Wildlife in Buxa Tiger Reserve

Year	BTR, West Division				BTR, East Division				Total
	Crop damage		Hut damage		Crop damage		Hut damage		Compen-sation paid in BTR (Rs.)
	No. of cases	Compen-sation paid (Rs.)	No. of cases	Compen-sation paid (Rs.)	No. of cases	Compen-sation paid (Rs.)	No. of cases	Compen-sation paid (Rs.)	
2005-06	675	270000.00	86	97200.00	967	363173.00	93	54600.00	784973
2006-07	708	318600.00	82	80400.00	897	390500.00	102	51350.00	840850
2007-08	723	289200.00	102	110800.00	1283	389200.00	490	157400.00	946600
2008-09	958	475350.00	108	122000.00	849	418400.00	107	52000.00	1067750.00
2009-10	800	395750.00	140	147850.00	1448	71520.00	90	106400.00	721520.00
2010-11	1303	775200.00	167	221000.00	768	425700.00	148	240500.00	1662400.00
2011-12	521	303500.00	219	308999.00	805	329300.00	113	186500.00	1128299.00
2012-13	1617	1109750.00	699	962750.00	2125	1074710.00	421	707270.00	3854480.00
Total	**7305**	**3937350**	**1603**	**2050999.00**	**9142**	**3462503**	**421**	**1556020.00**	**11006872.00**

Source: Tiger conservation plan, 2016-17 to 2026-27, DFD, East & West BTR Forest Office, Alipurduar

5.2 Economy

5.2.1 Labour Force Participation

The villagers of the sample households have been classified into main workers, marginal workers and non-workers. Table–5.14 (Appendix D) presents the labour force participation of the household of 17 sampled villages. It has been observed from the table that out of 4071 persons, main workers form only 35.57 percent, marginal workers 43.78 percent and non-workers constitute for 20.65 percent of the total villagers. In Suni Village, villagers have large number of main workers, followed by the Garo Basti, Gadhadhar, Bhutri forest basti, Balapara, Gudamdabri, Santrabari, Poro, and Adma and so on. The above table also explains the sex wise labour force participation among households where it has been shown that male and female main workers consists 18.72% and 18.45% respectively. Besides maximum male main worker found in Suni village and female main worker in Garo basti which is 25.28% and 29.12% respectively. In case of marginal workers, male workers are more than the female, but in some villages female workers are more in number than male i.e. in Santrabari, Lapraguri.

5.2.2 Occupational Structure of Working Family Members

An attempt has been made here to give an idea of the economic condition of the forest communities. A detail discussion has been prepared based on both primary and secondary occupation. The table–5.15 (Appendix D) describes the primary and secondary occupation of forest living communities. From the data it has been noticed that out of total 4071 persons of the total households, 98.27% are engaged in primary activities, 0.59% is in manufacturing, and service occupied only 1.14%. So it noticed that, villagers are depending on primary activity for livelihood where manufacturing and service is too less importance. The above table also explains the sex wise occupational status where it has been shown that 49.41% male and 48.86% female is engaged in primary activity. Besides maximum engagement of primary activity is found in Gadhadhar village which is 99.65% and minimum engagement is found in Lehra village which is 92.95%.

5.2.3 Income Pattern

Income is one of the important indicators for socio-economic study. Keeping in view on labour force participation, about land use and occupational structure, an emphasis has been given on income of the forest villagers living in different locations of the study area. For the purpose of analyzing the data, monthly income of the families are tabulated under different income group ranges as shown in the table–5.16, that is Rs. Below 5000, 5001-10000, 10001-25000, 25001-50000, 50001-75000, 75001-100000, and Rs. above 100000.

From the table–5.16 it apparent that out of total families, above half of the total families (66.86%) earn between Rs. 5001-10000. Another 20.39% families have income between Rs.10001-25000. There are only 6.61%, 2.84%, 1.71%, and 1.59% families whose monthly income ranges below Rs. 5000, Rs. 25001-50000, Rs. 50001-75000 and Rs. 75001-100000 group range respectively.

It is seen from the table–5.17 that majority of the households (93.51%) depend on primary activities i.e. on cultivation, NTFPs collection, agriculture labour, horticulture and their income fall in between below Rs.5000.00-50000.00, where 66.61% households have income from Rs. 5001.00-10000.00, 20.73% have income from Rs.10001.00-25000.00, 6.61% are in income from below Rs.5000.00-10000.00 and 1.71% are belongs to the group of Rs.25001.00-50000.00. About 4.44% household are earning from service sector where 2.85% households have income from Rs.50001.00-75001.00, and 1.59% have income from Rs. 75001.00-100000.00. Only 2.05% are engaged in manufacturing sector where household income ranges from Rs.10001.00-25000.00.

Table–5.16
Income Pattern of Sampled Households

S.No.	Forest Village	Income (Rs.) of sampled households							
		Total surveyed house hold	< 5000	5001-10000	10001-25000	25001-50000	50001-75000	75001-100000	>100000
1	Lehra	22	2 (9.09)	18 (81.82)	-	-	2 (9.09)	-	-
2	Suni	28	4 (14.29)	23 (82.14)	-	-	1 (3.57)	-	-
3	Garo Basti	72	7 (9.72)	51 (70.83)	10 (13.89)	2 (2.78)	-	2 (2.78)	-
4	Gadhadhar	63	5 (7.94)	47 (74.60)	10 (15.87)	-	1 (1.59)	-	-
5	Poro (N)	61	4 (6.56)	51 (83.60)	4 (6.56)	-	2 (3.28)	-	-
6	Nimati and Dabri	68	-	54 (79.41)	14 (20.59)	-	-	-	-
7	Gangutia H.A	55	6 (10.91)	25 (45.46)	19 (34.55)	2 (3.63)	2 (3.63)	1 (1.82)	-
8	Adma H.A	55	1 (1.82)	43 (78.18)	10 (18.18)	-	1 (1.82)	-	-
9	Raimatang H.A	55	3 (5.45)	33 (60.00)	15 (27.28)		1 (1.82)	3 (5.45)	-
10	Bhutri forest basti H.A	45	-	20 (44.44)	19 (42.22)	3 (6.68)	2 (4.44)	1 (2.22)	-
11	Gudamdabri	63	7 (11.11)	43 (68.25)	12 (19.05)	-	1 (1.59)	-	-
12	Chunabati H.A	54	6 (11.11)	38 (70.37)	8 (14.82)	-	1 (1.85)	1 (1.85)	-
13	Bhutiabasti	30	-	21 (69.99)	6 (20.00)	-	1 (3.34)	2 (6.67)	-
14	Sankosh	60	-	31 (51.66)	19 (31.67)	4 (6.67)	4 (6.67)	2 (3.33)	-
15	Lapraguri	47	5 (10.63)	33 (70.22)	6 (12.77)	-	2 (4.26)	1 (2.12)	-
16	Santrabari H.A	65	-	35 (53.86)	21 (32.31)	4 (6.15)	4 (6.15)	1 (1.53)	-
17	Balapara	35	8 (22.86)	21 (59.99)	6 (17.15)	-	-	-	-
	Total	**878** **100%**	**58** **6.61%**	**587** **66.86%**	**179** **20.39%**	**15** **1.71%**	**25** **2.84%**	**14** **1.59%**	**-**

% is given in brackets, H.A=High Altitude, (Prepared based on field survey, 2017)

Table–5.17
Income with Reference to Occupation

S.No.	Occupational Status (Village-wise)	Income (Rs.) of sampled households							
		< 5000	5001-10000	10001-25000	25001-50000	50001-75000	75001-100000	>100000	Total households
1	**Lehra Village**	-	-	-	-	-	-	-	**22**
	Primary	2(9.09)	15(68.18)	-	-	-	-	-	
	Manufacturing	-	-	3(13.64)	-	-	-	-	
	Service	-	-	-	-	2(9.09)	-	-	
2	**Suni Village**	-	-	-	-	-	-	-	**28**
	Primary	4(14.29)	23(82.14)	-	-	-	-	-	
	Manufacturing	-	-	-	-	-	-	-	
	Service	-	-	-	-	1(3.57)	-	-	
3	**Garo Basti Village**	-	-	-	-	-	-	-	**72**
	Primary	7(9.72)	51(70.83)	10(13.89)	2(2.78)	-	-	-	
	Manufacturing	-	-	-	-	-	-	-	
	Service	-	-	-	-	-	2(2.78)	-	
4	**Gadhadhar Village**	-	-	-	-	-	-	-	**63**
	Primary	5(7.94)	47(74.60)	10(15.87)	-	-	-	-	
	Manufacturing	-	-	-	-	-	-	-	
	Service	-	-	-	-	1(1.59)	-	-	
5	**Poro Village (N)**	-	-	-	-	-	-	-	**61**
	Primary	4(6.56)	51(83.60)	-	-	-	-	-	
	Manufacturing	-	-	4(6.56)	-	-	-	-	
	Service	-	-	-	-	2(3.28)	-	-	

S.No.	Occupational Status (Village-wise)	Income (Rs.) of sampled households							
		< 5000	5001-10000	10001-25000	25001-50000	50001-75000	75001-100000	>100000	Total households
6	**Nimati and Dabri Village**	-	-	-	-	-	-	-	68
	Primary	-	54(79.41)	11(16.18)	-	-	-	-	
	Manufacturing	-	-	3(4.41)	-	-	-	-	
	Service	-	-	-	-	-	-	-	
7	**Gangutia Village H.A**	-	-	-	-	-	-	-	55
	Primary	6(10.91)	25(45.46)	19(34.55)	2(3.63)	-	-	-	
	Manufacturing	-	-	-	-	-	-	-	
	Service	-	-	-	-	2(3.63)	1(1.82)	-	
8	**Adma Village H.A**	-	-	-	-	-	-	-	55
	Primary	1(1.82)	43(78.18)	10(18.18)	-	-	-	-	
	Manufacturing	-	-	-	-	-	-	-	
	Service	-	-	-	-	1(1.82)	-	-	
9	**Raimatang Village H.A**	-	-	-	-	-	-	-	55
	Primary	3(5.45)	33(60.00)	15(27.28)	-	-	-	-	
	Manufacturing	-	-	-	-	-	-	-	
	Service	-	-	-	-	1(1.82)	3(5.45)	-	
10	**Bhutri forest basti Village H.A**	-	-	-	-	-	-	-	45
	Primary	-	20(44.44)	19(42.22)	3(6.68)	-	-	-	
	Manufacturing	-	-	-	-	-	-	-	
	Service	-	-	-	-	2(4.44)	1(2.22)	-	

S.No.	Occupational Status (Village-wise)	Income (Rs.) of sampled households							
		< 5000	5001-10000	10001-25000	25001-50000	50001-75000	75001-100000	>100000	Total households
11	**Gudamdabri Village**	-	-	-	-	-	-	-	63
	Primary	7(11.11)	43(68.25)	12(19.05)	-	-	-	-	
	Manufacturing	-	-	-	-	-	-	-	
	Service	-	-	-	-	1(1.59)	-	-	
12	**Chunabati Village H.A**	-	-	-	-	-	-	-	54
	Primary	6(11.11)	38(70.37)	8(14.82)	-	-	-	-	
	Manufacturing	-	-	-	-	-	-	-	
	Service	-	-	-	-	1(1.85)	1(1.85)	-	
13	**Bhutiabasti Village H.A**	-	-	-	-	-	-	-	30
	Primary	-	21(69.99)	6(20.00)	-	-	-	-	
	Manufacturing	-	-	-	-	-	-	-	
	Service	-	-	-	-	1(3.34)	2(6.67)	-	
14	**Sankosh Village**	-	-	-	-	-	-	-	60
	Primary	-	31(51.66)	19(31.67)	4(6.67)	-	-	-	
	Manufacturing	-	-	-	-	-	-	-	
	Service	-	-	-	-	4(6.67)	2(3.33)	-	
15	**Lapraguri Village**	-	-	-	-	-	-	-	47
	Primary	5(10.63)	33(70.22)	2(4.26)	-	-	-	-	
	Manufacturing	-	-	4(8.51)	-	-	-	-	
	Service	-	-	-	-	2(4.26)	1(2.12)	-	

S.No.	Occupational Status (Village-wise)	Income (Rs.) of sampled households							
		< 5000	5001-10000	10001-25000	25001-50000	50001-75000	75001-100000	>100000	Total households
16	**Santrabari Village H.A**	-	-	-	-	-	-	-	65
	Primary	-	35(53.86)	21(32.31)	4(6.15)	-	-	-	
	Manufacturing	-	-	-	-	-	-	-	
	Service					4(6.15)	1(1.53)		
17	**Balapara Village**	-	-	-	-	-	-	-	35
	Primary	8(22.86)	21(59.99)	2(5.72)	-	-	-	-	
	Manufacturing	-	-	4(11.43)	-	-	-	-	
	Service	-	-	-	-	-	-	-	
	Overall result of Villagers								
	Primary	58(7.37)	584(74.21)	164(18.68)	15(1.71)	-	-	-	821(93.51)
	Manufacturing	-	-	18 (2.05)	-	-	-	-	18 (2.05)
	Service	-	-	-	-	25(3.18)	14(1.78)	-	39(4.44)
	Grand Total	**58**	**584**	**182**	**15**	**25**	**14**	**-**	**878**
		6.61%	**66.51%**	**20.73%**	**1.71%**	**2.85%**	**1.59%**		**100%**

H.A=High Altitude, (Prepared based on field survey, 2017)

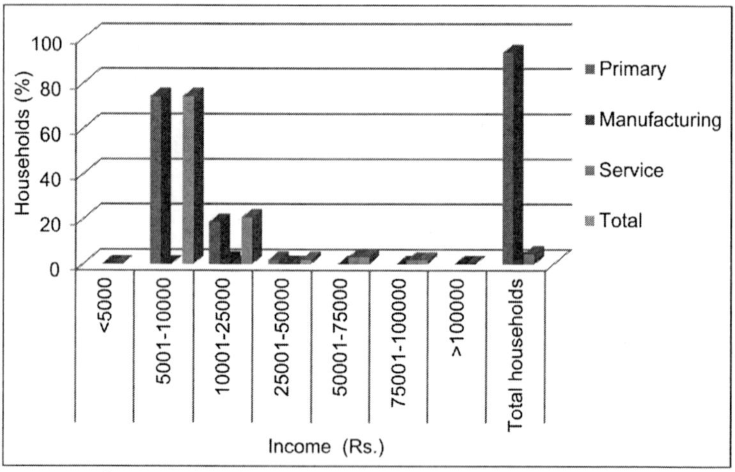

Fig. 5.8: Relation between Income and Occupation

5.2.4 Land Holding Capacity

The size of agricultural holding capacity depends on the climate and geographical conditions, partly upon the social institutions and laws, partly upon the techniques and methods of cultivation (Mamoria, 1995). The capacity of land holding of sampled households was stratified into marginal (<1.5 acre), small (1.51-2.00 acre), medium (2.01-2.50 acre) and high (>2.51 acre) and accordingly the studies were conducted and the results were analyzed, and is presented in table 5.18. It is clear that most of the sample households were found to be in medium category land holding capacity which accounted for 433 (49.32%) to the total sample households. The small category of land holding household were found to be quite less than median category, that is about 314 (35.76%) and the high and marginal land category were found to be less that is about 110 (12.53%) and 21 (2.39%). It is mentioned that the land owned by the households (forest villagers) were within the reserve forests wherein they were permitted to do agricultural operations to fulfill their livelihood needs as land agreement holder with Forest Department. Recently the Govt. of West Bengal took initiative to give their land right by issuing land patta of individual household especially for Schedule Tribe villagers (plate 5.4).

Table–5.18
Land Holding Capacity

S. No.	Forest village	Number of households with land holding (acre)				
		Marginal (<1.50)	**Small (1.51-2.00)**	**Medium (2.01-2.50)**	**High (>2.51)**	**Total House-holds**
1	Lehra	-	-	18	04	22
2	Suni	-	-	26	02	28
3	Garo Basti	-	-	61	11	72
4	Gadhadhar	-	-	45	18	63
5	Poro (N)	-	-	48	13	61
6	Nimati and Dabri	-	-	56	12	68
7	Gangutia H.A	03	52	-	-	55
8	Adma H.A	05	50	-	-	55
9	Raimatang H.A	04	51	-	-	55
10	Bhutri forest basti H.A	02	43	-	-	45
11	Gudamdabri	-	03	45	15	63
12	Chunabati H.A	03	51		-	54
13	Bhutiabasti	-	-	23	07	30
14	Sankosh	-	03	46	11	60
15	Lapraguri	-	-	34	13	47
16	Santrabari H.A	04	61	-	-	65
17	Balapara	-	-	31	04	35
	Total	**21**	**314**	**433**	**110**	**878**
	%	**2.39**	**35.76**	**49.32**	**12.53**	**100.00**

H.A=High Altitude, (Prepared based on field survey, 2017)

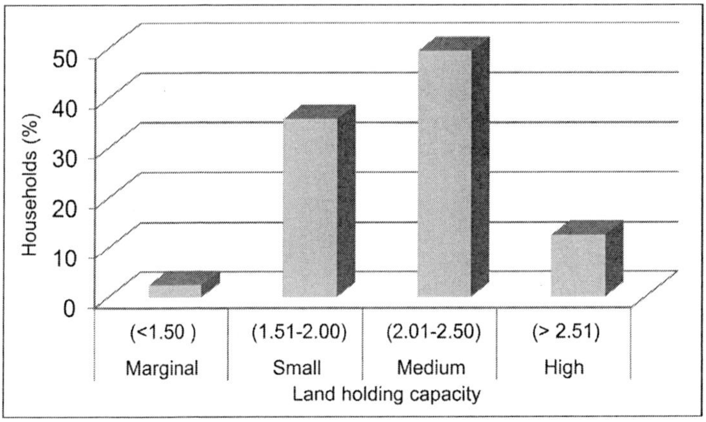

Fig. 5.9: Land Holding Capacity of Households

Table–5.19
Land Holding Status

S. No.	Forest village	Land holding status (Households-wise)			Uses of land (Households-wise)		Total sampled households
		Yes		No	For		
		Lease from Forest Dept.	Patta given from West Bengal Govt.		Agriculture	Agriculture & homestead	
1	Lehra	-	22 (100)	-	-	22	22 (100 %)
2	Suni	-	28 (100)	-	-	28	28 (100 %)
3	Garo Basti	42 (58.33)	30 (41.67)	-	-	72	72 (100 %)
4	Gadhadhar	-	63 (100)	-	-	63	63 (100 %)
5	Poro (N)	-	61 (100)	-	-	61	61(100 %)
6	Nimati and Dabri	-	68 (100)	-	-	68	68 (100 %)
7	Gangutia H.A	55 (100)	-	-	-	55	55 (100 %)
8	Adma H.A	55 (21.82)	-	-	-	55	55 (100 %)
9	Raimatang H.A	55 (41.82)	-	-	-	55	55 (100 %)
10	Bhutri F. basti H.A	45 (100)	-	-	-	45	45 (100 %)
11	Gudamdabri	-	63 (100)	-	-	63	63 (100 %)
12	Chunabati H.A	54 (100)	-	-	-	54	54 (100 %)
13	Bhutiabasti	30 (100)	-	-	-	30	30 (100 %)
14	Sankosh	60 (100)	-	-	-	60	60 (100 %)
15	Lapraguri	-	47 (100)	-	-	47	47 (100 %)
16	Santrabari H.A	65 (100)	-	-	-	65	65 (100 %)
17	Balapara	-	35 (100)	-	-	35	35 (100 %)
	Total	**461 (52.51%)**	**417 (47.49%)**	**-**	**-**	**878 (100%)**	**878 (100%)**

H.A=High Altitude, (Prepared based on field survey, 2017)

It is also noticed from the table–5.19 that 461 (52.51%) number of household don't have own proper document for the land and it is provided lease basis for agreement holder. The households who have proper document (land patta) have been accounted only for 417 (47.49%) number of total household.

5.2.5 The Livestock Situation and Asset

The forest villagers' livelihood security was closely associated with the agriculture and allied activities such as livestock farming, collection of fodders, collection of dry leaves, processing and sale of NTFPs etc. among these, the livestock raring and its assets are very important to support the economic impact. The animal population classified as adult cow, goats, pig and calves, their details were analysed and the results are given in table–5.20 below. Among various categories of livestock animals, the population of adult cow (both dry and milch) belongs to the top position which are found 44.78% (36.39 and 8.39) followed by pig, goat and claves where they have 27.88%, 17.62% and 9.72% respectively. It is depicted from the study that the cow and pig are most valuable animals and villagers were getting financial assistance by selling livestock within a regular interval of the year.

Table–5.20

Livestock Population (village-wise)

S.No.	Forest village	Adult Cow		Goat	Pig	Calves	Total
		Dry	Milch				
1	Lehra	15 (36.59)	6 (14.63)	13 (31.71)	-	7 (17.07)	41 (100)
2	Suni	19 (32.20)	8 (13.56)	23 (38.98)	-	9 (15.25)	59 (100)
3	Garo Basti	38 (30.89)	12 (9.76)	25 (20.33)	33 (26.83)	15 (12.20)	123
4	Gadhadhar	55 (34.81)	16 (10.17)	37 (23.42)	31 (19.62)	19 (12.02)	158 (100)
5	Poro (N)	46 (30.87)	14 (9.39)	32 (21.48)	41 (27.52)	16 (10.74)	149 (100)

6	Nimati and Dabri	75 (43.86)	18 (10.53)	34 (19.88)	24 (14.04)	20 (11.69)	171 (100)
7	Gangutia H.A	16 (24.24)	04 (6.06)	11 (16.67)	31 (46.97)	4 (6.06)	66 (100)
8	Adma H.A	21 (24.42)	05 (5.81)	17 (19.77)	37 (43.02)	6 (6.98)	86 (100)
9	Raimatang H.A	25 (27.78)	08 (8.89)	14 (15.56)	34 (37.78)	9 (9.99)	90 (100)
10	Bhutri forest basti H.A	35 (41.18)	06 (7.06)	11 (12.94)	26 (30.59)	7 (8.24)	85 (100)
11	Gudamdabri	51 (39.53)	12 (9.30)	16 (12.40)	36 (27.91)	14 (10.85)	129 (100)
12	Chunabati H.A	14 (23.33)	2 (3.33)	6 (10)	34 (56.67)	4 (6.67)	60 (100)
13	Bhutiabasti	25 (43.86)	-	9 (15.79)	23 (40.35)	-	57 (100)
14	Sankosh	71 (47.65)	10 (6.71)	23 (15.44)	33 (22.15)	12 (8.05)	149 (100)
15	Lapraguri	31 (41.33)	07 (9.33)	6 (7.99)	23 (30.67)	8 (10.67)	75 (100)
16	Santrabari H.A	42 (44.68)	5 (5.32)	7 (7.45)	35 (37.23)	5 (5.32)	94 (100)
17	Balapara	24 (36.92)	6 (9.23)	8 (12.31)	21 (32.31)	6 (9.23)	65 (100)
	Total	**603 (36.39%)**	**139 (8.39%)**	**292 (17.62%)**	**462 (27.88%)**	**161 (9.72%)**	**1657 (100%)**

H.A=High Altitude, (Prepared based on field survey, 2017)

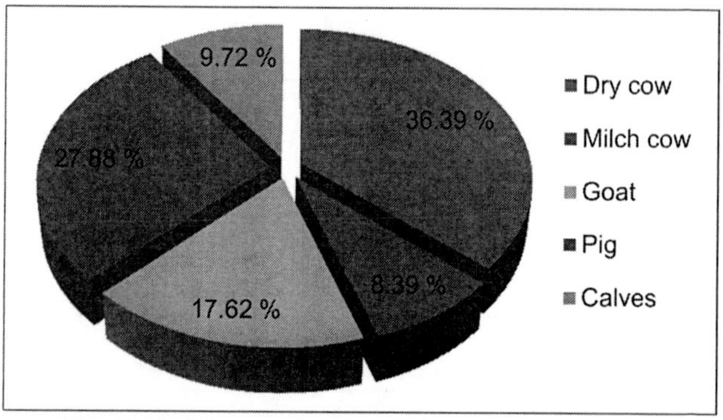

Fig. 5.10: Livestock Population of Households

5.2.6 Agricultural Pattern

In high land forest villages, mainly Adma, Chunabat, Santrabari, Gangutia, Bhutia basti, Raimatang and Bhutri village, step and shifting cultivation is being practiced (plate–5.5 and 5.6). The step is a technique of growing crops on sides of hill slope or by planting on terraces built into the slope though it is labour-intensive, the method has been deployed effectively to increase arable land in variable terrains and to decrease soil erosion and water loss (Bhattacharya et al., 2015). The shifting cultivation is an age-old agricultural practice among the tribes. It means the cultivation of a plot of land for temporary period and then leaves it fallow. It consists of clearing the forest slopes, burning the fallen trees and bushes, and broadcasting the seed in the ash covered soil (Hasnain, 2005). It is also reported that 32% of the states' geographical area (5316 sq.km) is under shifting cultivation (Tripathi, 2005). In these forest villages, the common cultivable edible plants are rice, maize, potato, raisakh, green chili, tomato, squash, leaf mustard, banana, pomelo, areca nut, large cardamom etc. In this connection it is reported that vegetable production was comparatively more environment friendly than food grains production on hill farms of Nepal (Pant & Pandey, 1999). Areca nut is the main cash crop of this area and an important economic source of horticulture farming. The households of forest villages used organic farming and cow-dung as manure. Although some pesticide and fertilizer is added to the fields as there is presence of pest attack in the agricultural areas.

Most of the houses in hill forest villages have cultivable lands adjacent to the houses and horticulture farming is done there. Since agricultural production is one and only prime economic sources of the villages hence they used to sell the foods, mainly vegetables in the local markets i.e. in Kalchini, Madarihat, Hamiltongaunj, Rajabhatkhawa markets.

The intensive subsistence farming is being practiced by the (plate–5.7) villages of low lying area and mainly they are Lera, Suni, Gadhadhar, Poro (N), Gudhamdabri, Garo basti,

Lapraguri, Nimti and Dabri, Sankosh, and Balapara village. The intensive subsistence agriculture is a method of growing food crops on even terraces of inside and nearby forests and the method has been employed effectively to fulfill self-requirements of the people of the area. The size of land holdings is small, use of maximum manual labour and traditional simple farm implements etc. are observed in this farming. The common cultivable edible plants are paddy, white, maize, potato, green chili, tomato, mustard, banana, areca nut, large cardamom, brinjal, laddish finger etc. Now villagers' used pesticide and fertilizer to get more agricultural production. The excess food and vegetable used to sell in the local markets periodically i.e. in Kalchini, Nimti bazar, Hamiltongaunj, Kumargaunj markets.

In conclusion, it can be said that, physical site and other natural environment directly and indirectly controlled livelihood entity of villagers. The forest households has been lived and adopted automatically to survive in this forest environment. Besides other important aspects of social customs and traits related to local ecology has been depicted here. It is noticed that there are some differences of agriculture, social customs and other anthropogenic activities between high altitude and low lying reside villagers; core area and fringe area forest villagers. The land use pattern, food habit, fuel used, house type, water storage facilities, type of NTFPs collection of household of high altitude area is differ from low-lying household. In the other side, difference also observed in land holding capacity, income pattern, occupational structure, livestock rearing and agriculture practices. In high land forest villages, mainly Adma, Chunabat, Santrabari, Gangutia, Bhutia basti, Raimatang and Bhutri village, step and shifting cultivation has been followed due to undulating and rugged surface feature. On the other hand the intensive subsistence farming is being followed by the villages of low lying area villagers i.e. in Lera, Suni, Gadhadhar, Poro (N), Gudhamdabri, Garo basti, Lapraguri, Nimti and Dabri, Sankosh, and Balapara village due to huge even land, fertile soil and available water facilities. The pipe line and spring water is the only source of water for high altitude villagers' but in low-lying villagers' are used well and tube well to fulfil demand of water. Finally it is depicted that although villagers adapted to their surrounding environment but income, education, housing, culture etc of high altitude households are comparatively fall behind than low lying households, and it is due to lack of job opportunity, education institution, agricultural land, accessibility of the high altitude villagers.

6 Chapter — Villager's Dependency on Forest Resource

6.1 Introduction

In general, forest villagers lived in fringe and interior of forests areas with fairly and dense forest cover. The forests of this study area is not only a source of employment and income for but also it provides so many Non Timber Forest Products (NTFPs) to the local forest villagers and fringe people which make forest an great contributor to the rural economy. It also plays an important role to get shape of villagers separate social and cultural life. Villagers living in forest depend upon forest for a variety of goods and livelihood needs. These includes collection of edible fruits, tubers, roots flowers and leaves for food and medicines; firewood for both selling and cooking purpose; wood materials for agricultural implements, house construction and fencing; fodder (grass and leave) for livestock and grazing of livestock in forests; and collection of a range of marketable Non-Timber Forest Products (NTFPs).

Several NTFPs were found to be extracted in the different study sites of KFD of Burdwan District, 23 major types of Non-Timber Forest Products (NTFPs) were recorded during survey at the present observation which includes different forms of grass, dyes, honey, oil, wax, resin, gum, bamboo, broom, food items (leaf, fruit, seed, herb, stem), paper, basket, cotton, brush, ornamental, worship, leaves (sal, kendu, datepalm), marriage rituals, sap and flour (Bauri, et al., 2015). It is observed that more than 54% of total families are sustaining livelihoods from sell of Non-Timber Forest Products (NTFPs). In addition, poor and marginalized villagers use small timber for edible roots and tubers, thatch for roof; house construction; mushrooms, leaf litter and leaves, fruits and flowers as alternative of staple foods especially during lean seasons; medicinal plants for healing etc. (Das, 2005). Here the activities of forests and dependency of villagers has been analyzed and summarized on the basis of data and information collected from the field survey of sample households of flowers, tubers, roots and leaves for food and medicines; firewood for own use cooking and selling purpose in the market; timber and branches for agricultural implements, house construction and fencing; fodder (grass and leave) for livestock and grazing of livestock in forests; and collection of a range of marketable non-timber forest products.

6.2 Forest as Source of Non-Timber Forest Products (NTFPs)

The Non-Timber Forest Product (NTFPs) has been defined, all biological materials, other than timber, which are being collected from forests for human use purpose. It may be included firewood (which is not timber), fodder (grass and leave), fruits, flowers, tubers, roots and dry leaves, green leaves for fuel, food and medicines; resins, roots, herbal plants, gums, honey. According to Shvidenko et al. (2005), Non-wood forest products (NTFPs) are defined as goods of biological origin other than timber wood, obtained from forests, other forests land, and from trees outside the forests. Ii can be classified in a number of broad categories based on their end use: fodder for domestic animals; medicines; perfumes and cosmetics; edible products; colorants; utensils, and construction materials; handicrafts, ornamentals; and exudates like gums, resins, and latex. Overall, it plays a vital role in the everyday life and social well-being of hundreds of millions of people worldwide besides in the national economies of many countries (Shvidenko et al., 2005). The type, number and nature of NTFPs vary from one geographical area to another based on the physical conditions. Considering the socio-cultural importance of NTFPs in forests livelihoods, Wickens (1991) believes that NTFPs are all the biological components that may be turned out from natural ecosystems, managed plantations, etc. and be marketed, be used within the household, or have cultural, religious and social importance. The NTFPs have an important role in forests livelihoods in the south-western part of the State (Tewari and Campbell, 1995). The NTFPs have a great importance within the household economy of forest villagers. In India over 50 million villagers are depends on NTFPs for cash income and other subsistence (Hegde et al., 1996). The poor condition of road and transportation system, distance among remote forest villages and the local market and service centre, limited availability of manufacturing and consuming products are reasons for the high levels of dependence on NTFPs of forest inhabitants. It is because of these reasons; the importance of NTFPs for household needs in the interior forest villages of Alipurduar District is distinctly higher. So forest villagers are highly depending on the collection of NTFPs for their domestic as well as commercial purpose. In this connection it can be mentioned that as per the forest working plan prescription, collection of Minor Forest Produces (MFPs) or Non-Timber Forest Produce (NTFPs) of any kind is allowed from any part of the forests but no quarry for sand, gravel and stone should be made without previous approval of the Divisional Forest Officer or Local Range or Beat officer. There are many NTFPs available in the forests of this study area but no systematic study is conducted regarding the quantity of NTFP available and its regeneration status. There is no definite extraction procedure adopted for its collection. Very easily forest villagers go inside the forest and collect NTFPs according to their collection capacity and demand. The importance of NTFPs may be classified in to two categories; i. NTFPs for household needs for livelihood, ii. NTFPs for commercial or marketing purposes by which villagers earning money to fulfil their livelihood demand. The some important NTFPs which have been collected by villagers are bamboo, pan leaves, dry branches, dry leaves, purundi fruits, naglata, lycopodium stick, totola pods and seeds, lali fruit, odal fruit, fern bud, cane, cane fruits, simul floss and floral axis, mahogony floral axis, broom stick, golden and sponge mushrooms and thatch etc. Besides, there are some medicinal plants which are being seldom used by villagers to recover diseases such as fever, bone and join fracture, stomach, skin diseases and insect bite etc.

Based on the commercial and domestic importance, details of the amount of NTFPs collection, market value, availability as well as valuable NTFPs are given in the table below (table–6.1).

Respondents collect their fruits, fodder, firewood, branches and leaves from surrounding forest. However more than half of the villagers are entirely dependent on NTFPs of forest, while others associates with agricultural and horticulture practice in their own agreement land or engage as agricultural labour and tea garden wage labourers. Besides, everyday, at least one person from each household goes into the contiguous forest to collect green fodder for livestock, leaves, dry branches as well as firewood for fuel and other purpose. Villagers also employed to collect cane, cane fruits, bark, bamboo, roots, leaves of sal, teak, simul, gamaree for commercial purpose as well as own consumption during whole of the year. Each household picked up 360 to 400 sack of leaf per year. Villagers are engaged whole of the year to collect green leaves mainly for livestock rearing. Dry leaves are mostly used as kitchen fuel purpose and very little for other purpose that is to make fencing and roof shading. Household earned between Rs. 900.00 to 1200.00 by selling cane and cane fruits per month, Rs. 200.00 to 250.00 by climber, Rs. 160.00 to 190.00 by grass, Rs. 240.00 to 300.00 by shrub, Rs. 150.00 to 190.00 by bamboo, Rs. 1000.00-to 1300.00 by firewood (table–6.1). Villagers also collected different kinds of fruit and flowers which are also used for households needs as well as selling purpose through which they could earned extra supporting amount by selling Haritaki, jam, Purundi from which they earned Rs. 8.00 to 10.00 per kg by Purundi, Rs.35.00 to 40.00 per kg by jam, Rs. 25.00 to 35.00 per kg by Haritaki and Rs. 35 per barra of Pan leaves.

Table–6.1
Some Important NTFPs Collected by Sampled Households

Name/Nature of Plants	Name of NTFPs	Season	Households use	Commercial use	Quantity of NTFPs Collected in a year/ household	Monetary value
Fire wood	Benches	All season	Yes	Yes	1800 kg to 2000 kg	Rs.10/kg
Tree	Leaf	Winter	Yes	No	360 to 400 sack	-
Bamboo	Stem	All season	Yes	Yes	20 to 25 piece	Rs. 90/ba
Grass/ fodder	Stem	All season	Yes	Yes	400 kg to 450 kg	Rs. 5/kg
Haritaki	Fruit	Summer	Yes	Yes	16 kg to 20 kg	Rs.20/kg
Shrub	Benches	Winter	Yes	Yes	360 kg to 400 kg	Rs.8/kg
Climber	Stem	Winter	Yes	Yes	300 kg to 350 kg	Rs.8/kg
Golden and Sponge Mushroom	Stem & flower	Winter	Yes	Yes	25 kg to 30 kg	Rs. 25/kg
Jam	Fruit	Summer	Yes	Yes	18 kg to 20 kg	Rs.25/kg
Cane	Stem fruit	All season	Yes	Yes	250 kg to 300 kg 15 kg to 18 kg	Rs. 45/kg Rs.10/kg
Orchards	Stem & flower	Winter	Yes	Yes	20 kg to 25 kg	Rs.12/kg
Pan	Leaves	Summer	Yes	Yes	25 to 30 barra	Rs35/barra
Medicinal Plants	Leaf & Stem	All season	Yes	No	5 kg to 7 kg	-
Purundi	Fruits	Summer	Yes		12 kg to 15 kg	Rs8/kg

(Prepared based on field survey, 2017)

6.2.1 Uses of Medicinal Plants

From field study total 121 numbers of species of plants were found to be used as medicinal purpose by forest villagers of Alipurduar District. The experience and uses of medicinal plants are being transmitted traditionally for first aid medicine of treatment from generation to generation. Medicinal plants are another set of important NTFPs that have been utilizing by human beings especially tribal people. A total 14 species of herbal plants belonging to 11 families were recorded that normally used to cure different ailments in the day-to-day life (Sarmah, 2010). The table–6.2 (Appendix D) of plants is arranged according to their scientific name, local name, parts used and medicinal uses for which disease. Among different plant parts used for the preparation of medicine (table–6.2), such as leaves of different trees were found to be the most frequently used plant parts to remove the diseases like as acalypha indica leaf for nasal and nounds, justicia adhatoda L. for chronic bronchitis, cough and cold, lippia alba (Mill.) for skin disease; roots of crinum amoenum were used to remove jaundice and diarrhea, glycosmis arborea DC for fever, hepatopathy, eczema, skin diseases, wounds, liver disorder; whole plant of ammannia baccifera for fever and child diseases, B. Ammannioides for bone fracture and menstrual disorder, bark of acacia catechu for stomachache, gmelina arborea for vomiting and Diarrhea etc. Besides rhizome, fruit, latex, flower, flower bud, root bark and stem of different trees also were used to remove various diseases.

6.3 Forest as Source of Fodder

The fodder is a prime food item of livestock and livestock rearing is depends on availability of fodder. In this study livestock rearing considered as an important sector and source of economy of forest villagers. The livestock is feeding and maintaining for milk, cash income by selling of old cow, calf, sheep, pig and goats, and also to provide organic manure for agricultural fields. The feeding, maintenance and rearing of livestock is impracticable without fodder which is consuming from the forest. In this connection it is reported that about 60% of buffaloes and cattle and 90% of goats and sheep populations' depended on forests for green fodder (Nayak, 2001). The quantity of fodder collecting and consuming from the nearby forest depends on number, size and variety of livestock, nature of feeding as well as quantity of fodder availability from the agricultural side. The livestock are both stall feed and open grazed. The buffalos are mostly stall feed while goats, cows and sheep are grazed openly.

The villagers obtained green and dry fodder from various sources and fed per day in summar and rainy season has been given in table–6.3, where average of each village has been calculated. It is seen that lowest per day quantity of dry fodder fed to livestock was 1.24 kg ± 0.85 kg which is noticed in Chunabati village where small size of the land holding capacity observed. While it was 4.54 kg ± 0.35 kg is recorded in Gadhadhar village which is maximum due to advantages low lying and plain area location as well as medium size of land holding capacity. The total quantity of dry fodder fed was collected from own agricultural lands and villagers fed by-products of different crops as dry fodder to animals. The lowest quantity (average) of green grass fodder and green leaves fodder obtained from field was 1.24 kg ± 0.89 kg and 0.92 kg ± 0.21kg per day which is noticed in Suni and Raimatang village respectively. While, the highest quantity (average) of green fodder of grass and leaves was 2.37 kg ± 0.65 kg and 2.55 kg ± 0.35 kg per day which is observed in Lehra and Garo Basti village respectively.

The lowest average quantity of green fodder of leaves received from forest was 2.35 kg ± 0.65 kg per day and 3.45 kg ± 0.82 kg per day in case of grass which is identified in Poro and Garo Basti village. The highest average quantity of green fodder of grass and leaves acquired from forests was 5.49 kg ± 0.39 kg and 5.47 kg ± 0.31 kg per day which has been found in Lehra and Adma village. A comparative line graph is (Fig. 6.1) shown the per day fodder collection of forest villagers between dry fodder from field and green fodder from forest in summer season. It is observed that the green fodder

Table–6.3

Fodder Collections in Summer Season for Livestock (kg/day)

S.No.	Forest village	Dry fodder		Green fodder			
		From field	From forest	From field		From forest	
		Grass	Leaves and Grass	Leaves	Grass	Leaves	Grass
1	Suni	2.23 ± 0.25	-	1.84 ± 0.47	1.24 ± 0.89	3.45 ± 0.93	4.38 ± 0.37
2	Garo Basti	3.42 ± 0.45	-	2.55 ± 0.35	1.57 ± 0.67	3.12 ± 0.25	3.45 ± 0.82
3	Lehra	3.55 ± 0.31	-	1.57 ± 0.75	2.37 ± 0.65	3.53 ± 0.89	5.49 ± 0.39
4	Nimati & Dabri	3.58 ± 0.15	-	1.57 ± 0.54	1.34 ± 0.56	3.52 ± 0.69	4.56 ± 0.25
5	Poro (N)	4.35 ± 0.32	-	-	-	2.35 ± 0.65	4.49 ± 0.85
6	Gadhadhar	4.54 ± 0.35	-	1.65 ± 0.87	2.27 ± 0.53	2.54 ± 0.38	3.56 ± 0.75
7	Gangutia H.A	2.56 ± 0.25	-	-	-	4.45 ± 0.32	4.78 ± 0.65
8	Adma H.A	2.67 ± 0.46	-	-	-	5.47± 0.31	4.89 ± 0.88
9	Chunabati H.A	1.24 ± 0.85	-	-	-	5.34 ± 0.33	4.66 ± 0.77
10	Bhutri F.basti H.A	1.56 ± 0.75	-	-	-	4.23 ± 0.69	3.59 ± 0.15
11	Raimatang H.A	2.23 ± 0.55	-	0.92 ± 0.21	1.26 ± 0.88	3.45 ± 0.66	5.34 ± 0.67
12	Santrabari H.A	2.67 ± 0.73	-	-	-	3.17± 0.95	4.78 ± 0.38
13	Gudamdabri	3.78 ± 0.38	-	-	-	4.56 ± 0.73	4.57 ± 0.25
14	Bhutiabasti	1.45 ± 0.37	-	-	-	4.12 ± 0.61	4.67 ± 0.81
15	Sankosh	3.35 ± 0.39	-	1.79 ± 0.27	1.62 ± 0.55	3.56 ± 0.71	4.43 ± 0.43
16	Balapara	3.59 ± 0.21	-	1.45 ± 0.31	1.29 ± 0.47	3.59 ± 0.37	5.23 ± 0.31
17	Lapraguri	2.45 ± 0.28	-	1.25 ± 0.39	1.34 ± 0.95	4.33 ± 0.64	3.65 ± 0.29
	Average	**2.89 ± 0.41**		**0.86 ± 0.24**	**0.84 ± 0.36**	**3.81 ± 0.59**	**4.50 ± 0.53**

N.B: (Mean ± SD), H.A=High altitude location.
H.A=High Altitude, (Prepared based on field survey, 2017)

line is located over the dry fodder line which referred that villagers collected and depended more on green forest fodder of forest than dry fodder in summer. The highest quantity of green fodder collection was 5.18 kg per day which is found in Adma and the lowest quantity obtained was 2.51 kg per day which is found in Gadhadhar village respectively.

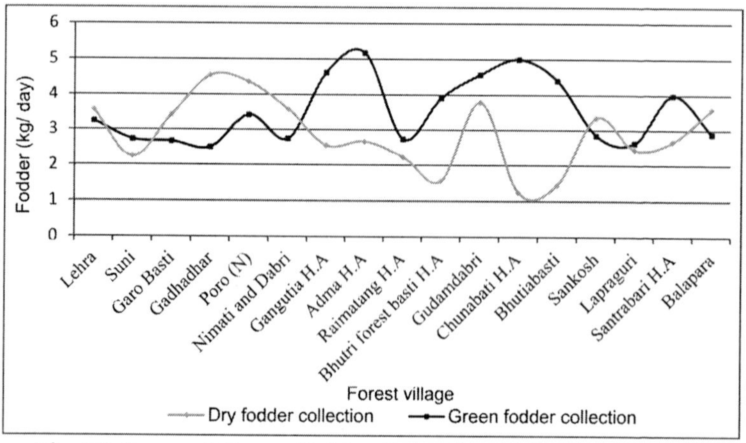

Fig. 6.1: Dry and Green Fodder Collection in Summer Season for Livestock (kg/day)

The fodder collection in winter season is presented in table 6.4, the analysis expressed that villagers collecting and feeding of dry fodder quantity is comparatively less in winter than summer season. The average highest quantity of dry fodder fed of grass was 4.98 kg ± 0.62 kg per day and lowest quantity was 1.78 kg ± 0.91 kg which is observed in Poro (N) and Chunabati respectively.

The per day maximum and minimum quantity of green fodder of leaves from field was 2.47 kg ± 0.17 kg and 0.76 kg ± 0.12 kg of Raimatang and Garo Basti respectively but in case of green grass fodder it was 2.27 kg ± 0.45 kg in Lehra and 1.14 kg ± 0.55 kg in Suni village. However it is also noticed that per day highest and lowest quantity of green fodder consumption of leaves from forest was 5.37 kg ± 0.21 kg and 2.24 kg ± 0.23 kg of Adma and Gadhadhar village respectively where as in case of green grass fodder it was 4.89 kg ± 0.49 kg in Lehra village and 2.95 kg ± 0.72 kg in Garo Basti. From

Table–6.4
Fodder Collection in Winter Season for Livestock (kg/day)

S.No.	Forest village	Dry fodder		Green fodder			
		From field	From forest	From field		From forest	
		Grass	Leaves and Grass	Leaves	Grass	Leaves	Grass
1	Suni	2.93 ± 0.65	-	1.51 ± 0.27	1.14 ± 0.55	3.15 ± 0.43	4.18 ± 0.32
2	Lehra	3.98 ± 0.39	-	1.37 ± 0.35	2.27 ± 0.45	3.13 ± 0.39	4.89 ± 0.49
3	Gadhadhar	4.94 ± 0.85	-	1.73 ± 0.52	2.21 ± 0.33	2.24 ± 0.23	3.26 ± 0.65
4	Garo Basti	3.88 ± 0.95	-	2.47 ± 0.17	1.47 ± 0.47	3.10 ± 0.15	2.95 ± 0.72
5	Nimati and Dabri	3.89 ± 0.65	-	1.47 ± 0.36	1.31 ± 0.54	3.32 ± 0.39	4.26 ± 0.21
6	Poro (N)	4.98 ± 0.62	-	-	-	2.25 ± 0.45	4.29 ± 0.15
7	Gangutia H.A	2.86 ± 0.35	-	-	-	4.35 ± 0.22	4.29 ± 0.35
8	Adma H.A	2.87 ± 0.56	-	-	-	5.37± 0.21	4.19 ± 0.78
9	Raimatang H.A	2.73 ± 0.82	-	0.76 ± 0.12	1.23 ± 0.37	3.25 ± 0.16	4.74 ± 0.47
10	Bhutri forest basti H.A	1.88 ± 0.87	-	-	-	4.21 ± 0.39	3.19 ± 0.25
11	Santrabari H.A	2.81 ± 0.82	-	-	-	2.97± 0.87	4.41 ± 0.48
12	Gudamdabri	3.93 ± 0.89	-	-	-	4.46 ± 0.63	3.97 ± 0.75
13	Chunabati H.A	1.78 ± 0.91	-	-	-	4.74 ± 0.53	3.86 ± 0.87
14	Balapara	3.90 ± 0.45	-	1.41 ± 0.21	1.19 ± 0.27	3.21 ± 0.33	4.73 ± 0.42
15	Sankosh	3.69 ± 0.73	-	1.69 ± 0.17	1.52 ± 0.51	3.56 ± 0.71	4.13 ± 0.33
16	Lapraguri	2.96 ± 0.78	-	1.21 ± 0.31	1.32 ± 0.75	3.93 ± 0.74	3.11 ± 0.19
17	Bhutiabasti	1.79 ± 0.57	-	-	-	3.82 ± 0.51	4.17 ± 0.21
	Average	**3.28 ± 0.69**		**1.51 ± 0.28**	**1.52 ± 0.47**	**3.59 ± 0.43**	**4.04 ± 0.45**

N.B: (Mean ± SD), H.A= High altitude location.
(Calculated based on field survey, 2017)

the above discussion it is acquired that amount of green leaves and grass collected from forests was significantly higher than that of leaves and grass obtained from field and other sources. However, field and owned land was the only source of dry fodder of villages under study while forest is the one and only source of green fodder for livestock. It is also identified that per day fodder collection of leaves and grass is more in summer comparatively than winter season. The graph (Fig. 6.2) shows the per day fodder (kg) collection of forest villagers where it is observed that the green fodder line is raised over the dry fodder line except Lehra, Suni, Garo and Gadhadhar village which indicated that villagers are depend more on green forest fodder of forest than dry fodder in winter. The average highest quantity of green fodder (leaves & grass) collection was 4.78 kg per day which is found in Adma and the lowest collection obtained was 2.36 kg per day which is found in Gadhadhar village respectively.

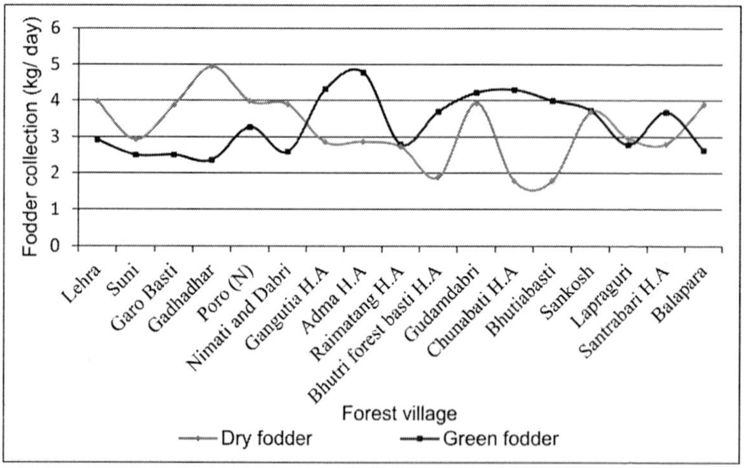

Fig. 6.2: Dry and Green Fodder Collection in Winter Season for Livestock (kg/day)

6.3.1 Time Spent and Distance Covered for Collection of Fodder from the Forest

The villagers moved toward nearest surroundings for dry and green fodder of animals which include uncultivated land, waste land, common land, pastures and forests. Where limited quantity of dry and green fodder is collected from agricultural field, common open land, and waste land; there green leaves, twigs and grasses are collected from forests. The forest is the prime source of green fodder and almost major portion of requirement obtained from the forests. Even forests has been utilized whole of the year and fodder is collected regularly for various purpose. The time spent of fodder consumption from the nearby forest has been considered in hours for per day and the number of days in a year. During calculation of the time of spent, hours, days have been considered which is given for fodder collection (table–6.5).

The average maximum and minimum time spent in collection of dry fodder from field is about 2.36 hrs ± 0.58 hrs and 1.19 hrs ± 0.57 hrs per day of households of Lapraguri and Raimatang villagers respectively and the average maximum and minimum days spent is about, 98.23 ± 3.89 days and 91.23 ± 3.47 days in a year which is identified in villagers of Balapara and Nimati and Dabri. Villagers were following both two sector of field and forest for green fodder. The average maximum and minimum time spent to the field is found in Garo Basti (1.10 ± 0.27 hrs/day) and Lehra (0.37 ± 0.31 hrs/day) villages as well as their average maximum and minimum day spent is observed about 97.32 ± 2.97 days/year (Garo Basti) and 81.23 ± 4.51 days/year (Lehra). Most of the green fodder of livestock requirement is being fulfilled from forest, so naturally they were spending maximum time to the forests than field to collect green fodder. The table 6.5 shows that The average maximum and minimum time spent to the forest in collection of green fodder is about 2.59 ± 0.36 hrs and 2.10 ± 0.14 hrs per day which identified in the household of Santrabari and Garo Basti village. And the average maximum and minimum day spent in collection of green fodder is about 324.43 ± 3.87 days/year and 226.24 ± 2.65 days/year which is found in Chunabati and Gadhadhar village.

Table–6.5
Time Spent to Collect Fodder

S.No.	Forest village	For Dry fodder		For Green fodder			
		Time spent to field	Time spent to field	Time spent to field		Time spent to field	
		hrs/day	days/year	hrs/day	days/year	hrs/day	days/year
1	Lehra	1.54 ± 0.59	94.23 ± 2.45	0.37 ± 0.31	81.23 ± 4.51	2.11 ± 0.23	275.45 ± 3.41
2	Suni	1.56 ± 0.53	92.43 ± 2.83	0.53 ± 0.24	84.53 ± 3.85	2.15 ± 0.11	297.23 ± 3.31
3	Garo Basti	2.12 ± 0.45	96.13 ± 3.95	1.10 ± 0.27	97.32 ± 2.97	2.10 ± 0.14	299.12 ± 3.42
4	Gadhadhar	2.14 ± 0.55	91.83 ± 2.56	0.73 ± 0.32	89.42 ± 3.71	2.21 ± 0.13	226.24 ± 2.65
5	Poro (N)	1.58 ± 0.42	95.23 ± 2.18	-	-	2.15 ± 0.41	306.31 ± 2.15
6	Nimati and Dabri	1.29 ± 0.45	91.23 ± 3.47	0.67 ± 0.33	85.56 ± 3.64	2.21 ± 0.31	302.34 ± 3.21
7	Gangutia H.A	-	-	-	-	2.35 ± 0.23	312.22 ± 3.39
8	Adma H.A	-	-	-	-	2.37± 0.25	321.31 ± 3.75
9	Raimatang H.A	1.19 ± 0.57	95.23 ± 3.28	0.47 ± 0.23	82.52 ± 3.34	2.25 ± 0.19	298.41 ± 3.43
10	Bhutri forest basti H.A	-		-	-	2.21 ± 0.49	310.71 ± 4.15
11	Gudamdabri	2.23 ± 0.56	96.23 ± 2.85	0.45 ± 0.33	84.57 ± 3.24	2.56 ± 0.47	286.33 ± 2.75
12	Chunabati H.A	-	-	-	-	2.54 ± 0.56	324.43 ± 3.87
13	Bhutiabasti	-	-	-	-	2.52 ± 0.52	308.47 ± 3.21
14	Sankosh	2.29 ± 0.52	97.23 ± 2.86	0.63 ± 0.47	81.32 ± 4.71	2.56 ± 0.54	289.89 ± 4.53
15	Lapraguri	2.36 ± 0.58	93.23 ± 3.90	1.00 ± 0.42	88.54 ± 2.85	2.53 ± 0.46	267.67 ± 3.19
16	Santrabari H.A	-	-	-	-	2.59 ± 0.36	301.23 ± 4.48
17	Balapara	1.21 ± 0.45	98.23 ± 3.89	0.71 ± 0.23	87.63 ± 3.42	2.21 ± 0.38	286.42 ± 3.42
	Average	**1.15 ± 0.45**	**61.25 ± 5.70**	**0.67 ± 0.32**	**86.24 ± 3.62**	**2.33 ± 0.34**	**294.93 ± 3.43**

N.B: (Mean ± SD), H.A= High altitude location.
(Calculated based on field survey, 2017)

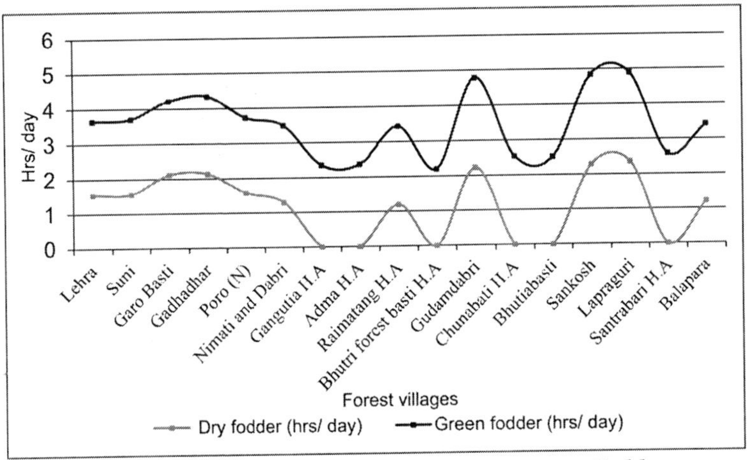

Fig. 6.3: Time Spent to Collect Dry and Green Fodder

The Fig. 6.3 shows that the line graph of time spent to the forest for green fodder is located over time spent for dry fodder from field which identified that villagers are very much depend on surrounding forest than field for fodder. There is a variation in distance covered in bringing dry fodder and green fodder from the field and forests. The table 6.6 shows that the average maximum and minimum distance covered in collection of dry fodder from field is about 2.96 ± 0.48 km/day and 1.08 ± 0.49 km/day of households of Lapraguri and Lehra villagers respectively. And the average maximum and minimum distance covered from forest is about, 284.20 ±7.56 km/ year and 101.52 ± 4.53 km/year which is identified in Balapara and Lehra villagers. The average maximum and minimum distance covered in collection of green fodder from field is about 2.86 ± 0.62 km/day and 1.07 ± 0.43 km/day which depicted in the household of Gadhadhar and Lehra village and it is 244.47 ± 9.65 km/year and 86.67 ± 5.45 km/year in the household of Balapara and Lehra villagers respectively. The average maximum and minimum distance covered in collection of green fodder from forests is about 1.04 ± 0.15 km/day and 0.21 ± 0.12 km/day which identified in the household of Gadhadhar and Bhutri forest basti village and it is 271.70 ± 11.46 km/year and 65.10 ± 4.37 km/year in the household of Gudamdabri and Bhutri forest basti respectively.

Table–6.6
Distance Covered to Collect Fodder

S.No.	Forest village	For Dry fodder		For Green fodder			
		Distance covered from field	Distance covered from field	Distance covered from field		Distance covered from field	
		km/day	km/year	km/day	km/year	km/day	km/year
1	Lehra	1.08 ± 0.49	101.52 ±4.53	1.07 ± 0.43	86.67 ± 5.45	0.75 ± 0.12	206.25 ± 13.13
2	Suni	1.23 ± 0.52	113.16 ±5.34	1.21 ± 0.65	101.64 ± 6.55	0.72 ± 0.10	213.84 ± 11.21
3	Garo Basti	1.48 ± 0.53	142.08 ±9.21	1.37 ± 0.17	132.89 ± 5.47	0.50 ± 0.11	149.50 ± 6.51
4	Gadhadhar	2.11 ± 0.85	192.01 ±3.31	2.11 ± 0.52	187.79 ± 8.33	1.04 ± 0.15	235.04 ± 12.44
5	Poro (N)	2.48 ± 0.93	235.60 ±4.51	-	-	0.25 ± 0.12	76.50 ± 4.13
6	Nimati & Dabri	1.59 ± 0.22	144.69 ±7.44	1.57 ± 0.55	133.45 ± 4.54	0.32 ± 0.16	96.64 ± 6.22
7	Gangutia H.A	-	-	-	-	0.35 ± 0.12	109.20 ± 8.32
8	Adma H.A	-		-	-	0.37± 0.11	118.77 ± 6.39
9	Raimatang H.A	2.73 ± 0.52	259.35 ±9.23	2.56 ± 0.19	209.92±10.34	0.25 ± 0.16	74.5 ± 4.35
10	Bhutri F. basti H.A	-	-	-	-	0.21 ± 0.12	65.10 ± 4.37
11	Gudamdabri	2.93 ± 0.69	281.28 ±5.73	2.86 ± 0.62	240.24 ± 9.76	0.95 ± 0.10	271.70 ± 11.46
12	Chunabati H.A	-	-	-	-	0.74 ± 0.13	239.76 ± 8.35
13	Bhutiabasti	-	-	-	-	0.82 ± 0.12	252.56 ± 10.14
14	Sankosh	2.69 ± 0.43	260.93 ±6.39	2.66 ± 0.19	215.46 ± 8.53	0.70 ± 0.14	202.30 ± 9.42
15	Lapraguri	2.96 ± 0.48	275.28 ±4.43	2.76 ± 0.58	242.88 ± 5.59	0.65 ± 0.14	173.55 ± 6.24
16	Santrabari H.A	-	-	-	-	0.55 ± 0.17	165.55 ± 8.23
17	Balapara	2.90 ± 0.42	284.20 ±7.56	2.81 ± 0.29	244.47 ± 9.65	0.80 ± 0.13	228.80 ± 12.31
	Average	**2.13 ± 0.57**	**208.19 ± 6.15**	**2.09 ± 0.42**	**179.54 ± 7.42**	**0.59 ± 0.13**	**169.39 ± 8.42**

N.B: (Mean ± SD), H.A=High altitude location.
H.A=High Altitude, (Prepared based on field survey, 2017)

6.4 Forest as Source of Fuel Wood

Forest villagers are collecting fire wood as prime NTFP from nearby forest to fulfil households need. Interestingly, all villagers are entirely dependent on forest wood for fuel. It is reported that the use of trees by small farmers in two villages in Eastern Gujarat where the direct uses of trees identified were fuel-wood, agricultural implements and house construction and providing a valuable additional source of income by sale. Households have become self-sufficient in fuel wood thereby saving of time spent on fuel wood collection (Conroy, 1994). A study based on information gathered from 743 households spread over eight states of India, reported that bulk of the rural energy (75.77 per cent) requirements was met by forest wood fuel (Prasad et al., 1999). Fuel wood is generally used for cooking of foods, preparation of food for animals and to keep the houses warm during winter season especially it is found among high altitude sited villages. The consumption of fire wood is found to different amount throughout the season. The table–6.7 gives an idea of fuel wood consumption of average of villages of household per day and per month during summer and winter season separately.

It is clear that villagers use substantially more quantity of fuel wood during winters than summer season. Thereafter consumption of fire wood recorded higher during winter season than summer. The average per day consumption of fire wood of each household was 3.99 ± 0.67 kg in winter and 3.29 ± 0.68 kg in summer. In winter the per day minimum and maximum quantity of fire wood consumption was 3.23 ± 0.98 kg and 4.96 ± 0.59 kg found in Lehra and Sankosh respectively where in summer it was 2.78 ± 0.81 kg and 4.03 ± 0.72 kg in Lapraguri and Adma. The consumption of fire wood per household per month recorded maximum of 145.68 ± 16.21 kg in Adma village and minimum 96.91 ± 29.42 kg in Lehra village in winter which was 120.91 ± 21.63 kg in Adma and 83.43 ± 24.31 kg in Lapraguri in summer season. In high altitude area of the Buxa hill where per household per day

Table–6.7
Season-wise Consumption of Fire-wood

S.No.	Forest village	Winter		Summer	
		kg/day	kg/month	kg/day	kg/month
1	Lehra	3.23 ± 0.98	96.91± 29.42	2.81 ± 0.54	84.32 ± 16.21
2	Suni	3.39 ± 0.74	101.69 ± 22.44	3.04 ± 0.43	91.30 ± 12.90
3	Garo Basti	3.78 ± 0.75	113.31 ± 22.51	3.31 ± 0.59	99.32 ± 17.72
4	Gadhadhar	3.76 ± 0.69	112.83 ± 20.73	2.96 ± 0.89	88.87 ± 26.74
5	Poro (N)	3.91 ± 0.84	117.23 ± 25.22	3.29 ± 0.72	98.65 ± 21.61
6	Nimati and Dabri	3.67 ± 0.40	110.12 ± 12.36	3.34 ± 0.47	100.32 ± 14.11
7	Gangutia H.A	4.76 ± 0.77	142.36 ± 23.76	3.98 ± 0.71	119.43 ± 21.33
8	Adma H.A	4.86 ± 0.54	145.68 ± 16.21	4.03 ± 0.72	120.91 ± 21.63
9	Raimatang H.A	3.36 ± 0.64	100.81 ± 19.28	3.08 ± 0.47	92.47 ± 14.11
10	Bhutri F. basti H.A	4.56 ± 0.51	136.87 ± 15.34	3.86 ± 0.79	115.85 ± 23.76
11	Gudamdabri	3.26 ± 0.67	97.83 ± 20.14	2.87 ± 0.76	86.11 ± 22.83
12	Chunabati H.A	4.79 ± 0.73	143.72 ± 21.91	3.46 ± 0.38	103.84 ± 11.45
13	Bhutiabasti	4.14 ± 0.75	124.11 ± 22.61	3.37 ± 0.67	101.21 ± 20.11
14	Sankosh	3.63 ± 0.59	108.89 ± 17.74	3.09 ± 0.89	92.82 ± 26.76
15	Lapraguri	3.36 ± 0.68	100.82 ± 20.41	2.78 ± 0.81	83.43 ± 24.31
16	Santrabari H.A	4.19 ± 0.61	125.65 ± 18.32	3.22 ± 0.78	96.48 ± 23.47
17	Balapara	3.89 ± 0.58	106.73 ± 17.45	2.94 ± 0.88	88.23 ± 26.41
	Average	**3.99 ± 0.67**	**119.74 ± 20.34**	**3.29 ± 0.68**	**98.64 ± 20.32**

N.B. (Mean ± SD), H.A=High altitude location.
(Calculated based on field survey, 2017)

average was recorded from 3.36 kg ± 0.61 kg to 4.86 kg ± 0.54 kg in winter and 3.22 ± 0.78 kg to 4.03 kg ± 0.72 in summer. It is important to note that the quantity of fire wood requirement is too high due to lack of alternative source of fuel energy such as kerosene, LPG, electricity and other sources. So villagers choose fire wood for daily use as only the alternative source of energy.

6.4.1 Type of Fuel-Wood Used

There are many different types of the fuel wood used by the villagers. The fuels are obtained in the forms of twigs, branches, dead dry wood, fallen wood and log wood. The villagers promote to use the wood which is available in the forest and suit to use easily as fuel. Most of the household used more than one types of fuel-wood such as dry leaves, branches and twigs. It was mostly the mixture of fallen dry wood and branches which most of the household used. As a matter of rights and concessions, the forest villagers are allowed to collect the dry leaves, dry fallen wood and small twigs and branches for fuel from nearby forest. The small logs of wood are also available but collecting in illegal way. At the aggregated level, as many as almost all of 878 households used dry or dead wood, branches and twigs as common fuel wood. But few of them used specific type more and more such as dry leaves, branches and logs. The information collected about the difference of fuel wood consumption reveals that in the high altitude where population is concentrated remotely around the forest, the fuel wood consumption is higher than plain area villagers and the Adma, Bhutri, Raimatang, Santrabari and Chunabati are such type of village. These villagers opted branches and logs as prime fuel. During field study for the information about fuel wood, the villagers were asked to indicate their preferred of fuel trees. In most of the cases they mentioned about locally suitable trees like sal, teak, simul, jarul as the most preferred trees. Since sal and teak are very common, widely grown trees and available, so almost all respondents preferred that leaves, branches and log of these trees as a good fuel. In the lower elevation area simul, jarul, sisoo were the most preferred trees.

6.4.2 Time Taken and Distance Covered for Fuel Wood Collection

The fuel wood collection is one of the most important activities of the villagers where fuel wood used for both consumption and selling purpose. The forest is the only single field of source for fuel wood since the contribution in fuel requirement is insignificant from any other source than forest. The households of each village covered a particular distances and spent sufficient time of the day for collecting fuel wood. Now they felt that the deforestation and run out of forests cover makes fuel collection more difficult. Therefore distances to be covered for fuel wood collection increased day by day consequently, more time is to be devoted by the inhabitants for this activity.

During field survey, it was reported that average hour utilized for collecting fuel-wood among households were 1 hrs to 2.30 hrs per day depending upon requirement, family size; and terrain characteristics and distance of the forest from the village. The average maximum and minimum time spending is identified on 2.09 ± 0.32 hrs/day and 1.04 ± 0.31 hrs/day of Chunabati and Lehra village respectively (table–6.8). It was also found that fuel wood collection requires 2 days to 3 days per week of each household and the average maximum and minimum days is on 129.57 ± 15.67 days/year and 95.23 ± 14.90 days/year of Bhutia basti and Lapraguri village respectively.

It was also reported that average distance covered for collecting fuel-wood were 0.42 km to 1.83 km per day depending upon forest density, season, terrain characteristics and distance of the forest from the village. The average maximum and minimum distance covered is identified on 1.83 ± 0.13 km/day and 0.42 ± 0.16 km/day in Balapara and Chunabati. It was also found that fuel wood collection requires 2 days to 3 days per week of each household and the average

Table–6.8
Time Taken and Distance Covered

S.No.	Forest village	Time Spent		Distance Covered	
		Hrs/day	Days/year	Km/day	km/year
1	Lehra	1.04 ± 0.31	104.23 ± 12.45	1.05 ± 0.22	127.92 ± 10.23
2	Suni	1.13 ± 0.32	112.43 ± 11.83	1.02 ± 0.12	114.24 ± 13.24
3	Garo Basti	1.32 ± 0.45	126.13 ± 13.95	0.75 ± 0.34	94.59 ± 9.32
4	Gadhadhar	1.14 ± 0.55	111.83 ± 10.56	1.54 ± 0.52	172.21 ± 16.14
5	Poro (N)	1.53 ± 0.42	105.23 ± 12.18	0.85 ± 0.41	89.45 ± 14.23
6	Nimati and Dabri	1.49 ± 0.41	121.23 ± 13.47	1.32 ± 0.46	160.02 ± 11.31
7	Gangutia H.A	1.56 ± 0.67	127.12 ± 18.57	0.65 ± 0.21	171.61 ± 12.33
8	Adma H.A	2.01 ± 0.67	109.23 ± 10.45	0.57 ± 0.15	258.87 ± 6.39
9	Raimatang H.A	1.12 ± 0.54	116.23 ± 13.28	1.05 ± 0.21	126.53 ± 14.35
10	Bhutri forest basti H.A	2.05 ± 0.23	103.53 ± 14.36	0.71 ± 0.32	94.21 ± 14.37
11	Gudamdabri	1.22 ± 0.52	117.23 ± 12.85	0.95 ± 0.11	111.36 ± 13.56
12	Chunabati H.A	2.09 ± 0.32	108.35 ± 13.56	0.42 ± 0.16	221.03 ± 6.45
13	Bhutiabasti	1.57 ± 0.58	129.57 ± 15.67	0.78 ± 0.26	274.68 ± 10.24
14	Sankosh	1.29 ± 0.51	107.23 ± 12.86	1.70 ± 0.23	182.29 ± 9.43
15	Lapraguri	1.36 ± 0.46	95.23 ± 14.90	1.75 ± 0.24	166.65 ± 8.54
16	Santrabari H.A	1.48 ± 0.45	98.74 ± 17.34	0.85 ± 0.27	162.92 ± 12.63
17	Balapara	1.21 ± 0.37	108.23 ± 16.89	1.83 ± 0.13	198.06 ± 5.34
	Average	**1.45 ± 0.46**	**111.87 ± 13.83**	**1.44 ± 0.33**	**160.39 ± 11.06**

N.B. (Mean ± SD), H.A=High altitude location.
H.A=High Altitude, (Prepared based on field survey, 2017)

maximum and minimum distance is on 274.68 ± 10.24 km/year and 94.21 ± 14.37 km/year of Bhutia basti and Bhutri forest basti respectively.

6.4.3 Relation between Fuel Wood Consumption and Distance

It is observed from the table–6.9, that villagers' of Chunabati and Balapara covered minimum and maximum distance of 12.6 km/month and maximum 54.9 km/month for fuel wood collection respectively where amount of fuel wood consumption is noticed 123.78 kg/month and 97.48 kg/month. So, it is clear that if distance of village is far away from forest cover, then consumption of fuel wood is decreased and if it is too closer then consumption of fuel wood is increased due to close proximity and less distance. This opposite relation also observed in other sampled villages. So it can be explained that there is negative correlation between distance covered and fuel wood consumption. These negative correlation relations are shown in the scatter diagram (Fig. 6.4) below along with regression line of estimated fuel wood consumption.

Table–6.9
Calculation of Estimated Fuel Wood Consumption in Respect of Distances Covered

S.No.	Forest village	Distance covered (km/month)	Fuel wood consumption (kg/month)	Estimated fuel wood consumption (kg/month) Yc = a +bx
1	Lehra	31.05	90.615	107.53
2	Suni	30.06	96.495	108.25
3	Garo Basti	22.50	106.32	113.70
4	Gadhadhar	46.20	100.85	96.61
5	Poro (N)	25.50	107.94	111.53
6	Nimati and Dabri	39.60	105.22	101.37
7	Gangutia H.A	19.50	130.895	115.86
8	Adma H.A	17.10	133.295	117.59
9	Raimatang H.A	31.50	96.64	107.21
10	Bhutri forest basti H.A	21.30	126.36	114.56

11	Gudamdabri	28.50	91.97	109.37
12	Chunabati H.A	12.60	123.78	120.83
13	Bhutiabasti	23.40	112.66	113.05
14	Sankosh	51.00	100.855	93.15
15	Lapraguri	52.50	92.125	92.07
16	Santrabari H.A	25.50	111.065	111.53
17	Balapara	54.90	97.48	90.34

H.A=High Altitude, (Prepared based on field survey, 2017)

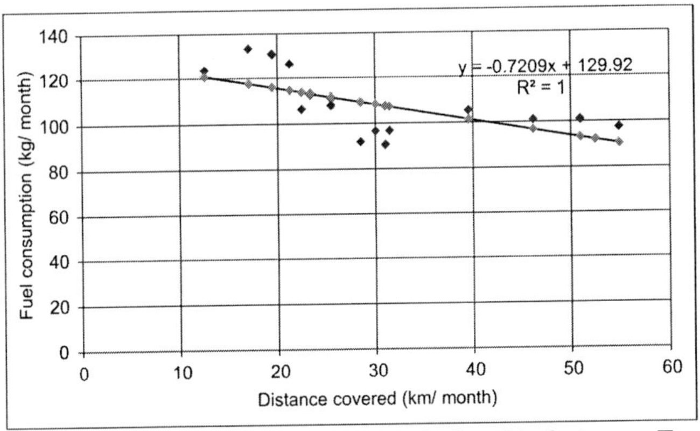

Fig. 6.4: Regression Line showing Relationship between Fuel-Wood consumption and distance covered

By looking the above scatter diagram (Fig. 6.4) it may be described that distance covered and fuel wood consumption are correlated. Further, correlation is negative because the trend of the points is downward going from the upper left side corner to the lower right side corner of the diagram. The diagram also indicates that the degree of relationship which is higher because the all plotted points are near to the trends line which shows perfect negative correlation ship between distance and fuel wood consumption. Although, Karl Pearsons's method applied and calculated where correlation coefficient value was '- 0.675', which again indicates high negative correlation between distance cover and fuel wood consumption.

6.5 Forest as Source of Timber

The timber is one of the important livelihood forest resources which are used for various purposes. In forest areas, timber and branches of trees are main element for house construction such as it is utilised for doors, windows, wall, platform and stair of houses. It is also used to prepare wood bridge, wooden tower, entresol and fence of house premise. Most of the houses are prepared as long heighted two storey houses where the timber of trees has been used as pillar of the house (plate–6.4). The ground floor is used as cattle shed and storage of fuel wood, water tank as well as garage for other purpose. Although, cattle shed is also made by wood besides the house separately to avoid the pollution. The first floor is allotted for the living purpose mainly as bed room, dining room, kitchen, open space. It is also stated that first floor is relatively save from the wild animal attack. The walls, windows, doors and floors of ground and first floor are made of wooden planks whereas stones and mud are used only for floor of ground floors and tins, polythene, banana leaves and other tree leaves are used for roof making purpose according to their economic capacity. A limited number of households use banana grass and other leaves as thatching but tin and wood is a common component for roofing purpose almost in all the cases. The required wood is either received from contiguous forest as free basis those are agreement holder or by paying concessional price or as a claim basis on traditional rights of forest inhabitants or auction price or labour or collected unauthorized way. The main woods used for house construction are sal, sisoo and teak which are available and lifelong in this climate.

6.5.1 Timber Used in House Construction

The obtained information from sampled survey about the number of households using wood for house construction such as doors, windows, walls and floors shows that as many as 87.70% of the households used tin and wood for house construction, 6.61% used thatched and wood, 5.69% used concrete wall with tin (table–6.10). The village wise percentage of households using timber for house construction varies from 100% to 17.86% where in Bhutiabasti, Gangutia, Bhutri forest basti and Lapraguri village it is covered 100% of using

Table–6.10

House Construction Material Used (village-wise)

S.No.	Forest village	Stone & Tin	Wood and Tin	Pucca (concrete with tin)	Thatched and wood	Tiled & wood	Total sampled households
1	Lehra	-	7 (31.82)	15 (68.18)	-	-	22 (100%)
2	Suni	-	5 (17.86)	23 (82.14)	-	-	28 (100%)
3	Garo Basti	-	65 (90.28)	-	7 (9.72)	-	72 (100%)
4	Gadhadhar	-	45 (71.43)	-	18 (28.57)	-	63 (100%)
5	Poro (N)	-	57 (93.44)	4 (6.56)	-	-	61(100%)
6	Nimati and Dabri	-	61 (89.71)	-	7 (10.29)		68 (100%)
7	Gangutia H.A	-	55 (100)	-	-	-	55 (100%)
8	Adma H.A	-	51 (92.73)	-	4 (7.27)	-	55 (100%)
9	Raimatang H.A	-	47 (85.45)	-	8 (14.55)	-	55 (100%)
10	Bhutri forest basti H.A	-	45 (100)	-	-	-	45 (100%)
11	Gudamdabri	-	58 (92.06)	-	5 (7.94)		63 (100%)
12	Chunabati H.A	-	52 (96.30)	-	2 (3.70)	-	54 (100%)
13	Bhutiabasti		30 (100)	-	-	-	30 (100%)
14	Sankosh	-	53 (88.33)	4 (6.67)	3 (5)	-	60 (100%)
15	Lapraguri	-	47 (100)	-	-	-	47 (100%)
16	Santrabari H.A		61 (93.85)	4 (6.15)	-	-	65 (100%)
17	Balapara	-	31 (88.57)	-	4 (11.42)	-	35 (100%)
	Total		**770 (87.70%)**	**50 (5.69%)**	**58 (6.61%)**		**878 (100%)**

H.A=High Altitude, (Prepared based on field survey, 2017)

timber. The Gitanjeeli project provided concrete wall house to all households of Suni and Lehra villages with tin shed so there are only 17.86% and 31.82% households who using timber for other purpose. Villages of high altitude such as household of Raimatang, Bhutiabasti, Gangutia, Adma, Santrabari and Chunabati used comparatively more timber than low-lying and plain area. Thus, it is noticed that the altitude is prime factor which enhanced timber used for house construction. Also the number of rooms, size of the family or settlement house type, however, has affected the use of timber. The households at higher elevations are forced and bound to utilise the forest wood as house construction material because of lack of alternatives of house building material such as bricks, irons, soils and cement at that location and for this inhabitants depends on plain area market of Kalchini, Alipurduar, Hamiltongaunj with any cost, although transport is a big obstacle for it. So it is identified, that types of trees, nature of terrain and availability of timber also recognizes as dependent factor of timber use.

6.5.2 Types of Trees Used as Source of Timber

The type of trees used as sources of timber has been collected through sampled study to consider the tree species which are most frequently used for timber. The respondents of 17 villagers specified different types of wood they used. Out of 878 respondents, about 553 households (62.98%) used both sal and teak, 124 households (14.12%) teak, sissu and sidha, 81 households (9.22%) sissu, odal, 73 households (8.31%) khair, Jarul and neem, 47 households (5.35%) sidha, semal, simul and neem etc. for house as well as other uses. The teak, sal and sisoo are popular timber in higher and middle altitudes household such as Adma, Chunabati of high altitude villagers and Sankosh, Santrabari, Raimatang, Gangutia and Bhutri forest basti of middle altitudes villagers while gamaree, khair, sidha and neem are very common used in lower altitudes areas. The sal and teak were popular and valuable tree species of timber for all respondents since its lifelong than other timber.

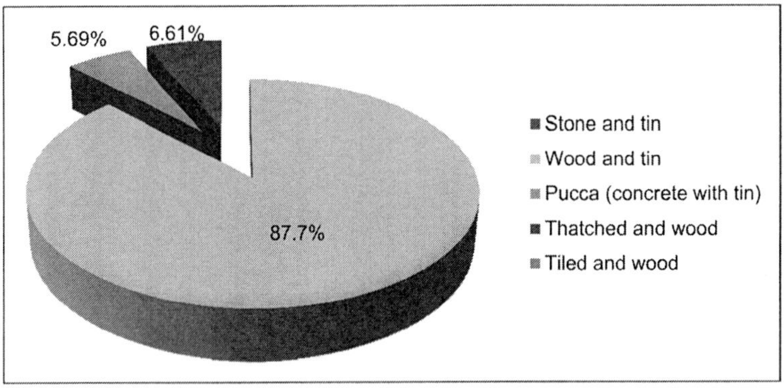

Fig. 6.5: House Construction Material Used

6.5.3 Methods of Obtaining Timber for House Construction

In 1894 cultivators were first allowed to settle in the forest in connection with the scheme of taungya sowings. About 1904 establishment of forest villages became a regular policy and very large numbers of forest villagers were allowed to settle in the forests of Alipurduar District (Das, 2000). Forest villagers were found very useful for undertaking cultural operations in the forest and also for fire protection purpose. Initially there was no sufficient control over the forest property and villagers within forest or near the forest had been consumed forest and forestland as common resource considering it as their own property. A villager might cultivate and number of cattle he might keep according to capacity (Ninth working plan of Jalpaiguri Forest Division, Vol. I, 2009).

In 1912 rules were made to limiting the cultivation and homestead land to 2.5 acres in plains, and 1.5 acres in hills per family (Das, 2000). Later the Indian Forest Act, 1927 was the important regulating act of the forests of India where village forest considered being included as a category of forest and extensive rights for fuel and fodder etc were allowed for villagers (Rahman, 2000). After the independence, the government has fixed a certain quantity of timber, called free grant, to be given to the forest villagers and residents of forest contiguous villages. As a result the forest villagers have been provided with wooden departmental quarters in most cases.

Table–6.11

Methods of obtaining timber for house construction (households-wise)

S.No.	Forest village	Free grant basis	Concessional price basis	Auction basis	Purchase from markets	Un-authorized collection
1	Lehra	15 (68.18)	05 (22.73)	02 (9.09)	-	-
2	Suni	18 (64.29)	05 (17.86)	03 (10.71)	-	02 (7.14)
3	Garo Basti	64 (88.89)	05 (6.94)	-	-	03 (4.17)
4	Gadhadhar	50 (79.37)	11 (17.46)	-	-	02 (3.17)
5	Poro (N)	54 (88.52)	03 (4.92)	4 (6.56)	-	-
6	Nimati and Dabri	60 (88.24)	5 (7.35)	03 (4.41)	-	-
7	Gangutia H.A	53 (96.36)	02 (3.64)	-	-	
8	Adma H.A	51 (92.73)	3 (5.45)	-	-	01 (1.82)
9	Raimatang H.A	44 (80.00)	7 (12.72)	02 (3.64)	-	02 (3.64)
10	Bhutri forest basti H.A	39 (86.67)	5 (11.11)	-	-	01 (2.22)
11	Gudamdabri	54 (85.71)	5 (7.95)	02 (3.17)		02 (3.17)
12	Chunabati H.A	50 (92.60)	2 (3.70)	-	-	02 (3.70)
13	Bhutiabasti	27 (89.99)	03 (9.99)	-	-	-
14	Sankosh	54 (90.00)	3(5.00)	3 (5.00)	-	-
15	Lapraguri	44 (93.62)	-	-	-	03 (6.38)
16	Santrabari H.A	62 (95.38)	-	3 (4.62)	-	-
17	Balapara	32 (91.43)	3 (8.57)	-	-	-
	Average	**771**	**67**	**22**		**18**
	%	**87.81 %**	**7.63 %**	**2.51 %**		**2.05 %**

H.A=High altitude location, (Calculated by the researcher based on field survey, 2017).

Constructions of wooden huts have been started from the year 1947-48 and have continued till 1960-61 (Das, 2000). Forest villagers cultivate their land and rare large number of cattle. Later the villagers are also permitted to get additional timber on concessional price as an agreement holder for certain small demands (PD) like repairing of houses, extra room purpose, fence making, pillar making or other agricultural implements. Besides if the demands of timber needs of the households are not fulfilled through these methods, the additional amount is to be complete by either buying the timber at commercial rates, or auction basis or through unauthorized gathering from the nearby forest.

It is observed that 87.81% of households obtained the timber as free grant through forest department for house construction (table–6.11). Another 7.63% of the households purchased at concessional price through negotiation with the local forest office for extra demand; and 2.51% collected through auction basis as well as 2.05% of households were engaged to fulfil other extra needs of timber in unauthorized way. It is observed that average 186.92 ± 3.98 cft. timbers obtained as free grant through forest department for house construction (table–6.12). Another 10.50 ± 2.23 cft purchased at concessional price after negotiation with the local forest office, 2.11 ± 0.57 cft collected through auction basis and 0.35 ± 0.04 cft timbers collected in unauthorized way to fulfil extra demand. The consumption of timber wood per household as free grant basis recorded maximum of 202.45 ± 3.21 cft in Lapraguri village and minimum 176.55 ± 4.78 cft in Lehra village, concessional price basis it is 15.59 ± 2.56 cft in Raimatang village and 09.12 ± 1.43 cft in Chunabati village, auction basis it is 5.97 ± 0.91 cft in Raimatang and 2.21 ± 1.25 cft in Poro (N) and in unauthorized way it is 0.95 ± 0.075 cft in Adma and 0.38 ± 0.091 cft in Suni. There is no option observed in purchase of wood from the market.

6.5.4 The Quantity of Timber Required for House Construction

The quantity of timber used by households and for how

Table–6.12
Amount of Timber Obtained for House Construction (Households-Wise)

S.No.	Forest village	Free grant basis (cft)	Concessional price basis (cft)	Auction basis (cft)	Purchase from markets (cft)	Un-authorized collection (cft)
1	Lehra	176.55 ± 4.78	14.57 ± 2.26	5.92 ± 1.25	-	-
2	Suni	179.23 ± 3.35	12.59 ± 3.06	4.84 ± 1.47	-	0.38 ± 0.091
3	Garo Basti	183.42 ± 4.41	10.49 ± 3.41	-	-	0.57 ± 0.085
4	Gadhadhar	181.54 ± 3.55	9.78 ± 1.86	-	-	0.76 ± 0.077
5	Poro (N)	184.35 ± 4.36	11.23 ± 2.12	2.21 ± 1.25	-	-
6	Nimati and Dabri	183.58 ± 3.45	12.21 ± 2.32	2.57 ± 0.94	-	-
7	Gangutia H.A	195.26 ± 3.75	9.48 ± 2.46	-	-	-
8	Adma H.A	196.61 ± 4.26	10.52 ± 1.77	-	-	0.95 ± 0.075
9	Raimatang H.A	185.23 ± 3.35	15.59 ± 2.56	5.97 ± 0.91	-	0.43 ± 0.083
10	Bhutri F. basti H.A	194.31 ± 3.86	11.76 ± 2.87	-	-	0.48 ± 0.086
11	Gudamdabri	179.89 ± 5.31	14.53 ± 2.92	2.87 ± 1.11	-	0.78 ± 0.079
12	Chunabati H.A	197.23 ± 4.45	09.12 ± 1.43	-	-	0.77 ± 0.036
13	Bhutiabasti	181.45 ± 3.38	12.54 ± 2.41	-	-	-
14	Sankosh	176.95 ± 4.32	14.93 ± 3.56	5.79 ± 0.97	-	-
15	Lapraguri	202.45 ± 3.21	-	-	-	0.79 ± 0.065
16	Santrabari H.A	200.67 ± 4.63	-	3.61 ± 1.25	-	-
17	Balapara	183.89 ± 3.26	09.21 ± 2.87	-	-	-
	Average	**186.92 ± 3.98**	**10.50 ± 2.23**	**2.11 ± 0.57**	**-**	**0.35 ± 0.04**

N.B. (Mean ± SD), H.A=High altitude location, (Calculated based on field survey, 2017).

long the wood stayed lasts as houses material and the time at which replacement require, all is depend on age and height of trees. The trees which have 5 feet to 10 feet girth measured and at a height of 35 feet to 45 feet are considered as standard and good quality timber for construction. The number of trees are depends on the good tree species such as if the species are simul, jarul, khai, sidha and neem, then the number of trees required will be more as compared to other trees of sal, teak, sissu etc.

Table–6.13
Amount of timber used and replacement in house construction

S.No.	Forest Village	Amount of timber (cft) used for house construction (per household)	Average period for replacement of timber (years)
1	Lehra	197.04 ± 8.29	45.81 ± 4.54
2	Suni	197.04 ± 7.97	41.21 ± 3.43
3	Garo Basti	194.48 ± 7.91	39.01 ± 4.59
4	Gadhadhar	192.08 ± 5.49	42.96 ± 3.89
5	Poro (N)	197.79 ± 7.73	46.12 ± 5.72
6	Nimati and Dabri	198.36 ± 6.71	43.41 ± 4.47
7	Gangutia H.A	204.74 ± 6.21	35.98 ± 4.71
8	Adma H.A	208.08 ± 6.11	34.03 ± 2.72
9	Raimatang H.A	207.22 ± 6.90	46.76 ± 4.47
10	Bhutri forest basti H.A	206.55 ± 6.82	33.86 ± 5.79
11	Gudamdabri	198.07 ± 9.42	39.87 ± 4.76
12	Chunabati H.A	207.12 ± 5.92	33.46 ± 4.38
13	Bhutiabasti	193.99 ± 5.79	51.04 ± 2.67
14	Sankosh	197.67 ± 8.85	43.76 ± 3.89
15	Lapraguri	203.24 ± 3.28	52.78 ± 2.81
16	Santrabari H.A	204.28 ± 5.88	37.88 ± 3.78
17	Balapara	193.10 ± 6.13	42.94 ± 4.88
	Average	**200.06 ± 6.82**	**41.70 ± 4.21**

N.B. (Mean ± SD), H.A=High Altitude
(Calculated based on field survey, 2017)

The average sort out in this study, however, gives an idea of the quantity of timber wood required in different locations and altitudes. The quantity of timber used is more in high altitude than in low-lying and plain area. The availability and types of timber, terrain character, climate and non-availability of alternatives are responsible factors for the variation of consumption of wood. The villagers' of Gangutia, Bhutri forest basti, Bhutiabasti, Adma, Raimatang, Chunabati, Santrabari and Lapraguri consumed more quantity of timber because it is the only available material for construction and all types of rooms are made by woods. While the bricks, woods, tins, bamboos are used as house materials in comparatively low lying and plain region and such villages are Gadhadhar, Nimati and Dabri, Gudamdabri and Garo Basti. The average used amount of timber wood per household for house construction is recorded of 200.06 ± 6.82 cft and average number of years for replacement of timber is 41.70 ± 4.21 years (table–6.13). The average maximum and minimum amount of timber used for house construction (per household) is identified of 208.08 ± 6.11 cft in Adma and 193.10 ± 6.13 cft in Balapara. The timbers has been used for the construction of houses is generally changed after the damaged of about more or less between 33 to 53 years as stated by respondents and average maximum and minimum number of years for replacement of timber is observed 52.78 ± 2.81 years in Lapraguri and 33.46 ± 4.38 years in Chunabati village.

6.6 Other Wood Needs and The Use of Forest

There are some special needs which are being fulfilled by collection of branches and woods from the neighbouring forest. The needs of agriculture related implements such as harrows for cultivation, wood plough and rod poles of wood for vegetable creepers and fence, sit benches for house and shop and bulk fire wood for the occasional purpose such as wedding ceremony, birth party and cremation activity etc. have been fulfilled by forest wood. The huge quantity of wood needed for cultural and social ceremonies although it depends on size and number of invitees of occasion. Therefore, villagers could not able to response the actual fire wood requirement. However, it has been depicted that an average of 5 to 6 quintal of extra fire wood is needed for each of these kinds of occasions.

Relatives of organizers either contribute some amount of wood or pay for it individually or go together to the nearby forest to collect required amount of wood through unauthorized way. Although sometimes the concerned family collects it on concessional rate by taking permission from local forest authority/beat and range office as forest agreement holder. The requirement of forest wood as well as small branches for agricultural appliance is a common phenomenon and for that purpose almost 4 to 5 small size trees are acquired for each household every year as respondents replied during field survey. It is also mentioned that branches of trees are mainly used to making hedges and protective poles around the agricultural field. Again this required amount of branches has been received after granting permission or through negotiation with local office of Forest Department, but in most of the time, villagers enter to surrounding forest and collect it through illegal or invisible way.

6.7 Forest as Source of Employment

Forest villagers never thought their livelihood economy and existence without forests. It is, however, considered that the forest offered more or less some employment opportunity to for their livelihood. Forest, no doubt generates a considerable amount of income but most of its income gone to the Government side through silviculture tree felling by Forest Department. Even most of the permanent workers, contractors come from outside who were deployed for tree felling, lumbering works, as a result villagers do not get financial assistance except casual or contractual basis work of labour. Although the FPCs and EDCs members of Joint forest Management committee (JFMC) are getting financial support through beneficiaries sharing of different activities, nursery, plantation, cleaning of weeds, loan for farming work etc. During the field survey it has also been identified that about 141 household members out of 878 household (chapter–8 and table–8.31) were engaged in forestry activities being member of FPCs and EDCs committees, Self Help Group members, or employed as casual, contractual labour for official activities such as nursery supervisor, day and night guard, seed collectors, tourist guide etc. In this connection it is reported that for almost six months in a year, the tribals in Western Ghat Zone of Maharashtra were engaged. Due to uninterrupted rain in the rainy seasons, the tribals got relatively better employment in the summer off-farm works such as hunting, collection of NTFPs and works under employment guarantee scheme. The forest plays alone and offered them for more than 30% of the total man days (Suryawanshi, 1992).

The analysis indicated that forest villagers are very much depended upon forests for basic livelihood needs. The NTFPs is very much inevitable for villagers' economic support. So gathering and selling of NTFPs are the permanent source of income for forests inhabitants of this area. The study also revealed that the forest is used as prime source of green fodder for livestock grazing and the cattle feeding on plants, leaves, grass and twigs; and the grass, leaves and twigs are cut off to be brought home for further used. It is to be noted that fuel wood is the common source of domestic energy for forest villagers and forest is the only source of fuel wood and except it, villagers' daily life may be stopped any time. It is also clear that timber is the prime forest produce which also used as component of house construction as well as to make doors, windows, walls, pillar, upper floors, stairs, agricultural tools, fence etc. Besides the study showed that a good number of the collected plants has been used for the treatment of multiple diseases, such as Andrographis paniculata (kalmegh; Chirata) are used for the treatment of stomach, fever, liver, skin and ulcer diseases; Cadiospermum helicacabum (Lataphatkari; Sibjhul; Bhado) for the treatment of rheumatism, snake bite diseases; and other more than 100 plants are used to treat many diseases.

7 Chapter Villager's Perception

7.1 Introduction

The socio-economic life of the forest villagers is so intimately interrelated and intermixed with forests that by now villagers and forests have become inseparable words. The forest is an only single prime factor for which the physical, economic, socio-economic and cultural environment of forest villagers affects directly and indirectly. Earlier days the relationship between forest and human revealed itself a kind of easy accessibility and independent movement of villagers in the neighbourhood forests. Since the demands of villagers were limited and economy of forest villages was based on self-supporting subsistence economy hence they could satisfy their meagre wants by hunting, food-gathering, minor forest produce and primitive cultivation. In that way, an ecological balance was sustained by reproduction and natural growth of forest species in the huge forest areas. Later, excess dependence pattern, over exploitation and unsustainable practice, increasing and extension of family size and changing cultural attitude have brought increasing pressure on forests. Therefore free gift of nature of unlimited quantity presently considered limited resource since more exploitation than regeneration and natural growth. Socio-economic changes (human population growth and dynamics, economic growth, consumption and trade, inequality and poverty) and biophysical changes (conversion and fragmentation of natural habitats, climate change, biodiversity loss and hydrological change) are the main causes affecting natural resources (Barber et al., 2004). Hence pressure on forests was increased so the free movements of villagers were restricted by the forest authority. Besides due to laws enforced by the Forest

Department, the rights of villagers on forest and forest resource are reduced day by day along with their chances of making a livelihood from their natural habitat. Another side during last few decades, the rate of deforestation increased very fast due to which the question of great threat to ecological equilibrium raised. It is reported that the Eastern Himalaya is a 'Bio-diversity Hotspot' as well as 'Eco-crisis zone' (Brooks et al., 2006). The impact has been realized in decrease in rainfall, increase in temperature, increase conflict between wild and human and dried up of jhora, waterfalls and rivers etc. On account of this it can be reported that the ecosystems of this region have been imbalanced as well as fragmented due to economic development, migration and population increase along with climatic change (Beniston, 2003). Fragmentation and fragility often cause mass wasting, landslides and soil erosion, other geo-climatic problems (Tewari, 2000). The 'chipko movement' is one of the results of realization of forest degradation with the objective of saving the forest cover from commercial exploitation. In the British period forest resources were consumed in unrestricted way by the forest inhabitants. But when the independent government of India took control the forest, the forest inhabitants were given certain rights and concessions based on their agreement and traditional use of forest in the nearby regions. All this issues brought into focus through the question and an attempt has been made from the view point of villagers by analyzing their perception of the problems in this chapter.

7.2 Extension of the Forest

The most significant matter connecting between the villagers and their forest related activities is the extent of the forest cover itself. To realize the changes taking place in the extent and composition of forest, the respondents were asked about the changes in forest cover and the changes in the density and type of vegetation. The villagers were also asked regarding presence of natural vegetation in surrounding area of village and on their own land to assess the extent of contribution and performance to non-timber and timber product needs of the villagers from their own sources of capacity.

7.2.1 Trees Belonging to the Household and Surrounding Area of the Household

The information collected discloses that as many as 351 households (39.98%) of the total sample) do not have even a single naturally grown tree on their own land. Other 527 respondents (60.02%) could specify the minimum 5 to 20 number of trees on the land owned by them. It is clear that the proportion of households having trees is more in higher altitude villagers' such as Adma, Chunabati, Gangutia and Bhutri and in case of those households having average and less number of trees on their land observed in the lower and plain altitude which is prominent in Gadhadhar, Lehra, Gudamdabri and Garo Basti village. Behind this lacking of open agricultural land is the prime cause where a small amount of open space also used for cultivation, giving more priority to agriculture than the forest. On the other hand demand of non-timber forest products and other forest related product is more at higher altitudes so, villagers are compelling to maintain and grow larger number of naturally green trees on their own land. It is also clear that the proportion of households having trees on surrounding of other and Government land is 664 (75.63%) of the total respondents and only 214 household (24.37%) are free from surrounding of trees. Almost 76% are within the forest cover and only 24% have adjacent area. So they have to spend time and covered distance for forest.

Table–7.1
Natural trees on the land belonging to the households and surrounding area of the households

S.No.	Forest village	Trees on own land		Trees on surrounding of the households		Total sampled households
		Yes	No	Yes	No	
1	Lehra	14	08	16	06	22

2	Suni	16	12	18	10	28
3	Garo Basti	39	33	51	21	72
4	Gadhadhar	35	28	28	35	63
5	Poro (N)	24	37	61	-	61
6	Nimati and Dabri	36	32	41	27	68
7	Gangutia H.A	31	24	55	-	55
8	Adma H.A	34	21	55	-	55
9	Raimatang H.A	36	19	41	14	55
10	Bhutri forest basti H.A	29	16	45	-	45
11	Gudamdabri	41	22	34	29	63
12	Chunabati H.A	33	21	54	-	54
13	Bhutiabasti	23	07	30	-	30
14	Sankosh	41	19	35	25	60
15	Lapraguri	31	16	26	21	47
16	Santrabari H.A	43	22	47	18	65
17	Balapara	21	14	27	08	35
	Total	**527** (60.02%)	**351** (39.98%)	**664** (75.63%)	**214** (24.37%)	**878** (100%)

H.A=High Altitude, (Prepared based on field survey, 2017)

7.2.2 Trees in the Village

It was rather wondering to find out that there were as many as 351 households (39.98%) who could not specify the minimum number of trees in their own land. In their native and inhabitant location where trees are of highest importance, the ignorance of activities regarding of trees among the villagers was not expected. It has been also noticed the fact that although large proportion of all kind of demands are fulfilled from the forest but less significance on plantation activities of trees in the villager own land was identified. Only grown trees inside and adjacent of the villages are either fruit trees like mango tree, flower trees and which have very much less contribution to fulfil villagers demands of fuel, fodder and timber. The presence of natural trees in the villages is more in higher altitude and less number of trees observed in the lower and plain altitude area. The personal trees in the villages are not comprehended by the residents to be affecting their social life. As results not enough attention is given to planting the trees in the village locations.

7.2.3 Change in Forest Cover

The villagers were asked to recognize their perception regarding forest coverage change, density and composition of trees in the surrounding forest areas and respondents were given about perception of such changes. All respondents gave their reply based on perception and knowledge regarding forest situation prevailing about before 30 years ago and present day scenario (table–7.2). There were 722 (82.23%) households who opined that forest cover situation is worse today than before, and due to plantation, check on forest felling, and illegal cutting, the condition of forests is now being improved. But there were 156 (17.77%) respondents, who still felt that, no development or change has been observed in the forest coverage in last two decades.

Out of total respondents, 783 (89.18 %) were of the opinion that the forest cover was better stocked, dense jungle about 25-30 years ago and there had been continuous deterioration and degradation in the forest cover. Although 95 household (10.82 %) were opined that forest cover situation was very good in three decades before. It is also noted that altogether high altitude and plain area respondents felt that forest situation was better in the sense of area coverage, density of trees in 30 years ago than today. According to researchers observation most deterioration and degradation area was noticed in plain area than hill forest due to more pressure of

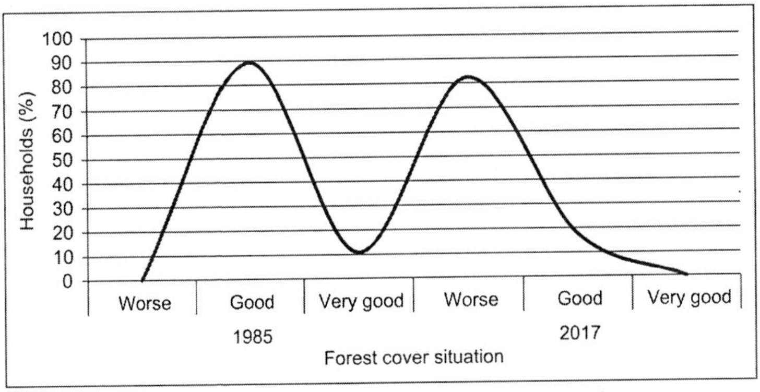

Fig. 7.1: Perception on Forest Cover Change

Table–7.2

Perception of respondents about forest cover 1985 and 2017

S.No.	Forest village	1985			2017			Total
		Worse	Good	Very good	Worse	Good	Very good	sampled households
1	Lehra	-	15	7	22	-	-	22
2	Suni	-	25	03	28	-	-	28
3	Garo Basti	-	60	12	70	02	-	72
4	Gadhadhar	-	53	10	63	-	-	63
5	Poro (N)	-	52	09	58	03	-	61
6	Nimati and Dabri	-	61	07	63	05	-	68
7	Gangutia H.A	-	51	04	41	14	-	55
8	Adma H.A	-	49	06	38	17	-	55
9	Raimatang H.A	-	47	08	39	16	-	55
10	Bhutri F. basti H.A	-	42	03	32	13	-	45
11	Gudamdabri	-	60	03	56	07	-	63
12	Chunabati H.A	-	51	03	35	19	-	54
13	Bhutiabasti	-	28	02	26	04	-	30
14	Sankosh	-	53	07	41	19	-	60
15	Lapraguri	-	44	03	39	08	-	47
16	Santrabari H.A	-	61	04	36	29	-	65
17	Balapara	-	31	04	35	-	-	35
	Total	**-**	**783 (89.18)**	**95 (10.82)**	**722 (82.23)**	**156 (17.77)**	**-**	**878 (100%)**
			878 (100%)			**878 (100%)**		

H.A=High Altitude, (Prepared based on field survey, 2017)

anthropogenic activities such as road construction, electrification, extension of agricultural and homestead area.

7.3 Type of Trees Felled

The villagers were asked to recognize their perception regarding the types of trees felled mostly, and the respondents were given about perception of tree felled questions. Among the 878 respondents, 397 respondents (45.22%) named sal and 376 (42.82%) referred teak as the dominant felled tree type. The 93 households (10.59%) were of the opinion that sisoo, simul and gamari are tree which felled regularly. Rest of the respondents gave opinion that all types of trees are felled for commercial needs.

7.3.1 Period of Tree Felling

The process of felling had been going on in different forests sectors of the region in varying magnitudes in the past. Although villagers were asked to specify the period of tree felling according to their knowledge and information gathered from seniors or ancestors which they could remember during observation.

Out of 878 respondents (table–7.3), 459 respondents (52.28%) were of the opinion that maximum tree felling in their area has been occurred between 1970 and 1990, 234 respondents (26.65%) fixed that in 1950-70 was the period of initial stage of tree felling after independence although it

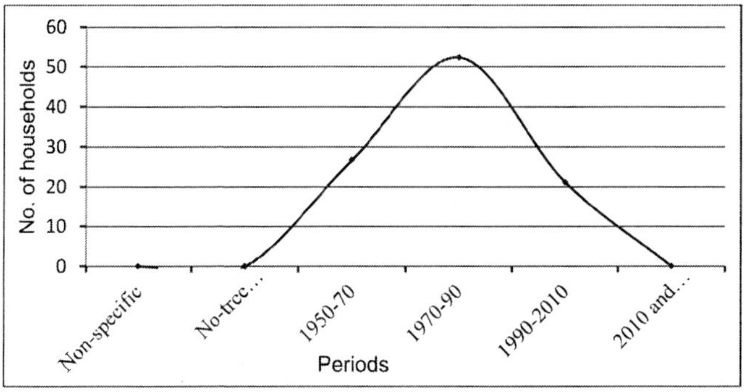

Fig. 7.2: Tree Felling Periods

Table–7.3
Response about Period of Tree Felling

S.No.	Forest village	Period of tree felling						Total
		Non-specific	No-tree felling	1950-70	1970-90	1990-2010	2010 and onwards	sampled households
1	Lehra	-	-	08	11	03	-	22
2	Suni	-	-	06	17	05	-	28
3	Garo Basti	-	-	19	45	08	-	72
4	Gadhadhar	-	-	16	43	04	-	63
5	Poro (N)	-	-	12	38	11	-	61
6	Nimati and Dabri	-	-	14	41	13	-	68
7	Gangutia H.A	-	-	11	31	13	-	55
8	Adma H.A	-	-	13	30	12	-	55
9	Raimatang H.A	-	-	15	29	11	-	55
10	Bhutri F. basti H.A	-	-	12	25	08	-	45
11	Gudamdabri	-	-	21	31	11	-	63
12	Chunabati H.A	-	-	14	22	18	-	54
13	Bhutiabasti	-	-	12	15	03	-	30
14	Sankosh	-	-	17	23	20	-	60
15	Lapraguri	-	-	13	25	09	-	47
16	Santrabari H.A	-	-	24	18	23	-	65
17	Balapara	-	-	07	15	13	-	35
	Total	**-**	**-**	**234** (26.65%)	**459** (52.28%)	**185** (21.07%)	**-**	**878** (100%)

H.A=High Altitude, (Prepared based on field survey, 2017)

was started by the British Government before independence. As many as 185 (21.07%) reported that there was no maximum felling occurred in between 1990-2010 than 1970-90. The felling shows a decreasing trend as the altitude increases. The respondents reported that at lower altitudes there was large scale felling in their area than high altitude.

7.3.2 Responsibility of Tree Felling

It is observed that the scale of tree felling has mostly taken place in lower altitude reserved forest area. The forest department auctions trees to be felled and most of the felling is done by contractors. The villagers' response had been collected to know about responsibilities for tree felling. The results indicate that the villagers are divided in their opinion about fixing these responsibilities. While 52.28% (459) of total respondents who opined and felt that government and forest officials were responsible for it, 15.38% (135 respondents) fixed the responsibilities with the contractors and 32.35% (284 respondents) opined that illegal cutting of trees by outsiders, lacking of awareness of forest department on illegal cutting, jointly responsible.

7.3.3 Regional Background of Contractors and Labourers

There is no direct involvement of forest villagers even in the process of commercial felling of trees either as contractors, labourers or any other tree felling activities. It has been observed that while 538 (61.28%) respondents were of the opinion that contractors and labourers were coming from regional service centres such as Alipurduar, Siliguri, Jalpaiguri, Kochbehar and Dhupguri and another 254 (28.93%) respondents fixed their opinion that contractors' came from outside of the locality. And only 86 (9.79%) respondents fixed contractors' background as local level. The same situation also observed in case of labourers. As many as 557 (63.44%) of respondents fixed their opinion that tree felling labourers were brought outside of the region such as Nepal, Bhutan, Bihar, Assam and Uttar Pradesh as the labourers from these regions are considered to be cheap in lumbering than local labour and, therefore, contractors prefer them. On the other side 189 villagers (21.53%) opined that the labourers were regional while 132 respondents (15.03%) commented the background of labourers as local means labours are supplied from forest villages and from fringe areas. The interaction between labourers-contractors with villagers was generally very poor.

7.3.4 Destination of Timber

Majority of the respondents remembered that trees were felled and transported outside the region to be used for different purpose. Almost all the Duars towns and service centres e.g. Alipurduar, Kalcnini, Hamiltonguanj, Hasimara, Madarihat and Birpara are timber collection centers. But forest villagers do not know the actual destination of the timber which originating from their locality. In general, the respondents in Lehra, Suni, Gadhadhar, Garo basti, Poro, Nimti and Dabri village said Assam, Bangladesh, Bhutan, Nepal, Jalpaiguri, Kolkata and Siliguri as the destination of timber whereas respondent in Gangutia, Adma, Raimatang, Bhutri Forest basti, Gudamdabri villagers mentioned Bhutan, and North-Frontier states are the major market and destinations. Very few respondents identified the local residents of Alipurduar District and North Bengal as the possible destination. The timbers are supplied all above mentioned destinations where woods have demand as furniture and house construction materials. Although in the 19th century the Indian Railway bought large number of sal timber for sleepers of railway lines. Besides according to the forest report, the produce of the forests mainly timber is exported not only to Calcutta and Bihar but also it sent to the Bhutan, Bangladesh and to the some areas in the Northern India. The entire production of the plywood timber is also very saleable and a few factories situated in the Duars and Siliguri consume the plywood. Presently plywood is allotted to West Bengal plywood and Allied Products Ltd (WBPAPL). The match wood timber is purchased by the Western India Match Co. (WIMCO) of Calcutta. There is also a very keen demand for Khair trees for manufacture of Katha. Out of 878 respondents 569 respondents (64.81%) reporting that Bhutan, Bangladesh, Assam and other North Eastern states and Nepal and 309 respondents (35.19%) named Siliguri, Jalpaiguri, Alipurduar and Calcutta, Kishanganj of Bihar as centers where timbers was transported for various purposes such as for plywood, furniture, house material, gun industry, railway sleeper etc. The above discussion shows that, though, the forest villagers are very much worried about tree felling and deforestation in their native environment but do not feel devoted to go into various aspects of this activities through forest may be protected. Only they are saying that villagers have no direct role in either cutting of trees or in actual process of felling.

7.4 Response to Local Needs

The observation of the feeling of the villagers' needs and their fulfilment is very important. The demand of forest resources and supply or stocks mechanism are of absolute importance to the forest villagers. They fulfil their livelihood demands of fuel by gathering grasses, fuel wood, bamboo, dry leaves, dry branches, and fodder by green leaves of branches and timber by felling the trees. All demand has been fulfilled by free-grant and although sometime paid nominal price for timber, as well as the extra demand is met either by illegal cutting or purchasing. In this part attempt has been made to analyze the respondent's perception on the tree felling, stock, and fodder related subject.

7.4.1 Tree Felling by the Villagers

The villagers are not support to cut any tree even they have been unapproved from trimming branches of trees beyond a particular thickness. Although they are not allowed to collect green leaves and woods from the forests. The villagers are allowed to collect dry branches of woods, fallen dry leaves, dry roots, grass etc which are sufficient to fulfil their certain requirements. The respondents were asked about involvement in trees felling but they refused their involvement by unauthorized way. Few of them allow the fact that unauthorized tree felling has been done on a limited amount at the time of any celebration of the society. It has been noticed that only 44 (5.01%) respondents were supported and engaged to cut the trees through illegal way, but they could not specify the actual demand or numbers (table–7.4). On the other hand 834 (94.99%) respondents opted that they were not supported and engaged to cut the trees by illegal way even they remarked illegal felling are mainly the cause of outside of the forest people who are not emotionally connected with forests environment. It was noticed that as the altitude decrease, the number of inhabitants' engagement in illegal felling also increases. There are some causes behind this occurrence e.g. at lower altitude it is easy to getting timber due to its more even surface, and there is no alternative available except the timber from the forests for house materials, fuels, agricultural implements, unemployment of villagers where timbers and dry branches give some earning etc.

Table–7.4
Villagers Acceptance on Illegal Tree Felling

S.No.	Forest village	Illegal tree felling		Total sampled
		Yes	No	Households
1	Lehra	-	22	22
2	Suni	-	28	28
3	Garo Basti	-	72	72
4	Gadhadhar	-	63	63
5	Poro (N)	03	58	61
6	Nimati and Dabri	-	68	68
7	Gangutia H.A	07	48	55
8	Adma H.A	06	49	55
9	Raimatang H.A	03	52	55
10	Bhutri forest basti H.A	07	38	45
11	Gudamdabri	-	63	63
12	Chunabati H.A	05	49	54
13	Bhutiabasti	04	26	30
14	Sankosh	03	57	60
15	Lapraguri	-	47	47
16	Santrabari H.A	06	59	65

17	Balapara	-	35	35
	Total	**44 (5.01%)**	**834 (94.99%)**	**878 (100%)**

H.A=High Altitude, (Prepared based on field survey, 2017)

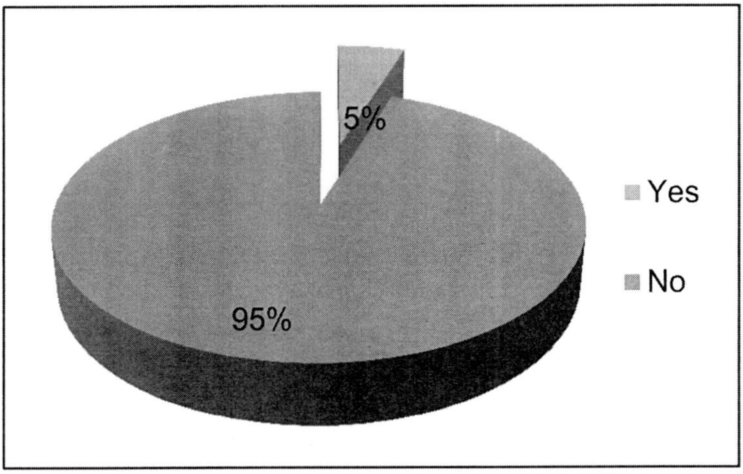

Fig. 7.3: Villagers acceptance on illegal tree felling.

7.4.2 Perception about Present and Future Forest Stock

During the field observation the respondents were asked to know the feeling of villagers about the present and future forest stock. Out of 878 respondents (table–7.5), 215 (24.49%) respondents gave positive response to the question pertaining to the adequacy of present stock in meeting their demands. They opined and hope that if the forests are used only by forest residents, the growth and annual increment in the forest will be enough for them. As many as 663 (75.51%) reported that at present forest stock is insufficient and there will a dangerous situation for wild life and them if it not protected now. Further, opined that there is no need to felling of trees as it is sufficient and dead wood, leaves, branches etc. are always been available for local use. The respondents in high altitudinal zone opined that the forest stock is sufficient as compared to the respondents in lower altitudinal zone or plain area. This, once again shows the huge pressure, illegal tree felling, high encroachment of outside people on plain forest. Although huge pressure and dependence has been observed of forest of villagers on higher altitudes but villagers seemed it is now under control.

Table–7.5
Villagers Perception about Present Forest Stock

S.No.	Forest village	Adequacy stock		Inadequacy stock		Total sampled house-holds
		Yes	No	Yes	No	
1	Lehra	-	-	22	-	22
2	Suni	-	-	28	-	28
3	Garo Basti	-	-	72	-	72
4	Gadhadhar	-	-	63	-	63
5	Poro (N)	11	-	50	-	61
6	Nimati and Dabri	-	-	68	-	68
7	Gangutia H.A	31	-	24	-	55
8	Adma H.A	23	-	32	-	55
9	Raimatang H.A	29	-	26	-	55
10	Bhutri F. basti H.A	32	-	13	-	45
11	Gudamdabri	-	-	63	-	63
12	Chunabati H.A	34	-	20	-	54
13	Bhutiabasti	13	-	17	-	30
14	Sankosh	11	-	49	-	60
15	Lapraguri	-	-	47	-	47
16	Santrabari H.A	31	-	34	-	65
17	Balapara	-	-	35	-	35
	Total	**215 (24.49%)**	**-**	**663 (75.51%)**	**-**	**878 (100%)**

H.A=High Altitude, (Prepared based on field survey, 2017)

7.4.3 The Causes for Not Growing The Fodder Crops

More or less all families of the forest villagers rearing livestock for livelihood support. These livestock animals besides open grazing, needs additional feed during night time. The respondents opined that they did not grow any fodder crops separately for livestock. They could use only the crop residue as fodder such as paddy, corn thatches. The absence of agricultural land is the only most important cause behind less interest and not growing the fodder trees for animals. Therefore it was, necessary to know about the sources of fodder which was asked to the respondents.

There are 67.65% respondents (table–7.6) who realized lacking of agricultural land as the main reason. About 24.95 % of the respondents perceived that lacking of food crop is a factor of less interest in fodder crops. While 7.40% gave negative response due to paucity of irrigation. From above observation it is noted that due to unavailability of fodder crops for feeding and since fodder has been collected constantly from the forest, so an enormous pressure also has been faced by the nearby forests.

7.4.4 Perception about Forest Values

The forest values have been considered here as concepts of the demand value, related to forests. In this sense, the value of forests is referred as relates to the functions or purposes or demand, for villagers use. In this study, by analyzing different services of forests in this area, the value of forests has been divided into two broad types such as i. economic value, and ii. ecological and environmental value. The economic value of the forest means its ability to provide demands related to villagers livelihood subsistence and income, for example uses of natural resources such as food, fodder, bamboo, fruit, cane and medicinal products etc. The ecological and environmental value means, functions and services of forest, such as protection of water resources or restoration of soil fertility, soil erosion, landslides, climate change etc. For better understanding of forest values to the villagers, each group of values were subdivided into specific values according to their demand related to the forests (table–7.7). Specific values of forest were explained to the respondents such as in food, timber, climate, worship etc and asked for opinion what benefit came from the forest to them, or what they can get from the forest, or what activities can they do in the forests.

Table–7.6

Villagers perception about causes for not growing fodder crop

S.No.	Forest village	Causes for not growing the Fodder crop				Total
		Lacking of land	Lacking of food crop	Unsuitable climate	Paucity of irrigation	sampled households
1	Lehra	14	06	-	02	22
2	Suni	17	04	-	07	28
3	Garo Basti	43	24	-	05	72
4	Gadhadhar	47	13	-	03	63
5	Poro (N)	36	17	-	08	61
6	Nimati and Dabri	44	15	-	09	68
7	Gangutia H.A	31	13	-	11	55
8	Adma H.A	45	10	-	-	55
9	Raimatang H.A	39	16	-	-	55
10	Bhutri F. basti H.A	35	10	-	-	45
11	Gudamdabri	37	26	-	-	63
12	Chunabati H.A	46	08	-	-	54
13	Bhutiabasti	23	07	-	-	30
14	Sankosh	42	12	-	06	60
15	Lapraguri	23	16	-	08	47
16	Santrabari H.A	51	14	-	-	65
17	Balapara	21	08	-	06	35
	Total	**594** (67.65%)	**219** (24.95%)	**-**	**65** (7.40%)	**878** (100%)

H.A=High Altitude, (Prepared based on field survey, 2017)

Table–7.7
Description of Forest Values

Value type	Code	Forest values	Description	Ranked according to villagers opinion
Economic value	F.V 1	Grass/Fodder	Villagers, who are forest dependent, collected dry and green grass as food of livestock from forests such as grass of Kucho, Kans, Thatch.	R-4
	F.V 2	Firewood	Firewood for daily day cooking fuel mainly collected from the forest; especially it is consumed for warming the house in winter season.	R-1
	F.V 3	Timber	Timber and wood vines collected from the forests for construction of house materials such as pillar, wall, door, window, etc guard wall, fence, bridges, and towers and so on.	R-2
	F.V 4	Livestock rearing	Forest is used as field of livestock rearing mainly cows and goat.	R-6
	F.V 5	Bamboo	Bamboo from forests is collected and used to build houses, walls, and fence and also to make house furniture.	R-7

Value type	Code	Forest values	Description	Ranked according to villagers opinion
	F.V 6	Medicinal plants	Villagers collecting different plants as medicinal purpose from the forests to be cure from disease like fever, skin disease, bone fracture etc.	R-8
	F.V 7	Leaf	Green leaves used as fodder for livestock and dry leaves used for fuel and fertilizer purpose in the vegetable or rice fields.	R-16
	F.V 8	Ecotourism	Forests areas are developed for ecotourism industry which bringing extra household income through tourist guide and home stay business for forest villagers.	R-10
	F.V 9	Cane	Cane is gathered from forests and it is mainly used to build house furniture such as chair, table and fence purpose.	R-9
	F.V 10	Golden and Sponge Mushroom	It is an edible herb collected by villagers and consumed as vegetable curry.	R-15

Value type	Code	Forest values	Description	Ranked according to villagers opinion
	F.V 11	Orchards	Orchards and Inflorescence is collected from different species for decorative purpose.	R-19
	F.V 12	Fruit	Myrobalan (Amlaki), peach, fig fruit, jackfruit, Mango etc. are collected from forest.	R-11
	F.V 13	Climbers	It has many used, such as for fencing of agricultural field, as edible food for cows and goat and also used for rope purpose. Satmula, Manjito, Bantarul, Gila, Sikakai, Dhundhal, Jangli San, Bet etc. are different types of climber in this area.	R-3
Ecological and Environmental value	F.V 14	Water source	Inside the forest there are many natural perennial springs and reservoir, and forests help to preserve perennial water conservation.	R-5
	F.V 15	Clean air	Forests clarify air dust, reduce CO2 and air pollutants give them pollution less fresh environment.	R-18
	F.V 16	Soil protection	Root systems of trees of forests prevent soil erosion.	R-14

Value type	Code	Forest values	Description	Ranked according to villagers opinion
	F.V 17	Landside protection	Landslides are being prevented by forests trees through root systems of trees.	R-20
	F.V 18	Windbreak	Forests reduce wind speeds and protect villagers' house and properties from storm.	R-17
	F.V 19	Climate	Climate is directly and indirectly controlled by forest, and it provides comfortable weather regionally through enough rainfall, controlling temperature by tree canopy.	R-12
	F.V 20	Fertility of soil	Soil erosion preventing, dry leaves, and dead wood composition from the forests, which also improves fertility of soil.	R-13

(Prepared based on field survey, 2017)

Villagers were asked to rank their perception on forest values according to the importance and after taking opinion, 20 ranks of forest values have been noticed and presented here (table–7.7). It is noted that most of the economic values that were mentioned in the table get much more importance and ranked than ecological and environmental values. However villagers were very much concerned about environment issues. Since ecological as well as environmental values of water source (ranked 5), climate (ranked 12), fertility of soil (ranked 13), soil protection (ranked 14) clean air (rank 18) etc. also get position. So it proves that villagers now very much concern about natural environment as well as forest ecosystem which is related to future livelihood needs.

Table–7.8
Opinion of Villagers on Forest Value

S.No.	Forest village	Opinion of villagers on forest value (no. of households)			
		Economic value		Ecological and Environmental value	
		Yes	No	Yes	No
1	Lehra	17	05	13	09
2	Suni	22	06	24	04
3	Garo Basti	64	08	57	15
4	Gadhadhar	57	06	51	12
5	Poro (N)	53	08	47	14
6	Nimati and Dabri	61	07	54	14
7	Gangutia H.A	49	06	47	08
8	Adma H.A	51	04	46	09
9	Raimatang H.A	48	07	43	12
10	Bhutri forest basti H.A	41	04	37	08
11	Gudamdabri	56	07	58	05
12	Chunabati H.A	48	06	43	11
13	Bhutiabasti	24	06	22	08
14	Sankosh	53	07	51	09
15	Lapraguri	42	05	38	09

16	Santrabari H.A	59	06	56	09
17	Balapara	31	04	32	03
	Total	**776**	**102**	**719**	**159**
	%	**88.38**	**11.62**	**81.89**	**18.11**

H.A=High Altitude, (Prepared based on field survey, 2017)

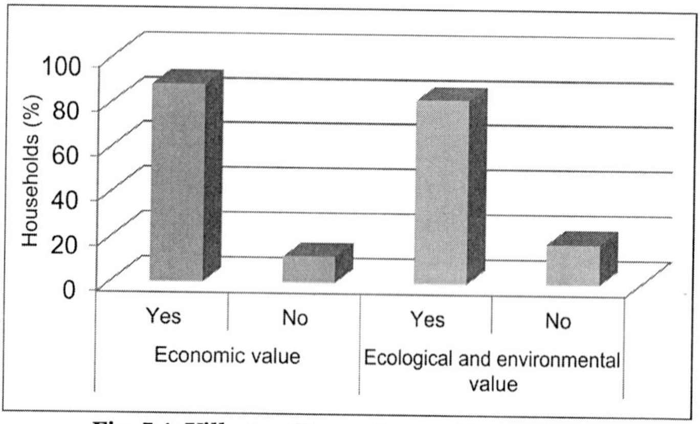

Fig. 7.4: Villagers Perception on Forest Value

The villagers were asked separately about economic as well as for ecological and environmental values where there are about 88.38% respondents (table–7.8) who gave much more importance in economic value of forests and about

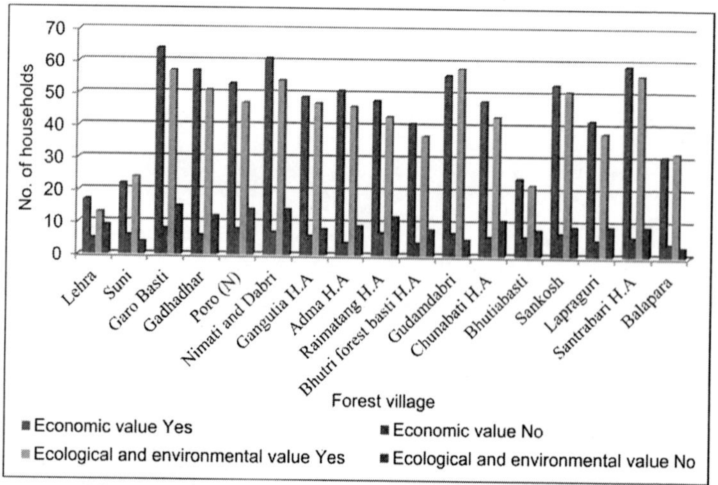

Fig. 7.5: Village-wise Perceptions on Forest Value

81.89% opined in favour of ecological value. From above observation it is clear that directly or indirectly villagers are very much dependent on forest for economic activity and due to which forest have been facing tremendous pressure of economic related work although respondents were also very much serious about deterioration of forest environment and gave importance on ecological and environmental values.

7.5 Perception about the Effect of Forest on Ecological Changes

At present the forest resource utilization and developmental of society played as a prime factor for environmental changes in any forest region. Forest can influence regional and local weather and climate via a number of different mechanisms (Betts, 2006). There are innumerable adverse effects of the changes in forest cover and forest area shrinkage on ecological conditions. Even in the world environment has suddenly a lot of changes due to rapid rate deforestation. Dokuchaev (1892) and Kasatkin (1927) in Rusia, and Zon (1935) in the United States, among others, held that a forested area would provide effective moistening of the atmosphere by transpiration to significantly increase precipitation. Dokchaev promoted afforestation of the Russia steppes to prevent drought (Golding, 1970). Now a day the effect of forest cover change is more prominent through ecological imbalance due to fast deforestation such as extinct and endangered of wild animals, regular conflict of man-animal, more or less rainfall, temperature, landslides and scarcity of water sources etc. In this study, an effort has been made to take opinion of feeling of respondents about forest role in ecological control. The villagers were asked about their perception and feeling of forest role on environment change. About 878 villagers were engaged to give response on it. In the table 7.9 shows that while 0.91% was not very specific, there were 7.74% of the respondents who felt that presently trees do not affect on environmental change at all. And about 91.35% of the respondents were consented about the influence of forests on the environment.

Table–7.9
Perception about the Impact of Forest on Ecological Changes

S.No.	Forest village	Impact of forest on ecological changes			Total sampled
		Not specific	Effect of forest	Not feel any change	house-holds
1	Lehra	-	19	03	22
2	Suni	-	25	03	28
3	Garo Basti	05	61	06	72
4	Gadhadhar	-	59	04	63
5	Poro (N)	03	56	02	61
6	Nimati and Dabri	-	63	05	68
7	Gangutia H.A	-	49	06	55
8	Adma H.A	-	52	03	55
9	Raimatang H.A	-	47	08	55
10	Bhutri forest basti H.A	-	43	02	45
11	Gudamdabri	-	57	06	63
12	Chunabati H.A	-	51	03	54
13	Bhutiabasti	-	30	-	30
14	Sankosh	-	54	06	60
15	Lapraguri	-	47	-	47
16	Santrabari H.A	-	60	05	65
17	Balapara	-	29	06	35
	Total	**8 (0.91%)**	**802 (91.35%)**	**68 (7.74%)**	**878 (100%)**

H.A=High Altitude, (Prepared based on field survey, 2017)

7.5.1 Impacts of Forest Cover Change on Rainfall

The impact of forests on local rainfall situations of any areas is quite apparent and approved. In any macro, meso or micro level region, the forest plays a vital role to determine the rainfall characteristics and other environmental phenomena. The moisture amount of air above the forests becomes larger, which could factor affecting convection, cloud formation and an enhancement of rainfall (Millan, 2005). Depending on the scale and pattern of afforestation or deforestation rainfall can either be enhanced or reduced (Sanderson et al., 2012). It is also estimated that about half of the rainfall in the Amazon area originates as moisture content supplied by the forests (Silvas Dias et al., 2009).

Table–7.10
Perception about The Impact of Forest on Rainfall Changes

S. No.	Forest village	Impact of forest on rainfall changes within 10 years			
		No change in Rainfall	Rainfall Irregular	Rainfall decreased	Rainfall increased
1	Lehra	-	09	13	-
2	Suni	-	05	23	-
3	Garo Basti	-	21	51	-
4	Gadhadhar	-	19	44	-
5	Poro (N)	03	26	32	-
6	Nimati and Dabri	05	14	49	-
7	Gangutia H.A	07	12	36	-
8	Adma H.A	08	09	38	-
9	Raimatang H.A	-	14	41	-
10	Bhutri forest basti H.A	04	09	32	-
11	Gudamdabri	-	16	47	-
12	Chunabati H.A	06	11	37	-
13	Bhutiabasti	-	06	24	-
14	Sankosh	-	14	46	-
15	Lapraguri	-	13	34	-
16	Santrabari H.A	-	10	55	-
17	Balapara	-	06	29	-
	Total	**33 (3.76%)**	**214 (24.37%)**	**631 (71.87%)**	**0%**

H.A=High Altitude, (Prepared based on field survey, 2017)

The table–7.10 reveals perception of respondents about the impact of forest on rainfall changes. Among the respondents 3.76% commented that no change in rainfall has been occurred over the past 10 years and it is opined only by the villagers who were in high altitude and dense forest respondents.

About 71.87% of the respondents announced that amount of rainfall has decreased over the past 10 years; whereas 24.37% noticed it is now uncertainty and irregularity at the time of rainy season. According to the villagers' opinion, it is noticed that the rainfall behaviour has become uncertain for the past few decades. It either comes early or late or comes in increased or decreased intensity which affect their normal life. Surprisingly not a single respondent felt increase in rainfall. The analysis also shows that the respondents comments on drastically decreased of rainfall were mostly comes from decrease and less dense forest, shrinkage of forest cover, lower altitude and plain area residents.

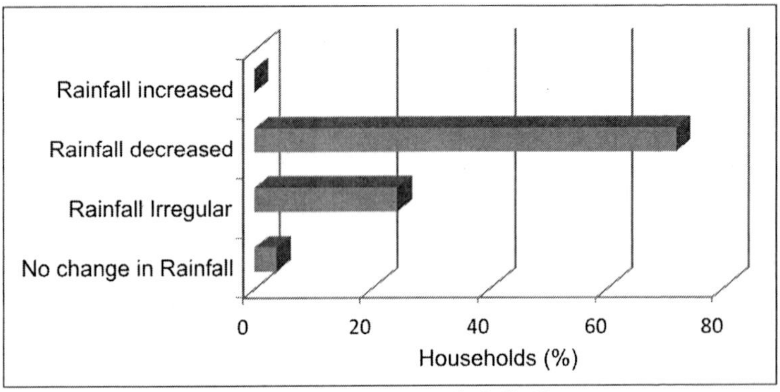

Fig. 7.6: Perception on Rainfall Changes

7.5.2 Effect of Forest on Temperature

The perception of respondents about changes in normal temperature due to changes in forest cover had been observed by asking question during field study. It is referred that forest also absorb water from soils via their roots and release it into the atmosphere, a process called evapotranspiration, which has various impacts on weather and climate (Von Randow et al., 2004). Boreal forest has large effects on local temperature and of the three main forest types, the largest influence on global mean temperature (Bonan, 2008). And interestingly it is observed that respondents opined reverse relation between rainfall and temperature, where they noticed that rainfall has been perceived as decreasing over one decade, the temperature has reportedly increased. The field investigation has revealed that out of the total 878 respondents, 71 (8.08%) opined that no change in temperature has been felt, 623 (70.96%) felt increase in normal temperature while 184 (20.96%) are of the

Table–7.11
Perception about the Impact of Forest on Temperature Changes

S.No.	Forest village	Impact of forest on temperature changes within 10 years			
		No change in temperature	Temperature decreased	Temperature increased	Fluctuate temperature in seasons
1	Lehra	-	-	17	05
2	Suni	-	-	20	08
3	Garo Basti	-	-	49	23
4	Gadhadhar	-	-	47	16
5	Poro (N)	-	-	40	21
6	Nimati and Dabri	-	-	56	12
7	Gangutia H.A	13	-	36	06
8	Adma H.A	11	-	42	02
9	Raimatang H.A	-	-	38	17
10	Bhutri F. basti H.A	07	-	29	09
11	Gudamdabri	-	-	42	21
12	Chunabati H.A	14	-	32	08
13	Bhutiabasti	04	-	21	05
14	Sankosh	-	-	51	09
15	Lapraguri	13	-	27	07
16	Santrabari H.A	09	-	48	08
17	Balapara	-	-	28	07
	Total	**71** (8.08%)	**-**	**623** (70.96%)	**184** (20.96%)

H.A=High Altitude, (Prepared based on field survey, 2017)

notice that the normal temperature has fluctuated in different seasons over the last 10 years (table–7.11).

Among the respondents who were in high altitude and dense forest respondents they perceived that no change in temperature has been occurred over the past 10 years in their surroundings. But respondents who were on plain and less dense forest area; they felt fluctuation and increase of temperature in their locality.

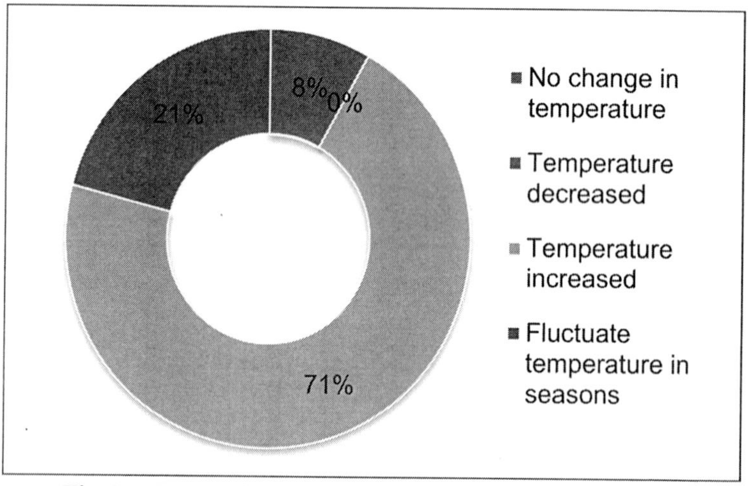

Fig. 7.7: Perception on Temperature Changes for Forest Shrinkage

7.5.3 Impact of Forest Cover Change on Landslide

Vegetation cover plays an important role to protect landslides. The trees on hill slopes and beside of river banks control the force in the flow of water and consequently reduces landslide and soil erosion. Deep-rooted shrubs and trees can reduce the incidence of shallow firstly moving landslides by strengthening soil stratas and improving drainage and transpiration via extensive root systems also reduces soil water content and landslide risk (Sidle et al., 2006). Due to forest felling and thinning of the forest cover in this area, the river bank erosion and landslides in the high altitude area generally increased. Therefore respondents were, asked to give opinions on this subject. The table–7.12 that

Table–7.12
Perception about the Impact of Forest on Landslide and Erosion

S. No.	Forest village	Impact of forest on landslides changes within 10 years			
		No change in landslides/ erosion	Landslides/ erosion increased	Landslides/ erosion decreased	No specific idea
1	Lehra	-	05	-	17
2	Suni	-	09	-	19
3	Garo Basti	-	33	-	39
4	Gadhadhar	04	23	-	36
5	Poro (N)	07	31	-	23
6	Nimati and Dabri	09	27	-	32
7	Gangutia H.A	05	41	-	09
8	Adma H.A	03	49	-	03
9	Raimatang H.A	04	43	-	08
10	Bhutri forest basti	03	38	-	04
11	Gudamdabri	-	26	-	37
12	Chunabati H.A	04	47	-	03
13	Bhutiabasti	05	22	-	03
14	Sankosh	07	41	-	12
15	Lapraguri	04	34	-	09
16	Santrabari H.A	05	52	-	08
17	Balapara	03	26	-	06
	Total	**63 (7.18%)**	**547 (62.30%)**	**-**	**268 (30.52%)**

H.A=High Altitude, (Prepared based on field survey, 2017)

about 268 (30.52%) respondents did not give any reply since they have no idea about landslide and erosion; and 63 (7.18%) were of opinion in no change in landslides or erosion intensity, while 547 (62.30%) villagers' were of the opinion that landslides have increased in recent past. None of single respondents felt decrease in landslides. As a whole, villagers were not so much concerned about landslides and erosion as there has been no major occurrence in their neighbourhoods in lower altitude villages. The maximum respondents who felt increase in landslides and erosion are belong to the villages from high altitudes of the area such as Chunabati, Adma, and Santarbari village.

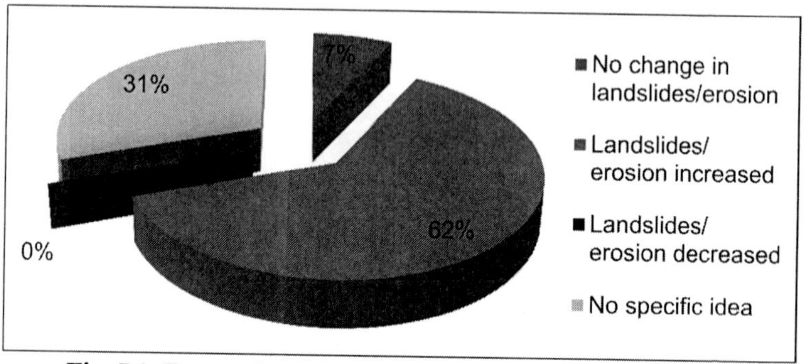

Fig. 7.8: Perception on Impact of Landslide and Erosion for Tree Felling

7.5.4 Effect of Forest on Water Sources

In hill and plain forests areas the natural sources of water such as river, lake, reservoir and springs, seasonal water channels has prime importance to the forest villagers. The deforestation or tree felling in the catchment areas of water bodies affects the water availability in springs, seasonal reservoir and small rivers. These forest acts a very active role in the local hydrological cycle. They capture water from rainfall, and also harvest water directly from wind (i.e. advective) or convective-driven clouds (Bruijnzeel, 2001). During the field investigation, respondents were asked to specify the changes in availability of water source and duration of water presence in local water bodies. Out of total respondents, 112 (12.75%) did not have any idea about impact of forest cover change on source of water while 38 respondents (4.33%) were opined that no change in water sources is noticed by them (table–7.13). Besides there was not a single respondents who perceived that water sources not drying up/dried while 728 (82.92%) opined that water sources have dried up as well as the amount of water in the local water bodies has shrunk. It is noticed that the high altitude villagers were so much concerned about drying up of springs and small natural reservoir especially in winter season, whereas villagers of low altitude who replied that most of the rivers drying up and in volume of flow is day by day shrinking.

Table–7.13

Perception about the Impact of Forest on Water Source

S.No.	Forest village	Impact of forest on water source changes within 10 years			
		No change in water source	water sources drying up/dried	water sources not drying up/dried	No specific idea
1	Lehra	-	15	-	07
2	Suni	-	23	-	05
3	Garo Basti	09	43	-	20
4	Gadhadhar	04	52	-	07
5	Poro (N)	07	48	-	06
6	Nimati and Dabri	05	54	-	09
7	Gangutia H.A	-	47	-	08
8	Adma H.A	-	52	-	03
9	Raimatang H.A	-	48	-	07
10	Bhutri F. basti H.A	-	41	-	04
11	Gudamdabri	08	46	-	09
12	Chunabati H.A	-	51	-	03
13	Bhutiabasti	-	28	-	02
14	Sankosh	05	49	-	06
15	Lapraguri	-	42	-	05
16	Santrabari H.A	-	58	-	07
17	Balapara	-	31	-	04
	Total	**38 (4.33%)**	**728 (82.92%)**	**-**	**112 (12.75%)**

H.A=High Altitude, (Prepared based on field survey, 2017)

Most of the respondents perceived that deforestation has affected the water bodies and sub-surface water. In some cases it is indicated that the felling of sal and teak trees as reduced the water in winter springs because these tree helps soil in absorbing a lot of water which is released subsequently after rainy season. The fe1ling of mixed vegetation cover is responsible for reduction in water in natural sources.

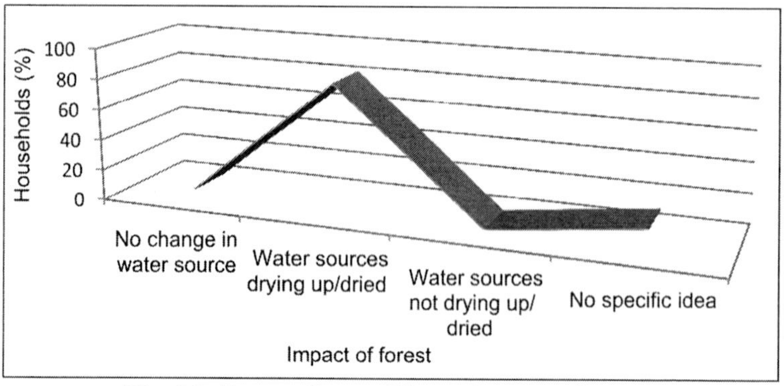

Fig. 7.9: Perception on Water Source Changes

7.5.5 Forest and Other Ecological Aspects

Besides the above aspects, the villagers felt few important impacts of forests on ecology of this area. It is reported by villagers of low lying altitude area that due to deforestation, landslide and erosion has been increased which is responsible for shrinking of river beds and sudden flood have become frequent in the area. In connection it is argued that the ongoing climatic change would produce significant impacts on natural hazards, river flows, flood and ecosystem composition and biodiversity, structure, and function and human livelihoods (Parmesan, 2006). The respondents of plain area felt that deforestation has led to more wild animal attack to the men happened in a regular interval.

7.6 Reasons for Forest Destruction, Its Responsibilities and Solutions

During the field study, an attempt had been made to prepare the villagers opinions regarding causes of forest area shrinkage and destruction, the responsibility of this destruction and the possible solutions. In general studies on forest problems of any region, a number of causes such as felling of trees for different purpose of development activities, over grazing, expansion of agriculture field etc have been mentioned as the prime causes of forest degradation. By considering these ideas, it is important to know the opinions of the forest villagers through the question regarding shrinkage of forest area, decrease of density of forest and solutions of the problems of it.

7.6.1 Reasons of Forest Area Shrinkage and Destruction

About the question of forest area shrinkage and destruction, as many as main 5 reasons were mentioned by the villagers, almost all respondents gave one prime reason or single reason but some of them opined more than one reason.

Large scale tree felling is mentioned as the most important single reason for forests destruction and shrinkage by 368 (41.91%) out of 878 respondents. About 228 (25.97%) respondents opined that illegal felling by outsiders; poachers are main culprit for forest destruction, whereas 125 (14.24%) villagers viewed day by day increase in village population as the major reason for forest destruction. About 41 (4.67%) respondents viewed natural calamities (fire, landslide) as the reason for forest destruction, whereas 116 (13.21%) respondents considered rail way and road construction as

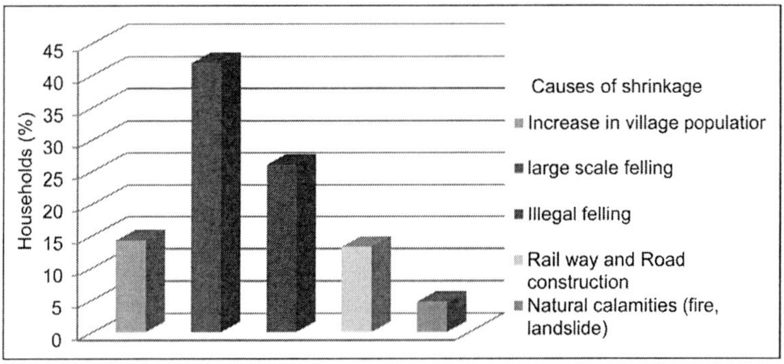

Fig. 7.10: Perception on Causes of Forest Area Shrinkage

Table–7.14

Perception about Reasons of Forest Shrinkage and Destruction

S. No.	Forest village	Different opinions of respondents				
		Increase in village population	Large scale felling	Illegal felling	Railway and Road construction	Natural calamities (fire, landslide)
1	Lehra	05	13	04	-	-
2	Suni	07	19	02	-	-
3	Garo Basti	19	25	07	21	-
4	Gadhadhar	06	20	18	14	05
5	Poro (N)	13	34	02	12	-
6	Nimati and Dabri	15	27	14	12	-
7	Gangutia H.A	06	25	15	05	04
8	Adma H.A	07	22	17	03	06
9	Raimatang H.A	05	19	21	07	03
10	Bhutri F. basti H.A	07	13	16	04	05
11	Gudamdabri	08	25	19	11	-
12	Chunabati H.A	06	23	20	-	05
13	Bhutiabasti	-	12	12	04	02
14	Sankosh	07	24	18	06	05
15	Lapraguri	06	22	14	05	-
16	Santrabari H.A	08	24	20	07	06
17	Balapara	-	21	09	05	-
	Total	**125 (14.24%)**	**368 (41.91%)**	**228 (25.97%)**	**116 (13.21%)**	**41 (4.67%)**

H.A=High Altitude, (Prepared based on field survey, 2017)

main damaging factors. The villagers in lower lying altitude were so much concerned about forest destruction and opined that large scale felling, rail way and road construction, and illegal felling are major responsible factors which has been occurred in their neighborhoods. While villagers of high altitude viewed that increase in village population and natural calamities (fire, landslide) also involved and considered as responsible factor to the forest destruction in high altitudes area.

7.6.2 Responsibility for Forest Shrinkage and Destruction

An attempt had been made to view about the responsibility of the persons or agency that responsible for forest destruction the study area. In the table 7.15 shows that out of these 878 respondents, 516 (58.77%) give the blame on Forest Department for allowing large scale felling to fulfil Government or agencies needs as well as not taking proper care of the forest to prohibit illegal felling and poaching. About 162 (18.45%) respondents give the blame on villagers own self for destruction through green leaves collection, braches collection, excessive grazing and overall careless use. While 165 respondents (18.79%) have blamed contractor who helped forest official for large scale felling also insist fringe and local people for illegal and uncontrolled large scale felling. A few respondents put the blame on natural calamities and it was 35 (3.99%) respondents who blamed nature hazards such as fire, landslide for destruction.

Table–7.15
Perception about Responsibility of Forest Shrinkage and Destruction

S. No.	Forest village	Different opinions of respondents			
		Forest villagers	Forest Department	Contractors	Others
1	Lehra	07	15	-	-
2	Suni	05	21	02	-
3	Garo Basti	13	36	19	04
4	Gadhadhar	11	35	14	03

5	Poro (N)	10	37	12	02
6	Nimati and Dabri	13	39	16	-
7	Gangutia H.A	09	33	08	05
8	Adma H.A	07	39	06	03
9	Raimatang H.A	14	31	07	03
10	Bhutri forest basti H.A	12	24	09	-
11	Gudamdabri	13	31	15	04
12	Chunabati H.A	05	36	11	02
13	Bhutiabasti	04	21	05	-
14	Sankosh	10	32	12	06
15	Lapraguri	11	26	10	-
16	Santrabari H.A	15	37	13	-
17	Balapara	03	23	06	03
	Total	**162 (18.45%)**	**516 (58.77%)**	**165 (18.79%)**	**35 (3.99%)**

H.A=High Altitude, (Prepared based on field survey, 2017)

7.6.3 Solution of Problems

With the perception of forest related environmental as well as other problems and by considering the critical situations of the surrounding forests, the respondents gave some separate suggestions about proper care of the forests. Among 878 respondents, 218 (24.83%) respondents (table–7.16) opined that more and more afforestation is the only good and easy way of solution of forest problems in the area. About 342 (38.95%) respondents were of the opinion that serious awareness of the Forest Department should have been taken for proper care of the forest by implementing Government projects accordingly. While 158 (17.99%) respondents suggested to control of illegal felling by implementing hard and fast rules and laws, and also proposed heavy fine on the offenders must be imposed. It was thought by 111 (12.64%) respondents that ban and restriction on large scale felling can save the forest area and should have taken step about it strictly, whereas 49 (5.59%) respondents suggested to awareness of villagers own self and they felt that alternatives sources of fuel and fodder should be made available to protect the forest.

Table–7.16

Perception about Solution of Forest Area Shrinkage and Destruction

S.No.	Forest village	Different opinions of respondents				
		Afforestation	Serious awareness of Forest Department	Control of illegal felling	Restriction on large scale felling	Awareness of villagers
1	Lehra	05	13	02	02	-
2	Suni	07	14	04	03	-
3	Garo Basti	16	29	09	13	05
4	Gadhadhar	09	22	13	11	08
5	Poro (N)	18	21	08	10	04
6	Nimati and Dabri	22	23	11	07	05
7	Gangutia H.A	15	25	07	05	03
8	Adma H.A	12	24	10	06	03
9	Raimatang H.A	14	18	13	08	02
10	Bhutri F. basti H.A	11	14	11	06	03
11	Gudamdabri	18	22	14	09	-
12	Chunabati H.A	12	21	15	04	02
13	Bhutiabasti	08	10	05	04	03
14	Sankosh	16	25	12	05	02
15	Lapraguri	11	21	07	03	05
16	Santrabari H.A	17	26	10	08	04
17	Balapara	07	14	07	07	-
	Total	**218** (24.83%)	**342** (38.95%)	**158** (17.99%)	**111** (12.64%)	**49** (5.59%)

H.A=High Altitude, (Prepared based on field survey, 2017)

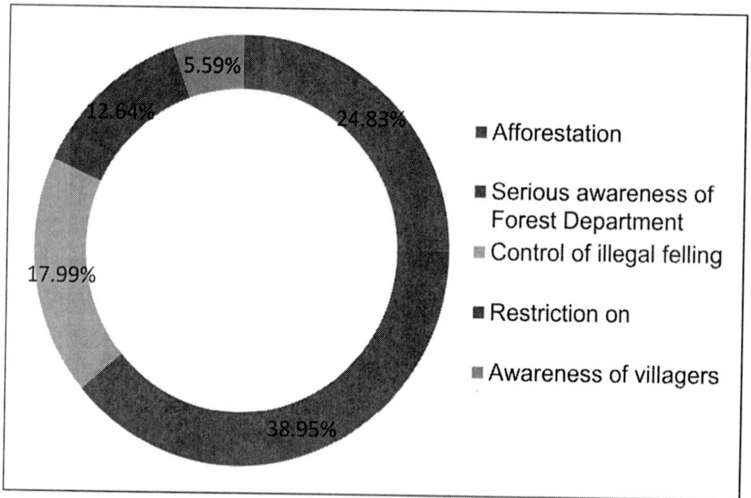

Fig. 7.11: Perception on Solution of Forest Area Shrinkage

In this chapter an attempt had been made regarding perception of villagers on forests value and other forest and environment related perception, problem and suggestion. Villagers opined that forests cover condition is very much worse today than before, and should have been checked by plantation, stop of bulk felling and illegal cutting to improve forest density and shrinkage of forests cover. They felt that government and forest officials are responsible for regional tree felling. Besides, illegal cutting of trees by outsiders, lacking of awareness of forest department is also responsible for shrinkage of forest cover, deterioration and deforestation. Most of the respondents were serious about the impact of deforestation on local environment. They also felt that shrinkage of forests cover and decrease of density are the main causes behind abnormal change of local and regional weather and climate as well as quickly dried up of water bodies, landslides, fluctuation in normal temperature seasonally etc. Finally it may be concluded that forests is an important factors of controlling weather and climate, source of biodiversity, providing habitats for many unique plant and animal species, and home for forests villagers or indigenous peoples.

8
Chapter Joint Forest Management Activity

8.1 Origin of Joint Forest Management (JFM)

The West Bengal has been a beginner of the Joint Forestry Management (JFM) movement in India (Roy, et al., 2001). The JFM (a form of participatory forest management) has been widely adopted in West Bengal, especially in degraded lateritic soil areas of south West Bengal. In 1972, an Indian forester, namely A.K. Banerjee, from Midnapore, had taken a pilot project in West Bengal known as the Arabari socio-economic project where six hundred and eighteen families from eleven villages participated in degraded forest for rehabilitation (Roy, el al., 2001). In this context it is reported that the beginning of JFM thinking around 1975 (in West Bengal) was the realization by the forest officials that it is impossible to protect and regenerate forest without local inhabitants support (Joshi, 2000). In this period, there was no legal support in forest policies and laws for involving local villagers in forest management. The project was neither sponsored by any other NGO or agency nor by the Government. The Arabari socio-economic project was extensively accepted in several parts of West Bengal and its apparent success contributed to a large extent to the development of the 1988 Indian Forest Policy. With the introduction of the 1988 Forest Policy, informal participation of indigenous communities in forest management was converted to Joint Forestry Management (JFM). Under this system, the West Bengal Forest Department in alliance with the village-based Forest Protection Committees (FPCs) started managing forests. The official ground for JFM was prepared by the National Forest Policy of 1988 which planed local villagers' involvement, particularly of women, in meeting basic forests related needs and in managing forest resources. This was followed in 1990 by a circular from Ministry of Environment and Forests (MOEF) providing guidelines for participation of village communities and NGOs in regeneration of degraded and shrinkage forestcover. The National Forest Policy of 1988 and the JFM resolution of 1990 combined with state level resolutions acknowledged the need to give greater rights and authority to forest and fringe villager community groups related to forest. It has been pointed out that Joint Forest Management (JFM) is being increasingly suggested as a solution to the protection of forest in India and other developing countries (Khanna, 1994). The primary objective of Joint Forest Management (JFM) is to secure sustainable use of forest resources to meet villagers demand in proper way while ensuring sustainability of environmental. The central premise is that local men and women who are dependent on forests have the greatest stakeholder in sustainable forest management. The policy envisages a process of joint management of forest by the local people and the State Government, who would share the responsibility for managing the forest resource and the benefits accruing from this. Under Joint Forest management (JFM), local bodies or village communities are assigned with the management and protection of nearby forest. The communities of different parts of rural India have organized formal and informal groups for forest protection and management in states of Orissa, Bihar, Rajasthan, Gujarat, Karnataka, Haryana, Madhya Pradesh and Punjab. While some are formed by state Forest Departments, some are sponsored by local Government or NGO programmes e.g. Gram Panchayets in different names such as Groups of Village Elders (VE), Village Forest Protection Committees (VFPC), Village Councils' (VC), Village Youth Clubs (VYC) in Orissa, Forest Cooperative Societies (FCS) in Himachal Pradesh, Van Panchayats (VP) in UP hills, Forest Protection Committees FPC), Eco-Development committees (EDC) in West Bengal.

8.2 Joint Forest Management in West Bengal

The West Bengal Forest Department (WBFD) is involved

in administration and management of one of the largest forest area of the country. The total forest area is 11879 sq. km which is around 1.55% of the country. In order to have better administrative control in the Forest Department, there are 18 Forest Circles (FC), 58 Territorial Divisions (TD), 474 Territorial Forest Ranges (TFR), and 762 Beats (State Forest Report, 2010-11) in the state.

8.2.1 Joint Forest Management Committees (Government of West Bengal, Forest Department)

West Bengal is the beginner state for initiating Joint Forest Management project (JFMP). This movement of JFM project had its genesis at Arabari administrative area in Midnapur District of West Bengal where forest villages were encouraged to rejuvenate 1,186 hectare of runied sal forest by roping in participation through a set of functions of employment generation and sharing of NTFPs from such forests. This was followed by the adoption of the Government's decision in 1989 to share 25% of net profit for participated local people. In1996, Eco-Development Committee (EDCs) was also established keeping assistance of the forest villagers and fringe people in protection and development of Wildlife Protected Areas (WLPA). The Government Notifications on the resolutions on JFM project including the composition of Forest Protection Committee (FPCs) and Eco-Development Committee (EDCs), the duties and functions of beneficiaries of FPCs and EDCs, sharing benefits etc. have been disclosed locally and circulated amongst the targeted communities of the JFM movement in West Bengal (State Forest Report, 2011-2011). The main objective of JFM was to promote maximum local villagers participation in protection, management and enhance of forest cover. Subsequently, India Eco-Development Project (IDP) implemented in Buxa Tiger Reserve (BTR) and UNDP in Sunderban Tiger Reserve (STR) came as a gracious to carry on with the process of concentration of JFM project (State Forest Report, 2011-2011). As on 31st March 2012, there are 4281 Forest Protection Commitees (FPCs) in the West Bengal consisting total 498808 members protecting the total forest cover over 567599.00 hectare (table–8.1) and total numbers of Eco-Development Committees (EDCs) are 117 consisting of 27575 members protecting 82008.09 hectare of protected areas (table–8.2). For maintenance of assets and taking up village development activities in FPCs areas, the members of FPCs are encouraged to create funds of their own and many of the Forest Protection Committees have already developed substantial fund which also applied for developmental purposes. The Self-Help Groups among the members of FPCs have been made to promote various income generation and vocational functions utilizing fund from own savings as well as bank loans where available and necessary and such Self-Help Group operations are found to be very encouraging mainly for women as they are able to earn supplement for the livelihood needs of their families and society. There is no denying that performances of FPCs and EDCs may differ from area to area with different physical and social parameters.

8.3 Joint Forest Management in Alipurduar District

The Buxa Tiger Reserve (BTR) of Alipurduar District came under conservation in 1983. The Field Director (FD) is the head of the BTR administration under the Principal Chief Conservator of Forests (PCCF), Government of West Bengal. Besides, there are two Deputy Field Director (DFD) under Field Director of BTR to control administrative functions at local level these are DFD, BTR East and DFD, BTR West Division who are also in-charge of forest range offices. Sequencly forest Range officers control Beat Offices and villages under their field in the protected area of the forests.

8.3.1 FPCs and EDCs Activities in Alipurduar District

There are two main committee of JFM in Alipurduar District for villagers' participation at local level either directly or indirectly through SHGs. Such committees are Eco-Development Committees (EDCs) and Forest Protection Committees (FPCs). The executive bodies of EDCs and FPCs have been formed by common members selected or elected for four years by members through general meeting. The

Table–8.1

Status of Joint Forest Management Committee in West Bengal (Forest Protection Committees)

Zone	Division	Total no. of FPC	Area protected (Ha.)	No. of members					
				Male	Female	Total	SC	ST	Others
	Kalimpong	64	26237.86	3582	195	3777	204	875	2698
	Kurseong	45	13091.08	4311	10058	14369	430	1219	12720
	Darjeeling	74	14412.88	3864	426	4290	139	107	4044
Duars-Terai	Jalpaiguri	63	20284.16	11431	638	12069	5255	3399	3415
	Coochbehar	26	4102.90	2932	209	3141	1497	517	1127
	BTR (E)	17	9331.09	3340	103	3443	1548	1334	561
	BTR (W)	33	25595.80	4064	489	4553	768	2563	1222
	Wildlife III	25	6681.70	3738	171	3909	708	1958	1243
	Baikunthapur	64	12898.91	5978	129	6107	4475	628	1004
North Bengal	Raiganj	21	1162.6	1727	74	1801	864	412	525
plains	Malda	04	210	543	18	561	261	296	04
South Bengal	Midnapur	363	45956.45	48038	2801	50839	10130	9186	31522
	Jhargram	474	52179.31	38254	2449	40703	9135	14906	16662
	Nadia-Msd.	12	916.24	957	44	1001	246	254	501

Zone	Division	Total no. of FPC	Area protected (Ha.)	No. of members					
				Male	Female	Total	SC	ST	Others
	Kharagpur	254	27437.65	18421	12281	30702	6950	9504	14248
	Bankura (S)	630	44460.37	53977	4857	58834	14189	18411	26234
	Bankura (N)	540	43514.44	50560	2083	52643	19837	7912	24894
	Rupnarayan	213	26397.78	26331	1343	27674	6419	7814	13441
	Panchet	231	28466.18	27328	1562	28890	11033	4674	13183
	Kangsabati (N)	244	17641.2	23578	881	24469	5677	8089	10693
	Purulia	213	30729.22	20741	867	21608	6012	4944	8652
	Kangsabati (S)	305	25168.8	29561	569	30130	10899	4293	14938
	Burdwan	74	20239.38	16914	2940	19854	7371	5771	6712
	Durgapur	24	2436.439	1957	1964	3921	1112	1405	1404
	Howrah	04	479.08	815	319	1134	537	238	359
	Birbhum	194	10376.39	16608	347	16955	6028	5463	5464
	Purba Medinipur	19	1813.11	4760	1097	5857	1256	50	4551
Estuarine	Sundarban T.R	11	12844	3958	107	4065	3642	254	169
	24-Parganas (s)	40	43534	10801	10718	21519	11830	514	9175
Total		**4281**	**567599**	**439069**	**59739**	**498808**	**148453**	**118990**	**231365**

Source: State Forest Report, 2012-2013.

Table–8.2

Status of Joint Forest Management Committee in West Bengal (Eco-Development Committees)

Zone	Division	Name of P.A	Total no. of EDC	Area protected (Ha.)	No. of members					
					Male	Female	Total	SC	ST	Others
Hilly	Wildlife I	Maha nanda WLS	15	12405.55	2552	2088	4640	1284	992	2346
		Singalila N.P	01	350.00	63	72	135	0	59	76
		Senchal WLS	15	4114.72	1587	1196	2783	92	1442	1249
	Wildlife II	Chapramari WLS	01	960.31	47	1	48	4	8	36
		Gorumara N.P	10	6315.17	1792	51	1843	458	569	816
		Neora valley N.P	06	5594.17	1526	1414	2940	283	758	1899
Duars-Terai	BTR (E)	BTR	14	23534.97	1454	173	1627	223	612	792
	BTR (W)	All EDC transferred to FPC	00	00	00	00	00	00	00	
	Wildlife III	Jaldapara WLS	33	15986.53	6846	1604	8450	3452	2346	2652

Zone	Division	Name of P.A	Total no. of EDC	Area protected (Ha.)	No. of members					
					Male	Female	Total	SC	ST	Others
North Bengal	Raiganj	Kulik WLS	03	130.00	193	21	214	172	30	12
	Nadia-Msd. plains	Bethuadahari WLS	01	66.67	96	6	102	55	-	47
	Birbhum	Ballavpur WLS	04	200.00	276	34	310	9	196	105
Estuarine	Sunder-ban T.R	Sundarban T.R	14	12350.00	3993	490	4483	4047	108	328
Total			**117**	**82008.09**	**20425**	**7150**	**27575**	**10079**	**7120**	**10376**

Source: State Forest Report, 2012-2013

EDCs and FPCs are fully engaged with execution of the government forest conservation programme. But for the interest of villagers, they can alter the forest conservation plan of Forest Department, although it is the subject to the Government approval. The EDCs will exist always inside core area of wildlife sanctuaries and national parks and in reserved forest area with rich bio-diversity, while FPCs mostly formed in degraded forests cover of fringes or buffer forests of a protected area or reserved area. The EDCs of BTR were formulated by the State G.O No. 3841-for/ fr/6/11m-7/95) in June 1996, on the other hand, the FPCs have a prior origin from the State Government JFMP in the 1980s.

The total protected forest area of the Buxa Tiger Reserve (BTR), East Division is 32612.88 hectare. There are 26 Revenue Village (R.V) and 18 forest village belongs in this division where approximately 20,000 human population inhabitated. There are total 31 Joint Forest Management Committees of which 17 are belongs to FPCs and 14 are from EDCs that are running in operation of different forestry activities in this division. The total FPCs members within this division is about 5070, out of which 1773 are SC, 1947 are ST and 1336 members are includes in General or Other category. There are total 210 Self Help Groups (SHGs) that are operated different livelihood activity jointly with JFMc. The FPCs and EDCs have arranged total 29 micro plans which are under preparation. The total protected forest area of the Buxa Tiger Reserve (BTR), West Division is 36607.41 hectare. There are 23 Revenue Village (R.V) and 20 forest villages belong to this division where approximately 28,000 human populations are inhabitated. There are total 31 Joint Forest Management Committees of which 24 are belongs to FPCs and only 07 are from EDCs that are running in operation of different forestry activities. The total FPCs members within this division are about 3722, out of which 775 are SC, 2901 are ST and 46 members are from General category. There are total 187 Self Help Groups (SHGs) that are operated jointly with JFMC in different livelihood activity. The FPCs and EDCs have arranged total 31 micro plans which are under preparation.

There are several village as well as forest development activities done by FPCs and EDCs in BTR in collaboration with Forest Department, local panchayet and other NGOs which are as followed:

a. Training on tailoring, furniture making by cane, weaving, bag making, apiculture, toy making, HYV agriculture practices, tourist guides, farming and cattle rearing.
b. Nursery for providing seeding to the villagers and various institutions for plantation.
c. Infrastructure development through construction and maintenance of earthen road, wooden bridge, culvert, school building and pipe line as well as other source of drinking water supply.
d. Village electrification and extension in all forest villages.
e. Construction of house for forest villagers through Govt. Housing project.
f. Distribution of furniture to the forest village primary schools.

Table–8.3
JFMCs and Other Details of FPCs and EDCs in Alipurduar District

Buxa Tiger Reserve, East Division		
1.	No. of JFMC (FPCs)	31
2.	No. of Revenue Villages	26
3.	No. of Forest Villages	18
4.	No. of members under JFMC (FPCs)	Total members-5070, (SC-1773, ST-1947, Others-1336)
5.	Total human population	20000 approx.
6.	Total cattle population (cow, goat, sheep, buffalo)	50350 approx.
7.	Total forest area protected (in ha.)	32612.88ha
8.	No. of micro plans prepared & under preparation	29

9.	No. of SHG	210
	Buxa Tiger Reserve, West Division	
1.	No. of JFMC (FPCs and EDCs)	24+ 07 = 31
2.	No. of Revenue Villages	23
3.	No. of Forest Villages	20
4.	No. of members under JFMC (FPCs and EDCs)	Total members - 4166, (SC-901, ST-3219, General- 46)
5.	Total human population	28000 apx.
6.	Total cattle population (cow, goat, sheep, buffalo)	60,000 approx.
7.	Total forest area protected (in ha.)	36607.41 ha
8.	No. of micro plans prepared & under preparation	31
9.	No. of SHG	187
	Jalpaiguri Forest Division	
1.	No. of JFMC (FPCs)	04
2.	No. of Forest Villages	04
3.	No. of members under JFMC (FPCs)	Total members - 654, (SC-333, ST-95, Others-226)

Source: Tiger conservation plan, 2016-17 to 2026-27, DFD, East & West BTR Forest Office, Alipurduar, 9th working plan, Vol. I, Jalpaiguri Forest Division, 2008-09.

There are total 66 EDCs and FPCs altogether in Alipurduar District along with BTR East, West Division and Jalpaiguri Forest Division. Each EDCs or FPCs has its control over more than one village. Based on the tenancy of land, villages of FPCs and EDCs fall into three categories such as (a) Forest Villages (FV), (b) Fixed Demand Holding (FDH) villages and (c) Revenue Villages (RV). (Tiger conservation plan, 2016-17 to 2026-27, BTR F.D Office Alipurduar).

Total numbers of FPCs in East division of BTR are 31(after conversion of 14 EDCs to FPCs) where 34032.34

hectare forested area has been protected and maintained by these committees. Total FPCs members of this division are 5070, out of which 4847 members are male and 223 FPC members are female. Among these FPC members, 1773 are SC, 1747 are ST and others comprise 1336 (table–8.4).

In West Division of BTR, total number of FPC is 24 where total 15694.85 hectare protected area belongs to this forest division. Total FPC members of this division are 3722 out of which 3676 members are male and 119 members are female, of which 775 are SC, 2901 are ST and GEN comprise 46 (table–8.5).

Total number of EDCs, in BTR West Division is 07, where 10809.17 hectare protected forest area is covered for forestry activity. Total EDC members of this division are 444, out of which 405 members are male and 39 members are female, where 126 are SC, 318 are ST (table–8.6).

Division wise details of FPCs and EDCs committees, Self-Help Groups (SHG) of forest villages of Alipurduar District is show in the table–8.7, table–8.8 and table–8.9 respectively.

Table–8.8
Number of Self-Help Groups (SHG)

Name of the Division	Number of Groups	Woman Groups	Man Groups
Jaldapara Wl Division (including Jaldapara NP)	149	110	39
Buxa Tiger Reserve (East)	210	210	0
Buxa Tiger Reserve (West)	187	172	15
Total	**546**	**492**	**54**

Source: Tiger conservation plan, 2016-17 to 2026-27, DFD, East & West BTR Forest Office, Alipurduar, 9th working plan, Vol. I, Jalpaiguri Forest Division, 2008-09.

Table–8.4
Details of FPCs in BTR, East Division

Division	No. of FPCs presently formed	Area protected (Ha.)	No. of members					
			Male	Female	Total	SC	ST	GEN.
BTR, East	31	34032.34	4847	223	5070	1773	1947	1336

Source: Tiger conservation plan, 2016-17 to 2026-27, DFD, East & West BTR Forest Office, Alipurduar.

Table–8.5
Details of FPCs in BTR, West Division

Division	No. of FPCs presently formed	Area protected (Ha.)	No. of members					
			Male	Female	Total	SC	ST	GEN.
BTR, West	24	15694.85	3676	119	3722	775	2901	46

Source: Tiger conservation plan, 2016-17 to 2026-27, DFD, East & West BTR Forest Office, Alipurduar.

Table–8.6
Details of EDCs in BTR, West Division

Division	No. of EDC presently formed	Area protected (Ha.)	No. of members					
			Male	Female	Total	SC	ST	Others
BTR, West	07	10809.17	405	39	444	126	318	-

Source: Tiger conservation plan, 2016-17 to 2026-27, DFD, East & West BTR Forest Office, Alipurduar.

Table–8.7
Details of FPCs and EDCs in Alipurduar District

S. No.	Name of JFMC (EDCs/ FPCs)	Date of formation and Reg. No.	Range	No. of Members				Block/Comptt. protected	Area protected (Ha)
				SC	ST	Others	Total		
Buxa Tiger Reserve (East Division)									
1	Purba Salbari & Lapraguri FPC, JFMC	06. 06.97 9/F/V/-1	Bholka	185	103	46	334	Sb-6	336.8
2	Radhanagar Barobisha FPC, JFMC	06. 06.97 8/F/V/-1	Bholka	82	82	44	208	SB-5	334.8
3	Chengmari FPC, JFMC	06.06. 97 15/F/V/-2	Bholka	292	101	55	448	NB-5(P)	337.2
4	Madhya Haldibari FPC, JFMC	06. 06.97 14/F/V/-2	Bholka	260	52	10	322	NB-2,3 & PF land	571.6
5	Dakshin Haldibari FPC, JFMC	06. 06.97 13/F/V/-2	Bholka	176	43	62	281	NB-1(P), NB-(5)	288.60
6	Khutimari & Bengdoba FPC, JFMC	06. 06.97 16/F/V/-3	Bholka	02	72	81	155	SB-1, 2(B), 4, 3(a)	120.0
7	Ghoramara FPC, JFMC	06.06.97 11/F/V/-3	Bholka	60	124	17	201	SB-1, 4, 3(b)	605.6
8	Ghaksapara & Indubasti FPC, JFMC	06. 06. 97 17/F/V/-3	Bholka	125	105	0	230	SB-4, 3(a)	671.0

S. No.	Name of JFMC (EDCs/ FPCs)	Date of formation and Reg. No.	Range	No. of Members				Block/Comptt. protected	Area protected (Ha)
				SC	ST	Others	Total		
9	Balapara banabasti FPC, JFMC	06. 06.97 10/F/V/-4	Bholka	05	31	02	38	SB-1, 2(a), 3(b), NB(4), 5(P)	332.27
10	Kumargram FPC, JFMC	06. 06.97 04/E/K-1	Kumargram	01	13	42	56	KG-1 & 2	1051.39
11	Sankosh FPC JFMC,	06. 06.97 02/E/K-3	Kumargram	09	44	45	98	SK 1, 2 & 3	796.76
12	Newlands FPC JFMC,	06. 06. 97 01/E/K-2	Kumargram	12	19	09	40	NLS-1, 2	1295.41
13	Nurpur FPC, JFMC	06. 06. 97 03/E/J-01	Jainty (S)	81	127	56	264	JNT- 2(b), 3(a), 3(b), 6(a), 6(b), 7(a), 7(b)	1613.60
14	Jainty (F.D holding) FPC, JFMC	12.07.00 03/E/J-01	Jainty (N)	46	15	132	193	NRVK -5,6,7, PHK-1, 2(a), JNT-1, 2(a)	2395.79
15	Bhutiabasti FPC, JFMC	31.03.99 02/E/J-02	Jainty (S)	04	03	65	72	PHK-2, 3, RL, JNT 2(b)	1713.00
16	Buxa Road FPC (28th & 29th mile), JFMC	06. 06.97 05/E/B-1	Buxaduar	1	8	67	76	NRVK-1,2,3, 4,8,9	1657.00
17	Santrabari FPC, JFMC	06.06. 97 06/E/B/3	Buxaduar	7	18	45	70	STV-1,2,3,4	2273.20

S. No.	Name of JFMC (EDCs/ FPCs)	Date of formation and Reg. No.	Range	No. of Members				Block/Comptt. protected	Area protected (Ha)
				SC	ST	Others	Total		
18	Buxaduar FPC, JFMC	06. 06. 97 07/E/B-02	Buxaduar	24	111	23	158	TBGN-1,2,3,4	3099.58
19	Chunabati FPC, JFMC	06.06.97 08/E/B-04	Buxaduar	0	65	04	69	C.bhati-1,2,3	1978.40
20	Shiltong FPC, JFMC	06. 06. 97 01/E/S-1	S. Rydak	2	142	-	144	DH-1,2, SR-1(p) & 4	989.00
21	Paschim Changmari FPC	06.06.97 07/F/S/-4	S. Rydak	27	116	31	174	MKT-2 & 1(P)	662.00
22	Chipra Forest Basti FPC, JFMC	06.06.97 04/F/S/-2	S. Rydak	0	43	0	43	SR-5 & 7	538.04
23	Narathali FPC, JFMC	06.06.97 03/F/S/-3	S .Rydak	126	38	20	184	NRD-1,2	1287.11
24	Marakata FPC, JFMC	06.06.97 05/F/S/-4	S. Rydak	81	62	35	178	MKT-3 &1(P)	1755.00
25	Uttar Narathali FPC, JFMC	06.06.97 06/F/S-4	S. Rydak	38	0	96	134	MKT-4	201.94
26	Uttar Rampur FPC, JFMC	06.06.97 02/F/S-1	S. Rydak	06	159	28	193	SR-2,3	958.00
27	Chowkirbos FPC, JFMC	06.06.97 08/F/S-2	S. Rydak	81	62	33	176	DH-3, SR-6	509.00

S. No.	Name of JFMC (EDCs/ FPCs)	Date of formation and Reg. No.	Range	No. of Members				Block/Comptt. protected	Area protected (Ha)
				SC	ST	Others	Total		
28	Kartick FPC, JFMC	06.06.97 01/E/N/-1	N. Rydak	05	47	14	66	Kartick, Dhowla-RF, Chunia RF, Rahimabad	769.250
29	Teamari FPC, JFMC	06.06.97 02/E/N/-3	N. Rydak	02	08	24	34	CRD-3,4,5,6	1256.00
30	Kanjali Basti FPC, JFMC	06.06.97 03/E/N/-2	N. Rydak	22	58	148	228	CRD-1 & 2, NRD-3 & 4, JNT-Hatipota -II	2391.00
31	Turturi Khand Shanti FPC, JFMC	06.06.97 04/E/N-2	N. Rydak	11	76	116	203	BHT-1 &2, NRD-1 & 2	1244.00
Buxa Tiger Reserve (West Division)									
32	Gadadhar Banabasti F.V FPC, JFMC	15.02.97 16/FPC/ EDPO	East DPO	12	157	-	169	Gada-3 & 4	531.60
33	Uttar Dakshin Dhalkar R.V, FPC, JFMC	16.02.97 17/FPC/ EDPO	East DPO	43	221	-	264	Gada-1&2	496.80

S. No.	Name of JFMC (EDCs/ FPCs)	Date of formation and Reg. No.	Range	No. of Members				Block/Comptt. protected	Area protected (Ha)
				SC	ST	Others	Total		
34	Uttar Dakshin Sibkhata R.V, FPC, JFMC	01.01.98 24/FPC/ EDPO	East DPO	73	169	-	242	Gada-5&6	403.10
35	Uttar Dakshin Panialguri RV, FPC, JFMC	16.02.97 18/FPC/ EDPO	East DPO	0	68	-	68	Checko-3, 4,7,8	930.35
36	Checko Banabasti F.V FPC, JFMC	16.02.97 19/FPC/ EDPO	East DPO	4	193	-	197	Checko-5,6,9	817.60
37	Damanpur F.D, Holding FPC, JFMC	16.02.97 20/FPC/ EDPO	East DPO	2	14	-	16	DPO-7,8	598.70
38	Panijhora Banabasti F.V FPC, JFMC	16.02.97 20/FPC/ EDPO	East DPO	0	78	-	78	DPO-3,4	550.80
39	West Garam F.V & Satkodali FPC, JFMC	13.02.97 13/FPC/ WDPO	West DPO	-	55	-	55	Poro-3,4,8,9	1345.60
40	East Garam F.V, FPC, JFMC	13.02.97 14/FPC/ WDPO	West DPO	69	106	-	175	DPO-1, 5 (P), 6(P),9(P)	720.00

S. No.	Name of JFMC (EDCs/ FPCs)	Date of formation and Reg. No.	Range	No. of Members				Block/Comptt. protected	Area protected (Ha)
				SC	ST	Others	Total		
41	Uttar Jitpur R.V, FPC, JFMC	13.02.97 14/FPC/ WDPO	West DPO	25	14	-	39	Poro-2,5(P),7,10	606.00
42	Poro-Phoskadanga F.V, FPC, JFMC	06.07.92 01/FPC/ WDPO	West DPO	19	188	-	207	Pana-3	989.24
43	Panbari F.V, FPC, JFMC	17.04.96 05/FPC/ ERVK	ERVK	35	99	-	134	Pana-4	273.00
44	Dhamsibad R.V, FPC, JFMC	17.04.96 05/FPC/ ERVK	ERVK	10	49	-	59	Pana-10	380.00
45	Dakshin Panbari (20th mile) Banabasti F.V, FPC, JFMC	22.12.96 10/FPC/ ERVK	ERVK	79	55	-	134	Pana-10	227.00
46	Dangi R.V, FPC	25.01.97 11/FPC/ ERVK	ERVK	35	49	-	84	Pana-10	227.00
47	F.D holders (Merchanpara, B.S mill & Depot. Line R.V), FPC, JFMC	16.02.97 22/FPC/ WRVK	WRVK	12	99	-	111	SRVK-7,8,10	924.80

S. No.	Name of JFMC (EDCs/ FPCs)	Date of formation and Reg. No.	Range	No. of Members				Block/Comptt. protected	Area protected (Ha)
				SC	ST	Others	Total		
48	Garobasti & Pampu basti F.V, FPC, JFMC	24.02.9 22/FPC/ WRVK 7	WRVK	49	11	-	60	SRVK-15,16	950.00
49	Nimati-Domohani R.V, FPC, JFMC	11.11.96 07/FPC/ NMT	Nimati	159	229	-	388	Poro-1, 5	599.19
50	Uttar Patkapara R.V, FPC	11.11.96 08/FPC/ NMT	Nimati	15	40	-	55	Poro-6	358.30
51	Uttar Dakshin Latabari R.V, FPC, JFMC	11.11.96 09/FPC/ NMT	Nimati	10	331	-	341	Nimati-2,7	669.00
52	Nimati Banabasti F.V, FPC	12/FPC/ NMT	Nimati	20	212	-	232	Nimati -1	1011.20
53	Dalbadal F.V, FPC, JFMC	07.02.96							
		02/FPC/ HTG	HTG	38	35	-	73	GD-2(P), GD-1a, BB-3a, 3b,	881.30
54	Godamdabri F.V, FPC, JFMC	13.02.96 03/FPC/ HTG	HTG	35	229	-	264	GD-3a,3b, 2a, 2b, 4b	1046.67

S. No.	Name of JFMC (EDCs/ FPCs)	Date of formation and Reg. No.	Range	No. of Members				Block/Comptt. protected	Area protected (Ha)
				SC	ST	Others	Total		
55	Latabari R.V, FPC, JFMC	23.02.96 04/FPC/ HTG	HTG	31	200	46	277	GD-4a	157.60
56	Gopal-Bahadur basti R.V, EDC JFMC	03.09.96 01/EDC/ HTG	HTG	55	59	-	114	BB-1,2,4	1072.36
57	Khokla basti R.V, EDC, JFMC	10.02.97 02/ EDC/ HTG	HTG	12	66		78	Ranga-1a,1b, 2a, 2b, 3a,3b	908.22
58	Bhutri F.V, EDC JFMC	10.02.97 03/ EDC/ HTG	HTG	25	12		37	Bhutri-3,4,5	1505.57
59	Pana Forest Village, EDC JFMC	10.02.97 04/ EDC/ Pana	Pana	12	33		45	Pana-1a,1b, 2a,2b, 3, 4a, 4b	1337.21
60	Raimatang F.V, EDC, JFMC	10.02.97 05/ EDC/ Pana	Pana	09	21		30	RTG-1,2, 3,4,5(P)	1688.82
61	Adma F.V, EDC	10.02.97 06/ EDC/ Pana	Pana	08	69		77	Adma-1,2, 3,4,5	2481.47

S. No.	Name of JFMC (EDCs/ FPCs)	Date of formation and Reg. No.	Range	No. of Members				Block/Comptt. protected	Area protected (Ha)
				SC	ST	Others	Total		
62	Gangutia F.V, EDC, JFMC	10.02.97 07/EDC/ Pana	Pana	05	58		63	RTG-5(P),6, 7,8,9,10	1815.52
	Jalpaiguri Forest Division								
63	Lehra F.V, FPC	67/FPC	Dalgaon	0	24	0	24	2 (part) & 4	224.46
64	Suni F.V, FPC	64/FPC	Dalgaon	0	30	0	30	1 &3 (part)	218.34
65	East Dalgaon FPC	1/FPC	Dalgaon	204	15	03	222	2 (part)	62.52
66	West Dalgaon FPC	2/FPC	Dalgaon	129	26	223	378	1 & 3 (part)	83.95

Source: Tiger conservation plan, 2016-17 to 2026-27, DFD, East & West BTR Forest Office, Alipurduar, 9th working plan, Vol. I, Jalpaiguri Forest Division, 2008-09.

Table–8.9

Status of FPCs and EDCs under the Joint Forest Management of Alipurduar District

Name of the Division	Number of EDC	Number of FPC	Total (EDC+FPC)	Number of EDC members	Number of FPC members	Total members (EDC+FPC)	Total area protected in Ha.
Jalpaiguri Forest Division	00	04	04	00	654	654	589.27
Buxa Tiger Reserve (East)	00	31	31	00	5070	5070	34032.34
Buxa Tiger Reserve (West)	07	24	31	444	3722	4166	26504.02
Total	**07**	**59**	**66**	**444**	**9446**	**9890**	**61125.63**

Source: Tiger conservation plan, 2016-17 to 2026-27, DFD, East & West BTR Forest Office, Alipurduar, 9th working plan, Vol. I, Jalpaiguri Forest Division, 2008-09.

8.4 Plantation

The forest policy of West Bengal is guided by the National Forest Policy in which highest priority has been given on the conservation of bio-diversity along with local people's participation. It is expressed that philosophy of Joint Forest Management stands in stark contrast to conventional social forestry projects, which in fact have been based on the traditional development paradigms (Poffenberger, 1995). At present, JFM covers only the protection and maintenance of degraded forests. Villagers' participation may be, in future, expanded to include a number of other activities such as infrastructure development, biodiversity conservation, forest based-and small scale enterprises, rationalization of shifting cultivation, where villagers' participation can be practiced beneficially (Shukla, 2000). There are some general objectives of JFM, (a) such as conservation of bio-diversity, preservation of gene pool, and fragile ecosystem, (b) ecological amelioration of teak, sal and other degraded forest cover, (c) production of timber, non-timber and other forest resources from sal, teak plantation and restocking the timber, (c) forest protection and development as well as with capital accumulation and income of local people. With these objectives and strategies in view, the following working circles have been formulated for plantation.

1. Bio-diversity conservation working circle
2. Eco-development working circle
3. Sal working circle
4. Miscellaneous working circle

On the basis of the above objective, plantation has been extended and developed in different working circles for the period of ten years from 2007 to 2017.

It is noticed in the table 8.10 that maximum plantation area is recorded in bio-diversity working circle which is numerically 58475.02 hectare and it is followed by misc-working circle, sal working circle and eco-development working circle (table–8.11). The bio-diversity working circle

Table–8.10

Range-wise List of Plantation Area of Different Working Circles (up to 2010) in Alipurduar District

Range	Planted area of circles (Hectare)			
	Bio-diversity Working circle	Eco-development Working circle	Sal working circle	Misc. working circle
Dalgaon	-	-	306.61	-
Madarihat	-	456.21	-	321.90
Kumargram	3098.96	-	-	-
Bholka	1770.17	-	5.00	2113.64
South Rydak	4158.71	70.00	1112.13	284.00
North Rydak	7534.97	10.00	-	7.00
Jainti	10121.19	16.50	-	106.70
Buxaduar	8351.96	-	1783.48	37.00
Damanpur East	1382.04	50.00	-	3023.34
Damanpur West	1753.96	60.00	-	1821.55
Rajabhatkawa East	4243.07	-	-	700.29
Rajabhatkawa West	4042.28	40.00	1806.66	901.90
Nimati	1256.01	10.00	-	1866.21
Hamiltongunj	4812.19	60.00	-	950.49
Pana	5949.51	110.00	1297.85	-
Total	**58475.02**	**882.71**	**6311.73**	**12134.02**

Source: 9th Working plan of Jalpaiguri Forest Division, 2008-09

includes all the existing natural forest has to be primarily protected against illicit felling, degradation, exploitation etc and developed to take suitable measure. The total area planted under this working circle is about 58475.02 hectare. The plantation work has been done almost all ranges except Dangaon and Madarihat range. All the areas, having sal plantation are kept under sal working circle. These areas extended over West Rajabhatkhawa, Pana, Nimati and South Rydak ranges. The total area of 6311.73 hectare of this working circle is planted of forest tree among different blocks. The miscellaneous working circle comprises of mixed plantations under the different forest blocks in this study area such as South Rajabhatkhawa, Dima, Gudamdabri, Gadadhar, Nimati, Poro, Jainti, Hatipota etc. In this plantation mostly has Champa, Jarul, Mandane, Benteak, Lampatey, Toon, Pakasaj etc with teak being present in fair amount in pure to semi pure stands with some Chilaune, Chikrasi, Cham and Simul as admixture. The total planted area under this working circle is 12134.02 hectare. The Eco-development working circle primarily formed for faster biomass production to meet the fuel and fodder requirements of the fringe population, along with development and utilisation of NTFPs. It is arranged and managed with the help of the Forest Protection Committee (FPCs) and Eco-development Committees (EDCs). This working circle has been covered a total area of 882.71 hectare planted forest of mixed forest such as teak, sal, gamar, sisso, toon, minjiri, khair, etc. for fuel, timber and poles; and nebharo, dudhila, kathal, amloki, koel etc for fodder and napier, amliso, dinanath guinea etc for fodder grass.

8.5 Ecological, Economic and Social Activity of JFM in Sampled Forest Villages

The term livelihood connects the activities, assets and entitlements by which villagers prepare a good living condition. Assets, are termed as not only natural (water, land, fauna and flora) but also social (social network, family, community), economic (credits, savings employment, service), political (empowerment, participation), human (health, nutrition education, labour), infrastructure (school, college, health clinic, road network, training centre) etc. Forest has the potential to enhance the livelihood condition of forest villagers who are most underdeveloped in Indian society. In a study on joint forest management system in West Bengal, it is referred that the economic motive was the primary condition for participation of villagers in JFM programs (De, 1997). Hence, different sorts of livelihood functions are offered to the villagers through JFM targated programme as well as local Government or NGOs for villagers overall improvement, such as agriculture livelihood mainly training on horticulture practice, skill development, establishment of basic education institution, development of road network, small industry, plantation, infrastructure development, NTFPs, nursery, livestock rearing, elephant barrier fencing etc. It is noted that livelihood interventions are sensible efforts by an organization or agency to support or improve livelihood opportunities for a large number of villagers (Datta et al., 2004). The livelihood activity may be segmental, sectoral or spatial. These activities always intended to help economically backward villagers' of the forest and provide daily substance needs in a manner that is locally appropriate and environmentally sustainable. The efforts taken up by the JFM programme for income generating and resource development with subsequent betterment in the socio-economic condition of forest villagers and poverty reduction since the Govt. of India aided funds through JFM in the different states. According to Rangachari and Mukherji (2000) and Vedanand (2000), the JFM as a means to poverty alleviation in India as a part of integration of land use, in which plantation, pasture and agriculture are all fitted in an area unit as complementary activities. Besides it is stated that many states felt that the time has come for an instance shift in the role of Joint Forest Management (JFM) with greater attention now to be given for poverty alleviation of forest villagers by undertaking more offer of income generating activities (National workshop on JFM, 2011). The survey of forest villagers were conducted among the seventeen (17) villages of Alipurduar and Jalpaiguri District to obtain a picture of livelihood intervention done by JFM, local panchayet or NGOs for the improvement of villagers livelihood condition which are as follows:

8.5.1 Activity in Lera Village

Earlier, due to the prevailing tribal culture, the villagers were highly dependent on tree felling and selling wood to the local market, consumed tree benches as fuel for livelihood needs. After, with the introduction of JFM project, they were opted agriculture, agriculture labour as primary source of living by giving them patta of open forestland. In 2014, they were given patta of land of 1 to 3 acre each who are agreement holder from Government of West Bengal. The Forest Department also initiated some activities for overall improvement through operation of FPCs such as regeneration of plantation, forest clearance, nursery raising, construction of small dams, animal barrier, fence, water shed etc. Infra structure supports were made by the forest department providing concrete residential houses and community hall. Details are given in the table below.

8.5.2 Activity in Suni Village

The village is going towards development through self help group activity and their financial support to the family. The livelihoods were generated by installation of community deep tube wells, construction of boulder dam which protected soil erosion and agricultural land, community hall. The employment was generated in weeding out in plantation, insecticide application and manuring fertiliser in forestry. In the year 2013, villagers were given 'patta' of land of 1 to 3 acres land accordingly for residential purpose and to motivate agriculture practice. The infrastructure development was done by providing concrete residential houses to all agreement holder villagers through the 'Geetangali' project, un-metalled road construction, watch-tower constructed to follow elephant movement.

Table–8.11
Livelihood Activities in Lera Village

Livelihood Activities	Period (year)	Work done	Remarks
Agriculture related	2013	Land patta has been given to villagers for residential land and cultivable land for agreement holder by Forest Department, Govt. of West Bengal.	Only for ST agreement holder
skill building	2011	Trainings were organised for SHG members of villagers organised by local panchayet for preparation of cane furniture, and muri making.	
Infrastructure development	2006	A community hall has been constructed through forest village development scheme by panchayet for meeting and training of FPCs and SHGs and for other activity of villagers.	
	2013-14	A concrete building of Anganwari center had been constructed by Falakta Panchayet samiti funding by District ICDS cell.	
	2013-14	Concrete residential houses were provided to all agreement holders through the 'Geetangali' project by State Govt.	
Forest plantation	2016	Teak, khair-sisoo, sal plantation in 166.75 ha. of fringe side area of Alinagar forest.	
Livestock	Whole year	Pig, cow, goat, hen etc. rearing by ownself are allowed to nearby Alinagar forest.	

Livelihood Activities	Period (year)	Work done	Remarks
NTFPs	Based on season	Collection of Non Timber Forest Produce (NTFPs) is permissible and allowed for FPC members and others villagers. The chief NTFPs are cane, cane fruits, golden and sponge mushrooms, odal fruit, fern bud, simul floss, dry branches, honey and leaves etc.	But there is no definite harvesting procedure of it.
Animal barrier or elephant fence	2007	Wire fence had been made in western side of the village to protect wild attack.	
	2015	Digging of long narrow nali for elephant barrier in north-eastern side.	
Soil and water conservation	-	-	
Nursery and seed processing	Whole year	Nursery and seed processing for plantation (creation). It has been maintaining at Dalgaon range by forest staff during whole of the year and occasionally FPC members/ villagers were appointed as daily labour basis work.	
Small industry	-	-	
Horticulture	Whole year	Villagers have been practicing it through chilly, brinjal, edible roots, arums, beans, cucumber, and banana cultivation for selling and own need especially in winter season.	

(Prepared based on field survey, 2017)

Table–8.12

Livelihood Activities in Suni village

Livelihood Activities	Period (year)	Work done	Remarks
Agriculture	2015	Document of patta has been given to villagers for homestead and cultivable land for agreement holder Govt. of West Bengal.	Only for ST agreement holder
Skill building	2015 2017	Trainings on saving of men from wild animal by F.D and tailoring, weaving were organised for FPC and SHG members by local panchayet.	
Infrastructure development	2007	A community hall is constructed for meeting and training of FPCs and SHGs and other members.	
	2015	Concrete residential houses are made through the 'Geetangali' project funding by Govt. of West Bengal.and allotted to few villagers.	
	2016	A deep tube well has been installed as sources of drinking water for common uses.	
Forest plantation	2016	Teak, khair-sisoo, sal are planted in 150.85 ha. of fringe side area.	
Livestock	-	Pig, cow, goat, hen etc. rearing allowed in Alinagar forest for whole of the year.	
NTFPs	Based on season	Collection of Non Timber Forest Produce (NTFPs) is permissible and allowed only for FPC beneficiaries and other villagers. The chief NTFPs are bamboo, cane, cane fruits, naglata, golden and sponge mushrooms, odal fruit, fern bud, simul floss, dry branches, leaves etc. and it has been collected from Alinagar forests besides the village.	But there is no definite harvesting procedure of it.

Livelihood Activities	Period (year)	Work done	Remarks
Animal	2007	An elephant fence had been prepared in north to reduce elephant attack.	
barrier or elephant fence	2012	Digging of long narrow drain as elephant barrier in the north- east direction of the village.	
Soil and water conservation	2017	A boulder dam has been constructed in river bank of Suni as embankment as well as protection of soil erosion in western side of the village.	
Nursery and seed processing	Whole year	Nursery and seed processing for plantation (creation). It has been maintaining at Dalgaon range by forest officials during whole of the year and occasionally FPC members/villagers are appointed as daily wage labour basis work.	
Small industry	-	-	
Horticulture	Whole year and winter season	Villagers practicing it by cultivating chilly, bringal, potato, tomato, edible roots, beans, banana, pumpkin, cucumber, cultivation of other vegetables for selling and own consumption.	

(Prepared based on field survey, 2017)

8.5.3 Activity in Garo Basti

In the village the livelihood intervention was done in income generating and enhancing at the grass-root level as well as giving agricultural right of forest land and later forming the self help groups by providing micro-credit for horticulture and livestock farming. Villagers are being allowed for collecting NTFPs such as cane, bamboo, cane fruits, naglata, Lycopodium stick, golden and sponge mushrooms, odal fruit, fern bud, simul floss etc to support livelihood needs. To extend forest plantation, tree of teak, khair-sisoo, sal, has been planted in 103.85 ha. of fringe side area.

8.5.4 Activity in Gadhadhar Village

Villagers were opted agriculture and agriculture labour as primary source of living. To motivate them, they were given patta of land of 1 to 2.5 acre each of agreement holder by State Govt. through F.D. The attempt was also made in awareness generation by different JFM programme and SHG training programme. The Forest Department also initiated employment through regeneration of different plantation related activity, forest clearance, nursery raising, construction of small dams, animal barrier, fence, water shed etc. from JFM funding and assistance. Infra structure supports were made through the connection of metalled road and providing community hall, and school building by local Government.

8.5.5 Activity in Poro (N) Village

The infrastructure facilities were provided by connecting electricity, enhancing drinking water supply, basic educational facility through free primary school, metalled and earthen roads facilities inside the village. The employments have been generated through self hand loom as well as the activities in tailoring, fishing, plantation, insecticide application and manuring fertilizer. In the year 2015 villagers were given 'patta' of land of 1 to 3 acres for residential as well as agricultural purpose to motivate agriculture practice. However villagers practicing horticulture such as chilly, brinjal, edible roots, cowpea, beans, cucumber,

Table–8.13
Livelihood Activities in Garo Basti

Livelihood Activities	Period (year)	Work done	Remarks
Agriculture	2015	Patta of land has been distributed to agreement holder for residential and cultivation permanently.	Only for ST agreement holder
Skill building	2014	Training was organised for FPC members regarding tailoring, weaving, fishing, micro plan project by Forest Department.	
Infrastructure development	2008	A primary school was established within the village for basic education for village children.	
	2013	An un-metalled road was constructed within forest area for villagers and it was also connected with local metalled road near Kaljani ridge more.	
Forest plantation	2017	Teak, khair-sisoo, sal plantation in 103.85 ha. of fringe side area.	
Livestock	Whole year	Pig, cow, goat, hen etc rearing by own self and it is allowed for whole of the year in West Rajabhatkhowa forest.	
NTFPs	Based on season	Members of FPC and other villagers are allowed to collect NTFPs. The chief NTFPs are tree branches, green and dry leaves, cane, cane fruits, naglata, Lycopodium stick, golden and sponge mushrooms, odal fruit, fern bud, simul floss bamboo etc and it is collecting from West Rajabhatkhowa forests.	But there is no definite harvesting procedure of it.

Livelihood Activities	Period (year)	Work done	Remarks
Animal barrier or elephant fence	2006	Two wooden watch towers constructed one in north and another is southern side of the village.	
	2014	Elephant fence of iron wire in north of the village.	
	2016	Digging of long narrow drain as elephant barrier west of the village.	
Soil and water conservation	-	-	
Nursery and seed processing	Whole year	Nursery and seed processing for plantation (creation). It has been maintaining at West Rajabhatkhowa range by forest staff during whole of the year and occasionally FPC members/ villagers are appointed as daily labour basis work.	
Small industry	-	-	
Horticulture	Whole year	Villagers practicing it by cultivating chilly, potato, brinjal, arums, beans, banana cultivation for selling and own need.	

H.A=High Altitude, (Prepared based on field survey, 2017)

Table–8.14
Livelihood Activities in Gadhadhar

Livelihood Activities	Period (year)	Work done	Remarks
Agriculture	2015	Land patta a document of land has been given to inhabitants for resident and cultivation for agreement holder of forest department.	Only for ST agreement holder
Capacity building	2013	Training were organised for FPC members on horticulture, fishing, tailoring, muri making and safe ways from wild animals attack by Forest Department.	
	2010	Concrete primary school building has been developed for better education.	
	2017	A deep tube well has been installed in the node of the village near beat office as sources of drinking water for all.	
Forest plantation	2015	Teak, khair-sisoo, sal plantation in 86.95 ha. of fringe side area.	
Livestock	Whole year	Pig, cow, goat, hen etc. rearing by ownself and cow and goat rearing are allowed to forest.	
NTFPs	Based on season	Collection of Non Timber Forest Produce (NTFPs) is permissible and allowed to FPC members and other villagers. The chief NTFPs are cane, cane fruits, flowers, green leave, tree branch, naglata, golden and sponge mushrooms, odal fruit, fern bud, simul floss etc and it is collecting from Damanpur forests.	But there is no definite harvesting procedure of it.

Livelihood Activities	Period (year)	Work done	Remarks
Animal barrier or elephant fence	2013	An iron wire elephant fence installed in north of the village.	
	2015	Wooden watch tower constructed north of the village to look wild movement and attack.	
Soil and water conservation	2017	Three concrete dam has been constructed beside road for embankment protection on Panijhora river.	
Nursery and seed processing	Whole year	It has been maintaining at Gadhadhar range by forest staff for whole of the year and occasionally FPC members/ villagers are appointed as daily wise basis.	
Small industry	-	-	
Horticulture	Whole year	Villagers practicing it by potato, tomato, chilly, brinjal, ladies finger, edible roots, arums, beans, parble, cultivation for selling and own need.	

(Prepared based on field survey, 2017)

Table–8.15
Livelihood Activities in Poro (N) Village

Livelihood Activities	Period (year)	Work done	Remarks
Agriculture	2015	A document of land patta has been provided for occupied homestead land and open cleared cultivable land those who have agreement with Forest Department by State Govt.	
Capacity building	2012	Procession, seedling distribution, tailoring, fishery training by FD.	
Infrastructure development	2012	One deep tube-well installed for drinking water supply by local Govt.	
	2013	Electricity supplied and connected to each village household through subsidy plan by Govt.	
	2016	A stone mixed non metal/ earthen road was constructed along north to south inside the village and connected with NH 31 of near Hatipota more.	
plantation	2017	Seed processing for plantation (creation and maintenance)	
Livestock	Whole year	Goat, pig, cow rearing by villagers ownself.	
NTFPs	Whole year	Members of FPC and other villagers are allowed to collect NTFPs. The chief NTFPs are green leaves, dry branches, naglata, Lycopodium stick, golden and sponge mushrooms, odal fruit, fern bud, simul floss, bamboo etc and it is collecting from Poro forests.	

Livelihood Activities	Period (year)	Work done	Remarks
Animal barrier or elephant fence	2012, 2014	Elephant proof trench/fence made east and west of the village by FD, also a wooden watch tower constructed southern side of the village by Panchayet.	
Soil and water conservation	-	-	
Nursery	Whole year	It has been maintaining through forest staffs of East Poro beat office during whole of the year and occasionally villagers are appointed as daily labour basis work.	
Small industry	Whole year	Some villagers (Mech and Rava) have own hand loom (Sedagra and takuri machine) and these are still running to provide their traditional clothes for family and their socxiety.	
Horticulture	Whole year	Villagers practicing it through chilly, brinjal, edible roots, arums, banana, betel nut, beans, cultivation to earn money.	

(Prepared based on field survey, 2017)

ginger, pumpkin, banana etc. are being cultivated for their own and for selling purpose. Details of some activities are given in the table–8.16.

8.5.6 Activity in Nimati and Dabri Village

The better livelihoods were generated through the installation of electricity, two community tube wells, setup of school for basic education, connection of un-metalled road. The employments have been created through agriculture, plantation, fencing and horticulture, livestock practice etc. Details of some works are given in the table below.

8.5.7 Activity in Gangutia Village

The infrastructure supports were made by the installation of electricity connection, metalled road construction, water drain construction, boulder dam, elephant proof trench, fence etc. through interference of local Government as well as JFM committee. Although Forest Department (FD) organised capacity building programmes to enhance villagers' skills and such programmes are procession, seedling distribution, and drama, sit drawing, essay and quiz. The nursery and seed processing for plantation (creation) has also been maintaining at Gangutia range by forest staff during whole of the year and occasionally EDC members or villagers are appointed as daily wage basis labour work.

8.5.8 Activity in Adma Village

The horticulture and livestock farming practice is the main income generating source for this high altitude village inhabitant. Sometimes they are collecting NTFPs such as bamboo, dry leaves and branches, mere trifle, naglata, golden and sponge mushrooms, odal fruit, fern bud, simul floss etc. as secondary source. Pipe line connection has been installed from Bhutan reservoirs as well as rivers and springs for drinking water supply and other purpose. The infrastructure developments were done through renovation of hill foot track way by villagers through 100 days panchayet scheme, setting up one health sub-centre (satellite clinic) opened by village

Table–8.16
Livelihood Activities in Nimati and Dabri

Livelihood Activities	Period (year)	Work done	Remarks
Agriculture	2014	Land patta has not been given to the villagers but they replied during survey time that it was under process to give.	
Capacity building	2013	Different trainings were organised for FPC and SHG members by local panchayet regarding process to avail Govt. loan, micro plan for animal husbandry, fishing and poultry farming.	
Infrastructure development	2008	A free primary school has been established at Nimati.	
	2013	Earthen road is constructed and connected from village to road which is running between Kalchini to Nimati more.	
	2015	Installation of two community tube wells in Nimati and Dabri through Panchayet fund.	
	2016	Installation and extension of electricity connection up to Dabri.	
Forest plantation	2017	Teak, khair-sisoo, sal plantation in 102.48 ha. of fringe side area.	
Livestock	Whole year	Pig, cow, goat, hen etc. rearing by ownself although in some case funding provided by FD.	

Livelihood Activities	Period (year)	Work done	Remarks
NTFPs	Based on season	Collection of Non Timber Forest Produce (NTFP) is permissible and allowed for FPC members and other inhabitants. The chief NTFPs are fruits, flowers, green and dry leaves, golden and sponge mushrooms, odal fruit, fern bud, simul floss etc and it is collecting from Nimati forests.	But there is no definite harvesting procedure of it.
Animal barrier or elephant fence	2015	An iron wire elephant fence repared in east of the village.	
	2017	Digging of long narrow drain for elephant barrier besides south east of the village.	
Soil and water conservation	2016	Three boulder dam has been constructed on river bank of Basra for embankment protection in north of the village.	
Nursery and seed processing	Whole year	It has been maintaining at West Poro range by forest office during whole of the year and occasionally FPC members/ villagers are appointed as daily labour basis work.	
Small industry	Whole year	Women of Rava community have own hand loom (Sedagra and takuri machine) and they practiced it to make and provide their traditional clothes for the society.	
Horticulture	Whole year	Villagers practicing it through cultivation of potato, cucumber, chilly, brinjal, edible roots, arums, beans, banana, betel nut for selling and own consumption.	

(Prepared based on field survey, 2017)

Table–8.17
Livelihood Activities in Gangutia

Livelihood Activities	Period (year)	Work done	Remarks
Agriculture related	2016	Paper of land Patta has been given to villagers for resident and cultivable land.	Only for ST agreement holder
Capacity Building	2015	Different kind of trainings were organised for EDC members to give idea of micro plan, agro-forestry, poultry farming by Forest Department.	
Infrastructure development	2007	A free primary school (Nepali medium) has been established for basic education of children.	
	2012	Electricity connection installation in each house.	
	2013	An earthen road is constructed inside the village and connected to metalled road which is going towards Kalchini market.	
Forest plantation	2017	Sal plantation, teak, khair-sisoo, in 79.23 ha. of fringe side area.	
Livestock	-	Pig, cow, goat, hen etc rearing by ownself.	
NTFPs	Based on season	Collection of non timber forest produce (NTFP) is permissible and allowed by EDC beneficiaries and other inhabitants. The chief NTFPs are tree branches, green leaves, golden and sponge mushrooms, fruit, fern bud, simul floss etc and it is collecting from Pana forests of BTR west.	But there is no definite harvesting procedure of it.

Livelihood Activities	Period (year)	Work done	Remarks
Animal	2006	A wooden watch tower constructed eastern side of the village.	
barrier or elephant	2012	Digging of long narrow concrete nali besides north of the village for Elephant barrier.	
fence	2016	An elephant fence in north of the village prepared by FD.	
Soil and water conservation	2017	A boulder dam has been constructed river bank of Pana river for embankment protection in west of the village.	
Nursery and seed processing	Whole year	Nursery and seed processing for plantation (creation). It has been maintaining at Gangutia range by forest staff during whole of the year and occasionally FPC members/ villagers are appointed as daily wage basis labour work.	
Small industry	-	-	
Horticulture	Whole year	Villagers practicing it through betel nut, chilly, brinjal, edible roots, tomato, potato, cabbage, cauliflower, arums, beans, banana cultivation for selling and own need.	

(Prepared based on field survey, 2017)

Table–8.18
Livelihood Activities in Adma

Livelihood Activities	Period (year)	Work done	Remarks
Agriculture	2015	Land patta 1 to 1.5 acre of residential and agricultural land has been provided to forest villagers.	Only for ST agreement holder
Capacity building	2012, 2013	Training of environmental consciousness, procession, agro-forestry, poultry farming was organised for EDC, SHG members and among villagers by local panchayet and FD.	
Infrastructure development	2007	A free primary school has been established by State Govt.	
	2011	One health sub-centre (satellite clinic) opened by village development committee with FPA, India, Kalchini Branch.	
	2012	A solar energy plant has installed funding by local MLA.	
	2015	Hilly foot track renovation done by villagers through 100 days scheme from Chunabati to Adma village for accessibility.	
	2016	Wooden and tin shading hut have been constructed for rest beside foot track in a particular interval by EDC.	
	2017	Electricity connection was under process.	
Forest plantation	2016	Khair-sisoo, teak, sal plantation in 71.23 ha. of fringe side area.	
Livestock	-	Pig, cow, goat, hen etc. rearing by own self and livestock are allowed whole of the year.	

Livelihood Activities	Period (year)	Work done	Remarks
NTFPs	Based on season	Collection of non timber forest produce (NTFP) is permissible and allowed by EDC members and other villagers. The chief NTFPs are green leaves, tree branches, bamboo, naglata, golden and sponge mushrooms, odal fruit, fern bud and it is collecting from Pana forests of BTR west.	But there is no definite harvesting procedure of it.
Animal barrier or elephant fence	-	Villagers reported that since the village is located at high altitude (746m) so there is no need to install any animal barrier.	
Soil and water conservation	2017	Lots of boulder dam has been constructed beside the foot track to protect the slide. Pipe line connection has been installed from Bhutan reservoir, rivers and springs to village for drinking water supply and other purpose.	
Nursery and seed processing	Whole year	Nursery and seed processing for plantation (creation). It has been maintaining at Adma beat by forest staff during whole of the year and occasionally FPC members/villagers are appointed as daily labour basis work.	
Small Industry	-	-	
Horticulture	Whole year	Villagers practicing it by cultivating cowpea plant, chilly, cauliflower, cabbage, brigal, pumpkin, mere trifle, beans, banana, and cucumber for selling and own consumtion purpose.	

(Prepared based on field survey, 2017)

development committee with FPA, installation of solar energy plants, electricity connection.

8.5.9 Activity in Raimatang

Infrastructure facilities were provided by enhancing drinking water facility, basic educational facility by free primary school, metalled and earthen roads facilities inside the village, watchtower construction. The employment was generated through the activities in plantation, insecticide application and manuring fertilizer. In the year 2015 villagers were given 'patta' of land of 1 to 1.5 acres of land for residential purpose and to motivate agriculture practice. Villagers practicing horticulture and by this chilly, brinjal, edible roots, cowpea, beans, cucumber, ginger, pumpkin, banana etc. are cultivating for their own need and for earning.

8.5.10 Activity in Bhutri Village

Land patta of forest land has been allotted for homestead and cultivation only for agreement holders to motivate towards agriculture and horticulture practice. The infrastructure supports were made through the installation of electricity connection, constructed cemented road along north to south the village also connected with pana river to Bhutri beat, water drain construction, boulder dam, elephant proof trench, fence etc. through JFM project and local Government. Beside the Forest Department organised capacity building programmes to enhance villagers' skills. Such programmes are procession, seedling distribution, and drama, sit drawing, essay, and quiz. Nursery and seed processing of plantation (creation) has been maintaining at Bhutri range by forest staff during whole of the year and although sometimes EDC members or villagers are appointed as daily labour basis work.

8.5.11 Activity in Gudamdabri

The agriculture, horticulture and livestock farming practice are the main livelihood source of villager. However they have been practicing of collection NTFPs such as cane,

Table–8.19
Livelihood Activities in Raimatang Village

Livelihood Activities	Period (year)	Work done	Remarks
Agriculture	2016	Land patta has been distributed to villagers for resident and cultivation purpose permanently from the State Govt.	Only for ST agreement holder
Capacity building	2014	Trainings were arranged for FPC and SHG and other members regarding animal husbandry, agro-forestry and micro plan by FD.	
Infrastructure development	2008	A free primary school has been established.	
	2008	One health sub-centre opened by Govt. of West Bengal, India.	
	2015	Extension of electricity connection in the houses managed by panchayet.	
Forest plantation	2017	Teak, khair-sisoo, sal plantation in 101.73 ha. of fringe side area.	
Livestock	-	Pig, cow, goat, hen etc rearing by ownself.	
NTFPs	Based on season	Collection of non timber forest produce (NTFP) is permissible and allowed by FDC beneficiaries and other villagers. The chief NTFPs are bamboo, green leaves, grass, tree branches, golden and sponge mushrooms, honey, hive, fern bud, simul floss etc and it is collecting from Pana forests of Buxa forest west.	But there is no definite harvesting procedure of it.

Livelihood Activities	Period (year)	Work done	Remarks
Animal barrier or elephant fence	2016	Elephant fence in north of the village.	
	2017	A wooden watch tower constructed eastern side of the village to follow animal movement.	
Soil and water conservation	2013	A boulder dam has been constructed besides west bank of Pana river near the village to reduce soil erosion and protection of landslide of river.	
	2016	Drinking water supply provided through pump well and deep tube well.	
Nursery and seed processing	Whole year	Nursery and seed processing for plantation (creation). It has been maintaining at Raimatang beat by forest staff during whole of the year and occasionally FPC members/villagers are appointed as daily labour basis work.	
Small industry	-	-	
Horticulture	Whole year	Villagers practicing it through chilly, cowpea, brinjal, edible roots, cucumber, beans, banana cultivation for own demand and surplus for selling to earn money.	

(Prepared based on field survey, 2017)

Table–8.20
Livelihood Activities in Bhutri Village

Livelihood Activities	Period (year)	Work done	Remarks
Agriculture	2017	Land patta has been given for homestead and cultivated land only for agreement holder of ST communities, and others are under consideration.	
Capacity Building	2016	Training for EDCs, Self Help Group and other members has been organised by Forest Department for nursery, horticulture and NTFPs collection, agro-forestry.	
Infrastructure	2013	Electricity connection installed.	
Development	2015	One cemented road constructed inside the village from pana river to Bhutri beat and it is connected up to extreme North of the village towards Adma village.	
Forest plantation	-	Seed processing for plantation (creation)	
Livestock	-	Goat, pig, cow, hen rearing by own self, and cow and goat are allowed in the forest for whole of the year.	
NTFPs	Based on season	Collection of non wood forest produce (NWFP) is permissible and allowed by EDC members and other villagers. The chief NTFPs are bamboo, cane fruits, purundi fruits, pan leaves, green leaves, tree branches, Lycopodium stick, golden and sponge mushrooms, flowers, fern bud, hive, honey, broom stick, thatch etc and it is collecting from Bhutri forests.	But there is no definite harvesting procedure of it.

Livelihood Activities	Period (year)	Work done	Remarks
Animal Barrier or Elephant fence	2017	Elephant proof trench/ fence extreme northern side of village by FD.	
Soil and Water conservation	2017	A concrete dam has been constructed in river bank of Pana. Villagers followed one private pump tube well within the village for drinking water supply by paying own cost.	
Nursery	Whole of the year	It has been maintaining through forest staff during whole of the year but occasionally villagers are appointed as daily labour basis work.	At Bhutri beat
Small Industry	-	Did not practice	
Horticulture	Whole year	Villagers practicing it through cucumber, pumpkin, chilly, brinjal, edible roots, cowpea, beans, banana, betel-nut tree, ginger cultivation.	Elephants damaged it every year.

(Prepared based on field survey, 2017)

Table–8.21
Livelihood Activities in Gudamdabri

Livelihood Activities	Period (year)	Work done	Remarks
Agriculture	2015	Document of land patta of 2 to 3.5 acre has been given to villagers for homestead of resident and cultivation land of agreement holder by State Govt.	Only for ST agreement holder
Capacity building	2016	Training programmes were organised on muri making, tailoring, poultry farming for SHG members as well as villagers by panchayet along with F.D for a week.	
Infrastructure development	2008	A free primary school has been established.	
	2014	An earthen road has constructed along north to south within the village.	
	2017	One deep tube-well is installed to provide drinking water facility by village panchayet.	
	2017	Electricity connection has been extended for each household by subsidy scheme from Govt side.	
Forest plantation	2015	Teak, khair-sisoo, sal plantation in 109.56 ha. of fringe side area.	
Livestock	Whole year	Pig, cow, goat, hen etc rearing by ownself.	

Livelihood Activities	Period (year)	Work done	Remarks
NTFPs	Based on season	Collection of NTFPs is permissible and allowed by FPC members and other villagers. The chief NTFPs are bamboo, honey, hive, green leaves, tree branches, cane fruits, naglata, Lycopodium stick, golden and sponge mushrooms, odal fruit, fern bud, simul floss etc and it is collecting from Hamiltonganj forests of BTR.	But there is no definite harvesting procedure of it.
Animal barrier or elephant fence	2014	A wooden watch tower constructed north-eastern side of the village by FD.	
	2017	A long narrow cable wire installed south of the village as elephant barrier.	
Soil and water conservation	2017	A long boulder dam has been repaired and constructed on river bank of Kaljani for embankment and soil protection in east of the village.	
Nursery and seed processing	Whole year	Nursery and seed processing for plantation (creation). It has been maintaining at Hamiltonganj range by forest staff during whole of the year and occasionally FPC members/villagers has been appointed as daily labour basis work.	
Small industry	-	-	
Horticulture	Whole year	Villagers practicing it through parble, chilly, brinjal, edible roots, ladies-finger, banana cultivation for selling and own need.	

(Prepared based on field survey, 2017)

honey, naglata, Lycopodium stick, golden and sponge mushrooms, odal fruit, fern bud, simul floss etc. as secondary source. Despite, one deep tube-well is installed to provide drinking water facility and other purpose. The infrastructure developments were done through setting up of primary school, health sub-centre, installation of electricity connection and construction of stone mixed earthen road along north to south within the village. A boulder dam has been constructed river bank of Kaljani for embankment protection in east of the village.

8.5.12 Activity in Chunabati Village

The infrastructure developments have been developed by renovation of hill foot track way by villagers through 100 days scheme from Suntalabari to Chunabati village, setting up one health sub-centre (satellite clinic) opened by village development committee with FPA, installation of solar energy plants, electricity connection. The villagers are practicing horticulture and livestock farming as income generating source. However they are always employed as collecting NTFPs such as banana leaves, dry branches, cane, cane fruits, naglata, lycopodium stick, golden and sponge mushrooms, odal fruit, fern bud, simul floss etc. The pipe line connection has also been installed with Bhutan natural water reservoir, rivers or springs for drinking water supply and other uses.

8.5.13 Activity in Bhutia Basti

The Forest Department organised capacity building programmes for villagers to develop their skilled and such programmes are procession, seedling distribution, and drama, sit drawing, essay, and quiz. The infrastructure supports were developed through the installation of electricity, road construction, water drain construction, boulder dam, elephant proof trench, iron cable fence etc. Besides, other details are given in the table–8.24.

8.5.14 Activity in Sankosh Village

The livelihoods of villagers have been generated through

Table–8.22
Livelihood Activities in Chunabati Village

Livelihood Activities	Period (year)	Work done	Remarks
Agriculture	2015	Land patta of homestead occupied land and for cultivated land has been given to ST villagers only for residential as well as cultivation purpose. Still villagers practicing shifting cultivation by burning of forest.	
Capacity building	2013	Training and awareness programme on man-animal conflict were organised by Binnaguri squad range at Chunabati T.G, as well as other trainings such as poultry farming, agro-forestry, horticulture training were arranged by F.D.	At Chunabati T.G
Infrastructure development	1970	A free primary school of Nepali medium has been established by NGO,	
	2007	later under taken by Govt. renovated of class room in 2007.	
	2014	Hill foot track renovation done by villagers through 100 days scheme from Santarabari village to chunabati village.	
	2012	One health sub-centre (satellite clinic) opened by village development committee with FPA, India, Kalchini Branch.	
	2012	A solar energy plant has been installed.	
	2015	Electricity connection is under process.	
	2017	A well condition wooden bridge has been made across the foot track near Santrabari on river and boulder embankment has also been constructed beside the foot track to landslide protection.	

Livelihood Activities	Period (year)	Work done	Remarks
Forest plantation	-	-	
Livestock	-	Goat, pig, cow rearing by ownself.	
NTFPs	-	Collection of NTFP is permissible and allowed by EDC members and other villagers. The chief NTFPs are dry branches, green leaves, cane fruits, bamboo, purundi fruits, golden and sponge mushrooms, odal fruit, fern bud, simul floss, broom stick etc.	
Animal barrier or elephant fence	-	Since the village is at high altitude (746 m) so there is not any application for animal barrier.	
Soil and water conservation	2010	Pipe line connection has been installed from Bhutan reservoir, rivers and springs for drinking water supply and other uses.	
Nursery	During whole of the year	It has been maintaining at Buxaduar range by forest staff during whole of the year but occasionally FPC members/ villagers are appointed as daily labour basis work.	
Small industry	-	-	
Horticulture	-	Villagers practicing it for their own need and for selling to local period market by cultivating cowpea, pumpkin, chilly, brinjal, edible roots, beans, banana cultivation. Besides villagers is practicing flower cultivation for their own interest of house decoration.	

(Prepared based on field survey, 2017)

Table–8.23
Livelihood Activities in Bhutiabasti Village

Livelihood Activities	Period (year)	Work done	Remarks
Agriculture	2015	Land patta of forest occupied land has been given to the villagers for homestead and cultivated only who are scheduled tribe; villagers of unreserved category were under consideration.	
Capacity building	2013	Procession, seedling distribution, agro-forestry, poultry farming, Sit drawing, essay, driving, drama, tourist guide, quiz organised by F.D, Buxa Tiger Reserve.	
Infrastructure development	2009	Earthen Roads are constructed inside the village.	
	2010	Electricity connection is installed.	
	2012-13	One S.S.K is established for primary education.	
	2013	One metalled road has been made in south of the village along Jayanti river.	
	2016	A water drain constructed besides earthen road in the village.	
Forest plantation	-	Seed sands of silviculture of teak, gamar lampate in 23 hectare area.	
Livestock	-	Goat, pig, cow rearing by owns self.	

Livelihood Activities	Period (year)	Work done	Remarks
NTFPs	Based on season	Collection of NTFPs is permissible and allowed by EDC members and other villagers. The chief NTFPs are tree branches, green and dry leaves, cane fruits, purundi fruits, pan leaves, naglata, honey, golden and sponge mushrooms, odal fruit, fern bud, simul floss, broom stick, thatch etc. All these are collecting from nearby Buxa and Jainti forests.	
Animal barrier or elephant fence	2012	Elephant proof trench, fence was installed western and northern side of village.	
Soil and water conservation	2017	A long boulder dam has been constructed on river bank of Jainti for embankment protection in south of the village.	
Nursery	-	It has been maintaining at Jainti (south) range by forest staff during whole of the year and occasionally FPC members/villagers are appointed as daily labour basis work.	
Small Industry	-	-	
Horticulture	During whole year	Villagers practicing it mainly for earning money by farming of chilly, brigal, edible roots, cucumber, ginger, beans, cowpea, banana, flower, betel nut etc. cultivation.	

(Prepared based on field survey, 2017)

Table–8.24
Livelihood Activities in Sankosh Village

Livelihood Activities	Period (year)	Work done	Remarks
Agriculture related	2016	Land patta of forest occupied land has been given to the villagers for homestead and cultivation only who are scheduled tribe; villagers of unreserved category were under consideration.	
Capacity building	2015	Training on procession, driving, tailoring, agro-forestry, seedling distribution, muri making by machine organised by Buxa Tiger Reserve.	
Infrastructure development	2003	One wooden bridge has been made at the way of entrance of the village from kumargram local market by F.D.	
	2009	Un-metal/earthen roads are constructed inside the village.	
	2010	Electricity connection is installed.	
	2011	A long water drain constructed besides earthen road in the village.	
	2012-13	One additional S.S.K is established and before it Sankosh new primary school was already there.	
Forest plantation	-	Seed sands of silviculture of teak, gamar lampate in 23 hectare area.	
Livestock	-	Goat, pig, cow rearing by ownself.	

Livelihood Activities	Period (year)	Work done	Remarks
NTFPs	Based on season	Collection of NTFPs is permissible and allowed by EDC and other villagers. The chief NTFPs are dry leaves, dry tree branches, cane fruits, purundi fruits, pan leaves, hive, honey, naglata, lycopodium stick, golden and sponge mushrooms, fruits, flower, fern bud, simul floss, broom stick, thatch etc. All these are collecting from nearby Dhumpara forests.	
Animal barrier or elephant fence	2017	Elephant proof trench, fence northern and eastern side of village.	
Soil and water conservation	2016	Three deep tube-wells are made for drinking water supply, one at middle of the village and other two at school premise.	
Nursery	-	It has been maintaining at Kumargram range by forest staff during whole of the year and occasionally FPC members/villagers are appointed as daily labour basis work.	
Small industry	-	-	
Horticulture	During whole year	Villagers practicing it mainly for earning money through vegetables farming such as ladies finger, chilly, brinjal, edible roots, beans, pumpkin, banana, flower etc cultivation.	

(Prepared based on field survey, 2017)

the installation of three community tube-wells, construction of one wooden bridge, establishment of one additional S.S.K, and a Seventh Day Adventist Church by NGO, as well as electricity connection installed for better livelihood. The employment opportunities have been improved through agriculture and horticulture practice. In the year 2015 villagers were given 'patta' land of 1.5 to 3 acres for residential purpose as well as to motivate agriculture practice.

8.5.15 Activity in Lapraguri Village

The infrastructure development of Lapraguri village is being improved by enhancing drinking water facilities, basic educational facilities, un-metal/earthen roads facilities inside the village, watch tower constructed to follow elephant movement. The employment aminities have been generated through the activities of plantation, insecticide application and manuring fertilizer and clearing of weeds. In the year 2013 villagers were given 'patta' land of 1to 3 acres for residential purpose and to motivate agriculture practice. Villagers were practicing horticulture (chilly, brigal, edible roots, arums, beans, ginger, pumpkin, and banana) for ownself as well as for earning purpose.

8.5.16 Activity in Santrabari Village

The Forest Department organised capacity building programmes for villagers of Santarbari especially for members of FPC to develop their skilled and such programmes are procession, seedling distribution, and drama, sit drawing, essay, and quiz. The infrastructure supports were made through the installation of electricity, road construction, water drain construction, boulder dam, elephant proof trench, fence etc.

8.5.17 Activity in Balapara Village

The Forest Department organised different capacity building programmes for villagers of Balapara village especially for members of FPC to develop their skilled through tailoring, fishery training beside SHGs members training also organised

Table–8.25
Livelihood Activities in Lapraguri Village

Livelihood Activities	Period (year)	Work done	Remarks
Agriculture	2013	Land patta has been provided for occupied land of homestead and cultivation who were agreement holder of F.D.	
Capacity building	2011	Training of tailoring, fishery training, weaving and agro-forestry were arranged by FD.	
Infrastructure development	2006	One primary school is established for basic education of children.	
	2013	Un metal/earthen road was constructed inside the village.	
	2014	A wooden watch tower constructed to follow elephant movement.	
	2017	Two deep tubes well were installed for drinking water facilities.	
Forest plantation	2013	Seed processing for plantation (creation), benches clearance for maintenance.	
Livestock	Whole year	Goat, pig, cow rearing by dwellers own self.	
NTFPs	Based on season	Collection of NTFPs is permissible and allowed by FPC beneficiaries and other inhabitants. The chief NTFPs are dry tree branches, leaves, cane fruits, purundi fruits, flower, honey, hive, pan leaves, naglata, Lycopodium stick, golden and sponge mushrooms, odal fruit, fern bud, simul floss, broom stick, thatch etc and it has been collecting from Bholka forests.	

Livelihood Activities	Period (year)	Work done	Remarks
Animal barrier or elephant fence	2017	Elephant proof trench/fence northern side of village and power fencing has made to protect villagers from animals.	
Soil and water conservation	2016	A water drain has been constructed beside the road of the village.	
Nursery	During whole year	It has been maintaining at Bholka range by forest staff during whole of the year and occasionally **FPC** members/ villagers are appointed as daily labour basis work.	
Small industry	-	Some villagers (Mech) have own hand loom of self interest to provide their traditional clothes.	
Horticulture	Whole year	Villagers practicing it through ginger, cowpea, chilly, brinjal, edible roots, beans, ginger, pumpkin, banana cultivation for their need and selling.	

(Prepared based on field survey, 2017)

Table–8.26
Livelihood Activities in Santrabari Village

Livelihood Activities	Period (year)	Work done	Remarks
Agriculture	2016	Land patta of homestead occupied land as well as agriculture purpose has been given to ST villagers only for residential and.	
Capacity building	2016	Awareness programme on herbivores census man-animal conflict organised by Binnaguri squad range, training on tourist guide, tailoring, agro-forestry by F.D.	
Infrastructure development	2004	Govt. aided primary school established.	
	2008	A metal road of about 25 km length has been extended from Kalchini to Santrabari village for better access by State Govt.	
	2014	Home stay tourist cottages were well decorated which directed by villagers ownself with the help of Forest Department.	
	2015	A periodic market has also been constructed by local panchayet.	
Forest plantation	2016	Seed sands of silviculture of teak, gamar and lampate in 13 ha. area.	
Livestock	whole year	Goat, pig, cow rearing by ownself.	
NTFPs	whole year	Collection of NTFPs is permissible and allowed by EDC members and other villagers. The chief NTFPs are tree branches, flower collection, cow pea, cane fruits, purundi fruits, pan leaves, naglata, lycopodium stick, golden and sponge mushrooms, odal fruit, fern bud, simul floss, broom stick, thatch etc.	

Livelihood Activities	Period (year)	Work done	Remarks
Animal barrier or elephant fence	2017	Proof trench and fence have made to prevent entry of elephant around the village.	
Soil and water conservation	2007	Pipe line connection has been installed from Bhutan reservior and springs for drinking water supply and other uses.	
	2016	Boulder barriers have constructed to protect river bank of Buxa Jhora.	
Nursery	whole of the year	It has been maintaining at Buxaduar range by forest staff during whole of the year but occasionally FPC members/ villagers are appointed as daily labour basis work to nurse.	
Small industry	-	-	
Horticulture	-	Villagers farming it for their own need and for selling to local market and such cultivation are betel nut, chilly, brinjal, spinach, cabbage, cowpea, edible roots, arums, beans, banana cultivation. Besides villagers practicing flower cultivation for their own interest of house decoration.	

(Prepared based on field survey, 2017)

Table–8.27
Livelihood Activities in Balapara Village

Livelihood Activities	Period (year)	Work done	Remarks
Agriculture	2014	Land patta has been given for homestead and cultivation only for agreement holder who belongs to ST community.	
Capacity building	2010	Training on tailoring, weaving agro-forestry and fishery training among villagers.	
	2011	SHGs training for earning opportunity by group activities of different works of the society organised by local panchayet.	
Infrastructure development	2008	One primary school is established for basic education.	
	2010	Electricity facility was connected.	
	2015	An earthen road constructed inside the village from east to west direction and connected to the metalled road.	
	2016	One deep tube was installed for drinking water supply and other uses.	
Forest plantation	2017	Teak, khair-sisoo, sal plantation in 77.67 ha. of fringe side area.	
Livestock	Whole year	Goat, pig, cow rearing by dwellers own self.	
NTFPs	Whole year	Collection of NTFPs is permissible and allowed by FPC members and other villagers. The chief NTFPs are tree branches, leaves, cane, bamboo, purundi fruits, pan leaves, naglata, golden and sponge mushrooms, odal fruit, fern bud, simul floss, broom stick, thatch etc. and it has been collecting from North Bhokla forests.	

Livelihood Activities	Period (year)	Work done	Remarks
Animal barrier or elephant fence	2017	Elephant proof trench/ fence northern and east side of village.	
Soil and water conservation	2013	A water drain has been constructed beside the road of the village.	
Nursery	Whole year	It has been maintaining at Balapara range by forest staff during whole of the year and occasionally FPC members/villagers are appointed as daily labour basis work.	
Small Industry	-	-	
Horticulture	Whole year	Villagers practicing it through by farming vegetables such as potato, tomato, chilly, brinjal, edible roots, arums, beans, ginger, pumpkin, banana cultivation for their need and selling.	

(Prepared based on field survey, 2017)

by local panchayet for better earning opportunity. The employment scopes were generated through agriculture and horticulture practice. In the year 2014 villagers were given 'patta' land of 2 to 3 acres for residential purpose as well as for agriculture practice. The infrastructure supports were made through the installation of electricity, road construction, water drain construction, boulder dam, elephant proof trench, fence etc.

In summary it is noted that, in the villages under study the JFM activities were intense in livelihood generation, be it agriculture, livestock, Non Timber Forest Products (NTFPs), employment in infrastructure development or forestry activities. For agriculture development, especially for increasing productivity, livelihood interventions were taken place in distributing 'pattas' (land ownership), micro credit for vegetable cultivation. The infrastructure development was done in road making, school building construction, pond deepening, solar energy installation, electricity connection, concrete house construction and so on. All these interventions produce employments in addition to other benefits in human resource development, cultivation, energy generation, social capital building etc. In forestry activities, plantations of various species were done to provide wage labouring for the labour class villagers. In live stock rearing and poultry farming micro credits were given to the members from NGOs, panchayets or other source. In case of NTFPs, no interventions were recorded in the villages under study. To protect forest area and soil erosion, many small boulder dams were constructed.

8.6 Villagers' Response on Joint Forest Management Activity

The villager's response is a necessary part of this study. It discloses perception and experiences about performance of JFM programme in their locality. The table–8.29 shows that out of 878 respondents, about 141 respondents (16.06%) opined as member of different sub-committee of JFM and among them 110 respondents (12.53%) are belonging in ST and only

Table–8.28
JFMC member

S.No.	Forest village	Total no. of respondents	JFMC member				Total JFMC member
			SC	ST	OBC	Gen	
1	Suni village	28	-	05	-	-	05
2	Gadhadhar	63	-	12	-	-	12
3	Lehra village	22	-	04	-	-	04
4	Garo Basti	72	-	09	-	05	14
5	Poro (N)	61	-	10	-	-	10
6	Nimati and Dabri	68	-	13	-	-	13
7	Chunabati H.A	54	-	07	-	-	07
8	Raimatang H.A	55	-	08	-	-	08
9	Gangutia H.A	55	-	02	-	09	11
10	Adma H.A	55	-	10	-	-	10
11	Bhutri F. basti H.A	45	-	04	-	-	04
12	Santrabari H.A	65	-	-	-	12	12
13	Gudamdabri	63	-	07	-	-	07
14	Bhutiabasti	30	-	00	-	00	06
15	Balapara	35	-	10	-	-	10
16	Sankosh	60	-	03	-	05	08
17	Lapraguri	47	-	06	-	-	06
	Total	**878** (100%)	**00**	**110** (12.53%)	**00**	**31** (3.53%)	**141** (16.06%)

(Prepared based on field survey, 2017)

31 (3.53%) are in GEN community. All respondents (members and non-members) gave their opinion and shared their experience regarding whatever activities and benefits gets from JFM project. It is noticed in Suni and Lera village that, there is deprivation sense among villagers in the form of non-payment and inactivity by FPCs (Forest Protection Committee), despite villagers' participation. Villagers viewed that forest is degraded due to illegal felling which is the main cause behind shrinkage and degradation of forest cover. Villagers of Adma, Raimatang, Bhutri, Gangutia, Santrabari and Chunabati village being located in high altitude of Buxa hill forest opined that period of employment in FPCs programme is very less and it is average only 5-8 days a month, although irregular for each month. So, villagers don't have attention in the JFMCs activities for sustaining livelihood needs as it provides less number of working days during the whole year. They felt better in engagement in alternative activities such as contour farming, shifting cultivation and marginal labour work in nearby Bhutan and other states. Nimati-Dabri, Balapara, Poro (N), Sankosh and Lapraguri villages have a great dependency on NTFPs collection. However villagers' participation in FPCs programme has not been presented at the satisfactory level due to lack of opportunity of sufficient income. The low altitude villagers' of Gudamdabri, Garo Basti and Gadhadhar village have less interest about JFM programme due to lack of sufficient income and uncertain job period and many of them migrated to other states such as Assam and Bihar, Delhi even in the Bhutan for several times a year for job as marginal labour. Besides these, frequent trampling of crops, less amount of compensation, loss of cooperative trust between Forest Department and FPCs members also responsible for lowers participation in JFMCs.

8.6.1 Forest Villagers' Participation and Expectation in JFM Project

In order to assess the extent of participation of forest villagers in JFM activities, the collected sampled data analysis has been prepared in table 8.30. It observed that out of 878 household, about 46.70% have viewed that the forest has been managed by the Forest Department itself and about 16.06% villagers are of the opinions that the forest is managed by JFM Committees (FPCs/EDCs) where 14.12% are engaged in participation meeting related to forest management programme and only about 10.60% are involved in plantation activities. Besides, about 8.31% were participated in the training programmes on different JFM scheme. The primary data also reveals that only 16.06% households are engaged and doing active role in Joint Forest Management as member of Forest Protection Committees and Eco-Development Committees. To find out causes behind non-membership and unwillingness to be as member in FPCs or EDCs, it has been seen that about 83.94% were of the opinion on the no guarantee of income as a beneficiary of Joint Forest Management Committees (JFMC) as well as income is not sufficient to fulfil livelihood needs. About 18.79% are of the opinion that the Forest Department now does not permit them to be a JFMC member, where 59.57% viewed to disagree due to unsecure and irregular income and 5.58% opined unwillingness of membership without any cause. In this context it is reported that 3/4th of the Village Forests Committee members (73.33%) viewed to low social participation followed by 20% with high social participation and 6.67% had moderate level of social participation for the development of forest (Sadashivaiah et al.2005). The different programmes of JFM must provided various financial benefits to its FPCs or EDCs beneficiaries and allow them to participate in decision making members. In spite of that, villager' performance and participation is not good and at the optimal level. In respect of benefit related subjects of JFM committee members, among 16.06% household members of JFM, about 9.80% of the beneficiaries are of the opinion that there is no guarantee of income although they have been benefited by collecting NTFPs and other 5.58% and 0.68% members are benefitted for participating in committees' process (FPCs/EDCs) and through forest product collection. However respondents expressed that villager should have been trained and intimated by the concerned authority on NTFPs collection, forest protection and conservation, micro planning projects, loan facility from different sections, about sustainable forest management and development. Villagers felt that whatever financial benefits gained by Forest Department but nominal amount benefit is allotted to the members of JFMC. Most of the FPCs and EDCs are on paper and registered only, there should be target oriented actions plan of JFM programme to get success and reach in goal within a certain period. Finally the researcher explored that villagers are below the poverty line and forest related activities are one of prime income source of the forest inhabitants in all sense. Thus forest contributes income in order to fulfil their needs of daily life providing fuel wood, timber and Non-Timber Forest Products (NTFPs) which villagers collecting through unsustainable way.

8.7 Women's Involvement in JFM

The Forest Policy of 1988 envisaged women's participation in the protection of forests. The rules of the Government of India (GOI) Order 1991 referred that at least two women should be on every village management committee in the JFM programmes. In 1998, an advisory committee to promote the involvement of women in the forestry sector was constituted by the Ministry of Environment and Forests (MOEF). It presented a number of recommendations which would enhance women's participation (GOI, 1999). Following these recommendations it was resolved that 50% of the members of the JFM General Body (GB) should be women and the attendance of at least 50% of women members should be requisite for calling a GB meeting. In the official JFM committees in all states, established for the implementation of the programme, there is a rule for necessary participation of a certain number of women from the concerned communities. However it has been observed that in many cases due to social, cultural and economic constraints the participation of women remains on paper only. And they usually play only a negligible role in the processes of planning and implementation.

Table–8.29
Villagers Participation statues in Joint Forest Management

Particulars	Forest village					
	Suni 1	Garo Basti 2	Gadhadhar 3	Poro (N) 4	Nimati Dabri 5	Lehra 6
1. Forest management						
Plantation activities	02	09	09	07	04	02
Participation in meeting	04	12	11	09	07	03
By Forest dept. Itself	14	26	24	28	32	11
Training programme attended	03	06	05	04	05	02
Awareness of micro planning	-	-	-	-	-	-
By forest protection committees (FPCs/EDCs)	05	14	12	10	13	04
None of these	00	05	02	03	07	00
Total	**28**	**72**	**63**	**61**	**68**	**22**
2. Membership of the committee						
No	23	58	51	51	55	18
Yes	05	14	12	10	13	04
Total	**28**	**72**	**63**	**61**	**68**	**22**

Particulars	Forest village					
	Suni 1	Garo Basti 2	Gadhadhar 3	Poro (N) 4	Nimati Dabri 5	Lehra 6
3. Role as a member						
Nominal member	02	08	06	06	06	02
Active member	03	06	06	04	07	02
Total	**05**	**14**	**12**	**10**	**13**	**04**
4. Reasons for non-membership						
Irregular earning	15	38	41	35	39	11
Unwillingness	01	05	03	05	07	00
Forest dept. did not allow	07	15	07	11	09	07
Total	**23**	**58**	**51**	**51**	**55**	**18**
5. Benefits as a members						
NTFPs collection	04	09	07	06	9	03
Participation in committees' process (FPCs/EDCs)	01	05	05	03	04	01
Contribution in forest product collection	00	00	00	00	00	00
No. benefits	00	00	00	00	00	00
Total	**05**	**14**	**12**	**10**	**13**	**04**

Particulars	Forest Village					
	Adma	Raimatang	Bhutri basti	Gudamdabri	Chunabati	Gangutia
	7	8	9	10	11	12
1. Forest management						
Plantation activities	04	09	06	06	05	06
Participation in meeting	06	07	11	06	07	09
By Forest Dept. Itself	28	26	21	32	28	24
Training programme attended	04	03	03	09	04	05
Awareness of micro planning	-	-	-	-	-	-
By forest protection Committees (FPCs/EDCs)	10	08	04	07	07	08
None of these	03	02	00	03	03	03
Total	**55**	**55**	**45**	**63**	**54**	**55**
2. Membership of the committee						
No	45	47	41	56	47	47
Yes	10	08	04	07	07	08
Total	**55**	**55**	**45**	**63**	**54**	**55**
3. Role as a member						
Nominal member	06	05	02	02	05	03
Active member	04	03	02	05	02	05
Total	**10**	**08**	**04**	**07**	**07**	**08**

Particulars	Forest Village					
	Adma 7	Raimatang 8	Bhutri basti 9	Gudamdabri 10	Chunabati 11	Gangutia 12
4. Reasons for non-membership						
Irregular earning	36	33	30	38	34	31
Unwillingness	02	03	03	06	00	04
Forest dept. did not allow	07	11	08	12	13	12
Total	**45**	**47**	**41**	**56**	**47**	**47**
5. Benefits as a members						
NTFPs collection	05	04	03	05	02	03
Participation in committees' process (FPCs/EDCs)	03	04	00	02	04	04
Contribution in forest product collection	02	00	01	00	01	01
No. benefits	00	00	00	00	00	00
Total	**10**	**08**	**04**	**07**	**07**	**08**

Particulars	Forest village					
	Sankosh 13	**Lapraguri 14**	**Santrabari 15**	**Balapara 16**	**Bhutia basti 17**	**Total (%)**
1. Forest management						
Plantation activities	06	05	08	03	02	93 (10.60)
Participation in meeting	09	10	06	04	03	124 (14.12)
By forest dept. Itself	31	23	32	16	14	410 (46.70)
Training programme attended	04	03	07	03	03	73 (8.31)
Awareness of micro planning	-	-	-	-	-	
By forest protection committees (FPCs/EDCs)	08	06	12	07	06	141 (16.06)
None of these	02	00	00	02	02	37 (4.21)
Total	**60**	**47**	**65**	**35**	**30**	**878 (100)**
2. Membership of the committee						
No	52	41	53	28	24	737 (83.94)
Yes	08	06	12	07	06	141 (16.06)
Total	**60**	**47**	**65**	**35**	**30**	**878 (100)**
3. Role as a member						
Nominal member	03	02	05	04	02	69 (7.86)
Active member	05	04	07	03	04	72 (8.20)
Total	**08**	**06**	**12**	**07**	**06**	**141 (16.06)**

Particulars	Forest village					
	Sankosh 13	Lapraguri 14	Santrabari 15	Balapara 16	Bhutia basti 17	Total (%)
4. Reasons for non-membership						
Irregular earning	35	29	38	21	19	523 (59.57)
Unwillingness	04	03	03	00	00	49 (5.58)
Forest dept. did not allow	13	09	12	07	05	165 (18.79)
Total	**52**	**41**	**53**	**28**	**24**	**737 (83.94)**
5. Benefits as a members						
NTFPs collection	06	05	07	05	03	86 (9.80)
Participation in committees' process (FPCs/EDCs)	02	01	05	02	03	49 (5.58)
Contribution in forest product collection	00	00	01	00	00	06 (0.68)
No. benefits	00	00	00	00	00	00
Total	**08**	**06**	**12**	**07**	**06**	**141 (16.06)**

(Prepared based on field survey, 2017)

8.7.1 Participation of Women in JFMC Activity of Sampled Forest Villages

The following table shows that out of 878 respondents, 141 respondents which is 16.06% of the total opined as member of different FPC and EDC of JFMC and among them only 19 respondents (13.48%) are belonging in female whereas 122 (86.52%) are in male (table–8.31).

Table–8.30

List of FPC/EDC members under the Joint Forest Management of sampled households

S.No.	Forest village	Total no. of respondents	Total JFMC member	Members under JFM	
				Male	Female
1	Lehra village	22	04	04	-
2	Suni village	28	05	04	01
3	Garo Basti	72	14	08	01
4	Gadhadhar	63	12	09	03
5	Poro (N)	61	10	10	-
6	Nimati and Dabri	68	13	10	03
7	Gangutia H.A	55	08	06	02
8	Adma H.A	55	10	09	01
9	Raimatang H.A	55	08	06	02
10	Bhutri F. basti H.A	45	04	04	-
11	Gudamdabri	63	07	07	-
12	Chunabati H.A	54	07	06	01
13	Bhutiabasti	30	06	04	02
14	Sankosh	60	08	06	02
15	Lapraguri	47	06	06	-
16	Santrabari H.A	65	12	10	02
17	Balapara	35	07	07	-
	Total	**878 (100%)**	**141 (16.06%)**	**122 (86.52%)**	**19 (13.48%)**

(Prepared based on field survey, 2017)

So it is very unfortunate that where JFM aims is to involve 50% women as major actors in forest management participatory programme but in particularly only 13.48% were engaged and there is a gender disparity occurred in addressing the constraints which prevent women from participating as equals to men.

8.7.2 Factors Affecting the Participation of Women

Reasons behind lacking of participation of women in the JFM programme can be summarised as following manner whatever observed during field survey. The women have lack of information about the surrounding forests area and even if they are knowledgeable about JFM, they are not taken seriously as eligible by the men. It was also observed that they were not very concern about the different scheme and benefits of JFM programmes. Besides their interest about the JFM activities are also too less as livelihood supports and economic gains are not sufficient to fulfil family needs. Moreover, the attitude of the office staffs of forest department is also responsible for such low participation of women villagers. As the government insists, so women are enlisted as members of FPC and EDC but female interests are not taken care of and the office staffs who are guided by their viewpoint of the dominant patriarchal order do not give much importance to the views and comments of the women.

In the same way men dominant FPC and EDC members' patriarchal system is the main cause behind the less interest of participation of women in the JFM programmes. It is noticed during survey that always men members felt that it is useless to spend time in understanding women's members' comment on issues such as NTFPs resource management, prevention of illegal poaching and cutting of trees etc as according to them women do not have any better knowledge than men that would be of valuable and applicable. Women felt that, it is the men who are able to perform as an importance member of FPC and EDC in forest protection; it is risky for women to enter the dense forests area although they are regularly gone to the forest to collect NTFPs as well as dry branches as fuel for cooking at home.

Most of women are of lower income groups or who are managing their household needs through daily basis labour wages which find it difficult to attend JFM meetings as this means loss of wages of the day. That's why they were rather gone to work than attend any JFM meetings. Besides due to domestic and other chars of family women find it extremely difficult to manage time for meetings which are often organised at times and venues inconvenient to women. There is a lack of female staff in the Forest Department, particularly at the field level activity. In addition to this who were employed do not wish to present in any meetings for extending JFM programme. Normally village women felt that it difficult to interact with the male staff every time who equally found it difficult to approach women or even to understand and incorporate their concerns and subjects.

8.8 Sustainability Issues of Sampled Forest Villages

It is referred that sustainable livelihood approach aims to promote a holistic vision of development that includes income generating activities, natural resource management, people's empowerment, use of appropriate technology, financial services and good governance (Kaushal and Kala, 2004). So in the context of sustainability, some issues are identified to reveal the performance and continuance of JFMC programme at the study villages. The issues affecting sustainability are describing in the following:

8.8.1 Sustainability Issues of Lera Village

1. The FPC of Lera FV has been formed with registration no. 67/ FPC covering area of 224.46 hectare forest of Dalgaon beat of Jalpaiguri Forest Division by taking total 24 members (table–8.8).
2. The function of JFM committee members (FPCs) is too less due to lack of job opportunity.
3. Every member have been provided concrete house to protect them from animal attack through 'Gitanjali project' of Jalpaiguri Forest Division.
4. The members have very low motivational level and they don't have interest to participate in the institutional level activities. Prime of the body (JFMC and FD) are always dominating as decision making.
5. Members are aware about their rights and duties but they almost lost interest due to conflict with foresters in

relation to less payment and activities, and with fringe villagers due to illegal tree felling.

6. Members' participation has decreased and especially among women it is nil. They are aware of the importance of the forest in their daily day life but have lost faith on the Forest Department (FD) in spite of attending different trainings on skill development programme. None of them have shown interest on specific training as livelihood or earning source since they are more interest in wage earning in different source.
7. Dominance of casual staffs of the Forest Department seen in all the activities of JFMC.
8. In earning opportunity from nursing, plantation and cleaning of forest JFMC activities are not satisfactory level.
9. Man-animal or man-elephant conflict is a common issue in Lera village. Somewhere persons killed, injured by wild animals, and somewhere damage to crops by wild animals, damage to live- stock by wild animals, damage to huts caused by wild animals, damage of semi-permanent house (G.I. sheet or Tali roof), damage of permanent house with RCC roof etc. State Government provided assistance and compensate through Forest Department (FD) for the losses. But it has very nominal in amount and some time it has taken very long time to paid compensation for victims. The Forest Department did not do anything more for villagers benefit.

8.8.2 Sustainability Issues of Suni Village

1. The FPC of Suni FV has been formed with registration no. 64/ FPC covering area of 218.34 hectare forest of Dalgaon beat of Jalpaiguri Forest Division by taking total 30 members (table–8.8).
2. The members have very low motivational level and they don't interest to participate in the institutional level (FPCs) activities.
3. Members are aware about their rights and duties but they almost lost interest due to conflict with Forest Department (FD) in connection to less payment, and with fringe villagers due to illegal tree felling.

4. Women members' participation has decreased. They are aware of the importance of the forest in their daily day life but have lost faith on the Forest Department (FD) due to few month jobs and less income opportunity in spite of attending different trainings on skill development programme.
5. None of them have shown interest on specific training as livelihood or earning source since they are more interest in wage earning in different source.
6. Dominance of casual staffs of the forest department seen in all the activities of JFMC.
7. In nursing, plantation and cleaning of forest JFMC activities are not satisfactory level in relation to income.

8.8.3 Sustainability Issues of Garobasti

1. The FPC of Garo basti and Puma basti FV has been formed in 24th February, 1997 covering area of 950.00 hectare forest of West Rajabhatkhowa of west BTR division by taking total 216 members (table–8.8).
2. The village has developed after electrification although it is too near to District highway of Hasimara-Kalchini road. Villagers are belongs to Oraon, Rava tribe and Nepali.
3. The JFM gives the members maximum one month job opportunity which did not fulfil their livelihood demand. So villagers are engaged mainly in agriculture, horticulture, daily labour work during whole of the year, although sometimes JFMCs are provided seed and other financial assistance for agriculture.
4. Some group of members formed SHGs, who are engaged in the mid-day meal cooking of primary school.
5. Man-elephant conflict is an important issue in this village. Persons injured, killed, damage to huts or damage crops by elephants, and somewhere live-stock by wild animals. State Government provided assistance and compensate through Forest Department (FD) for the losses. The victims getting compensation very less in amount and in some case it is too delayed. The Forest Department did not do anything more for villagers benefit.

8.8.4 Sustainability Issues of Gadhadhar Village

1. The FPC of Gadhadhar banabasti FV has been formed in 15th February, 1997 covering area of 531.60 hectare forest of Gadhadhar beat of west BTR division by taking total 157 members (table–8.8).
2. Members' participation has decreased especially among women. They are aware of the importance of the forest in their daily day life but have lost faith on the Forest Department (FD) in spite of attending different trainings on skill development programme. None of them have shown interest on specific training as livelihood or earning source since they are more interest in wage earning in different source.
3. Dominance of casual staffs of the forest department seen in all the activities of JFMC.
4. In earning opportunity from nursing, tailoring, fishing, plantation and cleaning of forest JFMC activities are not satisfactory level.
5. Not many activities have been done by the JFMC in the past years. Few infrastructure development works were carried out in the village such as metalled village path, fence of forest boundary near village, wooden tower etc.

8.8.5 Sustainability Issues of Poro (North) Village

1. The FPC of Poro-Phoskadanga FV has been formed in 6th July, 1992 covering area of 989.24 hectare forest of east poro beat of west BTR division by taking total 204 members (table–8.8).
2. The village has developed after electrification although it is so near to NH31 road. All the villagers are belongs to Rava tribe.
3. The function of JFM committee is too less. They are not interested to participate actively in JFM due to short period of working days and less financial benefits.
4. The villagers are affected by elephants daily. The elephants damaged and ruined inhabitants' crops, residential houses, school buildings every year. There is no solution of these problems.

5. The members have very low motivational level and they don't participate in the FPC and other institutional level activities since it has fewer wages and have only one to two month job opportunity, especially among women villagers' not a single member registered in FPC/EDC of JFM.

8.8.6 Sustainability Issues of Nimati and Dabri Village

1. The FPC of Nimati banabasti FV has been formed in 1st February, 1997 covering area of 1011.20 hectare forest of Nimati beat of west BTR division by taking total 120 members (table–8.8).
2. Not many activities have been done by the FPC members in the past years. Although some infrastructure development works were carried out in the village such as earthen path, primary school, fence of forest boundary near village, boulder fence, community building construction etc.
3. The JFM provided only one month job opportunity which did not fulfil inhabitant's livelihood demand. So they are engaged and spent maximum time in horticulture, agriculture, tea garden labour during the year.
4. The members did not get any loan from Govt. or any NGOs to promote their livelihood needs in spite of their backward situation.

8.8.7 Sustainability Issues of Gangutia Village

1. The EDC of Gangutia FV has been formed in 10th February, 1997 covering area of 1815.52 hectare forest of west BTR division by taking total 68 members (table–8.8).
2. The village is located in fringe forest of Buxa Duar of east zone and it is above 306 meter high from MSL. It has only one means of accessibility that is un-metalled footpath in the dense forest.
3. Some infrastructure development works were carried out in the village such as earthen path, primary school, fence of forest boundary near village, boulder fence in the river bank, community building construction etc.

4. There is severe scarcity of drinking water in this village and inhabitants are collecting water from springs of hills by pipe lines.
5. The JFM gives the members maximum one month job opportunity which did not fulfil their livelihood demand. So they are engaged by horticulture, agriculture labour, tea garden labour and poultry farming etc during the year.
6. The villagers are extremely affected by elephants and leopards attack. Mainly elephants damaged and ruined their vegetables, crops and houses properties in a regular interval of the year.

8.8.8 Sustainability Issues of Adma Village

1. The EDC of Adma FV has been formed in 10th February, 1997 covering area of 2481.47 hectare forest of west BTR division by taking total 64 members (table–8.8).
2. This village is located in dense forest of Buxa hill zone and it is above 846 meter high from MSL. It has no means of accessibility except footpath in the dense forest.
3. There is electricity installation in the village although a solar energy plant has been installed by local panchayet through MLA fund without any involvement of FD.
4. There is acute scarcity of drinking water in this village. Villagers are collecting water from springs of Bhutan hills by pipe lines connection.
5. Primary school, boulder fence beside the river bank and foot track, community building etc. has been constructed for development.
6. They have less interest and don't participate in the JFMC or other institutional level activities since it has fewer wages and have only one month job opportunity so inhabitants are engaged as daily labour, in horticulture, pig and poultry farming.

8.8.9 Sustainability Issues of Raimatang Village

1. The EDC of Raimatang FV has been formed in 10th February, 1997 covering area of 1688.82 hectare forest of

Raimatang beat, BTR west by taking total 68 members (table–8.8).

2. The village is located in dense forest of Buxa Duar of east zone and it is above 487 meter high from MSL. It has no means of accessibility except footpath in the dense forest.
3. Primary school, fence of forest boundary near village, boulder fence beside the river bank, community building etc. has been constructed.
4. The villagers are extremely affected by elephants and leopards. The elephants damaged and ruined their vegetables, crops and houses which occurred every year. Leopard poaching their live-stocks. There is no alternative solution of these problems still.
5. There is acute scarcity of drinking water in this village. They are collecting water from springs, jhoras which coming from Bhutan hills by pipe lines.
6. The villagers have less interest and they don't participate in the JFMC or other institutional level activities since it has fewer wages and have only one month job opportunity. Most of the villagers' are appointed as tea garden labour of nearby tea estates and others are gone outside of the state as factory labour.

8.8.10 Sustainability Issues of Bhutri Forest Basti Village

1. The EDC of Bhutri FV has been formed in 10th February, 1997 covering area of 1505.57 hectare forest of Bhutri beat, BTR west by taking total 45 members (table 8.8).
2. Not many activities have been done by the JFMC in the past years. Few infrastructure development works were carried out in the village such as village earthen path, fence of forest boundary near village etc.
3. There is scarcity of drinking water which is really extreme as it is on the Buxa foot hill zone where surface and subsurface layer is totally impermeable rock. Only a member has a deep machine pump from where all the members purchase and collect drinking water of 100 liters for the cost of 40 rupee. In spite of that the forest department has totally unconcern about it.

4. The villagers are unaware of JFMC works, because of being an illiterate and not a single woman participate as member of FPC or EDC.
5. The JFM gives the members maximum one month job opportunity which did not fulfil their livelihood demand. So they are engaged in horticulture, agriculture, daily labour, sometime labour of tea garden etc. during the year. The JFM programme unable to provide employment in the villagers and members' whole of the year.
6. Some group of members formed SHG, who are engaged in the mid-day meal cooking of primary.
7. Some of the members have got associated with NGO for which they got ambulance from the MLA fund. It is helping to carry serious patient from their remote area to Kalchini, Alipurduar or other better places for treatment. Although in that case there is no involvement of Forest Department here.
8. The members did not get any loan from Govt. or any NGOs to promote their livelihood needs in spite of their backward situation.
9. Man-elephant conflict is an important issue in Bhutri Forest Basti. Persons injured, killed, damage to huts or damage crops by elephants, and somewhere live-stocks by wild animals. State Government provided assistance and compensate through Forest Department (FD) for the losses. The victims getting compensation very less in amount and in some case it is too delayed.

8.8.11 Sustainability Issues of Gudamdabri Village

1. The FPC of Gudamdabri FV has been formed in 13th February, 1996 covering area of 1046.67 hectare forest of Gudamdabri beat, BTR west division by taking total 257 members (table–8.8).
2. The village is moving towards developed after preparation of metalled road and connection of electricity. Most of the villagers are belongs to Mech tribes and others are Santal, Nepali.
3. The inhabitants have very low motivational level and they don't wise to participate in the institutional level activities

such as FPCs and EDCs, since it has fewer wages and have only one month job opportunity.

4. There is no engagement of women as beneficiary of FPC or EDC from this village.
5. The villagers are being attacked by wild animals especially by elephants. The elephants damaged and ruined agricultural crops, houses property every year. There is no alternative solution of these problems still day except precaution taken by watch tower.
6. The village have many self-help groups for providing employments to the members. So somehow villagers did not bother in co-operation of forest activities.

8.8.12 Sustainability Issues of Chunabati Village

1. The FPC of Chunabati FV has been formed in 6th June, 1997 covering area of 1978.40 hectare forest of east BTR division by taking total 70 members (table–8.8).
2. The function of JFM committee is too less and few of the villagers have membership in FPC of JFM programme.
3. The villagers have less interest and they don't participate in the JFMC or other institutional level activities since it has fewer wages and have only one month job opportunity.
4. Not many activities have been done by the JFMC in the past years. There is no infrastructure development works were carried out in the village except foot path, tin shading besides foot path, wooden bridge, boulder and stone wall to protect slide of foot path.
5. There is no electricity facility in this village. For that cause solar energy plants installed by local panchayet through MLA fund although during survey it was under process.
6. The village is located in Buxa hill of 887 meter top and it has no means of accessibility except hilly track footpath. From the very beginning foot track had been made by villagers and now it is renovated by local panchayet with the help of 100 days labour fund. The FD still unconcern about it.

8.8.13 Sustainability Issues of Bhutia Basti

1. The EDC of Bhutia Basti FV has been formed in 31th March, 1999 covering area of 1713.00 hectare Bhutia basti beat forest of east BTR division by taking total 72 members (table–8.8).
2. The village has developed after installation of metalled road. Most of the villagers are belongs to Nepali community and others are santal, Bhutia.
3. The village is located in middle of the forest of Buxa Duar and too near of right bank of Jayanti River, it is above 256 meter high from MSL. It has only one means of accessibility that is un-metalled footpath which is connected to the Jayanti market.
4. All sustainability related forest work has been done by FD independently without involving JFMC members. There is a conflict between FD and local members to promote the programme. In 2016 the Govt. of West Bengal offered with compensation to shift their houses but villagers did not agree to leave although few of them shifted to other place.
5. Not many activities have been done by the JFMC in the past years. There is no infrastructure development works were carried out in the village except village path, fence of forest boundary near village, boulder and stone wall in the bank of river Jayanti.

8.8.14 Sustainability Issues of Sankosh Village

1. The FPC of Sankosh FV has been formed in 6th June, 1997 covering area of 1105.21 hectare forest of Sankosh beat of east BTR division by taking total 98 members (table–8.8).
2. The villagers are extremely disturbed by elephants and leopards attack. The elephants damaged and ruined their vegetables, food crops and houses every year. Leopard poaching their live-stocks. There is no alternative solution of these problems except rehabilitation although it has complexity.

3. All sustainability related forest work has been done by FD independently without involving JFMC members. So there is a conflict between FD and local members to promote the programme.
4. The JFM gives maximum one month job opportunity for villagers which did not fulfil their livelihood demand. So they are engaged in horticulture, agriculture, daily labour, and sometime labour of tea garden nearby garden during the year.
5. There are many self-help groups in this village formed independently and are providing employments to the members. So somehow villagers have non co-operation with forest activities.
6. The Forest Department did not renew members of Eco-Development Committee (EDC).

8.8.15 Sustainability Issues of Lapraguri Village

1. The Purba Salbari/ Bholka and Lapraguri FV FPC have been formed in 6th June, 1997 covering area of 336.80 hectare forest of Barobisa beat of east BTR division by taking total 334 members (table–8.8).
2. There is no member from woman inhabitants has been registered as beneficiary of JFMC. That means females participation is almost absent and is being neglected in sustainability issues.
3. Primary school, boulder fence beside the river bank and earthen road, community building etc has been constructed for development.
4. The members have very low motivational level and they don't participate in the institutional level activities since it has fewer wages and have only one month job opportunity.
5. The members have many Self Help Group for providing employments to the members. So somehow villagers did not bother in co-operation of forest activities.
6. The villagers are affected by elephants. The elephants damaged and ruined crops, houses every year. There is no alternative solution of these problems.

8.8.16 Sustainability Issues of Santrabari Village

1. The FPC of Santrabari FV has been formed in 6th June, 1997 covering area of 2319.59 hectare forest of Santrabari beat of east BTR division by taking total 70 members (table–8.8).
2. The village has developed after installation of metalled road. Most of the villagers are belongs to Nepali community and few of them are santal, Bhutia and others.
3. The village is located in core area of dense forest of east middle duars zone and it is above 467 meter high from MSL. It has well of accessibility road for its tourist spot importance (Buxa fort).
4. The villagers are daily affected by elephants attack. The elephants damaged and ruined their vegetables, food crops and houses property. There is no alternative solution of these problems except rehabilitation which not accepted by villagers'.
5. There are many EDCs and self-help groups in this village formed independently and which supporting of employments to the members.
6. The Forest Department did not renew members of Eco-Development Committee (EDC).
7. There is scarcity of drinking water in this village. They are collecting water from springs coming from Bhutan hill by pipe lines.

8.8.17 Sustainability Issues of Balapara Village

1. The FPC of Balapara FV has been formed in 6th June, 1997 covering area of 1332.27 hectare of forest of Balapara of east BTR division by taking total 40 members (table–8.8).
2. There is not a single female's participation as member of JFMC from this village.
3. Somewhere, sustainability related forest work has been done by FD directly without involving FPCs members. So there is a conflict between FD and JFMC members to promote the programme.

4. The JFM gives approximately one month job opportunity during whole of the year which never fulfils their livelihood demand. So they are engaged in agriculture, horticulture, daily labour, and sometime labour of tea garden nearby garden.
5. The villagers are extremely disturbed and affected by wild animals especially by elephants attack. The elephants damaged and ruined their vegetables, food crops school buildings and houses property every year. There is no alternative solution of these problems except precaution taken by seeing movement of animals from watch tower.

In conclusion, the following subjects are summed up from the above discussion. The medium of hopeful infrastructural development has not been installed as well as less institutional activities are noted which can enhance financial condition of villagers. The JFM members (FPCs and EDCs) are getting fewer interests as there is no regular source of income and employment opportunity to fulfil their needs. Besides whatever financial benefit gained by Forest Department but less amount benefit of share is distributed amongst the members of Joint Forest Management Committees (JFM). Due to this, fewer number of resident are found as member of Joint Forest Management Committee as well as a rare number of members plays active role in JFM Programme. The women members' engagement in JFM is too much less and whatever members already have also decreasing day by day. The villagers are unity in their livelihood concern and no ethnic conflict are emerging also observed. There are lack of planning and funding in JFM in respect of forest and village development. Lack of co-operation among stake holders (SHG, NGO) and forest department (FD) also noticed. Villagers have no sufficient ideas about of sustainable method of collection of NTFPs, conservation and protection of forest, awareness of micro planning etc. Most of the JFM committees are on paper only, so there is a need of activity and target oriented actions of JFM programme to achieve its goal within a certain period in this study area.

9 Chapter — Summary, Conclusion and Suggestion

9.1 Summary of the Research Findings

In this research study, all socio-economic aspects of forest villagers' have been discussed critically, based on the information collected from the research field as the report is a critical assessment of the situation. However, the entire thesis is grouped into nine chapters to find out actual situation which prevailing among them. The systematic field observation, not only provided correct data about the background and the existing situation but also giving a evident idea about the forest villagers' residing different altitude in same forest environment. Further, by systematic investigations of all the field information both quantitative and qualitative, necessary analysis has also been prepared so that the description of major events of villagers' life may discuss in separate chapters. This may give an idea about socio-economic characteristics of forest villagers' in respect to the forest and forest resource utilization such as villagers' dependency on forest as well as collection of Non-Timber Forest Product (NTFP), role of JFM for the protection of forests and villagers development, and to show ecological adaptation and changes among forest villagers' in Alipurduar District. Besides, it has main thrust to examine the villagers' relation with forest and their perception of problems associated with forest. It has also been attempted to suggest the ways to relieve the problems of forest villagers.

In the introduction (chapter 1), the researcher describes the details of hypothesis, methodology and what to be researched from forest villagers' who live in forests of same environment. Details of methodology, sources of primary and secondary data, other schedules etc. have been put just to give clear picture which prevailed and attracted others. The analysis of first chapter has been done on the basis of primary as well as secondary level data. The published and unpublished data from government forest office and other sources have been used to present geographical personality, forest profile and location of forest villages of the study area. The primary data containing to economic and socio-cultural dimensions of local environment and its inhabitants, dependency on forests, collection and use of non-timber forests resource, adaptation and perception of villagers on forest etc were generated through scheduled source.

Chapter 2 contains of the details of geographical setting of the Alipurduar District. Here details of administrative setup, relief, water bodies, climatic characteristics, soil, natural vegetation, details of demographic picture of the study area and economy etc. has been described. The area belongs to variety of climate, topography, soil and natural vegetation due to its wide altitudinal range from below 100 meters in south to over 800 meters in north. Geologically it is the foot hill zone of Greater Himalaya and mainly controlled by the altitude where climate of the region varies from tropical to sub-tropical type. The distribution of natural vegetation has also been influenced by altitude, climate and soil. The four vegetation zones have been identified which are (a) Riverine forests (b) Plains forests (c) Hill forests (d) Savannah forests. Besides close to the streams and moist pockets occurs a type of evergreen forests known as tropical evergreen forests. The area of the District has a preponderance of rural population where majority of the population, nearly 79.38% (about 11.83 lakh) lives in rural area and 20.62% (about 3.07 lakh) population live in the urban area (according to 2011 census).

Chapter 3 describes the details of forest profile as well as forest villagers' panorama. Here administrative setup of forest divisions, area coverage, forest resource product and utilisation, and important aspects of the forest villagers' life and culture has been depicted. As good number of tribal living, their mode of living, social customs and other religious festivals associated with agriculture, economy and forest have been described carefully. Manner and customs related to forest as well as many anthropogenic interactions (illegal cutting, man-animal conflict, forest fire, threatened and illegal trade of wildlife etc) have been depicted just to give a clear picture of the villagers' dependency and intervention on of forest in the locality under study.

Chapter 4 gives the details of field observations related information of demography as well as socio-economy of villagers of forests. Here demographic character such as age-sex composition, ethnic composition, dominant tribal group, family size and type, and migration; and social aspects such as language, educational status, religions and beliefs, and marital status etc. have been depicted diligently.

Chapter 5 is an elaborate analysis of various adaptation sides of sampled forest villagers. The site and location of forest villagers has a profound impact on the life style which they have to adapt according to their capacity. So the manner, customs and behaviour related to forest environment i.e. land use, food habit, fuel used, source of water facilities, house types and forest based economy i.e. income pattern, occupation, landholding capacity, livestock asset and agriculture as well as farming have been analysed to give the idea of livelihood adaptation power and economy of forest villagers in locality of the study area.

Chapter 6 describes the details of forest villagers' dependency on forests. Villagers are primarily depend on forests for number of forest resources like fodder, fuel, fruit, timber and minor forest products etc. Here the effort has been made to show the details of collection of forest resources such consumption of Non-Timber Forest Product (NTFPs), fodder, timber, fuel wood as well as time spent and distanced covered for collection of these resources.

Chapter 7 gives details of field observations related information of perception of villagers' as well as environment related views which also connected with villagers' socio-economic livelihood entities. Villagers' perception i.e. change in forest cover in the years, period of tree felled, perception about present and future forest stock, about forest values as well as environment related views such as perception about the effect of forest on ecological changes, reasons for shrinkage of forest area, destruction, its responsibilities and solutions etc. have been depicted carefully.

In the chapter 8, the researcher describes the details about key issues and supporting activities of Joint Forest Management project in Alipurduar District. Activities of FPCs and EDCs members in JFM, ecological, economic and social activity of JFM project, villagers' Response on Joint Forest Management activity, villagers' participation and expectation in forest management, women's involvement in JFM etc. have been put forward just to give clear picture about the real status of implementation of JFM pilot project for the development of forest villagers in this area.

Here, chapter 9, which is conclusion, all these have been critically assessed and what to be done for betterment of forest villagers has been suggested. All these given suggestions might be helpful to the social workers, project planners, social scientists and others who involved directly or indirectly for causes of the sustainable development of the forest villagers.

Various data, tables and charts have been documented to have a very clear idea of the situation of socio-economic characteristics of these forest villagers. For that purpose the study is made to analysis socio-economic characteristics of forest villagers' in respect to the forest and forest resource utilization as well as villagers' relation with forest and their perception of problems associated with forests also analyzed. It has also been attempted to suggest the ways to recover the associated problems of forest villagers.

The analysis has been done based on of primary as well as secondary level data. The data from government forest office and other sources have been used to present geographical information such as administrative set up, forest, soil, river, climate, forest villages, and demographic features of the study area. The primary data containing to socio-economic and socio-cultural dimensions of forest villagers were generated through questionnaire source. The area belongs to variety of climate, topography, soil and natural vegetation due to its wide variation natural activities and difference of altitudinal range from south to north. Geologically it is the foot hill zone of Greater Himalaya and mainly controlled by the altitude where climate of the area varies from tropical to sub-tropical type.

The distribution of natural vegetation has also been influenced by altitude, climate and soil. The four vegetation zones have been identified which are (a) Riverine forests- The Riverine forests are of mixed type, main trees are Khair (Acacia catechu), Sissoo (Dalbergia Sissoo), Premna species, Salmalia malabarica, Albizzzia species, and Gmelina arborea etc. (b) Plains forests- the Plains forests are Semal, Khair, Asathwa (Ficus religios), Neem (Melia azadirachta), Amlaki (phyllanthus emblica), Radha chura (Poinciana regia), Debdaru (Polyalthia longifolia), Guava (Psideim guyava), Arjuna (Terminalia arjuna), Hartaki (Terminalia arjuna) etc. (c) Hill forests-The hill forests of this District include some important species of Toona ciliate, Castanopsis specia, Acrocarpus fraxinifolius, Durabanga Sonneratioides, Ailanthus grandis and Mours Laevigata. (d) Savannah forests- Savannah forests covered small area in the District. Common savannah forests species of grasses that are found include the Saccharum species, Erianthus species, Imperata cylindrical, Phragmites karka, Arundo donax and Neyraudia reynaudiana. Besides close to the streams and moist pockets occurs a type of evergreen forests known as tropical evergreen forests, tropical trees of which are Aesculus assamica, Eugenia Formosa, Dillenia indica, Castanopsis species, Talauma hodgsoni, Pinanga gracilis, and Myristica species.

The area of the District has a preponderance of rural population where majority of the population, nearly 79.38%

(about 11.83 lakh) lives in rural area and 20.62% (about 3.07 lakh) population live in the urban area (according to 2011 census). The agriculture, by far, occupies the dominant sector of the economy as 93.51% of sampled workers are engaged in primary sector such as agriculture, farming, livestock rearing, while only 2.05 per cent is engaged in the secondary and 4.44% in tertiary sector (table–5.17). There is a referable feature in women section that is the higher female participation especially in agriculture as the cultivators, non-timber forest resource collection labour. The dependence on agriculture especially in horticulture farming practice increasing in higher altitudes village area where interior areas of low altitude food crop practicing is more visible.

The 17 sample forest villages were selected from different altitude and location area for detailed study of demography and social condition, adaptation to forest environment and economic characteristics of the inhabitants, their dependency, perception and participation in Joint Forest Management. In order to understand villagers' impact on the nature of relationship between villagers and forests, the socio-economic characteristics of the villages have been studied by selecting low and high altitude village. The majority of the respondents could respond about the unemployment, less number of higher education institution, lacking of metal roads and electric connection in the forest cover. About 49.20% households have family size of between 4 to 6 persons and the proportion of large families with more than 10 persons occupied only 0.57 % household (table 4.11). The economic characteristics of the households reveal that there is higher female participation in all forest villages because of migration of able males from this area. Since the returns from the agriculture are low, quite a few members of the household of high altitude have to adopt other occupations e.g. labour, NTFPs collector, daily wage labour in nursery, seedling and plantation. The field survey shows that about 1.73 per cent of the working household members has some auxiliary other activity besides agriculture.

The agricultural land is considered as the major productive resource of inhabitants which is limited in this region especially in high altitude it is too less due to hilly terrain. The analysis showed that the average land holding capacity per household is 0.62 acres where the average land holding size is 1.0 acres in the lower altitude area and less than 0.50 acres in high altitude area. Only 3.18 per cent of total households possess more than 1.1-2 acres of land whereas 50.46 % possess less than 1 acres (table–5.18). The analysis of livestock population and assets shows that on an average one household has 1.89 cattle units. It is also noticed that the average number of cattle units increase with decrease in altitude.

The collection and pattern of forest resource utilization, inhabitants' access of forest resource has been studied at the ground level with the help of household survey. The forests have shared an important resource base in this region. Villagers depend on forest for a number of forest resources like fodder, fuel, fruit, timber and minor forest products etc. The effort has been made to evaluate demand and needs of these resources. The quantity of green fodder is available for an average of 9 months from forests and dry fodder is sufficient for an average of 3 months only from agricultural field. In this study, it is concluded that in addition of usual grazing, average green fodder of grass and leaves collection is 4.50 ± 0.53 kg and 3.81 ± 0.59 kg per day of a member of household from the forest whereas it is only 0.84 ± 0.36 kg and 0.86 ± 0.24 kg per day from the agricultural field. In case of dry fodder, average grass and leaves collection is about 2.89 ± 0.41kg from the agricultural field but it is nil from forest (table–6.3 of chapter 6). However the green fodder demanded to sustain the livestock supply is obtained from the forests by spending average 2.33 ± 0.34 hr a day one member of the household for 294.93 ± 3.43 days in a year. But it is only 0.67 ± 0.32 hrs a day and 86.24 ± 3.62 days in a year from field collection. For dry fodder, average grass and leaves collection time is about 1.15 ± 0.45hrs a day and 61.25 ± 5.70 days in a year (table–6.5). There are some variations in the distance covered for regional and altitudinal height difference, proximity to forest for trip of fodder collection. The villagers inside the forest and near proximity have to walk minimum distance (0.59 ± 0.13 km/day), and have to make maximum 2.09 ± 0.42 km/ day of the fringe villagers of low altitude to obtain the green fodder of forest (table–6.6).

Another great contribution of resource from the forest is in the form of fuel wood. It is the only one source of domestic fuel energy for forest villagers. According to the data collected from field survey, average consumption of fuel wood is about 119.74 ± 20.34 kg and 98.64 ± 20.32 kg per household per month in winter and in summer season respectively (table–6.7 of chapter 6). It is responsible for more fuel wood consumption for cooking as well as for water and room heating at high altitude and hill villagers due to comparatively low temperature whole of the year. The women and children were performed as fuel wood collector for their family. The fuels collecting from the forest in the forms of twigs, branches, and dead dry wood, fallen wood and log wood. Most of the household used dry leaves, branches and twigs as fuel. The study has shown that a lot of time has been spent by women and children in collecting the fuel wood although restrictions are ruled by Forest Department.

The timber is another forests' contribution used by villagers' as a major component material in house construction. As many as 770 (87.70%) of total households are used wood and tin for making roofs, walls and floors of houses (table–6.10). The quantity of timber used is more in high altitudes areas (400-800m) where household make wood-floor, wood wall, wood stairs and wood-roof. The non-availability of alternative building material and the prohibitive transport cost of bricks, tin and cement, leave the forest inhabitants with no alternative but to use timber easily.

The analysis has shown that timbers are only prime material used in construction of a house with other materials. The presences of forest helps the villagers to obtain the timber easily whether free of cost or as free grant or at concessional price from Forest Department. Although this are not sufficient to meet timber needs of the households because the timber quantity provided by Forest Department is fixed on the basis of agreement holder of households existing in villages. Since other members who are out of agreement have to purchase extra timber according to their needs. The analysis shows that 87.81% of the households used free grant timber, 7.63% used as concessional based priced timber, 2.51% used on auction purchase basis, 2.05% household collected timber through un-authorize way (table–6.11). In addition to this the villagers required huge amount of fuel wood for family programmes and social ceremonies such as birth day, wedding, poles for vegetable creepers and stocking of dry fodder; fencing of fields, wood for agricultural implements etc. So wood and bunches for varieties of purposes is also collected from the surrounding forest area. From the above evaluation it is clear that forest contribution is unlimited to inhabitants in consideration of fodder, fuel and timber. The household obtained more and more timber and non-timber forest product according to their daily day needs. Except above facilities the study reveals that forest do not provide appropriate employment opportunities to local inhabitants. There are only few agreement household members who got some employment facility in forestry activities. Other few non agreement members were also getting job but it is very much irregular. The contribution of forest to the income level of households need is also not meaningful except for fodder, fuel and timber.

The present study has aimed to analyse the perception of local villagers about necessity of forest, related problems and solutions. A questionnaire was prepared to capture these valuable comments of inhabitants. The heads of household replied the questions about deforestation; local forest based needs, changes in the environment, awareness about their rights and concessions, attitude of officials', regarding unemployment, policy issues of Joint Forest Management and activities, reasons of frequent wild animal conflicts and solution ways of forest destruction.

The analysis shows that the perception of the individual is independent reflection of his or her dependence on forest and the intensity of the forest resource needs. The villagers were asked to recognize their perception regarding forest coverage, density and composition of trees in the surrounding forest areas, the respondents were given about perception of such changes. All respondents gave their reply based on perception and knowledge regarding past and present day forest situation. There were 82.23% households who opined that forest cover situation is worse today than before and there has been deterioration and degradation in the forest cover but there were 17.77% respondents, who still felt that, no development or change has been observed in the forest coverage in last two decades (table–7.2).

The study also shows that the forest and fringe inhabitant don't have any role in the process of deforestation and degradation of forests but they are directly affected and faced many problem by this deforestation. The inhabitants felt the impact of deforestation when there were large numbers of man-animal conflict occurred in their surrounding areas. Through this study, an attempt has been made to get the villagers' response about the causes of tree felling, type of trees felled, process of deforestation, period of tree felling, and the agency responsible for tree felling. Besides this as a supplementary question, villagers were also asked about the background of contractors, local market for woods, labourers engaged for felling and the actual destination of the wood. To recognize the reasons of tree felling, villagers were asked to reply the reasons of tree felling, as they perceived to report. Out of total respondents, 65.03 % respondents disclose their perception about reasons of tree felling, and thought that trees were felled for use of outside of the region. They have opined that the native and local residents have no share in felled trees and they have seen all the timber and wood being taken out of the region. However most of the older respondents expressed that large scale of trees were felled in the British period for their own needs, tea plantation and agricultural land for labours, later after independence huge amount of sal trees were felled for railway sleeper need. Among them 9.79% opined that at present illegal cutting of trees, illegal removal of fire wood and NTFPs, illegal grazing and encroachment are the prime causes of tree felled. It is quite significant to note that 8.88% respondents felt that road construction and extension of width of NH 34, railway line of NJP to Alipurduar Junction of North Frontier Railway Division within the dense forest, dam construction along river bank or extension of area under tea and agriculture are the reasons of large scale tree felling. However it has been noticed that only 5.01% respondents were supported and engaged to cut the trees through illegal way, but they could not specify the actual demand or numbers. On the other hand 94.99% respondents opted that they were not supported and engaged to cut the trees by illegal way even they remarked illegal felling are mainly the cause of outside of the forest people who are not emotionally connected with forest (table–7.4).

Villagers gave their perception on forest values according to the importance and after taking opinion it is noted that most of the economic values such as food, fodder, bamboo, fruit, cane medicinal products etc. were get much more importance than ecological values (such as protection of water resources or restoration of soil fertility, soil erosion, landslides, climate change). Although, they gave high ranked opinion on climate change and clean air value by giving more importance. So it proves that villagers now very much concern about forest environment. There are 81.44% respondents who gave much more importance in economic value of forests, where 16.17% opined in favour of ecological value and only 2.39% (table 7.7 of chapter 6) gave importance of forests on social and cultural value. From above observation it is clear that directly or indirectly villagers are very much dependent on forest for economic support and due to lack of other alternatives economic activity, forests have been facing tremendous pressure of economic related work although few respondents of them were very much serious about deterioration of forest cover and environment which provide them all sort of needs.

The villagers were asked about their perception and feeling of forest role on environment change. About 0.91% was not very specifying their comment, there were 7.74% of the respondents who feel that presently trees do not affect on environmental change at all. And about 91.35% of the respondents were consented about the influence of forest on the environment by referring increasing normal temperature and decreasing amount of normal rainfall in this area (table–7.9). It also reveals that 3.76% respondents commented on no change in rainfall over the past 10 years and it is opined only by the villagers who were resided in high altitude and dense forests. About 71.87% of the respondents announced that rainfall has decreased over the past 10 years, whereas 24.37% noticed it is now uncertainty and irregularity at the time of rainy season (table–7.10). According to the villagers' opinion, it is noticed that the rainfall behaviour has become uncertain for the past decade.

The perception of respondents about changes in normal temperature due to changes in forest cover had been tried to observe by asking questions. The field investigation has revealed that out of the total respondents, 8.08% opined that no change in temperature has been felt, 70.96% felt increase in normal temperature while 20.96% are of the notice that the normal temperature has fluctuated in different seasons over the last 10 years (table–7.11).

Due to forest felling and thinning of the forest cover in this area, the river bank erosion and landslides in the high altitude area generally increased. Therefore respondents were asked to give opinions on this subject. About 30.52% respondents did not give any reply since they have no idea about landslide and erosion; and 7.18% were of opinion in no change in landslides or erosion intensity. While 62.30% were of the opinion that landslides have increased in recent past. None of single respondents feel decrease in landslides (table–7.12).

An important aspect of the study was to understand the villagers' response regarding reasons of forest destruction, responsibility of this destruction and likely solutions. The field investigation reveals that a variety of causes have been perceived by respondents as its reasons. According to their opinion large scale tree felling is mentioned as the most important single reason for forest destruction and shrinkage by 41.91% out of 878 respondents. About 25.97% respondents opined that illegal felling by outsiders and poachers are main culprit for forest destruction, whereas 14.24% villagers viewed day by day increase in village population as the major reason for forest destruction. About 4.67% respondents viewed natural calamities (fire, landslide) as the reason for forest destructions; whereas 13.21% respondents considered rail way and road construction as main damaging factors (table–7.14). The villagers in lower altitude were so much concerned about forest destruction and opined that large scale felling, rail way and road construction and illegal felling are major responsible factors which has been occurred in their neighbourhoods, while villagers of high altitude viewed that increase in village population and natural calamities (fire, landslide) also involved and considered as responsible factor to the forest destruction in high altitudes area.

With the perception of forest related problems and by considering the critical situations of the surrounding forests, the respondents gave some separate suggestions about proper care of the forests. Among total respondents, 24.83% respondents opined that more and more afforestation is one and only good way of solution of forests problems in the area. About 38.95% respondents were of the opinion that serious awareness of the Forest Department should have been taken for proper care of the forests by implementing Government projects accordingly. While 17.99% respondents suggested to control strictly of illegal felling by implementing hard and fast laws, and also proposed heavy fine on the offenders must be imposed. It was thought by12.64% respondents that ban and restriction on large scale felling can save the forest area and should have taken step about it strictly, whereas 5.59% respondents suggested to awareness of villagers own self and they felt that alternatives sources of fuel and fodder should be made available to protect the forests (table–7.16).

The major finding of this research is 'sustainable livelihood of forest villagers' in which different favourable steps, obstacles and interventions were observed which was done by JFM, NGO's, local panchayet or others. The sustainable livelihood steps are the allotment of open and fairly open forest land for agriculture, collection and uses of non-timber forest products, permission livestock rearing, forestry activities, infra-structure development and nursery etc. For agricultural development and to reduce pressure on forest and fringe area, ownership of 1.5 to 2.5 acre of forest land has been distributed to the forest villagers by giving "patta" on forest land. The employment generation were done through infra-structure development like ecotourism, tourist guide, electricity connection, establishment of primary school as well as school building for children of each forest village, construction of metalled, earthen road which are connected with local market and main roads so on. In plantation activities different types of species were planted and wage labouring provided to the villagers. Many concrete walls and check dams had been constructed to protect river bank erosion, soil erosion, land slide and water conservation.

The study also tried to understand coherent relation between socio-economic conditions of forest villagers and their participation in different programmes of the Joint Forest Management (JFM) through sustainable view point. The JFM programme has been implemented over two decades in this state as well as in this study area. This JFM project opened up many avenues for forests as well as villagers development but a number of issues have been identified to sustain the programme from social, economic, political and technical point of view. From the social point of view, though the women are important stake holder but their participation was not good and satisfactory level. Number of women participation is decreasing day by day since lack of attempts and approaches had been made to empower the women.

Similarly the forest departments' dominance and influence is found more than the villagers/beneficiaries in case of the process and progress of different project related work. Lack of belongingness is observed among the forest villagers towards forest department. The EDCs, FPCs and other communities' leadership and activities is not observed so much active. The JFM members are getting fewer interests as there is no regular source of income and employment opportunity in this programme. Moreover forest officials didn't co-operate properly about villagers' compensation and other project installation issues. Almost in all forest villages, villagers engaged with SHGs, NGOs and Missionary activities since villagers getting ideas, funds, skilled opportunities etc. comparatively than Forest Department. There are many economic activities have been generated through different project of JFM, such as assistance of intensive agriculture farm, horticulture, NTFPs processing, value-addition and marketing, nursery of small plants and medical plants, cleaning of forest, sal and teak plantation of felling area, seed handling. But members are not properly appointed to work in these working circles and less number of villagers/ members sometimes has been engaged in these schemes due to which villagers are indifferent regarding JFM projects.

There is no available irrigation system, micro-credit schemes which are arranged in favour of villagers for cultivation, poultry farming and live-stock rearing. The skill building programmes were arranged but villagers as well as beneficiaries were not interested to implement the skill due to its lack of income opportunity. The application of micro enterprise of different sections is not properly organised for achieving sustainable livelihood of villagers. Financial assistance is an important side for mobilizing the remote inhabitants. But there is no micro-financial aid/projects which is essential and have to be started immediately without hard and fast rules.

In the very recent days due to implementation of NREGS, hundred days scheme infra-structural development had been taken place. But the income generating point of view infrastructural development is not satisfactory level and it has to be enhanced in different sectors relared with forestry so that sustainable livelihood can promote in this area.

The villagers are in huge troubles due to attack of wild animals specially elephants and leopards regularly which is now burning issue and there is no alternative ways or plans except compensation of damage materials provided by the Forest Department. The man-animals conflict has been increasing rapidly which is now a big environmental problem of imbalance of bio-diversity in this study area and challenge of environmentalists. So there have a deep thinking of planners to find out the way of sustainability of living for both forest villagers and wild animals for better future.

9.2 Suggestions

In the study area NTFPs collection provides substantial employment as well as income opportunities for forest villagers. So forest villagers, who are residing for more than 100 years, are collecting NTFPs from forest to sustain daily needs of the households. Hence number of species as well as quantity of NTFPs collection for both consumption and sale is increased appreciably over the years, reflecting dependence on forest by villagers to sustain family needs due to less employment opportunity. However forest resource decline is also reported due to commercial extraction, logging, fire hazards and excessive extraction of timber and Non-timber forests products. These are prime causes of imbalanced between forests and NTFPs based resources with extraction and income. In order to avoid the sudden bad consequences, there should be a strong step for scientific management and strict monitoring between timber and NTFPs yields with extraction rates of forest resources to maintain stabilization. Besides, villagers and fringe people should also be informed about the ill effects of excessive extraction of forest resource, man-made fire in the forest, and illegal cutting and collection of NTFPs, fire protection should be proactively followed by the Forest Department involving core and fringe inhabitants.

Scientific studies have to be carried out to evaluate the short and long run impact of NTFPs extractions on forests and ecosystem. Based on serious future impact, villagers should have to be educated on sustainable ways of harvesting NTFPs.

Research is also required on different harvesting mechanisms as such knowledge will ensure sustainable harvesting of resources, which in turn can contribute to the economic well-being of the villagers and involve them in the conservation of forest ecosystem and biodiversity. However, NTFPs activities should be based on participatory planning and management, where socio-cultural issues play an important role in the sustainability of the NTFPs resource base. Besides Research is also necessary on the environmental aspects of NTFPs such as distribution, regeneration pattern, growth rates, yield in different forest types of the area and silvicultural mechanisms for managing multiple products. The extraction and utilization rates over time and different seasons need to be explored over a period to identify trends or patterns in yield and use of NTFPs and other forest resource.

Villagers who are primary collectors are highly dependent on vendor/agents for NTFPs sale. As a result, they are not getting proper remunerative price for collection, since local vendor have the monopoly and control over the NTFPs trade. The vendor/agents reportedly followed misappropriate weighting of the products, providing them less purchase amount and retained higher margins through sales. Therefore concerned local authorities of vendors should be appointed by the local Govt. to ensure fair practices and appropriate price in the trade of NTFPs as well as explore the possibilities of increasing price benefit to the villagers.

At present villagers used forest woods, branches, green and dry leaves etc. to fulfill the fuel need, house construction and demands of other agricultural materials. To reduce the pressure and sustain the forest non vulnerable, state and central government should provide alternative of fuel such as LPG, concrete pillar, tins, bricks for house construction and other metal agricultural materials in free basis for certain period.

There is continuous threat of loss of agricultural products (food crops) due to depredation of elephant, wild boar and monkey. This crop raid by wild animals over agricultural farm is a major issue which is confining and controlling agricultural activities of the villagers. So immediately Government should ensure proper compensation for the loss and take up effective preventive measure against crop raids, although forest authority must take steps to enrich trees as well as fodders of animal food inside the forest by plantation, to reduce crop raid of animals. Besides other some preventive measures may be taken to reduce conflicts, such as by creating maximum no. of elephant proof trenches as physical barrier in vulnerable area, erection solar energy fencing, forming advisory committee to forest village, fringe village as well as to tea gardens for effective management of leopard straying outside, training of EDC and FPC members forming village wise small squards to provide immediate response etc.

The preventive measures to reduce incidence of elephant, bison and other animals killing by train may be implemented in the following way, such as restriction of trains speed within 20 to 25 km/hr. Local villagers as well as EDC and FPC members of forest villages may be trained and employed permanently or daily basis to track the movement of animals and immediately its information should be informed to concern railway authority for necessary action. Meeting should be arranged regularly to exchange information among Forest Department, Railway Board and movement trackers. Under pass may be constructed in animal corridor and vulnerable area across the railway track. Advanced technologies may be installed to alert the loco pilots regarding the presence of animals near the track. Besides clearing of bushes and vegetation up to 30 meter all along track side must be maintained by Forest Department.

Hand loom small-scale industry of cane furniture,

bamboo furniture and small showcase wood materials on cooperative basis could set up in this area so that maximum profits would go directly to primary producer as NTFPs extraction increased considerably in recent years. Furthermore, women Self Help Groups (SHG) can be engaged as selling agents for hand loom and NTFPs for more profits at ground level. Also village tourism through home stay basis may be initiated in potential forest village areas with full cooperation of Forest Department as well as JFM projects.

At present the forest laws prevent extraction and gave some restriction on NTFPs in the National Parks and Wildlife sanctuaries. In such a situation, forest inhabitants should be given suitable alternative sources of livelihood opportunities outside the forest area and also government should explore the possibility for voluntary rehabilitation or relocations outside the forest by giving attractive compensation and alternative job of reliable income source.

The concerned government authorities should ensure that the benefits of the development policies and programs targeted by the central and state government only at the forest villagers should successfully reach to the actual needy forest inhabitants. Besides health consciousness, knowledge of education about environment and forest, and transport and other infrastructures facilities should be ensured to villagers within the available provisions of forest area.

The funds provided for projects and working period of projects is too less, which have to be increased immediately with proper planning and guide based on local issues. Now the planning is prepared by the outside Govt. employee or officers or by thinkers or planner who don't have ideas about local demand, attitude, opportunity and environment. So the micro plans for inhabitants should have to be prepared and implemented on the basis of local demand, attitude, opportunity and environment along with villagers' maximum co-operation for sustainability issues. Otherwise in preparation of awareness building, skill development, infrastructure development and other development related interventions would be unsuccessful, which is very much apparent at present in case of earlier project plan and implementation in this study area.

9.3 Limitations of the Research Findings

There are some limitations in this research finding. The reasons behind these limitations were geographical as well as anthropogenic. As the research has been conducted on the socio-economically backward forests villagers' as well as geo-physically foot hill remote areas of the Bhutan of north eastern India, the availability of data and information was not at all very easy. Attempts have been made to manage data and information as much possible from the range office reports, District forest and state forest reports. However, it cannot be said that the data and information whatever collected, have been related and referred to in the research work. There are very limited sources of information on the forestry and forest-people relationships of these tropical deciduous forests. For administrative boundary, area, JFM activities and other documents of beat, range, and division have been collected from several government reports, Forest Department reports, District Statistical Handbook reports, and reports on project work by NGOs and research organisations, journal publications, books and newspaper articles. However, there is very limited work has been undertaken and evaluated the importance of NTFPs in forests socio-economic life and how these products can take a constructive role in tropical deciduous forest villagers' development and management. Therefore, there are limitations in terms of literature and background information available.

For this research, almost three months pilot study and five months full fieldwork have been conducted. Due to the limitations of poor accessibility within the interior and dense forest area, it is felt that the periods of fieldwork were insufficient. The problem of transportation in the field area posed a tremendous problem in terms of completing the research within the scheduled time. During the arrangement for interviews, household surveys and group discussions, a special effort had to put to encourage female and child members of forest tribes who were felt uneasy and avoid participating with outsiders. Although some of female and child members have shared their experiences, but still there is a space to improve it. As the study area is in dense and fairly dense forest cover and the accessibility is too poor so the wild animal attacks were quite noticeable in the research area. In fact, during the progress of field work, suddenly an elephant attack took place on the way of survey near Bhutia basti forest village. Therefore, the Forest Department was not allowing me to access to interior forest villages without proper protection, prior notice and guide in the core area. The researcher is thankful to the Forest Department for help hand in this regard. A flash flood also happened in Pana River when researcher has gone to survey in Bhutri forest basti. There is no any kind of transport line except rugged foot track to go Adma and Chunabati forest village of Buxa hill forest. So it was tough to manage for field survey as 2.30 hours to 3.00 hours trekking and walking taken to reach there from transport line. However, the situation adversely affected day-to-day social life of forest villagers and simultaneously this also influenced on the research work, which was conducted about these communities.

9.4 Implementation of the Research Findings in Different Forest Areas

Keeping in mind all the limitations of this research, it can be said that, this research is going to be the first piece of research which enclose all the aspects of forest villagers such as demography and social status, adaptation in forest environment and economy, dependency, perception, forest livelihoods with fuel wood and NTFPs, and forest management of the tropical deciduous forest of North Bengal. Although, it is true that with the variations in forest character and availability of forest resources, nature and characteristics, and livelihood of villagers varies from place to place. Even, the results of this work can be referred to for the similar type of forest villagers' research for other regions. There are some basic aspects of forestry and dependency, forest cultures and in forest management strategy. Therefore, the findings of this research may be used for similar forest areas with a little modification according to the respective native forest villagers' characteristics. To save the forest ecosystem and biodiversity, this research has been discussed in details with special reference to Joint Forest Managements' system and which are available in the tropical deciduous forest of North Bengal. Appropriate harvesting of NTFPs can reduce the dependence on timber, fuel wood and other products. Excess large scale tree feeling, illegal timber cutting always creates problems in the inhabitants of forests, where thousands of different forest community villagers live within or at the fringe of the forests. It is because of the poor economic conditions, these forest villagers cannot manage any other alternative source of fuel. So, selling firewood is only a good business for the marginal forest villagers as the demand of firewood is also higher outside and fringe forest area. For earning, they go to the forest to collect firewood as they are sure that they will be able to sell it. Therefore, the protection of forest cover it is necessary to control timber and non-timber product collection. But it is not very easy to control timber and NTFPs collection without offering an alternative source of income to forest villagers. In this situation, scientific harvesting of NTFPs and sustainable uses of it can do an important role in protecting the forests cover, providing an alternative source of income for forest villagers.

The research has interpreted the collection strategies of forest resources, way of storage facilities and how marketing channels of NTFPs connected from the ground level to the ultimate purchasers. The idea, themes, findings and suggestions can be useful for the improvement of socio-economically backward forest inhabitants of other countries. The economic development of forest villagers could help to protect the forests of North Bengal. The introductions of government policies are not enough to improve financial situation in this regard. It has to be ensured that forest policies are working intensively for the fiscal growth of forest villagers and other beneficiaries. A sense of ownership over forest resources including fuel wood, timber, NTFPs and others could inspire forest villagers to protect the forest cover of North Bengal. Proper education regarding the importance of forests and forest products directed through Gram Panchayat (Block and village level government body) institutions could help to increase the consciousness among villagers. It is, however, also true that as the forest inhabitant have been living in these forest areas for the long periods. So they know better than outsiders about how they should collect fuel wood, timber, NTFPs and other resources, which products should collect and how much they should collect.

9.5 Further Research

The present research mainly focuses on socio-economic characteristics of forest villagers, where social status, adaptation in the forests, dependency and perception has been analysed. In future, however, consumption of resources and sustainable harvesting of forest products, socio-economic impact of deforestation on forest inhabitants can arrange in a parallel way for the development of forest inhabitants. Research can also be conducted on other social aspects such as women's participation in JFM programme and their development, and other JFM policies applied on forest communities' development such as ecological and socio-economic impact assessment of villagers' Eco-Development Committee (EDC) and Forest Protection Committee (FPC). No doubt, the forest has played an important role in the life of forest villagers, but the action is not always same way for all. The activities of forest villagers' also differ on the forest environment and forest character. Besides, there are many several type socio-economic practices among different forest communities which can be included in the research separately. Moreover, forests and particularly those people live in the forest should not be studied only from the aspect of forestry and environment, but at the same time, other forest communities such as backward tribe communities should receive equal advantage in research. For the overall improvement of socio economic circumstance of marginal forest villagers and forest resource management, a research is needed that connects historical view, development, economics and environmental related local policy making perspectives. The discovery of the historical views of man-environment interactions, the study of contemporary socio-economic issues of forest inhabitants related to forest and forest products harvesting can be considered as an important features in terms of future relevant policy making. This research will intend to present an overall idea about natural resource harvesting and marginal livelihoods of villagers in terms of forest resources which are available in the tropical-deciduous forest of North Bengal.

Bibliography

Allen, B.C., Gait, E.A., Allen, C.G.H., & Howard, H.F., 2001: *Gazetteer of Bengal and North-East India,* Mittal Publications, New Delhi.pp.1-23.

Banerjee, B., 1964: *Morphological Regions of West Bengal,* in Geographical Review of India, vol. 26, pp. 119-12.

Barber, C. V., Miller K. R., Boness M., 2004: *Securing protected areas in the face of global change: issues and strategies,* IUCN, Gland, Switzerland and Cambridge, UK. pp. 45-62.

Bardhan, P., 2002: *The Environmental Impact of Poverty: Evidence from Firewood Collection in Rural Nepal,* World Bank, December, 12, p. 24-60.

Bauri, T., Palit, D., & Mukherjee, A., 2015: *Livelihood Dependency of Rural People utilizing Non-Timber Forest Product (NTFPs) in a Moist Deciduous Forests Zone, West Bengal, India,* International Journal of Advanced Research (2015), Vol. 3, Issue 4, pp. 1021-1032.

Beniston, M., 2003: *Climate Change in Mountain regions: a review of possible impacts,* Climate change, pp. 5-31.

Betts, R.A., 2006: *Forcing and feedbacks by land ecosystem changes on climate change,* J. Phys. IV France, pp. 123-146, doi: 10.1051/jp4: 2006139009.

Bhattacharya, P., Kandya, A. K., and Kumar, K.N. K., 2008: *Joint Forest Management in India, Vol. 1 and II,* Aavishkar Publishers, Distributors, 1st Ed. Jaipur, India, pp.145, 262,365, 443, 591.

Bhattacharya, S., Ghosh G., Banerjee T., Goswami S., Das P., 2015: *Socio-Environmental Survey of an Ecologically Important Hamlet of Darjeeling District West Bengal,*

India, International Letters of Natural Sciences 33 (2015), pp. 51-72.

Bonan, G.B., 2008: *Forests and climate change: Forcings, feedbacks, and the climate benefits of forests Science,* 320, 1444-1449, doi: 10.1126/science.1155121.

Brooks, T.M., RA, Mettermeier, GAB, da Fonseca., 2006: *Global Biodiversity conservation priorities,* Science. Vol. 313, pp. 58-61.

Bruijnzeel, L.A., 2004: *Hydrology of tropical Montane cloud forests: a reassessment.* Land Use Wat. Res., Vol.1, pp. 1-18.

Campbell, J.Y., Tewari, and D.D., 1995: *Increased development of non-timber forest products in India: Some issues and concerns,* J. Sustain, for, 3(1), pp. 53-79.

Chauhan, T. S., 1987: *Agriculture Geography: A Case study of Rajasthan State,* Academic Publishers, Jaipur, p. 41.

Conroy, C., 1994: *Contribution of Farm Forestry to Rural Households: A Case Study from Eastern Gujarat,* Wasteland News, Vol. 9 (2), pp. 45-64.

Das Gupta, S., 1988: *Tribal Women (In) Understanding the Tribal Dilemma. Tribal Women and Forest Dweller Economy,* Indian Social Institute, New Delhi.

Das, B.K., 2005: *Role of NTFPs among forest villagers in a protected area of West Bengal,* Journal of Human Ecology, 18(2): pp.129-136.

Das, K., 2013: *Man-Elephant Conflicts in North Bengal,* Conservator of Forests, Wildlife (Headquarters) West Bengal, pp. 1-26.

Das, S. C., 2000: *Management-cum-working plan of Buxa Tiger Reserve,* 2000-01 to 2009-2010, Forest Department, Govt. of West Bengal, Vol. I, pp. 10-11. 69-70, 77, 90-91, 111, 112-113, 120-121, 261-263, 347.

Dash, A.J., 1947: *Darjeeling Gazetteer, Bengal Government press, Alipur,* West Bengal and the first reprinted by N.L. Publishers, Shibmandir, Siliguri (2011), West Bengal.

Datta, S., Vijaya, M., Gitali, T., 2004: *A Resource Book for Livelihood Promotion,* Hyderabad, Basix and New Economics Foundation, pp. 34-36.

De, H.K., 1997: *Joint Forest Management for Sustainable Development,* Ph.D. Thesis, Indian Agricultural Research Institute, New Delhi, P. 98.

Debnath, S., 2010: *The Dooars in Historical Transition,* Shiv Mandir, Siliguri, N. L. Publishers, p. 137, 147.

Directorate of Census Operations West Bengal, 2011: *District Census Handbook,* West Bengal, Series 20, Part XII-A, Census of India, 2011, pp. 1-80, Avl at: https://indikosh.com/dist/708755/alipurduar, retrieved on dated 14.08.2016.

District Census Handbook, Jalpaiguri, 2011: *Village and Town Wise Primary Census Abstract* (PCA), Directorate of Census Operations, West Bengal, series-20, part XII-B, pp. 1-28.

Fernandes, W., Geeta Menon, and Philip Viegas, 1988: *Forests, environment and tribal economy: deforestation, impoverishment and marginalisation in Orissa,* Indian Social Institute, New Delhi, pp. 27-37.

Forest survey of India, Eastern Zone, Calcutta, 1999: *Report on forest resources of Jalpaiguri District,* West Bengal, p. 9.

Gadgil, M., and K.C. Malhotra, 1982: *Ecology of a pastoral caste: Gavli dhangars of peninsular India, Human Ecology,* Vol.10, No. 2.

Ghosh, A., 2003: *History and Culture of the Oraon Tribe, some aspects of their Social Life,* Mohit Publication, pp. 237-245.

Giri, H. H., 1976: *Land Utilization Survey: District Gonda,* Shivalaya Prakashan, Gorakhpur, Uttar Pradesh, p. 92.

Golding, D.L., 1970: *The Effects of Forests on Precipitation,* The Forestry Chronicle, p. 398.

Goswami, S.N., 2002: *Farm Planning in Hills of Meghalaya*

for Augmentation of Income and Employment Vis-A-Vis Preservation of Natural Resource Base, Indian Journal of Agricultural Economics, 57(2), pp. 211-223.

Government of India, 1960: *Report of the Scheduled Areas and Scheduled Tribe Commission 1960,* Government of India, New Delhi, pp. 2-4.

Govt. of India, 2006: *Annual report of Ministry of Environment and Forests,* 2005-06, pp. 32-34, Avl at: http://www.envfor.nic.in/sites/default/files/annualreport/pdf, retrieved on 19.12.2013.

Govt. of India, 2009: *Annual report of Ministry of Environment and Forests,* 2008-09, pp. 36-38, Avl. at: http://www.envfor.nic.in/sites/default/files/annualreport/pdf, retrieved on 19.12.2013.

Govt. of West Bengal, 2009: *Ninth working plan of Jalpaiguri Forest Division,* Directorate of Forest, Vol. I, 2008-09, pp. 10, 55, 61-62, 123-125.

Govt. of West Bengal, 2011: *Statistical Handbook of Jalpaiguri District,* Bureau of Applied Economics and Statistics, 2010-11, pp. 11-12.

Govt. of West Bengal, 2012: *State Forest Report,* 2011-2012, Directorate of Forests, pp. 13, 30-33, 65-78.

Govt. of West Bengal, 2013: *State Forest Report,* 2012-2013, Directorate of Forests, pp. 13-18, 24-25, 71-72.

Govt. of West Bengal, 2016: West Bengal, Agriculture Contingency Plan for District: Alipurduar, Avl. at: http://agricoop.nic.in/sites/default/files/WestBengal%2019-Alipurduar 01.04.2016.pdf, retrieved on 28th November 2016.

Govt. of West Bengal, 2018: *Statistical Handbook of Jalpaiguri District,* Bureau of Applied Economics and Statistics, 2010-11, pp. 3-4.

Grunning, J. F., 1911: *Eastern Bengal and Assam District Gazetteers, Jalpaiguri,* First reprinted by N.L. Publishers, Siliguri, 2008, pp. 11-15, 38-42, 44-58, 86-90.

Hasnain, N., 2005: *Tribal India,* 7th reprint (sixth edition) by Palaka Prakashan, New Delhi, India pp. 74-75, 161-209, 211. 208.

Hauser, P.M., et al., 1959: *The Study of Population: An Inventory Appraisal,* university of Chicago Press, p. 12.

Hegde, R., Suryaprakash, S., Achoth, L., and Bawa, K. S., 1996: *Extraction of Non-Timber Forest Products in the Forests of Biligiri Rangan Hills, India,* 1. Contribution to Rural Income, Economic Botany, Vol. 50, No. 3 (Jul-Sep., 1996), Published by: Springer on behalf of New York Botanical Garden Press, pp. 243-251.

Hotchkiss, D., & Kumar, S.K., 1988: *Consequences of Deforestation for Women's Time Allocation, Agricultural Production and Nutrition in Hill Area of Nepal,* International Food Policy Research Institute, Washington, D.C. p. 123.

J.V, Bhaskar., Rai, K., 2016: Tiger Conservation Plan, 2016-17 to 2026-27, pp. 93-94, 215, 222-223, 225-226, 227-241, 273-274, 439, 447-450.

Jose, U.V., 2000: *Rava-English dictionary khurangnala. Guwahati:* Don Bosco Publication, p. 17.

Joshi, A., 2000: *Roots of change: Frontline Workers and Policy Reform in West Bengal Unpublished Ph.D. Thesis Submitted to Madras Institute of Technology,* Chennai.

Kant, S., and Mehta, N. G., 1993: *A forest Based Tribal Economy-A Case Study of Motisinghloti Village,* Forest, Trees and People Newsletter, No. 20: pp. 34-39.

Kar, A., (Ed.) 2003: *Kirat Bhumi, Jalpaiguri Zila Sankalan* (second part), p. 435, 625-716.

Karmakar, M., 2011: *A Geographical Outline of North Bengal,* First Edn, N.L. Publishers, Shivmandir, Siliguri, pp. 114-116, 142-207.

Kaushal, K.K., and J.C. Kala, 2004: *Applying the sustainable livelihood approach to Joint Forest Management Projects in India,* International Forestry Review, Vol. 6 (1), 2004, pp 13-14.

Khanna, P., 1994: *Research Agenda for Joint Management. Indian Forester,* 120 (7), pp. 564-569.

Khullar D.R., 2002: *Geography,* Saraswati House, Delhi, pp. 237-238.

Kinhal, G.A., 2002: *Participatory Forest Management: Creating Options for Sustainability, Proceedings of Workshop on Joint Forest Management and Watershed Development,* Jointly organized by Tamil Nadu Forest Department and Srinivasan Service Trust during 21-22nd January 2002, pp. 26-31.

Kolay, S.K., 2000: Ecology, economy and tribal development, Mohit Publication, 1st Ed., New Delhi, p. 149.

Kothari, Ashish, 1995: *Peoples' participation in the conservation biodiversity.*

Kulkarni, S., 1987: *Forest Legislation and Tribals:* Comments on Forest Policy Resolution, Economic and Political Weekly 12th December, p. 4.

Mahapatra, A., 1992: *Forest dwellers dependence on forest, a case study of pauribhuinya tribe of Orissa,* Journal of Rural development, 11(6), pp. 863-872.

Malhotra, K. C., Deb, D., Dutta, M.,Vasulu, T. S.,Yadav, G., and Adhikari, M., 1991: *Role of Non-Timber Forest Produce in village economy, A Household Survey in Jamboni Range,* Indian Institute of Bio-social Research and Development, Calcutta, pp. 88-108.

Mamoria, C. B., 1995: *Agricultural Problems in India,* Kitab Mahal Publications, P. 142.

Manoj, K., Bhattacharyya, R., and Padhy, P.K., 2013: *Forest and wildlife scenarios of Northern West Bengal, India: A Review,* International Research Journal of Biological Sciences, July, Vol. 2(7), pp. 70-79.

Mehta, N. G., and Kant, S., 1993: *A forest Based Tribal Economy-A Case Study of Motisinghloti Village,* Forest, Trees and People Newsletter, No. 20, pp. 34-39.

Millan, M.M., et al., 2005: *Climatic feedbacks and*

desertification: the Mediterranean model, J. Climate, pp. 684-701.

Ministry of Home Affairs, GOI, 2001: *Census of India 2001,* Registrar General & Census Commissioner, Office of the Registrar General India, New Delhi.

Misri, B., 1995: Range and Forest Grazing in the Himalaya, In: Singh, P. (ed.) *Workshop Proceedings, Temperate Asia Pasture and Fodder Sub-Regional Working Group,* Kathmandu, pp. 28-33.

Mukherji, S.D., and Rangachari, C.S., 2000: *Old Roots New Shoots: A Study of Joint Forest Management in Andhra Pradesh,* Ford Foundation, New Delhi, pp. 354-356

Natarajan, I., 1996: *Trends in Fuel Wood Consumption in Rural India,* NCAER, New Delhi, pp. 41-47.

National Council for Applied Economic Research, 1989: *Household, income and its disposition,* National Council of Applied Economic Research, New Delhi, p. 12.

National workshop on JFM, 2011: *Development of Poverty alleviation activities. Proceedings,* FRI, Dehradun, Chapter IV, June 27-28, 2011, page 7, para 4.3

Nayak, Bibhudatta, 2001: *Economic-Ecologic values of an Indian Forests: A Case Study,* Indian Journal of Agricultural Economics, Vol. 56 (3), pp. 325-334.

Niyamatullah, M., 1984: *The plans which supplement the food of tribals in M.P,* in Patnaik (ed.) readings on tribal development administration, Nutrition, Health and Culture, THRJ, Bhubaneswar.

O' Malley, LSS, O., 1907: *Bengal District Gazetteers,* Darjeeling, the Bengal Secretariat Book Depot, Calcutta.

Palanna, V.K., 2005: *The current socio economic status of the project beneficiaries in Hassan,* Gulbarga and Davanagere Districts, My Forest. 41(2), pp. 177-180.

Pandey, A.P., and Sathyanarayana, V.V., 1981: *Income savings and investment behavior of small farmers in Chaka Block,* Allahabad District, U.P. Financing Agriculture. 13 (2), pp. 31-32.

Pandey, V.K., and Pant, K.P., 1999: *Minimizing environmental problems in hill agriculture of Nepal through multi objective farm planting,* Indian Journal of Agricultural Economics. 54(1), pp. 79-92.

Pant, K.P., and Pandey, V.K., 1999: *Minimizing environmental problems in hill agriculture of Nepal through multi objective farm planting,* Indian Journal of Agricultural Economics. 54 (1): pp. 79-92.

Parmesan, C., 2006: *Ecological and evolutionary responses to recent climate change,* Annual Review of Ecology, Evolution, and Systematics, Vol. 37, pp. 637-669.

Philip, V., and Geeta M., 1985: *The cost of deforestation,* Social Action, vol.35, October-December.

Poffenberger, M., 1990: *Joint Management of Forest Lands, Experiences from South Asia,* Ford Foundation, New Delhi.

Poffenberger, M., 1995: *India's Forest Keepers, Society for Promotion of Wasteland development,* New Delhi, p. 16.

Prasad R.R., and M.P. Jahagirdar, 1993: *Tribal Situation in forest villages: Changing subsistence strategies and adaptation,* New Delhi, Discovery Publishing House, pp. 214-215.

Prasad, B.N., 1985: *Regional Non Wood Forest Product Industries,* Forest Industries Development Group, Asia Pacific Region, FAO, Kualalampur.

Prasad, R., Majumdar, N.B., Bhattacharaya, P., Phukan, B.R.R. and Singh, S.P., 1999: *Wood fuel trade in India. Paper presented in the National Training Workshop on Wood fuel trade in India held at Indian Institute of Forest Management,* February, Bhopal, 17-19.

Raghupathy, D., 2005: *Forest dependants' socio economic appraisal and their needs in plains area of Mysore and Chamraja Nagar Districts of Karnataka,* My Forests, 41(2A) pp. 341-345.

Rahman, L. M., 2000: *The Forest Act, 1927* (Act No. xvi of 1927), p. 22.

Rai, R.S., and Parthiban, K.T., 1994: *Trees on farm land–their effects on soil fertility,* Annals of Forestry, 2(1), pp. 44-51.

Rangachari, C.S., and Mukherji, S.D., 2000: *Old Roots New Shoots: A Study of Joint Forest Management in Andhra Pradesh,* Ford Foundation, New Delhi, pp. 78-80.

Rao, N.G., 1988: *Role of Non-Timber Forest Products in tribals of Andhra Pradesh,* Indian Journal of Agricultural Economics, 38(2), pp. 72-79.

Ravi, P.C., G.S. Mahadevaiah and M.D. Muthamma., 2006: *Livelihood dependence on Non-Timber Forest Products: A study of Jenukurumba tribes in South India,* Proceedings of the International Association of Agricultural Economists Conference Held at Gold Coast, Australia, August 12-18, 2006.

Roy, B., 1961: *District Census Handbook, Jalpaiguri,* Calcutta, West Bengal, pp. 1-28.

Roy, P., 2010: *Sub-Himalayan Region of West Bengal-An Introduction to Anthropology, Ethnographic, Linguistic and Culture,* Uttarloke, Siliguri, pp. 23-32.

Roy, S., Dutta, M., and Bandyopadhyay, S., 2001: *Joint Forest Management and Forest Protection Committees: Negotiation Systems and the Design of Incentives-A Case Study of West Bengal,* pp. 5-6.

Sadashivaiah, A.S., Gangadarappa, N.R., Kenchappa, M., Ganesamoorthi, S., Sanjeev, M.V. and Nagesha, G., 2005: *Critical analysis of JFPM and extension strategies for educating VFC members in Tumkur and Chitradurga Districts,* My Forest. 41(2), pp. 195-212.

Sanderson, M., Santini, M., Valentini, R., and Pope, E., 2012: *Relationships between forests and weather,* EC Directorate General of the Environment, Met office, headly centre, pp. 6-8.

Sarin M., and Springate, B.O., 2010: *India's Forest Rights Act-The anatomy of a necessary but not sufficient institutional reform,* pp. 7, 10, 11.

Sarmah, R., 2010: *Commonly used Non-Timber Forest Products (NTFPs) by the Lisu tribe in Changlang District of Arunachal Pradesh, India,* Sibsagar college teachers' research journal Vol. 5, pp. 68-77.

Sengutpa, N., 1988: *Reappraising tribal movements-Ill, the Economic Basis,* Economic and Political Weekly, 21st May.

Shukla, R.S., 2000: *Forestry for Tribal Development,* A.H. Wheeler & Co. Ltd., New Delhi, pp 67-68.

Shvidenko, A., Barber, C. V. & Persson, R., 2005: *Forest and Woodland Systems (Current State and Trends Assessment) (online), Millennium Ecosystem Assessment,* World Resources Institute: Washington, USA. Avl. at: http:// www. maweb.org/documents/document.290.Aspx.pdf, retrieved on 25th May 2015, p. 605.

Sidle, R.C., Ziegler, A.D., Negishi, J.N., Nik, A.R., Siew, R. and Turkelboom, F., 2006: *Erosion processes in steep terrain-Truths, myths, and uncertainties related to forest management in Southeast Asia.* Forest Ecology and Management, Vol. 224, Issues 1-2, pp. 199-225.

Silva Dias, M.A., Avissar, R., and Silva Dias, P., 2009: *Modeling the regional and remote climatic impact of deforestation. In: Amazonia and Global Change,* Vol. 186 (Eds Keller M, Bustamante M, Gash J, Silva Dias P, pp. 251-260, AGU, Geo-physical Monograph Series, Washington, DC, Avl. at: http://www.agu.org/books/gm/v186/#thumb, retrieved on 05.05.2016.

Singh, A., Bhattacharya, p., Vyas, p., and Roy, S., 2010: *Contribution of NTFPs in the Livelihood of Mangrove Forest Dwellers of Sundarban,* Journal of Human Ecology 29(3), pp. 191-200.

Singh, Jasbir, 1974: *The Green Revolution in India: How Green it is,* Vishal Publication, pp. 23-37.

Singh, L.R., and Pandey, V.K., 1992: *A case study on agro-economics aspects of tribal farmers of plateau region, Bihar,* Indian Journal of Agricultural Economics. 47(3), p. 417.

Singh, T.P., and Sethi, P., 2001: *Village resource development as an incentive to sustain the Joint Forest Management Programme,* Indian Forester, 127(11), pp. 1215-1222.

Sinha, S.P., 1987: *Forest village in Bihar: An analysis of their present status,* in S.P. Sinha (ed.) Tribals and Forests, Govt. of Bihar, welfare department, BTWRI, Ranchi p. 297.

Sonowal C.J., 2007: *Demographic transition of tribal people in forest villages of Assam,* studies of tribals, 5(1), pp. 47-58.

Suryawanshi, D., 1992: *A study on employment, income and household economy of tribals in Western Ghat Zone of Maharashtra,* Indian Journal of Agricultural Economics, 47(3): pp. 427-428.

Tiwari, P.C., 2000: *Land use changes in Himalaya and their impact on the plains ecosystem: need for sustainable land use,* Land Use Policy vol. 17, pp. 101-111.

Tripathi, S.P., 2005: *Status of Joint Forest Management in Nagaland.* Indian Forester, September, pp. 1158-1170.

UNDP, 1997: *Human development report,* Oxford University Press, New York.

Von Randow, C., et al., 2004: *Comparative measurements and seasonal variations in energy and carbon exchange over forest and pasture in south west Amazonia.* Theor, Appl. Climatol, pp. 5-26.

Vyas, A. K., 1994: *An Introduction to Agriculture,* Rupa Books, Private Limited, Jaipur, p. 20.

Wickens, G. E., 1991: *Management issues for development of non-timber forest products,* Unasylva, 42(165), p. 38. Avl. at: http://www.fao.org/docrep/u2440e/u2440e02.htm#manage%20issues%20for%20development%20of%20non%20timber%20forest20products, retrieved on 26th November 2015.

Appendix–A

List of Other Related Publications

1. *Issues and Challenges of the Forest Villagers and Joint Forest Management: A case study of Alipurduar District,West Bengal*– Tarun Das & Dr. Deepak Kr. Mandal, **Indian Journal of Spatial Science,** (EISSN: 2249 - 4316), Autumn Issue, 10 (2), 2019 pp. 20 - 30.

2. *Influence of Mass Media and Cultural Changes of Forest Villagers' in Alipurduar District of West Bengal, India*– Tarun Das, **Glocal Issues in Contemporary Art, Culture and Society,** (ISBN: 978-81-8211-143-1), 2017, pp. 117-199.

3. *Forest degradation and forest change detection using Remote Sensing and GIS in Jalpaiguri and Alipurduar District (Duars) of West Bengal*– Tarun Das & Dr. Deepak Kr. Mandal, **Geographical Thoughts,** (ISSN: 2229-466X), Vol. 14, 2016, pp. 191-199.

4. *Environmental vulnerability of Duars: A case study of Jalpaiguri and Alipurduar district of West Bengal, India*– Tarun Das, **Major Environmental Issues: Vulnerability and Impacts** (ISBN: 978-93-84671-30-3), 2015, pp. 143-153.

5. *Cultural ecology and Influence of modern mass media: A case study on tribals of the Dooars, Jalpaiguri*– Tarun Das, **Wesleyan Journal of Research,** (ISSN: 0975-1386) vol. 5, No. 1, June, 2012, pp. 10-19.

6. *Garuchira village tourism and its impact: A forest village case study, Madarihat block, Jalpaiguri*– Tarun Das,

Journal of Landscape systems and Ecological studies BY ILEE, (ISBN: 0971-4170), 2012, pp. pp. 433-439.

7. *Ecological Vulnerability and Human impact on the Biodiversity of Dooars region: A brief overview*–Tarun Das, **Journal of Geo-Environment observer,** (ISSN: 2277-6141), Vol.1, No. 2, October, 2012, pp. 89-94.

Appendix–B

Questionnaire for Sample Forest Village Information

Name of Village: ....
Beat: .... Range: ....

1. General characteristics:

a. Panchayat: ....
Forest Panchayat (if part of any): ....
Block: .... District: ....

b. No. of households: 1991 .... 2001 ....
2011 .... 2015 ....

c. Total population:
i. (1991) Male: .... Female: ....,
ii. (2001) Male: .... Female: ....,
iii. (2011) Male: .... Female: ....

d. Distance from: Un-metalled road: ....
Metalled road: ....
Nearest town/Market name: ....
Distance: ....

e. Social Amenities:

i. Educational: PR/HI/HS/IN/GR: ....
ii. Medical: PHC/DIS/HOS: ....
iii. Veterinary Centre: SMC/AIC/VH: ....
iv. Electrified: YES/No,
How many houses have electricity (%): ....
v. Source Drinking water: TP/SP/ST/TW/PD: ....
Distance: ....
vi. Irrigated: Yes/No,
Seasonal/Permanent, How much area irrigated (%):
....

2. Physical Characteristics:

a. Altitude (approximate in m): ....,
b. Site: VE/HS/HT/IF/BF: ....,
c. Nature of Settlement: COM/SCA/NUC: ....,
d. Geographic Location: ....,
e. Relief: ....,
f. Characteristics natural vegetation: TCD/STP/HMT, Dominant species: ....

Natural vegetation

Forest type	Botanical Mane	Local Name	Utility for Villagers

Medicinal plants

Forest type	Botanical Mane	Local Name	Utility for Villagers

Abbreviations: Educational: Pr-Primary, HI-Higher Secondary, HS-High School, IN-Intermediate, GR-Graduate and above; Medical: PHC-Primary health centre, DIS-Dispensary, HOS-Hospital, Veterinary centre: SMC-Stockman Centre,· AIC-Artificial Insemination Centre, VH-Veterinary hospital, Drinking water: TP-Tapped, SP-Spring, ST-Stream, TW- Tube well, PD-Pond, .Site: VE-Valley, HS-Hill slope, HT-Hilltop, IF-Inside of forest, BF- Beside the forest, Nature or settlement: COM-Compact, SCA-Scattered, NUC-Nucleated, Natural vegetation: TCD-Tropical deciduous, STP-Sub-tropical Pine, HMT-Himalayan Moist Temperate.

g. Soils: (Valley) Type: ...., depth: ....,
Erosional status: NE/SL/ME/SE/VSE
(Upland) Type: ...., depth: ....,
Erosional Status: NE/SL/ME/SE/VSE
(Plane) Type: ...., depth: ....,

Erosional Status: NE/SL/ME/SE/VSE

h. Climate: Rainfall: ....

Temperature: ....

3. Economic Characteristics:

a. Land use (i) Reporting area (ii) Forests (iii) Cultural waste

(iv) Fallow land: ....

(v) Darren and uncultivable waste: ....

(vi) Land put to non-agricultural use: ....

(vii) Pastures and grazing land: ....

(vii) Area under groves and orchards: ....

(ix) Net area sown: ....

(x) Area sown more than once: ....

b. Industrial/Household industrial establishment

Type of Industry	Raw material	Source of Raw material	Distance of raw material	Source of power	No. of person employed	Nature of employment offered		Use of end product
						Perma-nent	Seas-onal	

4. Development activities and the forest (respondent, Pradhan /Sabhapati of Village Panchayat)

Nature of Activity	Effects on the forest	other beneficial effects	Damaging effects	Suggestions
Road construction				
Electricity Transmission Line				
Dam construction (a) catchment (b) Command				
School/Hospital/ veterinary/other construction				
Industrialization				
Urbanization				
Any other forests effects				

5. Evaluation of the methods tried to minimize/recover the damage to biomass

Activity	Year of initiation	Area Planted	Displacemet Of old species	Trees of land utilized	Control over land	Control over Product	Result Success	Result Failure	Reason for result	Benefits for the villagers	Opinion about Programme G/B/N
Plantation in village/ Panchayat land											
Plantation in civil/soya communal forests											
Plantation in Reserved Forests											
Social Forestry											
Horticulture											

6. Efforts made for efficient use alternative source of energy

	Year of beginning	No. installed	Result	Reasons	Suggestions
(i) Improved chulha					
(ii) Biogas/Gobar gas plants					
(iii) Solar devices					
(iv) water mills					
(v) wind mills					
(vi) others					

Abbreviations: Type of land utilized: AG-Agricultural, PA-Pasture, CSF-Vivil Soyam Forest, WL-Waste Land, RS-Road side, Control over land/Produce: I-individual, VP-village Panchayat, G-Government, Reasons for result: GP/BP-Good/bad planning, PI/NPI-proper/improver implementation, CM/NM-Careful/No monitoring, VA/VS-Villager's Opposition/support, AB/ND-Available benefits/no benefits. Benefits for Villagers: FU-Fuel FO-Fodder, TI-Timber, FR-Fruit, EM-Employment, E N-Environmental benefits. Opinion about Programme: G-Good, B-Bad, N-No comment.

Appendix–C

Questionnaire for Sample Household Survey of Forest Villagers

Village: ...., Beat: ....,
Range: ...., Block: ....

1. a. Name of the head of the household: ....
b. S/W/O: ....
c. Community: ....
d. Religion: ....
e. Caste: ...., Sub-caste: ....
f. Language: Nepali/Bangla/Adivashi: ....
g. Customs: ....

2. Family Members (including head):

S.No.	Name	Age	Sex	Relation with head	Education	Marital status	Occupation Main Type	Marginal Type	Non-Worker Type	Income (Rs.)
1.										
2.										

3. Migrated: Yes/No, If yes, cause of migration: ...., Inmigration/Outmigration: ....

4. Family Size: i) Below 5 member ii) 5 to 10 member iii) Above 10 member

5. Family Type: i) Single ii) Jointly iii) Extended

6. Electrified: Yes/No,

7. a) Source of drinking water: TP/SP/ST/Others: ....,
b) Distance covered: ....

8. Food Habit: ....,

9. House Type: (a) Tile; (b) Thatched (c) Hut (d) Wood/ Pucca ....

10. House pattern: Macha/Ground level/other

11. No. of Rooms: ....
    a) Bed .... b) Kitchen .... c) Others ....

12. Fuel used: a) Forest wood b) Coal c) Kerosene d) Gas e) Cow Dung

13. Water facilities: a) Canal b) Tube well c) Well d) River e) Spring and Pipe line f) Tap g) Others

14. Proximity of water sources: ....,
    Water Storage Facilities: ....

15. Dependency on forests produces: Yes/No: ....

16. a) Altitude of house (approximate in m): ....,
b) Site of the house: VE/HS/HT/IF/BF: ....
c) Nature of Settlement: COM/SCA/NUC: ....

17. Characteristics of natural vegetation: TCD/STP/HMT
    Dominant species: ....

18. Conflict with wild animals:

a) Any of the family member livestock were attacked by wild animals? Yes/No
b) Name of animals: Elephant/Tiger/Leopards/others if any: ....
c) Any wild animal destroyed the crops? Yes/No
d) Damage of House/Crops/Cattle/Death,
   Rs. amount of damage: ....
e) Compensation from Panchayet/Govt./Forest Dept.,
   Amount: ....

19. Agriculture

a. Land holding

Amount owned of Land	Leased	Patta	Cultivable	Fallow	Barren & uncultivable waste land	Pastures & Grazing	Cultiable & Homestead

b. Cropping pattern

S.No.	Crop	Area	Irrigated/ unirrigated	Yield	How much of total demand met by crop	Total Straw	Proportion of (months) fodder demand met by this produce	Grain-fodder ratio	others
Rabi Season (_______ to ______ month)									
1									
2									
Kharif Season (_______ to ______ month)									
1									
2									
Other Season (_______ to ______ month)									
1									
2									

c. Plantation of fruit crops/medicinal plants/farming

Name of the crop	Year of initiation	Area planted	What is displaced (crop)	Type of land utilized	Available products	Monetary gains as compared to earlier crops	Other benefits	Suggestions
i.								
ii								

20. Livestock

Animal	Adult	Calves	Use	Values	fodder source		Time spent and distance covered		Suggested alternatives
					SF	GR	Time	Distance	
Bullocks									
Cows									
Buffaloes									
Sheep									
Goats									
Mules/Horses									
Pigs									
Poultry									
Others									

Livestock: Fodder Source: SF-Stall-fed, GR- razing.

21. Use of forests (timber)

Purpose	Timber used for				Quantity of wood (timber required)		Time spent and distance covered timber		Way of obtaining
	Roof	Walls/ sides	Doors/ window	Floor/ Stairs	Quantity	Types	Time	Distance	
Living house									
Cattle shed									
Furniture									
Agricultural tool/ implements									
Fuel									
Others use (Birth/Wedding/ Cremation etc.)									

Abbreviations: Livestock: use: AG-Agricultural, MI-Milk, ME-Meat, TR-Transport, FR-Fertilizer. Source of fodder: FR-Forest, FL-Farm-land, VL-Village common land. Nature of Feeding: GR-Grazing SF-Stall fed. Use of Forests the Way acquired: FG-Free grant, CP-concessional price, FC-Free collected, PU-Purchased

22. Other uses of the forests (source of non-timber forest products)

Use/Purpose	Type	Quantity/ Season	Time spent and distance covered		self-consumption/ selling	Commercial Value/ monitory value	Processing	
			Time	Distance			Local	Outside
Fruits								
Medicinal herbs								
Seeds								
Tanning material								
Terpentine oil/ other oils								
Fire-wood for selling								
Fodder								
Fuel								
Other use (wax, Honey, medicinal plants, hunting)								

23. Cooking and heating

Chulha in operation in a day (hrs)		wood consumed		Nature of fuel wood utilized	Source of fuel-wood	Time taken and distance covered for fuel collection				The way acquired	Good fuel	Alternatives
		winter	summer									
Summer	winter					Summer		winter				
						Distance	Time	Distance	Time			

24. Forests as source of employment

i). From forest or nearby forest

Type of employment	No. of employment days		Employing agency			Income	No. of Working days	Suggestions
	Permanent	seasonal	Self	Contractor	Govt.			

i) Are you going to outside for employment: Yes/No
if yes, from where and why : ....,

25. Evaluation of forest-related activities in the life of the household

(i) Total time spend in forest-related activities: ....
(ii) Contribution in i) Fuel needs ii) Fodder needs iii) Timber needs iv) Employment

Abbreviations: cooking: Nature of Fuel wood: Lo-Log, TWB-Twigs and branches, OW-Dead dry woo, Source of Fuel: FL-Farmland, V1-Village Land. Employment: Agency: SE-Self, Co-Contractor, GO: Government, FR-Forest

26. Perception of the individual regarding different aspects of forestry activities

a. Extent of the forest
(i) No. of natural trees in own land: ....
(ii) No. of natural trees in surrounding of household ....
and the village ....
(iii) What was the situation 30 years ago? Same/Better/Very Good/Worse
(iv) What is the situation in present day? Same/Better/Very Good/Worse
(iv) Has there been any change in type of trees? Yes/No
If yes, what new trees replaced old? Old/New

b. Deforestation
(i) When did the maximum tree felling take place? ....
(ii) What type of trees felled? ....
(iii) Why the trees are felled?
(a) For Silviculture purpose
(b) For export to outside region
(c) For local use
(d) Others (construction etc.)
(iv) Who is responsible for tree felling?
(a) Govt./Forest Deptt./Forest Corporation
(b) Contractor
(c) Local people
(d) Others

(v) What is the socio-regional background of contractors?
  (a) Local
  (b) Regional
  (c) Outsiders

(vi) What is the regional background of labourers employed?
  (a) Local
  (b) Regional
  (c) Outsiders

(vii) To which place, is the wood/timber taken? ....

c. Response to local needs:

(i) Do the villagers cut trees? Yes/No

(ii) What type of trees you get in free grant and concessional price?
  a) Free grant: ....
  b) Concessional price: ....

(iii) How many trees can be taken and for what purpose?

(iv) Do you think that present forest structure is sufficient/ appropriate to meet your fodder, fuel and timber needs: Yes/No
  If yes, so, why: ....
  If no, so why: ....

(v) If not, what type of trees and how many, would you suggest to fulfill your annual demand?
  Type: .... Number: ....

(vi) Why fodder crop is not grown?
  (a) Enough land is not available even for cereals
  (b) Free fodder is available from the forest areas
  (c) As most of the animals are sent for grazing the fodder need at home is not felt
  (d) Any other cause

d. Changes in the environment

(i) Do you think that the trees affect the environment? Yes/No

(ii) Do you think that the trees affect the Rainfall? Yes/No

(iii) Do you think that the trees affect the Temperature? Yes/ No

(iv) Do you think that the trees affect the Land slide? Yes/No

(v) Do you think that the trees affect the water source? Yes/No

e. Awareness about forest movement/other movements to save the forest
   (i) Its genesis
   (ii) Main demands
   (iii) Present conditions
   (iv) Did it have some impact in your area?
   (v) What Impact?

f. Perception about forest values

(i) Do you think that forest have values? If Yes, then which value
   i) Economic value
   ii) Ecological value
   iii) Social and Cultural value

(ii) If, Economic value then opted for (a) Grass/Fodder (b) Firewood (c) Timber (d) Livestock rearing (e) Bamboo (f) Medicinal plants (g) Leaf (h) Ecotourism (i) Cane (j) Climbers (k) Fruit (l) Golden and Sponge Mushroom (m) Orchards (n) others

(iii) If Ecological value then opted for (a) Water source (b) Clean air (c) Soil protection (d) Landside protection (e) Wind break (f) Climate (g) Fertility of soil (h) others.

(iv) If Social and Cultural value opted for (a) Hunting festival (b) Worship (h) others

g. Awareness about rights and concessions

(i) What are your rights in the forests?

(ii) Has there been any change in these rights and concessions: Yes/No

(iii) What and since when change has come?

(iv) Why this change has been brought?
   (a) To protect the forests from illegal cutting by villagers
   (b) To speed up the growth being hampered by grazing, fuel collection and other uses by the villagers
   (c) To get control over large areas and materials for revenue
   (d) To maintain ecological balance
   e) Any other

(vii) How the forest needs of people of plains regarding be met? ....

(viii) For what purpose the forests are being managed?

a) Environmental,

b) Revenue,

c) Developmental,

d) Other

(ix) Who is getting the benefit of present management system?

(a) Government/Forest Department/Forest Corporation.

(b) Contractors

(c) Local People

(d) Local leaders/politicians

(xi) Are you aware of Govt. policies regarding forests conservation? Yes/No

(xii) Do you feel that the policies are correct? Yes/ No

(xiii) What changes are brought?

(xiv) Are you aware of Forest Conservation Act 2006? If yes, what it is?

h. Attitude of forest officials towards forest village community

(i) Which forest official you deal with? ....

(ii) For what purpose/problem? ....

(iii) What is their response? Yes/No

(iv) Do the higher officials take initiative to solve these problems? Yes/No

(v) Do the officials seek villager's cooperation? Yes/No

(vi) For what purpose? ....

(vii) What is the villager's response? Favorable/not favorable

(viii) Why such response ....

(ix) Do the officials discuss about Govt. policies? Yes/No

i. Awareness about other problems and your attitude

(i) Do you think following are the reasons of forest destruction?

(a) Increase in village population

(b) Deforestation by large scale felling

(c) Extension of Agriculture

(d) Grazing
(d) Illegal felling
(e) Rail way and Road
(f) construction
(g) Natural calamities (fire, landslide)
(f) Other

(ii) Who is directly responsible for forest destruction?
(a) Forest villagers
(b) Forest Department
(c) Contractors
(d) Others

(iii) What is solution according to you?
(a) Afforestation
(b) Serious awareness of Forest Department
(c) Control of illegal felling
(d) Restriction on large scale felling
(e) Awareness of villagers

27. Villagers and Joint Forest Management

(i) Do you know the joint forest management?

(ii) Are you a member of Joint forest management? Yes/ No, If yes which committee
a) FPC
b) EDC
c) Other

(iii) Name of the FPC/EDC where you engaged?

(iv) What type of sustainability works done in your village by JFM committee?

(v) Are you playing role in the committee as active member?

(vi) Reasons for non-membership
a) Unwillingness
b) Forest dept. did not allow
c) Irregular earning
d) Others

(vii) What kind of Benefits got as a member
a) Contribution in forest product collection
b) Participation in committees' process (FPC/EDC)
c) NTFPs collection
d) No Benefits?

(viii) What kind of livelihood activities done by JFM programme and when?

(ix) Weather forest is managed by

a) Forest department itself
b) By forest protection committees (FPC/EDC)
c) Participation in meeting
(d) Plantation activities
(e) Awareness of micro planning
(f) Training programme attended
(g) None of these
(h) others

(x) Are you getting benefits from JFM? Yes/ No, If yes, what kind of benefit

a) Environmental
b) Economical
c) others

(xi) Are you engaged in the plantation program? Yes/No

(xii) Is JFM success for protection of forest? Yes /No

(xiii) Is official of JFM cooperating with forest villagers?

(xiv) Are you a member of Self Help Group? Yes/No.

N.B: Other remarks if any:..

Signature of the surveyor

Appendix–D

Table–3.13

Statement of annual out tern of Timbers and Fire wood in different forest block

S.No.	Block & Comptt.	Year of CFC	Area Opett (in ha.)	Out turn of Timber Sal (m^3)	Out turn of Timber Misc. (m^3)	Out turn of Timber Total	Out turn of firewood Sal (m^3)	Out turn of firewood Misc. (m^3)	Out turn of firewood Total	Timber	Firewood
1	Panbari	Buxa Division 1990-91	2	0	29.64	29.64	0	63	63	350 m^3	65 Stack
2	Gadadhar		10	55.70	437.54	493.24	9	165	174		
3	DPO-6		12.14	8.85	882.92	891.78	2	550	552		
4	SRVK-10		27	350.37	2754.10	3104.48	176	2364	2540		
5	Nimati-I,II&II(A)		25.85	3973.84	273.64	4247.48	821	113	934		
6	Raimatang		2	160.15	0	160.15	52	0	52		
	TOTAL					**8926.79**			**4315**		
7	Gadadhar-2	Buxa Division 1991-92	8.2	1033.88	655.21	1689.10	213	259	472	350 m^3	65 Stack
8	Panbari		8.4	0.201	261.75	261.95	0	253	253		
9	Nimati		17.76	2489.73	655.81	3145.55	223	262	485		
10	Poro		5.65	19.827	254.17	273.99	9	209	218		
11	DPO-6		18.66	0	990.72	990.72	0	558	558		
	TOTAL					**6361.32**					

S.No.	Block & Comptt.	Year of CFC	Area Opett (in ha.)	Out turn of Timber			Out turn of firewood				
				Sal (m^3)	Misc. (m^3)	Total	Sal (m^3)	Misc. (m^3)	Total	Timber	Firewood
12	SRVK-15(1921 PH)	Buxa Division 1992-93	28.19	2.225	2459.20	2461.43	0	2333	2333	350 m^3	65 Stack
13	Raimatang (1916 & 1917 Plantation		3.52	222.65	392.36	615.01	55	159	214		
14	Gadadhar-4(1932)		7.78	7.44	95.76	103.21	0	138	138		
15	Panbari-10(1928)		9.29	51.62	123.66	175.29	0	325	325		
16	SB-5(1928)		4.25	0	344.18	344.18	0	184	184		
17	SB-2		4.45	53.54	567.78	621.32	0	410	410		
18	Poro-8(1932)		10.93	0	1109.71	1109.71	0	970	970		
19	DPO-6(1932)		10.12	6.56	656.58	663.15	0	281	281		
20	Poro-310 (1923, 1924 & 1930Pltn.)		27.77	46.89	517.32	564.21	10	712	722		
21	Nimati-1(1925 & 1926 pltn.)		17.38	2536.57	24.05	2560.63	521	6	527		
	TOTAL					**9218.18**			**6104**		

S.No.	Block & Comptt.	Year of CFC	Area Opett (in ha.)	Out turn of Timber			Out turn of firewood				
				Sal (m^3)	Misc. (m^3)	Total	Sal (m^3)	Misc. (m^3)	Total	Timber	Firewood
22	SRVK-10	BTR 1993-94	28	117.88	2612.93	2730.82	21	2171	2192	350 m^3	65 stacks
23	SRVK-9		20	42.25	1676.74	1719	4	1864	1868		
24	RTG ADMA-4		8	512.68	296.21	808.89	116	87	203		
25	Nimati-1(1927 & 1928 pltn.)		22.43	5552.19	373.95	5926.14	479	206	685		
26	Poro-1		25	12.09	537.22	549.31	22	510	532		
27	Poro-8		4.21	165.79	267.18	432.98	25	194	219		
28	DPO-6(1933pltn.)		9.31	0	852.02	852.02	0	590	590		
29	SB-5(1926,1932,1933&193)			13.68	113.95	310.28	424.23	39	381	420	
30	SB-4(1933pltn.)		3.23	0	340.58	340.58	0	265	265		
31	SB-2(a)(1933pltn.)		0	113.98	916.08	1030.07	32	826	858		
32	Gadadhar-4(1932)		18.2	26.22	1220.68	1246.90	8	628	636		
	TOTAL					**16060.99**			**8468**		

S.No.	Block & Comptt.	Year of CFC	Area Opett (in ha.)	Out turn of Timber			Out turn of firewood				
				Sal (m^3)	Misc. (m^3)	Total	Sal (m^3)	Misc. (m^3)	Total	Timber	Firewood
33	Poro-7(1933-34)	BTR 1994-95	28	326	1179.20	1505.20	0	1426	1426	350m^3	65 stacks
34	DPO-8		9.80	92.75	846.97	939.73	49	794	843		
35	Poro-9		10	0	73.51	73.51	0	26	26		
36	Nimati-4		14	0	449.58	449.58	0	349	349		
37	Nimati-1		26	1636.01	937.83	2573.84	302	183	485		
38	Gadadhar-4(1932)		9.80	0	434.90	434.90	0	411	411		
39	Panbari-5		6	0	560.62	560.62	0	778	778		
40	Panbari-10		7	0	59.61	59.61	0	51	51		
41	Checko-8		12.20	9.95	302.97	312.93	2	163	165		
42	SB-2(a)		11.40	0	1083.86	1083.86	0	767	767		
43	SRVK-9		22	0	1823.22	1823.22	0	1840	1840		
44	SRVK-10		28	109.716	4914.107	5023.82	30	4398	4428		
	TOTAL					**14840.87**			**11569**		

S.No.	Block & Comptt.	Year of CFC	Area Opett (in ha.)	Out turn of Timber			Out turn of firewood				
				Sal (m^3)	Misc. (m^3)	Total	Sal (m^3)	Misc. (m^3)	Total	Timber	Firewood
45	Nimati-1	BTR 1995-96	20.33	616.367	128.653	105.09	132	36	167	375m^3	70 stacks
46	Nimati-4		14	72.462	497.222	569.704	27	775	602		
47	Nimati-5		7	50.947	374.775	425.722	10	495	505		
48	Poro-9		8	0	252.985	252.985	0	158	158		
49	Poro-10(part-1)		6	0	51.287	51.287	0	46	46		
50	Poro-10 (Part-2)		14	0	34.771	34.771	0	68	68		
51	Panbari-10		7.3	0	116.640	118.64	0	240	240		
52	Panbari-5		1.5	0	93.074	93.074	0	39	39		
53	Checko-8		12.2	0	146.375	146.375	0	196	196		
54	DPO-6		8	0	52.672	52.672	0	60	60		
55	Gadadhar-4(1932)		8.9	5.802	490.299	496.101	4	212	215		
56	DPO-8		12.95	518.657	1337.125	1855.782	217	773	990		
57	SB-4 (1933 Pltn.)		1.6	0	96.620	96.620	0	77	77		
58	SB-5		2.02	1.224	121.190	122.414	0	138	138		
59	SRVK-9		18.5	11.017	1596.502	1607.519	0	1766	1765		
60	SRVK-15 (1921Pltn.)		10.13	522.073	942.41	1464.214	180	787	957		
61	NRVK-9		12	220.556	1232.844	1453.400	73	1311	1354		
	TOTAL					**9888.37**			**7819**		

S.No.	Block & Comptt.	Year of CFC	Area Opett (in ha.)	Out turn of Timber			Out turn of firewood				
				Sal (m^3)	Misc. (m^3)	Total	Sal (m^3)	Misc. (m^3)	Total	Timber	Firewood
62	Nimati-1	BTR (W) 1996-97	12.5	129.717	1013.693	1143.41	15	457	472	357m^3	70 stacks
63	Gadadhar-4(1932)		8.16	0	848.751	848.751	0	353	353		
64	Panbari-5		5.37	0.156	115.054	115.210	0	190	190		
65	Poro-7		14.74	0.11	899.136	899.246	0	1116	1116		
66	Nimati-5		7	140.402	421.972	562.374	45	555	600		
67	Nimati-4		13.72	357.146	1122.993	1480.139	98	1707	1805		
68	SRVK-15		9.35	1029.844	339.589	1369.433	407	238	645		
	TOTAL					**6418.563**			**5181**		
69	SB-2	BTR(E) 1996-97	2.02	0.661	291.408	292.069	0	130	130	357m^3	70 stacks
70	SB-4(1933pltn.)		2.83	0	101.685	101.685	0	60	60		
71	SB-5		3	0	134.715	134.715	0	140	140		

Source: Management-cum-working plan of BTR, 2000

Table–4.4
Age-Sex Composition

S.No.	Age Group	Male		Female		Both		Sex
		No. of persons	Percentage	No. of persons	Percentage	No. of persons	Percentage	Ratio
1	**Lehra**							
	0-14	09	9.68	11	11.83	20	21.51	1222.22
	15-29	16	17.20	14	15.05	30	32.26	875.00
	30-44	14	15.05	10	10.75	24	25.81	714.29
	45-59	07	7.53	04	4.30	11	11.83	571.42
	60 +	03	3.23	05	5.38	08	8.60	1666.67
	Sub-Total	**49**	**52.69**	**44**	**47.1**	**93**	**100**	**897.96**
2	**Suni**							
	0-14	16	12.60	13	10.23	29	22.83	812.50
	15-29	18	14.17	16	12.60	34	26.77	888.89
	30-44	14	11.02	11	8.66	25	19.69	785.71
	45-59	12	9.45	13	10.24	25	19.69	1083.33
	60 +	09	7.09	05	11.81	14	11.02	555.55
	Sub-Total	**69**	**54.33**	**58**	**45.67**	**127**	**100**	**840.57**
3	**Garo Basti**							
	0-14	38	11.55	35	10.64	73	22.19	921.05
	15-29	45	13.68	43	13.07	88	26.75	955.56
	30-44	41	12.46	38	11.55	79	24.01	926.83
	45-59	25	7.59	24	7.29	49	14.89	960.00
	60 +	21	6.38	19	5.78	40	12.16	904.76
	Sub-Total	**170**	**51.67**	**159**	**48.33**	**329**	**100**	**935.29**

S.No.	Age Group	Male		Female		Both		Sex
		No. of persons	Percentage	No. of persons	Percentage	No. of persons	Percentage	Ratio
4	**Gadhadhar**							
	0-14	45	12.93	39	11.20	84	24.14	866.67
	15-29	51	14.66	47	13.51	98	28.16	921.57
	30-44	34	9.77	37	10.63	71	20.40	1088.23
	45-59	28	8.05	26	7.47	54	15.52	928.57
	60 +	21	6.03	20	5.75	41	11.78	952.38
	Sub-Total	**179**	**51.44**	**169**	**48.56**	**348**	**100.00**	**944.13**
5	**Poro**							
	0-14	32	10.63	29	9.63	61	20.27	906.25
	15-29	36	11.96	34	11.29	70	23.26	944.44
	30-44	43	14.29	41	13.62	84	27.91	953.49
	45-59	26	8.64	22	7.31	48	15.95	846.15
	60 +	18	5.98	20	6.64	38	12.62	1111.11
	Sub-Total	**155**	**51.49**	**146**	**48.50**	**301**	**100**	**941.94**
6	**Nimati and Dabri**							
	0-14	45	12.22	41	11.14	86	23.36	911.11
	15-29	47	12.77	43	11.68	90	24.46	914.89
	30-44	42	11.41	39	10.59	81	22.01	928.57
	45-59	36	9.78	35	9.51	71	19.29	972.22
	60 +	21	5.70	19	5.16	40	10.87	904.76
	Sub-Total	**191**	**51.90**	**177**	**48.09**	**368**	**100.00**	**926.70**

S.No.	Age Group	Male		Female		Both		Sex
		No. of persons	Percentage	No. of persons	Percentage	No. of persons	Percentage	Ratio
7	**Gangutia**							
	0-14	27	12.86	29	13.81	56	26.67	1074.07
	15-29	32	15.23	26	12.38	58	27.61	812.5
	30-44	23	10.95	21	9.99	44	20.95	913.04
	45-59	18	8.57	14	6.67	32	15.24	777.78
	60 +	12	5.71	08	3.81	20	9.52	666.67
	Sub-Total	**112**	**53.33**	**98**	**46.67**	**210**	**100**	**875.00**
8	**Adma**							
	0-14	23	12.50	24	13.04	47	25.54	1043.48
	15-29	26	14.13	23	12.50	49	26.63	884.62
	30-44	21	11.41	22	11.96	43	23.37	1047.62
	45-59	17	9.24	14	7.61	31	16.85	823.53
	60 +	08	4.35	06	3.26	14	7.61	750.00
	Sub-Total	**95**	**51.63**	**89**	**48.37**	**184**	**100.00**	**936.84**
9	**Raimatang**							
	0-14	34	12.55	31	11.44	65	23.99	911.76
	15-29	37	13.65	32	11.81	69	25.46	864.86
	30-44	33	12.18	34	12.55	67	24.72	1030.30
	45-59	23	8.49	24	8.86	47	17.34	1043.48
	60 +	12	4.43	11	4.06	23	8.49	916.67
	Sub-Total	**139**	**51.29**	**132**	**48.71**	**271**	**100.00**	**949.64**

S.No.	Age Group	Male		Female		Both		Sex
		No. of persons	Percentage	No. of persons	Percentage	No. of persons	Percentage	Ratio
10	**Bhutri forest basti**							
	0-14	30	13.57	29	13.12	59	26.70	966.67
	15-29	25	11.31	27	12.22	52	23.53	1080.00
	30-44	26	11.76	24	10.86	50	22.62	923.07
	45-59	19	8.59	17	7.69	36	16.29	894.74
	60 +	13	5.88	11	4.98	24	10.86	846.15
	Sub-Total	**113**	**51.13**	**108**	**48.87**	**221**	**100.00**	**955.75**
11	**Gudamdabri**							
	0-14	34	13.55	35	13.94	69	27.49	1029.41
	15-29	28	11.16	25	9.96	53	21.11	892.85
	30-44	28	11.16	27	10.76	55	21.91	964.28
	45-59	21	8.37	19	7.57	40	15.93	904.76
	60 +	18	7.17	16	6.37	34	13.55	888.89
	Sub-Total	**129**	**51.39**	**122**	**48.61**	**251**	**100.00**	**945.74**
12	**Chunabati**							
	0-14	26	12.32	23	9.16	49	23.22	884.62
	15-29	29	13.74	26	10.36	55	26.06	896.55
	30-44	19	9.00	21	8.37	40	18.96	1105.26
	45-59	21	9.95	17	6.77	38	18.00	809.52
	60 +	14	6.64	15	5.98	29	13.74	1071.42
	Sub-Total	**109**	**51.66**	**102**	**48.34**	**211**	**100.00**	**935.78**

S.No.	Age Group	Male		Female		Both		Sex
		No. of persons	Percentage	No. of persons	Percentage	No. of persons	Percentage	Ratio
13	**Bhutiabasti**							
	0-14	16	12.03	17	12.78	33	24.81	1062.5
	15-29	17	12.78	15	11.28	32	24.06	882.35
	30-44	15	11.28	12	9.02	27	20.30	800.00
	45-59	13	9.77	11	8.27	24	18.04	846.15
	60 +	07	5.26	10	7.52	17	12.78	1428.57
	Sub-Total	**68**	**51.13**	**65**	**48.87**	**133**	**100.00**	**955.89**
14	**Sankosh**							
	0-14	44	13.29	40	12.08	84	25.38	909.09
	15-29	39	11.78	37	11.18	76	22.96	948.72
	30-44	37	11.18	38	11.48	75	22.66	1027.02
	45-59	34	10.27	31	9.37	65	19.64	911.76
	60 +	15	4.53	16	4.83	31	9.37	1066.67
	Sub-Total	**169**	**51.06**	**162**	**48.94**	**331**	**100.00**	**958.58**
15	**Lapraguri**							
	0-14	30	12.99	27	11.69	57	24.66	900.00
	15-29	26	11.26	27	11.69	53	22.94	1038.46
	30-44	24	10.39	22	9.53	46	19.91	916.67
	45-59	22	9.52	20	8.66	42	18.18	909.09
	60 +	16	6.93	17	7.26	33	14.29	1062.50
	Sub-Total	**118**	**51.08**	**113**	**48.92**	**231**	**100.00**	**957.63**

S.No.	Age Group	Male		Female		Both		Sex
		No. of persons	Percentage	No. of persons	Percentage	No. of persons	Percentage	Ratio
16	**Santrabari**							
	0-14	37	11.94	39	12.58	76	24.52	1054.05
	15-29	38	12.26	34	10.97	72	23.23	894.74
	30-44	32	10.32	31	9.99	63	20.32	968.75
	45-59	28	9.03	26	8.39	54	17.42	928.57
	60 +	24	7.74	21	6.77	45	14.52	875.00
	Sub-Total	**159**	**51.29**	**151**	**48.71**	**310**	**100.00**	**949.68**
17	**Balapara**							
	0-14	22	14.47	23	15.13	45	29.61	1045.45
	15-29	18	11.84	17	11.18	35	23.02	944.44
	30-44	17	11.18	15	9.87	32	21.05	882.35
	45-59	14	9.21	12	7.89	26	17.11	857.14
	60 +	7	4.61	7	4.61	14	9.21	1000.00
	Sub-Total	**78**	**51.32**	**74**	**48.68**	**152**	**100.00**	**948.72**
Grand	**Total**	**2102**	**51.63%**	**1969**	**48.37%**	**4071**	**100.00**	**936.73**

(Prepared by the researcher based on field survey, 2017).

Table–4.13
Education Status of Villagers

S.No.	Educational Level	Male		Female		Both	
		No. of persons	Percentage	No. of persons	Percentage	No. of persons	Percentage
1	**Lehra**						
	Illiterate	09	9.68	11	11.83	20	21.51
	Primary	36	38.71	31	33.33	67	72.04
	Secondary	04	4,30	02	2.15	06	6.45
	Higher Secondary	-	-	-	-	-	-
	Graduate and P.G	-	-	-	-	-	-
	Other Diploma	-	-	-	-	-	-
	Sub-Total	**49**	**52.69**	**44**	**47.1**	**93**	**100**
2	**Suni**						
	Illiterate	21	16.54	18	14.17	39	30.71
	Primary	41	32.28	38	29.92	79	62.21
	Secondary	05	3.94	02	1.57	07	5.51
	Higher Secondary	02	1.57	-	-	02	1.57
	Graduate and P.G	-	-	-	-	-	-
	Other Diploma	-	-	-	-	-	-
	Sub-Total	**69**	**54.33**	**58**	**45.67**	**127**	**100**
3	**Garo Basti**						
	Illiterate	42	12.77	35	10.64	77	23.40
	Primary	92	27.96	78	23.71	170	51.67
	Secondary	25	7.59	28	8.52	53	16.12

S.No.	Educational Level	Male		Female		Both	
		No. of persons	Percentage	No. of persons	Percentage	No. of persons	Percentage
	Higher Secondary	09	2.74	14	4.26	23	6.99
	Graduate	02	0.61	04	1.22	06	1.82
	P.G/Diploma	-	-	-	-	-	-
	Sub-Total	**170**	**51.67**	**159**	**48.33**	**329**	**100**
4	**Gadhadhar**						
	Illiterate	45	12.93	37	10.63	82	23.56
	Primary	102	29.31	94	27.01	196	56.32
	Secondary	24	9.77	27	7.76	51	14.66
	Higher Secondary	08	8.05	11	3.16	19	5.46
	Graduate	-	-	-	-	-	-
	P.G/Diploma	-	-	-	-	-	-
	Sub-Total	**179**	**51.44**	**169**	**48.56**	**348**	**100.00**
5	**Poro**						
	Illiterate	35	11.63	29	9.63	63	20.93
	Primary	70	23.56	58	19.27	128	42.52
	Secondary	37	12.29	40	13.29	78	25.92
	Higher Secondary	13	4.32	19	6.31	32	10.63
	Graduate	-	-	-	-	-	-
	P.G/Diploma	-	-	-	-	-	-
	Sub-Total	**155**	**51.49**	**146**	**48.50**	**301**	**100**

S.No.	Educational Level	Male		Female		Both	
		No. of persons	Percentage	No. of persons	Percentage	No. of persons	Percentage
6	**Nimati and Dabri**						
	Illiterate	45	12.22	41	11.14	86	23.36
	Primary	96	26.08	76	20.65	172	46.75
	Secondary	33	8.97	36	9.78	68	18.48
	Higher Secondary	15	4.07	20	5.43	36	9.78
	Graduate	02	0.54	04	1.08	06	1.63
	P.G/Diploma	-	-	-	-	-	-
	Sub-Total	**191**	**51.90**	**177**	**48.09**	**368**	**100.00**
7	**Gangutia**						
	Illiterate	27	12.86	29	13.81	56	26.67
	Primary	43	20.48	30	14.29	73	34.76
	Secondary	23	10.95	21	9.99	44	20.95
	Higher Secondary	14	6.67	16	7.62	30	14.29
	Graduate	05	2.38	02	0.95	07	3.33
	P.G/Diploma	-	-	-	-	-	-
	Sub-Total	**112**	**53.33**	**98**	**46.67**	**210**	**100**
8	**Adma**						
	Illiterate	26	14.13	24	13.04	50	27.18
	Primary	54	29.35	54	29.35	108	58.69
	Secondary	11	5.98	09	4.89	20	10.87
	Higher Secondary	04	9.24	02	7.61	06	3.26
	Graduate	-	-	-	-	-	-
	P.G/Diploma	-	-	-	-	-	-
	Sub-Total	**95**	**51.63**	**89**	**48.37**	**184**	**100.00**

S.No.	Educational Level	Male		Female		Both	
		No. of persons	Percentage	No. of persons	Percentage	No. of persons	Percentage
9	**Raimatang**						
	Illiterate	36	13.28	32	11.81	68	25.09
	Primary	62	22.88	58	21.40	120	44.29
	Secondary	22	8.12	24	8.86	46	16.97
	Higher Secondary	13	4.79	14	5.17	27	9.96
	Graduate	06	2.21	04	1.48	10	3.69
	P.G/Diploma	-	-	-	-	-	-
	Sub-Total	**139**	**51.29**	**132**	**48.71**	**271**	**100.00**
10	**Bhutri forest basti**						
	Illiterate	33	14.93	29	13.12	62	28.05
	Primary	46	20.81	51	23.08	97	43.89
	Secondary	21	9.50	20	9.05	41	18.56
	Higher Secondary	10	4.52	07	3.17	17	7.69
	Graduate	03	1.36	01	0.45	04	1.81
	P.G/Diploma	-	-	-	-	-	-
	Sub-Total	**113**	**51.13**	**108**	**48.87**	**221**	**100.00**
11	**Gudamdabri**						
	Illiterate	35	13.94	34	13.55	69	27.49
	Primary	62	24.70	56	22.31	118	47.01
	Secondary	21	8.37	23	9.16	44	17.53
	Higher Secondary	11	4.38	09	3.59	20	7.97
	Graduate	-	-	-	-	-	-
	P.G/Diploma	-	-	-	-	-	-
	Sub-Total	**129**	**51.39**	**122**	**48.61**	**251**	**100.00**

S.No.	Educational Level	Male		Female		Both	
		No. of persons	Percentage	No. of persons	Percentage	No. of persons	Percentage
12	**Chunabati**						
	Illiterate	32	15.17	29	13.74	61	28.91
	Primary	65	30.81	62	29.38	127	60.19
	Secondary	09	4.27	07	3.32	16	7.58
	Higher Secondary	03	1.42	04	1.89	07	3.32
	Graduate	-	-	-	-	-	-
	P.G/Diploma	-	-	-	-	-	-
	Sub-Total	**109**	**51.66**	**102**	**48.34**	**211**	**100.00**
13	**Bhutiabasti**						
	Illiterate	17	12.78	16	12.03	33	24.81
	Primary	30	22.56	26	19.55	56	42.11
	Secondary	15	11.28	12	9.02	27	20.30
	Higher Secondary	06	4.51	11	8.27	17	12.78
	Graduate	-	-	-	-	-	-
	P.G/Diploma	-	-	-	-	-	-
	Sub-Total	**68**	**51.13**	**65**	**48.87**	**133**	**100.00**
14	**Sankosh**						
	Illiterate	45	13.59	43	12.99	88	26.59
	Primary	75	22.66	70	21.15	145	43.81
	Secondary	31	9.37	29	8.76	60	18.13
	Higher Secondary	14	4.23	14	4.23	28	8.45
	Graduate	04	4.53	06	4.83	10	3.02
	P.G/Diploma	-	-	-	-	-	-
	Sub-Total	**169**	**51.06**	**162**	**48.94**	**331**	**100.00**

S.No.	Educational Level	Male		Female		Both	
		No. of persons	Percentage	No. of persons	Percentage	No. of persons	Percentage
15	**Lapraguri**						
	Illiterate	33	14.29	29	12.55	62	26.85
	Primary	70	30.30	66	28.57	136	58.87
	Secondary	13	5.63	15	6.49	28	12.12
	Higher Secondary	02	0.87	03	1.29	05	2.16
	Graduate	-	-	-	-	-	-
	P.G/Diploma	-	-	-	-	-	-
	Sub-Total	**118**	**51.08**	**113**	**48.92**	**231**	**100.00**
16	**Santrabari**						
	Illiterate	39	12.58	37	11.94	76	24.52
	Primary	68	21.94	58	18.71	126	40.65
	Secondary	32	10.32	33	10.65	65	20.96
	Higher Secondary	18	5.81	22	7.09	40	12.90
	Graduate	02	0.65	01	0.32	03	0.97
	P.G/Diploma	-	-	-	-	-	-
	Sub-Total	**159**	**51.29**	**151**	**48.71**	**310**	**100.00**

S.No.	Educational Level	Male		Female		Both	
		No. of persons	Percentage	No. of persons	Percentage	No. of persons	Percentage
17	**Balapara**						
	Illiterate	22	14.47	27	17.76	49	32.23
	Primary	38	24.99	33	21.71	71	46.71
	Secondary	14	9.21	12	7.89	26	17.11
	Higher Secondary	04	2.63	02	1.32	06	3.95
	Graduate	-	-	-	-	-	-
	P.G/Diploma	-	-	-	-	-	-
	Sub-Total	**78**	**51.32**	**74**	**48.68**	**152**	**100.00**
Grand Total		**2102**	**51.63**	**1969**	**48.37**	**4071**	**100.00**

Overall Education status

Educational Level	Male		Female		Both	
	No. of persons	Percentage	No. of persons	Percentage	No. of persons	Percentage
Illiterate	542	13.31	500	12.28	1042	25.59
Primary	1050	25.79	939	23.07	1989	48.87
Secondary	340	8.35	344	8.45	684	16.80
Higher Secondary	146	3.59	164	4.03	310	7.61
Graduate	24	0.59	22	0.54	46	1.13
P.G/Diploma	-	-	-	-	-	-
Total	**2102**	**51.63**	**1969**	**48.37**	**4071**	**100.00**

(Prepared by the researcher based on field survey, 2017).

Table–4.15
Relation between Occupation and Education among Forest Villagers

S. No.	Occupation	Illiterate		Literate											
				Primary		Secondary		H.S		Graduate		P.G/ Diploma		Total	
		M	F	M	F	M	F	M	F	M	F	M	F	M	F
1	**Lehra**														
	Agriculture	2	3	6	2	1	-	-	-	-	-	-	-	9	5
	Agricu.Lab/MFP	4	2	6	5	1	2	-	-	-	-	-	-	11	9
	Labour/MFP Colle.	2	3	6	6	-	-	-	-	-	-	-	-	8	9
	Lab./Livesto./MFP	1	3	10	12	1	-	-	-	-	-	-	-	12	15
	Service Job	-	-	-	-	1	-	-	-	-	-	-	-	1	-
	Students and oth.	-	-	8	6	-	-	-	-	-	-	-	-	8	6
	Sub-Total	**9**	**11**	**36**	**31**	**04**	**02**	-	-	-	-	-	-	**49**	**44**
2	**Suni**														
	Agriculture	3	-	3	-	-	-	1	-	-	-	-	-	7	-
	Agricu.Lab/MFP	8	6	13	11	2	1	-	-	-	-	-	-	23	18
	Labour/MFP Colle.	4	8	11	9	3	-	-	-	-	-	-	-	18	17
	Lab./Livesto./MFP	6	4	9	11	-	1	-	-	-	-	-	-	15	16
	Service	-	-	-	-	-	-	1	-	-	-	-	-	1	-
	Students and oth.	-	-	5	7	-	-	-	-	-	-	-	-	5	7
	Sub-Total	**21**	**18**	**41**	**38**	**5**	**2**	**2**	-	-	-	-	-	**69**	**58**

S. No.	Occupation	Illiterate		Literate											
				Primary		Secondary		H.S		Graduate		P.G/ Diploma		Total	
		M	F	M	F	M	F	M	F	M	F	M	F	M	F
3	**Garo Basti**														
	Agriculture	11	-	13	1	5	-	1	-	-	-	-	-	30	1
	Agricu.Lab/MFP	24	13	28	21	6	8	3	4	1	2	-	-	62	48
	Labour/MFP Colle.	4	15	22	24	7	5	1	4	-	1	-	-	34	49
	Lab./Livesto./MFP	3	7	9	10	3	10	3	5	-	1	-	-	18	33
	Service	-	-	-	-	-	-	1	1	1	-	-	-	2	1
	Students and oth.	-	-	20	22	4	5	-	-	-	-	-	-	24	27
	Sub-Total	**42**	**35**	**92**	**78**	**25**	**28**	**9**	**14**	**2**	**4**	**-**	**-**	**170**	**159**
4	**Gadhadhar**														
	Agriculture	13	-	25	11	2	-	2	-	-	-	-	-	42	11
	Agricu.Lab/MFP	10	14	27	23	6	8	1	3	-	-	-	-	44	48
	Labour/MFP Colle.	15	12	23	21	7	6	5	4	-	-	-	-	50	43
	Lab./Livesto./MFP	7	11	11	18	-	4	-	4	-	-	-	-	18	37
	Service	-	-	-	-	-	-	-	-	-	-	-	-	-	-
	Students and oth.	-	-	16	21	9	9	-	-	-	-	-	-	25	30
	Sub-Total	**45**	**37**	**102**	**94**	**24**	**27**	**8**	**11**	**-**	**-**	**-**	**-**	**179**	**169**
5	**Poro**														
	Agriculture	11	6	19	12	5	-	4	-	-	-	-	-	39	18
	Agricu.Lab/MFP	16	16	21	15	10	12	9	12	-	-	-	-	56	55
	Labour/MFP Colle.	5	4	12	11	17	20	-	5	-	-	-	-	34	40

S. No.	Occupation	Illiterate		Literate											
				Primary		Secondary		H.S		Graduate		P.G/ Diploma		Total	
		M	F	M	F	M	F	M	F	M	F	M	F	M	F
	Lab./Livesto./MFP	3	3	4	3	1	2	-	2	-	-	-	-	8	10
	Service	-	-	-	-	-	-	-	-	-	-	-	-	-	-
	Students and oth.	-	-	14	17	4	6	-	-	-	-	-	-	18	23
	Sub-Total	**35**	**29**	**70**	**58**	**37**	**40**	**13**	**19**	**-**	**-**	**-**	**-**	**155**	**146**
6	**Nimati and Dabri**														
	Agriculture	11	9	25	21	7	9	2	4	1	-	-	-	46	43
	Agricu.Lab/MFP	15	11	34	27	11	10	5	6	-	2	-	-	65	56
	Labour/MFP Colle.	14	16	17	13	4	6	3	2	-	2	-	-	38	39
	Lab./Livesto./MFP	5	5	8	5	3	4	1	2	-	-	-	-	17	16
	Service	-	-	-	-	-	-	-	1	1	-	-	-	1	1
	Students and oth.	-	-	12	10	8	7	4	5	-	-	-	-	24	22
	Sub-Total	**45**	**41**	**96**	**76**	**33**	**36**	**15**	**20**	**2**	**4**	**-**	**-**	**191**	**177**
7	**Gangutia**														
	Agriculture	8	4	7	5	4	3	2	1	1	-	-	-	22	13
	Agricu.Lab/MFP	12	15	13	11	9	6	4	5	3	1	-	-	41	38
	Labour/MFP Colle.	5	6	8	4	5	5	5	3	1	-	-	-	24	18
	Lab./Livesto./MFP	2	4	4	2	1	3	1	3	-	-	-	-	8	12
	Service	-	-	-	-	-	-	-	-	-	1	-	-	-	1
	Students and oth.	-	-	11	8	4	4	2	4	-	-	-	-	17	16
	Sub-Total	**27**	**29**	**43**	**30**	**23**	**21**	**14**	**16**	**5**	**2**	**-**	**-**	**112**	**98**

S. No.	Occupation	Illiterate		Literate											
				Primary		Secondary		H.S		Graduate		P.G/ Diploma		Total	
		M	F	M	F	M	F	M	F	M	F	M	F	M	F
8	**Adma**														
	Agriculture	4	2	5	3	-	-	-	1	-	-	-	-	9	6
	Agricu.Lab/MFP	8	9	19	21	2	3	2	-	-	-	-	-	31	33
	Labour/MFP Colle.	10	7	15	17	3	2	1	-	-	-	-	-	29	26
	Lab./Livesto./MFP	4	6	8	6	1	2	1	1	-	-	-	-	14	15
	Service	-	-	-	-	-	-	-	-	-	-	-	-	-	-
	Students and oth.	-	-	7	7	5	2	-	-	-	-	-	-	12	9
	Sub-Total	**26**	**24**	**54**	**54**	**11**	**09**	**4**	**2**	**-**	**-**	**-**	**-**	**95**	**89**
9	**Raimatang**														
	Agriculture	10	8	14	6	3	-	2	-	1	-	-	-	30	14
	Agricu.Lab/MFP	16	14	25	27	9	11	4	5	2	1	-	-	56	58
	Labour/MFP Colle.	6	7	11	9	4	5	3	2	1	1	-	-	25	24
	Lab./Livesto./MFP	4	3	-	6	2	4	1	3	-	1	-	-	7	17
	Service	-	-	-	-	-	-	-	2	1	1	-	-	1	3
	Students and oth.	-	-	12	10	4	4	3	2	1	-	-	-	20	16
	Sub-Total	**36**	**32**	**62**	**58**	**22**	**24**	**13**	**14**	**6**	**4**	**-**	**-**	**139**	**132**
10	**Bhutri forest basti**														
	Agriculture	8	5	11	7	3	-	1	-	-	-	-	-	23	12
	Agricu.Lab/MFP	12	15	18	21	7	6	4	3	2	-	-	-	43	45
	Labour/MFP Colle.	5	3	7	9	6	6	2	2	-	-	-	-	20	20

S. No.	Occupation	Illiterate		Literate											
				Primary		Secondary		H.S		Graduate		P.G/ Diploma		Total	
		M	F	M	F	M	F	M	F	M	F	M	F	M	F
	Lab./Livesto./MFP	8	6	4	6	2	3	1	1	1	-	-	-	16	16
	Service	-	-	-	-	-	-	-	-	-	1	-	-	-	1
	Students and oth.	-	-	6	8	3	5	2	1	-	-	-	-	11	14
	Sub-Total	**33**	**29**	**46**	**51**	**21**	**20**	**10**	**7**	**3**	**1**	**-**	**-**	**113**	**108**
11	**Gudamdabri**														
	Agriculture	7	3	12	9	3	2	-	2	-	-	-	-	35	16
	Agricu.Lab/MFP	13	16	21	16	9	11	6	3	-	-	-	-	49	46
	Labour/MFP Colle.	8	11	11	14	3	2	4	1	-	-	-	-	17	28
	Lab./Livesto./MFP	7	4	5	8	2	5	1	-	-	-	-	-	11	17
	Service	-	-	-	-	-	-	-	1	-	-	-	-	-	1
	Students and oth.	-	-	13	9	4	3	-	2	-	-	-	-	17	14
	Sub-Total	**35**	**34**	**62**	**56**	**21**	**23**	**11**	**9**	**-**	**-**	**-**	**-**	**129**	**122**
12	**Chunabati**														
	Agriculture	4	2	2	-	1	-	-	1	-	-	-	-	7	3
	Agricu.Lab/MFP	12	14	25	23	-	1	1	-	-	-	-	-	38	38
	Labour/MFP Colle.	9	7	17	19	1	1	-	1	-	-	-	-	27	28
	Lab./Livesto./MFP	7	6	14	16	2	2	-	-	-	-	-	-	23	24
	Service	-	-	-	-	1	-	-	-	-	-	-	-	1	-
	Students and oth.	-	-	7	4	4	3	2	2	-		-	-	13	9
	Sub-Total	**32**	**29**	**65**	**62**	**9**	**7**	**3**	**4**	**-**	**-**	**-**	**-**	**109**	**102**

S. No.	Occupation	Illiterate		Literate											
				Primary		Secondary		H.S		Graduate		P.G/ Diploma		Total	
		M	F	M	F	M	F	M	F	M	F	M	F	M	F
13	**Bhutiabasti**														
	Agriculture	3	-	2	-	1	-	-	2	-	-	-	-	6	2
	Agricu.Lab/MFP	6	7	12	10	5	3	2	3	-	-	-	-	25	23
	Labour/MFP Colle.	5	5	8	8	3	2	1	2	-	-	-	-	17	17
	Lab./Livesto./MFP	3	4	2	4	2	4	1	2	-	-	-	-	8	14
	Service	-	-	-	-	-	-	-	-	-	-	-	-	-	-
	Students and oth.	-	-	6	4	4	3	2	2	-	-	-	-	12	9
	Sub-Total	**17**	**16**	**30**	**26**	**15**	**12**	**6**	**11**	**-**	**-**	**-**	**-**	**68**	**65**
14	**Sankosh**														
	Agriculture	11	9	6	2	2	1	-	-	-	1	-	-	19	13
	Agricu.Lab/MFP	17	19	21	25	8	8	2	3	1	1	-	-	49	56
	Labour/MFP Colle.	8	6	18	12	10	5	2	2	-	1	-	-	38	26
	Lab./Livesto./MFP	9	9	16	20	6	8	6	4	1	2	-	-	38	43
	Service	-	-	-	-	-	-	-	1	-	1	-	-	-	2
	Students and oth.	-	-	14	11	5	7	4	4	2	-	-	-	25	22
	Sub-Total	**45**	**43**	**75**	**70**	**31**	**29**	**14**	**14**	**4**	**6**	**-**	**-**	**169**	**162**
15	**Lapraguri**														
	Agriculture	3	-	9	5	2	-	-	-	-	-	-	-	14	5
	Agricu.Lab/MFP	15	17	21	24	2	3	1	-	-	-	-	-	39	44
	Labour/MFP Colle.	6	8	13	11	2	5	-	1	-	-	-	-	21	25

S. No.	Occupation	Illiterate		Literate											
				Primary		Secondary		H.S		Graduate		P.G/ Diploma		Total	
		M	F	M	F	M	F	M	F	M	F	M	F	M	F
	Lab./Livesto./MFP	9	4	16	18	4	3	-	2			-	-	29	27
	Service	-	-	-	-	-	-	-	-	-	-	-	-	-	-
	Students and oth.	-	-	11	8	3	4	1	-	-	-	-	-	15	12
	Sub-Total	**33**	**29**	**70**	**66**	**13**	**15**	**2**	**3**	**-**	**-**	**-**	**-**	**118**	**113**
16	**Santrabari**														
	Agriculture	9	4	7	4	2	-	1	2	-	1	-	-	19	11
	Agricu.Lab/MFP	15	18	21	18	9	12	5	8	1		-	-	51	56
	Labour/MFP Colle.	8	9	16	13	11	8	3	6	1	-	-	-	39	36
	Lab./Livesto./MFP	7	6	8	10	4	6	4	3	-		-	-	23	25
	Service	-	-	-	-	-	-	1	1	-	-	-	-	1	1
	Students and oth.	-	-	16	13	6	7	4	2	-	-	-	-	26	22
	Sub-Total	**39**	**37**	**68**	**58**	**32**	**33**	**18**	**22**	**2**	**1**	**-**	**-**	**159**	**151**
17	**Balapara**														
	Agriculture	4	2	7	4	3	-	-	-	-	-	-	-	14	6
	Agricu.Lab/MFP	8	9	11	15	5	4	2	1	-	-	-	-	26	29
	Labour/MFP Colle.	4	7	7	4	-	3	-	1	-	-	-	-	11	15
	Lab./Livesto./MFP	6	9	6	5	3	2	1	-	-	-	-	-	16	16
	Service	-	-	-	-	-	-	-	-	-	-	-	-	-	-
	Students and oth.	-	-	7	5	3	3	1	-	-	-	-	-	11	8
	Sub-Total	**22**	**27**	**38**	**33**	**14**	**12**	**4**	**2**	**-**	**-**	**-**	**-**	**78**	**74**
Grand Total		**2102**		**51.63%**		**1969**		**48.37%**		**4071**		**100.00**			

	Overall Status													
	Illiterate		Primary		Secondary		H.S		Graduate		P.G/ Diploma		Total	
	M	**F**	**M**	**F**	**M**	**F**	**M**	**F**	**M**	**F**	**M**	**F**	**M**	**F**
Agriculture	122	57	173	92	44	15	16	13	3	2	-	-	358 8.79%	179 4.40%
	4.39%		**6.51%**		**1.45%**		**0.71**		**0.122**		**-**			
Agricu.Lab/MFP colle.	221	215	331	313	103	113	51	54	10	7	-	-	716 17.59%	702 17.24%
	10.71%		**15.82%**		**5.31%**		**2.58%**		**0.42**		**-**			
Labour/MFP Colle.	108	134	204	204	86	81	30	34	3	5	-	-	431 10.59%	458 11.25%
	5.94%		**10.02%**		**4.10%**		**1.57%**		**0.19%**		**-**			
Lab./Livesto./MFP	91	94	157	160	37	63	21	32	2	4	-	-	308 7.57%	353 8.67%
	4.54%		**7.79%**		**2.46%**		**1.30%**		**0.15%**		**-**			
Service	-	-	-	-	-	-	03	07	3	4	-	-	6 0.15%	11 0.27%
	-		**-**		**-**		**0.25%**		**0.17%**					

	Overall Status													
	Illiterate		Primary		Secondary		H.S		Graduate		P.G/ Diploma		Total	
	M	F	M	F	M	F	M	F	M	F	M	F	M	F
Students and others	-	-	185	170	70	72	25	24	3	-	-	-	283 6.95%	266 6.53%
	-		8.72%		3.49%		1.20%		0.074%		-			
Total	**542**	**500**	**1050**	**939**	**340**	**344**	**146**	**164**	**24**	**22**	**-**	**-**	**2102** **51.63%**	**1969** **48.37%**
	13.31	**12.28**	**25.79**	**23.07**	**8.35**	**8.45**	**3.59**	**4.03**	**0.59**	**0.54**	**-**	**-**		

(Prepared by the researcher based on field surveys, 2017).

Table–5.14
Status of Labour Force Participation

S.No.	Working Status (Village-Wise)	Male		Female		Total	
		No. of persons	Percentage	No. of persons	Percentage	No. of persons	Percentage
1	**Lehra Village**	-	-	-	-	-	-
	Main Worker	21	22.58	19	20.43	40	43.01
	Marginal Worker	16	17.21	15	16.13	31	33.33
	Non-Worker	12	12.90	10	10.75	22	23.66
	Total	**49**	**52.69**	**44**	**47.31**	**93**	**100.00**
2	**Suni Village**	-	-	-	-	-	-
	Main Worker	35	27.56	31	24.41	66	51.97
	Marginal Worker	25	19.69	21	16.54	46	36.22
	Non-Worker	09	7.08	06	4.72	15	11.81
	Total	**69**	**54.33**	**58**	**45.67**	**127**	**100.00**
3	**Garo Basti Village**	-	-	-	-	-	-
	Main Worker	89	27.05	81	24.62	170	51.67
	Marginal Worker	48	14.59	66	20.06	114	34.65
	Non-Worker	33	10.03	12	3.65	45	13.68
	Total	**170**	**51.67**	**159**	**48.33**	**329**	**100.00**
4	**Gadhadhar Village**	-	-	-	-	-	-
	Main Worker	78	22.41	71	20.40	149	42.82
	Marginal Worker	71	20.40	63	18.10	134	38.51
	Non-Worker	30	8.63	35	10.06	65	18.67
	Total	**179**	**51.44**	**169**	**48.56**	**348**	**100**

S.No.	Working Status	Male		Female		Total	
	(Village-Wise)	No. of persons	Percentage	No. of persons	Percentage	No. of persons	Percentage
5	**Poro Village**	-	-	-	-	-	-
	Main Worker	55	18.27	56	18.60	111	36.88
	Marginal Worker	73	24.25	69	22.92	142	47.18
	Non-Worker	27	8.97	21	6.98	48	15.94
	Total	**155**	**51.49**	**146**	**48.50**	**301**	**100**
6	**Nimati & Dabri Vill**	-	-	-	-	-	-
	Main Worker	71	19.29	69	18.75	140	38.04
	Marginal Worker	86	23.37	81	22.01	167	45.38
	Non-Worker	34	9.24	27	7.33	61	16.58
	Total	**191**	**51.90**	**177**	**48.09**	**368**	**100**
7	**Gangutia Village**	-	-	-	-	-	-
	Main Worker	34	16.19	30	14.29	64	30.48
	Marginal Worker	51	24.29	48	22.86	99	47.14
	Non-Worker	27	12.86	20	9.52	47	22.38
	Total	**112**	**53.33**	**98**	**46.67**	**210**	**100**
8	**Adma Village**	-	-	-	-	-	-
	Main Worker	23	12.50	21	11.41	44	23.91
	Marginal Worker	56	30.43	51	27.72	107	58.15
	Non-Worker	16	8.70	17	9.24	33	17.94
	Total	**95**	**51.63**	**89**	**48.37**	**184**	**100**

S.No.	Working Status	Male		Female		Total	
	(Village-Wise)	No. of persons	Percentage	No. of persons	Percentage	No. of persons	Percentage
9	**Raimatang Village**	-	-	-	-	-	-
	Main Worker	45	16.61	46	16.97	91	33.58
	Marginal Worker	72	26.57	69	25.46	141	52.03
	Non-Worker	22	8.11	17	6.28	39	14.39
	Total	**139**	**51.29**	**132**	**48.71**	**271**	**100**
10	**Bhutri F. basti Vill.**	-	-	-	-	-	-
	Main Worker	36	16.29	38	17.19	74	33.48
	Marginal Worker	66	29.86	62	28.06	128	57.92
	Non-Worker	11	4.98	08	3.62	19	8.60
	Total	**113**	**51.13**	**108**	**48.87**	**221**	**100**
11	**Gudamdabri Villag.**	-	-	-	-	-	-
	Main Worker	49	19.52	45	17.93	94	37.45
	Marginal Worker	66	26.29	64	25.50	130	51.79
	Non-Worker	14	5.58	13	5.18	27	10.76
	Total	**129**	**51.39**	**122**	**48.61**	**251**	**100**
12	**Chunabati Village**	-	-	-	-	-	-
	Main Worker	32	15.17	34	16.11	66	31.28
	Marginal Worker	58	27.49	54	25.59	112	53.08
	Non-Worker	19	9.00	14	6.64	33	15.64
	Total	**109**	**51.66**	**102**	**48.34**	**211**	**100**

S.No.	Working Status (Village-Wise)	Male		Female		Both	
		No. of persons	Percentage	No. of persons	Percentage	No. of persons	Percentage
13	**Bhutiabasti Village**	-	-	-	-	-	-
	Main Worker	24	18.04	26	19.55	50	37.59
	Marginal Worker	33	24.81	31	23.31	64	48.12
	Non-Worker	11	8.28	08	6.01	19	14.29
	Total	**68**	**51.13**	**65**	**48.87**	**133**	**100**
14	**Sankosh Village**	-	-	-	-	-	-
	Main Worker	65	19.64	62	18.73	127	38.37
	Marginal Worker	81	24.47	79	23.87	160	48.34
	Non-Worker	23	6.95	21	6.34	44	13.29
	Total	**169**	**51.06**	**162**	**48.94**	**331**	**100**
15	**Lapraguri Village**	-	-	-	-	-	-
	Main Worker	31	13.41	41	17.75	72	31.17
	Marginal Worker	47	20.35	49	21.21	96	41.56
	Non-Worker	40	17.32	23	9.96	63	27.27
	Total	**118**	**51.08**	**113**	**48.92**	**231**	**100**
16	**Santrabari Village**	-	-	-	-	-	-
	Main Worker	43	13.87	48	15.48	91	29.35
	Marginal Worker	77	24.84	81	26.13	158	50.97
	Non-Worker	39	12.58	22	7.10	61	19.68
	Total	**159**	**51.29**	**151**	**48.71**	**310**	**100**

S.No.	Working Status (Village-Wise)	Male		Female		Both	
		No. of persons	Percentage	No. of persons	Percentage	No. of persons	Percentage
17	**Balapara Village**	-	-	-	-	-	-
	Main Worker	31	20.39	33	21.71	64	42.11
	Marginal Worker	35	23.04	31	20.39	66	43.42
	Non-Worker	12	7.89	10	6.58	22	14.47
	Total	**78**	**51.32**	**74**	**48.68**	**152**	**100**
	Overall result of all villagers						
	Main Worker	762	18.72	751	18.45	1513	37.17
	Marginal Worker	961	23.61	934	22.94	1895	46.55
	Non-Worker	379	9.30	284	6.98	663	16.28
Grand	**Total**	**2102**	**51.63**	**1969**	**48.37**	**4071**	**100**

(Prepared by the researcher based on field survey, 2017)

Table–5.15
Occupational Structure of Working Family Members

S. No.	Occupational Status (Village-Wise)	Male		Female		Total	
		No. of persons	Percentage	No. of persons	Percentage	No. of persons	Percentage
1	**Lehra Village**	-	-	-	-	-	-
	Primary	35	49.29	31	43.66	66	92.95
	Manufacturing	-	-	3	4.23	3	4.23
	Service	2	2.82	-	-	2	2.82
	Total	**37**	**52.11**	**34**	**47.89**	**71**	**100**
2	**Suni Village**	-	-	-	-	-	-
	Primary	59	52.68	52	46.43	111	99.11
	Manufacturing	-	-	-	-	-	-
	Service	1	0.89	-	-	1	0.89
	Total	**60**	**53.57**	**52**	**46.43**	**112**	**100**
3	**Garo Basti Village**	-	-	-	-	-	-
	Primary	135	47.54	147	51.76	282	99.30
	Manufacturing	-	-	-	-	-	-
	Service	2	0.70	-	-	2	0.70
	Total	**137**	**48.24**	**147**	**51.76**	**284**	**100**
4	**Gadhadhar Village**	-	-	-	-	-	-
	Primary	148	52.30	134	47.35	282	99.65
	Manufacturing	-	-	-	-	-	-
	Service	1	0.35	-	-	1	0.35
	Total	**149**	**52.65**	**134**	**47.35**	**283**	**100**

S. No.	Occupational Status (Village-Wise)	Male		Female		Total	
		No. of persons	Percentage	No. of persons	Percentage	No. of persons	Percentage
5	**Poro Village**	-	-	-	-	-	-
	Primary	126	49.80	119	47.04	245	96.84
	Manufacturing	-	-	6	2.37	6	2.37
	Service	2	0.79	-	-	2	0.79
	Total	**128**	**50.59**	**125**	**49.41**	**253**	**100**
6	**Nimati and Dabri Village**	-	-	-	-	-	-
	Primary	157	51.14	147	47.88	304	99.02
	Manufacturing	-	-	3	0.98	3	0.98
	Service	-	-	-	-	-	-
	Total	**157**	**51.14**	**150**	**48.86**	**307**	**100**
7	**Gangutia Village**	-	-	-	-	-	-
	Primary	82	50.31	78	47.85	160	98.16
	Manufacturing	-	-	-	-	-	-
	Service	3	1.84	-	-	3	1.84
	Total	**85**	**52.15**	**78**	**47.85**	**163**	**100**
8	**Adma Village**	-	-	-	-	-	-
	Primary	78	51.66	72	47.68	150	99.34
	Manufacturing	-	-	-	-	-	-
	Service	1	0.66	-	-	1	0.66
	Total	**79**	**52.32**	**72**	**47.68**	**151**	**100**

S.	Occupational Status	Male		Female		Total	
No.	(Village-Wise)	No. of persons	Percentage	No. of persons	Percentage	No. of persons	Percentage
9	**Raimatang Village**	-	-	-	-	-	-
	Primary	113	48.71	115	49.57	228	98.28
	Manufacturing	-	-	-	-	-	-
	Service	4	1.72	-	-	4	1.72
	Total	**117**	**50.43**	**115**	**49.57**	**232**	**100**
10	**Bhutri Forest Basti Village**	-	-	-	-	-	-
	Primary	99	49.01	100	49.50	199	98.51
	Manufacturing	-	-	-	-	-	-
	Service	3	1.49	-	-	3	1.49
	Total	**102**	**50.50**	**100**	**49.50**	**202**	**100**
11	**Gudamdabri Village**	-	-	-	-	-	-
	Primary	114	50.89	109	48.66	223	99.55
	Manufacturing	-	-	-	-	-	-
	Service	1	0.45	-	-	1	0.45
	Total	**115**	**51.34**	**109**	**48.66**	**224**	**100**
12	**Chunabati Village**	-	-	-	-	-	-
	Primary	88	49.44	88	49.44	176	98.88
	Manufacturing	-	-	-	-	-	-
	Service	2	1.12	-	-	2	1.12
	Total	**90**	**50.56**	**88**	**49.44**	**178**	**100**

S. No.	Occupational Status (Village-Wise)	Male		Female		Total	
		No. of persons	Percentage	No. of persons	Percentage	No. of persons	Percentage
13	**Bhutiabasti Village**	-	-	-	-	-	-
	Primary	54	47.37	57	50.00	111	97.37
	Manufacturing	-	-	-	-	-	-
	Service	3	2.63	-	-	3	2.63
	Total	**57**	**50.00**	**57**	**50.00**	**114**	**100**
14	**Sankosh Village**	-	-	-	-	-	-
	Primary	140	48.78	141	49.13	281	97.91
	Manufacturing	-	-	-	-	-	-
	Service	6	2.09	-	-	6	2.09
	Total	**146**	**50.87**	**141**	**49.13**	**287**	**100**
15	**Lapraguri Village**	-	-	-	-	-	-
	Primary	75	44.64	86	51.19	161	95.83
	Manufacturing	-	-	4	2.38	4	2.38
	Service	3	1.79	-	-	3	1.79
	Total	**78**	**46.43**	**90**	**53.57**	**168**	**100**
16	**Santrabari Village**	-	-	-	-	-	-
	Primary	115	46.18	129	51.81	244	97.99
	Manufacturing	-	-	-	-	-	-
	Service	5	2.01	-	-	5	2.01
	Total	**120**	**48.19**	**129**	**51.81**	**249**	**100**

S. No.	Occupational Status (Village-Wise)	Male		Female		Total	
		No. of persons	Percentage	No. of persons	Percentage	No. of persons	Percentage
17	**Balapara Village**	-	-	-	-	-	-
	Primary	66	50.77	60	46.15	126	96.92
	Manufacturing	-	-	4	3.08	4	3.08
	Service	-	-	-	-	-	-
	Total	**66**	**50.77**	**64**	**49.23**	**130**	**100**
	Overall result of villagers						
	Primary	1684	49.41	1665	48.86	3349	98.27
	Manufacturing	00	00	20	0.59	20	0.59
	Service	39	1.14	00	00	39	1.14
Grand Total		**1723**	**50.55**	**1685**	**49.45**	**3408**	**100**

(Prepared by the researcher based on field survey, 2017).

Table–6.2
List of Medicinal Plants used by Forest Villagers

S.No.	Species	Local name	Parts Used	Medicinal Uses for
1	Andrographis paniculata	kalmegh; Chirata	Stem and leaf	Stomach, Fever, Liver, Skin and Ulcer
2	Hygrophila schulli	Kulekhara	Stem and leaf	Anemia
3	Acalypha Indica	-	Leaf	Nasal and Wounds
4	Acacia Catechu	-	Bark	Stomachache
5	Allium cepa	-	Bulb	Malaria, Asthma, Ear, eye and skin
6	A.Sativum	-	Bulb and clove	Eye, heart, asthma, ear paralysis pain
7	Azadirachta indica	-	All parts of plant	Toothache, skin, antidote, eye, diabetes, urinary, fever
8	Ammannia baccifera	-	Whole plant	Fever and child diseases
9	Argemone mexicana	-	Root and seed	Skin, Eye and expel worms
10	Baliospermum montanum	-	Root and seed	Pain, skin, piles, wounds, spleen, Jaundice and purgative.
11	Bauhinia purpurea	-	Root, leaf, bark and flower	Fever, headache, diarrhea, rheumatism
12	B. racemosa	-	Leaf	Diarrhea and Dysentery
13	B. variegate	-	Root, bud, bark and flower	Skin, diarrhea, worms, wounds, tuberculosis
14	B. ammannioides	-	Whole part	Bone fracture and menstrual disorder

S.No.	Species	Local name	Parts Used	Medicinal Uses for
15	Biophytum sensitivum	-	Stomach ache	Plant and seed
16	Boerhavia difusa	-	Root and leaf	Disorder of women, liver, blood, antidote and heart
17	Bombax ceiba	Simul; Panchu phang; Simal	Resin, gum and flowers	Diarrhea and disorders women
18	Butea monosperma	-	Root, bark, leaf flower and seed	Eye, blood, Diarrhea, typhoid, piles, skin disease
19	Caesalpinia bonduc	-	Bark, leaf, seed and seed oil	Fever, toothache, ear, diarrhea and bleeding
20	C. pulcherrima	-	Leaf and flower	Wounds febrifuge
21	Calotropis gigantea	-	Root, latex, leaf and flower	Wormsicide, fever, cholera, antidote, cough and cold
22	C. procera	-	Root, Rhizome and leaf	Toothache, antidote, asthma and cough
23	Cadiospermum helicacabum	Lataphatkari; Sibjhul; Bhado	Whole plant	Rheumatism, snake bite
24	Careya arborea	-	Bark, dried calyz and leaf	Stomachache, diarrhea, eye and swellings
25	Cassla fistula	-	Leaf, fruit and seed	Wormsicide, skin, toothache and fever
26	Crinum amoenum	Astachatur	Root	Jaundice and diarrhea.